MISSION COLLEGE
LEARNING RESOURCE SERVICES

Community Politics and Educational Change

Community Politics and Educational Change

Ten School Systems under Court Order

Charles V. Willie
Susan L. Greenblatt

LONGMAN

New York and London

COMMUNITY POLITICS AND EDUCATIONAL CHANGE:
Ten School Systems under Court Order

Longman Inc., New York
Associated companies, branches, and representatives
throughout the world

This work has developed under a grant from the U.S. Office of Education,
Department of Health, Education, and Welfare. However, the content does not
necessarily reflect the position of that agency, and no official endorsement of
these materials should be inferred.

Developmental Editor: Lane Akers
Editorial and Design Supervisor: Judith Hirsch
Cover Design: Dan Serrano
Manufacturing and Production Supervisor: Robin B. Besofsky
Composition: Jay's Publishers Services, Inc.
Printing and Binding: Book Crafters, Inc.

Manufactured in the United States of America

9 8 7 6 5 4 3 2 1

Library of Congress Cataloging in Publication Data

Willie, Charles Vert, 1927–
    Community politics and educational change.

    1. School integration–United States–Addresses, essays, lectures. 2. Education and state–
United States–Addresses, essays, lectures. 3. Discrimination in education–Law and legisla-
tion–United States–Addresses, essays, lectures. I. Greenblatt, Susan L., joint author.
II. Title.
LC214.2W53   370.19'342   80-11076
ISBN 0-582-28147-4

Contents

Contributors

Geoffrey P. Alpert is currently legal ombudsman for the Lane County, Oregon district attorney's office. He received his Ph.D. from Washington State University and has held academic appointments at the University of Texas at Dallas and the University of Colorado at Colorado Springs. He has also served as director of research for the Georgia Department of Corrections. He has contributed numerous articles to legal and sociological journals.

Michael Barndt received his Ph.D. in organizational behavior from Case Western Reserve University. He is currently an associate professor in the Department of Urban Affairs at the University of Wisconsin at Milwaukee. He is interested in neighborhood planning and citizen participation in urban affairs.

Pamela Bullard is a reporter/producer at WGBH Television in Boston, where she covered Boston school desegregation. Formerly she was a reporter and education editor, at the Boston *Herald American.* In 1977, she was awarded a fellowship at Yale Law School and earned a master's degree in the study of law. She has recently produced a documentary on the Massachusetts juvenile justice system and is coauthor of a book on desegregation in Boston to be published in 1980 by Little, Brown.

Amelia Cirilo-Medina received a doctorate in education from Texas A & M University. She has served as a consultant to school systems and has participated in educational research projects. She has recently published *A Comparative Analysis of Evaluative Theory and Practice for the Instructional Component of Bilingual Programs* (1978).

Elaine M. Clyburn, M.S.W., program director of social work at Villa Maria College, Erie, Pennsylvania, is an educator with interests in the areas of social welfare policy, child welfare, and community planning and change. She is also the author of *Crisis Intervention,* a training manual published by the American National Red Cross as part of its Art of Helping training series.

Rutledge M. Dennis is associate professor of sociology at Virginia Commonwealth University in Richmond. He is coeditor of *The Afro Americans: A Social Science Perspective* (1976) and has published articles in numerous journals. He received his B.S. from South Carolina State College and an M.A. and Ph.D. from Washington State University. His research and teaching interests center on theoretical sociology, complex organization, and social stratification.

Albert S. Foley, S.J., Ph.D. is director of the Human Relations Center and professor emeritus of sociology at Spring Hill College in Mobile, Alabama. He earned his doctorate in sociology at the University of North Carolina in 1950. He has been a member of the Alabama Advisory Committee for the United States Civil Rights Commission, president of the Alabama Council on Human Relations, and a fellow of the American Sociological Association. He was first president and is secretary-treasurer of the Mobile Committee for the Support of Public Education. He also serves as chairman of the Mobile Social Justice Commission.

Paul Geisel, Ph.D., is professor of urban affairs at the University of Texas at Arlington. He has conducted research and taught at Tuskegee Institute, the University of Pittsburgh, the Canadian Welfare Council, and Arizona State University. He has served as first executive director of the Dallas Alliance and as designer of the desegregation plan for Dallas His areas of interest include citizen involvement, community organization, systems planning, and coordinated service delivery. He has published several books and monographs and has served as a consultant to city governments, major school districts, and community agencies.

Joyce Marie Grant, Ed.D, is a member of the faculty of the Harvard Graduate School of Education and is former director of the Roxbury/Harvard School Program, a university/public school desegregation partnership. She has been active for many years in urban school improvement efforts as well as in community service programs, and is currently an administrator in the Boston School Department.

Susan L. Greenblatt, Ph.D., is a research associate and lecturer at the Harvard Graduate School of Education. She earned her doctorate in sociology from Boston College and has been involved in research on urban education, including issues related to school desegregation and citizen participation. She has published articles in several academic journals on school desegregation, planned change in education, and higher education. She has also served as a research consultant to various programs on juvenile delinquency and to desegregated public schools.

Joyce Miller Iutcovich is currently completing her Ph.D. in sociology. She is on the faculty of Villa Maria College in Erie, Pennsylvania and is also a research associate of the Northwest Institute of Research. She has been involved in research projects and evaluations for the Pennsylvania Governor's Justice Commission and the Council on the Prevention of Alcoholism and Drug Abuse. In 1975-1976, she was associated with the University of Sind in Pakistan, where she conducted a study on the perception of time. She has also presented papers and published articles on the problems of handicapped students within a college environment and on alcohol use and abuse among college students.

Rick Janka has been education reporter for *The Milwaukee Sentinel* for the last six years and has covered that city's court-ordered school desegregation. He is a graduate of the Marquette University College of Journalism. Janka has received awards for his reporting of public education in Milwaukee and its suburbs, from the Wisconsin Education Association Council, the Wisconsin School Board Association, and the Milwaukee Press Club. In 1978, he received a fellowship from the Ford Foundation and the Institute for Educational Leadership in Washington, D.C. to undertake a study on quality education. The study resulted in a handbook for parents to help them determine what makes a good teacher, principal, and school.

Dennis N. Mihelich is assistant professor of United States history and coordinator of the American Studies Program at Creighton University, Omaha, Nebraska. He holds a B.A. from Kent State University and an M.A. and Ph.D. from Case Western Reserve University. He is the author of several articles and conference papers dealing with black studies and the New Deal era.

Barry R. Morstain, associate professor in the College of Urban Affairs and Public Policy at the University of Delaware, received his Ph.D. in higher education from the University of California at Berkeley. He has published numerous articles on student and teacher educational orientations, adult learner motivations, and faculty development programs. He has consulted with state and federal educational agencies, including the Fund for the Improvement of Post-secondary Education. He is currently involved with the Society for Values in Higher Education, studying the creation and impact of faculty development teaching improvement projects at sixteen institutions. In New Castle County, Dr. Morstain worked with educational and community leaders on a planning process for the development of magnet and special focus programs in the public schools.

Fred Muskal received his Ph.D. in educational sociology from the University of Chicago and is currently associate professor in the School of Education, University of the Pacific, Stockton, California. He taught at inner-city schools in Chicago for several years and still works in classrooms as a staff development consultant. In addition, he is working on the sociology of the classroom and has begun developing a multidisciplinary approach to learning theory.

Ross L. Purdy earned his Ph.D. from the University of Southern California. Currently he is associate professor of sociology at Corpus Christi State University. His areas of specialization are demography, urban ecology, and criminology. He is now doing research on population decline and the effects of transportation on the redistribution of population in the United States.

Jeffrey A. Raffel received his Ph.D. in political science from the Massachusetts Institute of Technology. He is currently an associate professor at the College of Urban Affairs and Public Policy, University of Delaware. From November 1974 through October 1977, Dr. Raffel served as staff director to the Delaware Committee on The School Decision (DCSD), a group established to help prepare for metropolitan school desegregation. He is the author of a comprehensive political analysis of the Delaware desegregation process tentatively titled *The Politics of Metropolitan School Desegregation: The Delaware Case*, to be published by Temple University Press.

Harold M. Rose, Ph.D., is professor of geography and urban affairs at the University of Wisconsin-Milwaukee. His published works have focused primarily on black residential mobility. In 1974, Dr. Rose was awarded the Van Cleef memorial medal by the American Geographical Society for his contributions to urban geography. In 1976-1977 he served as president of the Association of American Geographers. Dr. Rose has served as a visiting professor at Washington University, Northwestern University, and the University of California at Los Angeles. In 1971, he was invited by the Polish Academy of Science to lecture at the Institute of Geography at Warsaw.

James A. Sartain, currently professor of sociology at the University of Richmond, received his Ph.D. from Vanderbilt University. He is an urban sociologist with interests in education, minorities, and demography. He was chairman of the Urban Team that studied "Resegregation in the Northside," a Richmond Public School/HEW research project. He was director of research for the NIMH/TRUST research project, "A Developmental Approach to Community Change" and served as a consultant between 1967 and 1973 for twenty-five public school systems undergoing desegregation. He recently spent his sabbatical studying new towns in Western Europe and the Soviet Union.

Judith Stoia is news editor of the Ten O'Clock News, a nightly newscast produced by WGBH TV in Boston. She worked as a reporter at WGBH for several years, specializing in Boston's desegregation experience. She produced several television specials on desegregation as well as numerous reports focusing on the effects of desegregation on Boston neighborhoods. She is coauthor of a book on desegregation in Boston to be published in 1980 by Little, Brown. She was a Nieman Fellow at Harvard University for the 1979-1980 academic year.

Donna Treadwell received a B.A. in psychology and sociology from the University of the Pacific in Stockton, California. During her undergraduate years she became involved in the Stockton community, assisting with several community-service projects such as the Special Olympics program and working with developmentally disabled children. She was also very active in campus organizations such as the Black Student Union and the Community Involvement Advisory Board.

Ashton Wesley Welch is assistant professor of history and coordinator of Black Studies at Creighton University, Omaha, Nebraska, where he lectures in African and Afro-American history. A graduate of Wilberforce University, he obtained a master's degree and a certificate of African studies from the University of Wisconsin, and recently submitted his doctoral thesis to the University of Birmingham (England). He did field work in Great Britain, Italy, the Ivory Coast, and Senegal. He is currently researching a work on the "American Middle West and the Civil Rights Revolution."

H. Ron White, a graduate of Howard University School of Law, is a practicing attorney in Dallas, Texas and has had extensive business, civic, and school desegregation experience. He is a member of the Texas State Bar and has served as lead counsel in school desegregation litigation in the U.S. Federal District Court, U.S. Court of Appeals for the Fifth Circuit, and in the U.S. Supreme Court. He has also served as a consultant to various organizations on school desegregation-related matters including coalition and consensus building, minority matriculation in the system, and minority leadership development.

Charles V. Willie, Ph.D., is professor of education and urban studies, Harvard Graduate School of Education. Former president of the Eastern Sociological Society, he is a member of the Council of the American Sociological Association and has served as a member of the board of directors of the Social Science Research Council. He was a member of President Carter's Commission on Mental Health. A court-appointed master in the Boston school desegregation case, he has served as an expert witness in the Dallas school desegregation case and as consultant to the Illinois Education Department. He has written several books, including *The Sociology of Urban Education.*

Foreword

Mary von Euler

As television cameras transmit images of conflict and protest across the country, the public sees desegregation as an event marked by burning school buses, adults spitting on small children, and other acts of violence. The prime concern of parents naturally turns to the safety of their children, and the reaction of policy makers is to stop the buses or to beef up security.

Sociologists Charles Willie and Susan Greenblatt start from the premise that a clearer understanding of the social processes during desegregation may lead to more enlightened and effective public policies. They began their study of community conflict and desegregation with a background of knowledge of social processes that went beyond the narrow view of desegregation as a single event that occurs the moment children are assigned to schools in accordance with particular racial ratios, or as a phenomenon related to how children get to school. They saw desegregation as a process of profound social change for schools and communities that was fundamental to the achievement of an equitable society. Thus from its inception in 1977 the study held promise of special usefulness to policy makers, planners, and practitioners engaged in formulating remedies for the courts.

Willie and Greenblatt's approach is through case studies of ten communities. Even nonsocial scientists will be interested in the authors' discussion of methodology—the effort to make findings from ten case studies generalizable to other cities; the perceptions made possible by knowledgeable interracial teams of researchers who have a stake in the local community and who assume the posture of detached concern; the broadening of traditional sociological approaches by placing desegregation in its historical and legal context. The methodology is based on a need to go beyond the events in order to understand human social systems and social change.

Social scientists can be most useful to policy makers, practitioners, and planners involved in designing desegregation remedies by illuminating the desegregation process. Rather than asking if desegregation is beneficial or harmful, Willie and Greenblatt ask how it happens and why. They view education in the context of dominant and subordinate groups in society that have different uses for schools. Litigation in the courts is one of the only ways in which minority subordinate groups—those without electoral power—can bring about peaceful social change so they will not be misused by the educational system.

An examination of the remedial process reveals that even after litigation, affluent whites frequently remain in total control, as courts, reluctant to become super school boards, resort to varying strategies for developing remedial plans. The authors examine the sequence of interactions between the judiciary and the community. Minority groups, as plaintiffs, usually provide the impetus for legal action. The courts provide a catalyst and leverage for change. Yet the governmental and social structures of the community constrain the process of implementation. Some community characteristics that appear to affect that process are the extent of the business community's interest in the public schools, whether there are divisions within the minority community that dissipate its effectiveness, and whether school boards are elected at large, rendering a sizable minority group virtually unrepresented.

Much depends upon the means that the courts choose for designing the desegregation plan, whether they rely on masters, court-appointed experts, compromises arrived at by different sorts of community coalitions, or the defendant school officials. If a broad spectrum of the community is injected early enough in the process and has some real authority, it can make a difference by giving various segments of the community a sense of ownership in the ultimate desegregation plan. Effective participation can mean that disruptive protest is unnecessary because the full range of community opinion is given some voice. Sometimes opposition is reduced because "effective participation" has meant that an influential middle-class group has ensured that its schools are omitted from a desegregation plan. However, the courts may ultimately find the exclusion to be unconstitutional, if the excluded schools are within the same court-ordered school district. (The Supreme Court has thus far protected most separate all-white suburbs).

The authors examine several hypotheses on the role of leadership in implementing desegregation. Mayors, legislators, police, and other officials have often exercised leadership for peaceful implementation, although sometimes they encourage protest. Antibusing groups are found to be ephemeral, especially when faced with leaders who present peaceful alternatives and when desegregation is patently inevitable. Not surprisingly, the authors point to the importance of political leaders who strongly endorse obedience to the law. The Omaha and Boston experiences are contrasting examples. Leadership in varying degrees provided by school systems in such cities as Milwaukee and Richmond successfully reduced community conflict. Thus the lessons for political leaders are obvious.

There are less obvious but equally useful lessons for the courts, as they go about their task of implementing school desegregation plans. It seems to be important to involve a broad range of citizens in the planning process. Community participation helps to prevent conflict and provides a continuing mechanism for educational decision making, so the plan once developed may in fact be implemented. Successful desegregation requires more than the absence of disruptions; it requires educational systems to respond to students whose needs have hitherto been ignored. Judges and policy makers will want to have more than these bare conclusions; they will want the fuller understanding that this study offers of the role of the community in desegregation as a process of social change.

PART I: HISTORICAL BACKGROUND

1

Power, Education, and Social Change: Persisting Issues

Charles V. Willie and Susan L. Greenblatt

As the United States moves through the final quarter of the twentieth century, it continues to experience the shock waves of school desegregation. With the exception of the Civil War, probably no event has shaken the nerve and tested the courage of this nation so much as the U.S. Supreme Court order in *Brown* v. *Board of Education* to end state-sanctioned discrimination in the public schools. In 1954, the court declared that "separate educational facilities are inherently unequal" and in 1955, it ordered the public schools to admit black plaintiffs and other children of the class that they represented "on a racially non-discriminatory basis with all deliberate speed" (*Brown* v. *Board of Education* 347 U.S. 483, 1954; 349 U.S. 294, 1955). Kluger assessed the impact of the court's decision this way: "Probably no case ever to come before the nation's highest tribunal affected more directly the minds, hearts, and daily lives of so many Americans" (1975:x).

Social scientists have discussed and debated the issue of desegregation endlessly in the quarter century that has passed since the *Brown* decision. Most studies of school desegregation have focused on the issue as a static phenomenon with little or no attention paid to the historical processes that have led various racial and ethnic groups to respond as they have to the processes and race relations accompanying desegregation. Yet the significant events in contemporary adaptations to court orders to desegregate reflect the experience racial groups have had in the past.

Minority groups have been treated as if their past were invisible. Because the nation had only a limited knowledge of the efforts and activities of black and brown populations in the past regarding race, education, and social change, it was unprepared to understand the motivation behind the combined court cases that eventually resulted in the *Brown* school desegregation decision of 1954.

As the discussion that follows will show, oppressed minority groups have used education as a means to achieve freedom and upward mobility.

DOMINANT AND SUBDOMINANT GROUPS
IN THE EDUCATIONAL SYSTEM

Dominant groups have used the educational system to achieve a number of goals, including preparation for political participation in a democracy, social control, and assimilation. Subdominant groups have used the educational system in an

3

attempt to change their status in society and to preserve their own cultural identity.

In all social relationships and in any social system, power is unequally distributed: there are dominant and subdominant people of power. If the dominant people of power fulfill their self-interests and at the same time hinder or block the subdominant people of power from fulfilling their self-interests, the system of interaction is unjust. Subdominants who are dissatisfied in one sytem can become dominants when they propose a new system and induce others to respond in a cooperative way. Individual people are not fixed in dominant or subdominant positions because of sex, race, wealth, or any other characteristic. Moreover, the fact that an individual or group is dominant in one situation does not mean that that individual or group will be dominant in all other situations.

In the early history of the United States, the educational system prepared elites for leadership, particularly political or religious. Thomas Jefferson was a very influential leader during this period, and his views on education were somewhat more progressive than other members of the dominant class at the time. Jefferson viewed education as a way of preventing tyranny and of recruiting leaders from the "unprivileged groups" (Malone 1948). His general plan to accomplish this in Virginia was to establish (a) a free school supported by public resources in every ward, (b) a tax-supported free school in each district for the continuing education of promising students identified by the ward schools, and (c) a publicly supported state university for the continuing education of the most promising students identified by the district schools (Jefferson 1813: 116–118). Ward schools provided the masses with "virtue and wisdom enough to manage the concerns of the society" (Jefferson 1813: 116). The state university, in Jefferson's plan, would prepare people for public-trust leadership roles. The district schools were intermediate and aided in the sifting and sorting process for the discovery of promising leaders.

Although Jefferson's plan was exceptional for that period of time, its scope was limited. It provided for only three years of free primary education; state support for further education was to be given only to exceptional students "raked from the rubbish annually" (Malone 1948: 283). Thus, Jefferson clearly viewed the educational system as a means of maintaining a stratification system while allowing a few exceptional low-status students to be upwardly mobile. Although his plan was a far cry from the contemporary ideals of mass education, there was general opposition on the part of dominants throughout the country to Jefferson's concept of education.

Prior to the Reconstruction period there were no free public schools in the South, with the possible exception of North Carolina, because dominant southerners feared that providing public education to the masses would disrupt the social structure. Public schools in the North during this period had the goal of socializing the poor and others not catered to by private religious schools so that they might conform to normative expectations (Katz 1971: 40). Beginning in the middle of the nineteenth century, the dominant people of power in the North, unlike Jefferson, looked upon public education as a form of indoctrination "to ensure social order" (Katz 1971: 37), "social unity" (Bremner 1971: 1095), and as a way of controlling vice (Ward 1883: 1104).

Many subdominant groups have successfully challenged the function of education as viewed by the dominants. For example, immigrants often sought to "assert the value of their culture by teaching their language to their children" in the public schools, in this way adapting public education to their own cultural designs (Tyack 1974). German people in Cincinnati won the right to conduct school in German from the Ohio legislature in 1840. The St. Louis German population won the same right in 1864. Between 1854 and 1877, eight mid-western states passed laws enabling local school boards to offer German language instruction. As German people became more assimilated and became members of the dominant culture, however, they dropped their demands for full bilingual education and instead merely sought German as an elective course in public high schools. In 1901, the German-American *Nationalbund* argued that "no foreign language should be taught in the American public schools simply because the pupils and patrons of the schools speak the foreign languages in question. If this principle will not be recognized, we will not only have German schools but Hungarian, Polish, and Italian schools as well" (pp. 106–109). Despite this warning, several immigrant groups variously pressed for the introduction of instruction in their languages. The position taken by the German people in opposing instruction in other foreign languages reveals a change in conception of the goals of education that was associated with a change in their own status in society.

That immigrant groups placed a high value on education is illustrated by a study conducted by Ayres (cited in Tyack 1974). In 1909, only 9 out of every 1,000 white children of immigrant parents were illiterate compared to 44 out of every 1,000 white children of native parents. Of children aged five to fourteen years who were in school 72 percent were among second-generation Americans, 69 percent were among foreign-born children, and 65 percent were among children of native parentage. It must be remembered that the minimal schooling of white, native southerners skews the figures for children of native parents: nevertheless, the percentages for immigrant Americans remain high.

Blacks in the United States represent a long history of respect for education. They have associated education with freedom and liberation rather than with indoctrination and conformity. Moreover, blacks have tended to look upon education as a ticket to full participation in society. That blacks in the United States over the years have associated education with freedom, liberation, and enlightenment for the public good is illustrated by a petition that was submitted by a group to the Massachusetts Legislature in 1787. The children of this group of black parents had been denied admission to the public schools because of their race. The petitioners said that they were requesting the legislature to provide for the education of their children so that they would not grow up "in ignorance in a land of gospel light." Moreover, the black parents then asserted that education is a right that all free persons ought to enjoy (Kluger 1975: xi). To these blacks, it was not so much their separation from whites that was a badge of inferiority, as the Supreme Court would contend 167 years later; it was denial of an opportunity to receive an equal education that caused them to feel not free.

In the first part of the nineteenth century in the South, according to W. E. B. DuBois, education was regarded by lower-class whites "as a luxury connected with wealth." In Jefferson's Virginia, "less than one-half the poor white children were attending any schools. . ." (DuBois 1969: 638–639). Before the Civil War, all southern states had laws making it illegal to instruct . . . blacks (Franklin 1967: 202). As for slaves, they could receive no education: "the laws on this point were explicit and severe" (DuBois 1969: 638).

As Binder (1974) points out, however, in the upper South, where the planter aristocracy predominated, the failure to develop a public school system was deliberate and purposeful. Fear of the effects of education on slaves and free blacks moved state governments to restrict the ability of blacks to get an education. As for a system of public education for the white population, "the powerful planter interests were not inclined to sponsor the growth of democracy through public education" (p. 16). This conservative, aristocratic impulse toward restricting the horizons of lower-class whites was especially prevalent in the years before 1830. Aristocratic whites, however, sent their children to private academies. By 1850, there were more private academies in the South than in New England or the Mid-Atlantic states.

Shortly after emancipation, the former slaves exhibited an insatiable desire for learning. Booker T. Washington said, "It was a whole race trying to go to school. Few were too young and none too old to make the attempt to learn. As fast as any kind of teacher could be secured, not only were day-schools filled, but night-schools as well" (quoted in DuBois 1969: 641–642).

DuBois reported that the public school systems in most southern states began with the enfranchisement of the Negro (1969: 648–649). The idea that the masses should be educated to participate effectively in the social order was mentioned by black parents in the North during the Revolutionary period. This idea was implemented by black legislators of the South during the Reconstruction period. All Americans owe a debt of gratitude to the state Reconstruction governments, some of which were dominated by blacks, for implementing a system of free public schools for all.

State conventions in the South during Reconstruction were often boycotted by white elites, but freedmen were represented. "With the numerical weight of their newly found citizenship so vital at the polls, Negroes had been able to accumulate sufficient representation at the various constitutional conventions to make their bid for a free public school system effective" (Bullock 1967: 59). The South Carolina convention of 1868 included a constitutional clause establishing public education for all youths regardless of color. The establishment of this system had been fought for intensively by the black delegates to the convention (Bullock 1967: 49). One historian of the Reconstruction called the South Carolina public law that authorized tax-supported schools open to all "the most beneficial legislation the State . . . has ever enacted" (quoted in DuBois 1969: 650). In 1868, black legislators initiated and supported resolutions that in 1870 resulted in the formation of a South Carolina State Board of Education to oversee the development of free local public school systems.

Similarly, in Alabama, the constitutional convention established a free school system with no mention of separate schools for blacks and whites. However, Alabama blacks did not seek integrated education but equal schools for blacks. In Mississippi in 1870, the state legislature, which was dominated by blacks and Republicans, passed a law establishing a public school system. In each of these instances poor, illiterate whites also benefited from the laws passed by the blacks.

In the middle of the twentieth century, black Americans still retained their vision of the educational system as a means of gaining full participation in society; this was the same idea the Massachusetts black parents expressed more than 150 years earlier. For example, the National Association for the Advancement of Colored People initiated a court case in Clarendon County, South Carolina, to gain better facilities for the schools for black children. This case evolved into a suit to end segregated education and eventually became one of the cases to reach the U.S. Supreme Court and to be decided jointly with the *Brown* case.

The South Carolina state president of the NAACP told a Clarendon County church meeting that "the surest measure of the force with which the white man's heel was still pressing the black man's face into the mud was the schools." Then he asserted that the black schools of South Carolina were a disgrace and concluded that "colored people could not rise until they got educated" (Kluger 1975: 13).

The opportunity to get an education in South Carolina in the late 1940s meant "equal treatment from top to bottom: buses, buildings, teachers, teachers' salaries, teaching materials - - everything the same [for blacks as for whites]; anything less was patently in violation of the Fourteenth Amendment," Thurgood Marshall [then Chief Counsel of the NAACP] explained (Kluger 1975: 18). Blacks in South Carolina did not ask for desegregation as a way of achieving equal education. They sought relief in the courts from the effects of discrimination. Whether desegregation was necessary to overcome the effects of discrimination was an issue the South Carolina blacks did not raise at the outset. Their goal was freedom from oppression as indicated by the opportunity to receive an education equal to that which whites received.

The case studies presented in this book are more recent examples of social change in the educational system initiated by subdominant groups. Not willing to endure the continuing unequal educational opportunities thrust upon them by dominants who control educational systems, blacks and Hispanics across the nation have utilized the judicial system to obtain their constitutional rights. The political processes discussed in the following chapters reveal how dominant and subdominant groups differentially use education and continue to battle over control of the educational system.

BIBLIOGRAPHY

Binder, Frederick. 1974. *The Age of the Common School.* New York: Wiley.

Bremner, Robert. 1971. "The School and American Society." In R. Bremner et al. (eds.), *Children and Youth in America, Volume II: 1866-1932.* Cambridge, Mass.: Harvard University Press.

Bullock, Henry Allen. 1967. *A History of Negro Education in the South.* Cambridge, Mass.: Harvard University Press.

DuBois, W. E. B. 1969. *Black Reconstruction in America.* New York: Atheneum. First published in 1935.

Franklin, John Hope. 1967. *From Slavery to Freedom.* 3rd ed. New York: Knopf.

Jefferson, Thomas. 1813. "Letter from Thomas Jefferson to John Adams on Natural Aristocracy." In Stuart Gerry Brown (ed.), *We Hold These Truths.* New York: Harper, 1941, pp. 114–118.

Katz, Michael B. 1971. *Class, Bureaucracy and Schools.* New York: Praeger.

Kluger, Richard. 1975. *Simple Justice.* New York: Knopf.

Malone, Dumas. 1948. *Jefferson and his Time.* Boston: Little Brown, vol. 1.

Tyack, David. 1974. *The One Best System.* Cambridge, Mass.: Harvard University Press.

Ward, Lester F. 1883. "The Need for State Authority in Education." In R. Bremner et al. (eds.), *Children and Youth in America, Volume II: 1866–1932.* Cambridge, Mass.: Harvard University Press, pp. 1104–1106.

2

School Desegregation: Racial Politics and Community Conflict Processes

Charles V. Willie and Susan L. Greenblatt

Scores of cities across the country have faced court orders to racially desegregate their public school systems. Social science research has failed to provide educational planners and community leaders with data that would help them achieve school desegregation without repeating the errors made previously in other cities. In an article devoted to this topic, Robert Crain (1976) lamented the failure of social scientists to conduct research studies that would provide practical guidelines for those faced with implementing school desegregation plans.

The failure of social scientists to document the political and social processes that lead to conflict is not applicable solely to the issue of school desegregation. According to sociologist Robin Williams, social scientists have been more likely to study conformity than conflict: "When group relations are relatively stable, the central problems that tend to monopolize research have to do with conformity, social patterning, enduring prejudices and stereotypes, and so on. When change becomes massive and rapid, one senses the lack of studies of leadership, political and legal processes, the exercise of power and authority, the sources of innovation, and the conditions generating collective protest" (1965: 13).

In the hope of providing some additional knowledge about community conflict processes, this book presents case studies of ten communities across the country that have implemented court-ordered plans to desegregate public school systems. Although we recognize that specific factors associated with school desegregation will limit the generalizability of the findings, we do believe that the findings may be applicable to other potential community conflict situations, particularly in the area of race relations.

The studies published in this book attempt to build on social theory and previous social research. Although community case studies have received much criticism from sociologists for not being replicable or comparable, we have made an effort to utilize the case study method in the hope of making some preliminary observations about community processes. Indeed, previous community case studies have furthered social science concepts and stimulated academic debate.

The activities revolving around school desegregation have only recently become viable research topics for social scientists. Social scientists have been studying attitudes toward racial desegregation since 1942, when the National Opinion Research Center (NORC) first conducted national surveys on this issue. The National Opinion Research Center has continued to survey Americans about their attitudes toward desegregation, and has found that many Americans have become more favorably disposed to racial integration over the years (Taylor et al. 1978). For example, in 1942, only 2 percent of white southerners favored school desegregation compared with 45 percent in 1970. In 1942, 40 percent of white northerners favored school desegregation compared with 83 percent in 1970 (Rothbart 1976: 343).

Attitudes are not always accurate predictors of behavior, however, and social science research has failed to adequately study the behavioral responses to legally mandated school desegregation. Most studies of school desegregation involve changes in students' grades, scores on standardized tests, and self-concepts at the end of one year of school desegregation. Few of these studies use control groups, and most are not comparable because their definitions of desegregation as well as their operational definitions of the dependent variables vary greatly. For an excellent review of the research findings see St. John (1975).

Another recent interest of social scientists is the phenomenon of white flight and how it relates, if at all, to school desegregation. The term white flight denotes the process of whites leaving the central cities for suburban areas and connotes the process of escaping from racially integrated settings. The debate among social scientists and lay persons alike regarding white flight continues, with some contending that there are not enough whites left in the central cities to afford racial desegregation of public schools (see Coleman 1975; Pettigrew and Green 1976).

Although the importance of the effects of racial desegregation on pupil achievement and demographic patterns cannot be denied, the major interest of this study is not in either of these two issues. Rather the major interest is the actions of various sectors of the community in relation to public school desegregation. The issue has been even more narrowly defined for purposes of this book to include only public school desegregation mandated by a court case ruling. This definition allows the study of a legally required process often rejected by many citizens of a community both individually and in groups. The reasons for rejection may in part be traced to the history of race relations in this country. However, the wide range of responses to court-ordered school desegregation in cities across the country leads us to reject history as the sole source of conflict over school desegregation.

Community reactions to court-ordered school desegregation may be compared with reactions to the attempt to fluoridate water supplies in many local communities that began about thirty years ago. Fluoridation became a controversial issue in many of the more than 3,000 communities involved. In their study of the fluoridation issue, Robert Crain and his associates (1969) noted that the explanation often put forth by social scientists for the high rate of rejection was that citizens used the fluoridation issue to tell the government, which had campaigned for fluoridation, to relinquish control over their lives. These citizens viewed "mass medication" as an invasion of their personal privacy. Crain and his colleagues noted further that the attempt to use alienation theory as an explanation of the conflict surrounding fluoridation failed to explain why some communities accepted fluoridation and other communities rejected it.

An analogy may be made between the fluoridation issue and the current issue of court-ordered school desegregation. Some cities have peacefully complied with the court's order for public school desegregation, whereas other cities have experienced school boycotts, protests, and violence. Citizens who rejected the court's authority in the area of school desegregation often campaigned against "forced busing," a term that is reminiscent of mass medication. The temptation to explain adverse reactions to court-ordered school desegregation by citing alienation theory again is not adequate. There is no evidence to support the notion that citizens are more alienated in Boston, a city that experienced great strife during its initial years of school desegregation, than in Milwaukee, a city that is often portrayed as a model of successful school desegregation.

The desegregation and fluoridation issues are of course different in many respects. Whether to fluoridate local water supplies was a decision made by local political leaders or by voters in a referendum. The decision to desegregate schools was (in the cities studied in this book) mandated by the court system, and in many instances the individual court cases reached the U.S. Supreme Court. The decision to desegregate was not made by political leaders or citizens. Furthermore, the school desegregation issue is one that involves the issue of race relations, whereas fluoridation does not. Thus, it would be expected that cleavages of the community concerning desegregation would be along racial lines, whereas in the fluoridation issue they would not.

Newspapers and other media outlets have alerted the country and the world to the fact that school desegregation has caused conflict and even violence in some of our major urban centers. The media have given shorter shrift to those cities that have desegregated their schools peacefully. It is the purpose of this study to document both the negative and the positive community processes that accompanied court orders to racially desegregate public schools. By studying the actions of individuals and groups who were key to the process, we hope to gain insight into factors that led to peaceful acceptance of school desegregation in some cities and violent resistance in other cities. Peaceful acceptance and violent resistance are two extremes of a continuum, and many cities may have accepted desegregation plans with only a moderate amount of protest. Furthermore, conflict often serves a positive function in bringing about necessary social change, and we expect to analyze our data in terms of both positive and negative effects that resulted from community conflict or the lack of conflict.

In order to study as wide a range of reactions to court-ordered school desegregation as possible within our financial limitations, we have selected ten diverse communities across the country as subjects of our study. The only common denominator of these ten communities is that they have received court orders to racially desegregate their public schools. We were not interested in what changes occurred within the school system as a result of the court order, but rather what happened within the community. The definition of desegregation varied by community and was usually defined by the court itself.

For purposes of this study we have intentionally failed to define successful school desegregation in either educational or political terms. This lack of an operational definition for success reflects what we view as society's failure to define successful school desegregation. Nonetheless, our analysis will necessarily reflect the notion that the desegregation process has not been successful when intergroup conflicts result in bodily harm or property damage.

The major approach of our study is to document the actions of various sectors of the community both historically and contemporarily in regard to the issue of public school desegregation. In so doing, we hope to uncover factors that will explain some of the variations in the responses that occurred in communities across the country.

Even though educational planners, politicians, and lay persons often contend that their own community is unique and therefore cannot be compared with other communities, as social scientists we reject this notion. Indeed, the overriding goal of social science is to predict patterns of human behavior at both the institutional and personal levels, and we are aware of no evidence that supports the contention that behavior within certain communities is not replicated in other comparable communities.

Furthermore, we view the community's response to court-ordered school desegregation as an impetus to major social change within the community. Because court-ordered desegregation involves issues of race relations and governmental authority versus individual rights, the processes set in motion by the court order are fraught with implications for new social roles and rights of various groups and individual actors. In addition, the possibility of confrontation and conflict among various sectors of the community is greatly increased when the court orders implementation of a process that is ideologically rejected by one or more segments of the community. Any understanding we may gain from studying the community processes that accompany school desegregation may further our understanding of community conflict surrounding other controversial social issues.

The goal of this study was the identification of the key actors and institutions that played major roles in the school desegregation process and the analysis of the effect of their actions and policies on the community's response to the implementation of a school desegregation plan. Selected as key to the process were the mayor, other elected politicians, the superintendent, the school board, the police, business and civic leaders, the mass media, formal voluntary organizations including civil rights groups, and citizens' boards appointed to assist with the desegregation process.

As Roland Warren (1969) has suggested, no community exists in isolation from the larger society; rather local communities are connected to the state and federal levels of organization on a vertical axis. The relationship of community leaders to the state and federal levels of organizations and government suggested the need to include the role·of the state department of education, the state legislature and the laws it mandated, and the governor, as well as federal intervention in the form of funding, technical assistance, and participation in the court case. In addition, the role of state and national levels of formal voluntary organizations was viewed as an important element in the process.

The demographic patterns of the community were also viewed as possible contributors to the community response to the school desegregation process. Thus, we denoted population changes, ethnic and racial distributions of the population, and annexations or secessions as variables to be studied. School enrollment patterns by race in both public and private schools were also considered as part of the overall demographic picture.

The variables discussed above were decided upon after reviewing the available research in the field of community processes and school desegregation. Although to our knowledge there had been no comparative community case studies of school systems faced with court-mandated school desegregation in recent years, we conjectured that studies of communities with attempts at voluntary school desegregation would reveal the key institutions and actors involved in the process. Notable exceptions, of course, would be the role of the judge and any masters or experts appointed by the court to assist with the implementation.

A pioneering work in the area of case studies in school desegregation was published by Robin Williams and Margaret Ryan in 1954. Williams and Ryan's study predated the *Brown* v. *Board of Education* U.S. Supreme Court decision and included twenty-four diverse communities across the country. Williams and Ryan concluded that many aspects of the planning process independent of the community's specific characteristics are important to the outcome of school desegregation. Included among these factors are the attitudes and actions of school board members and school administrators, the presence of national groups such as the NAACP, the establishment of citizen groups, the timing of the plan, the preparation of teachers and students, and the history of race relations in the community.

A more recent study by Robert Crain et al. (1968) included eight case studies of northern cities attempting to implement voluntary desegregation as well as New Orleans, which was under court mandate to desegregate. The major conclusion of this study was that the school board played the most important role in responding to the demand for desegregation, whereas the superintendent's role was less important. School boards that experienced internal conflicts were less likely to take action regarding desegregation, and cities that had appointed school board members were less likely to take action than those with elected school boards.

Many of the conclusions reached by Crain et al. were later contradicted in a study by David Kirby et al. (1973). Studying desegregation actions taken in ninety-one northern cities with a population of over 50,000 including at least 3,000 blacks, investigators conducted a quantitative analysis of the move to achieve voluntary school desegregation. Kirby's findings indicated that the superintendent does indeed play an important role in the desegregation process and that the actions of school board members are important whereas their attitudes are not. Desegregation was more likely to take place in cities that had fewer actors involved in the decision and when elites had greater control of the issue. White opposition was positively correlated with the amount of desegregation that took place. Perhaps the most significant finding of the study was that as the conflict intensified, elites withdrew from the controversy and blacks became divided.

It is important to note that the studies conducted by Crain, Kirby, and their associates took place in an earlier time period than the cases presented in this book. Both of these studies documented community processes beginning about 1960. The present study includes some southern cities such as Dallas and Mobile which had a first wave of school desegregation in the 1960s but which faced continued court challenges to the operation of their school systems through the middle 1970s. Indeed, the Dallas public school system was brought back to court to modify the remedy to its segregated system after the case study presented here was completed in the fall of 1977. Thus, the earlier works and the present work vary in their temporal settings. Over the years, the attitudes that various segments of the population hold toward racial integration have become more favorable to integration, as documented by the NORC studies mentioned earlier. It would seem logical that these changing attitudes would be reflected in the community's response to school desegregation.

Perhaps of even greater importance is the fact that the works of Williams and Ryan, Crain, Kirby, and their associates dealt with school desegregation that was more symbolic than real. The early efforts to desegregate public schools in the South allowed a few black students to enroll in previously all-white schools. Oftentimes, allowing the black students to enroll was all that actually occurred; lacking funds for bus fare or fearing hostile reactions on the part of the white students and faculty, most black students chose to remain in their all-black schools. Voluntary desegregation plans in the North were often initiated by school boards as a result of pressure placed by civil rights groups. These plans once again were largely based on open enrollment procedures of which few blacks were able to take advantage.

Public school desegregation in the 1970s has differed from this earlier type of desegregation. In 1968, the U.S. Supreme Court in *Green* v. *New Kent City School Board* (1968) declared that open enrollment plans were not legally adequate to desegregate schools because they had not resulted in desegregation. In the future, proposed remedies to eliminate segregated school systems were to be judged on their ability to actually desegregate schools. Thus, court cases following the *Green* case required that school officials prove that the remedies they were suggesting would actually work in terms of numerical desegregation. The case studies presented in this book document community reaction to actual school desegregation as opposed to token or symbolic desegregation.

It is reasonable to suppose that community reactions to actual school desegregation would be different from reactions to symbolic desegregation in a number of ways. On the one hand, it is possible to argue that symbolic desegregation paved the way for the actual desegregation that was to come and in a sense prepared the community for the inevitability of actual desegregation. This reasoning leads to the hypothesis that communities that had had earlier symbolic school desegregation would react more peacefully to actual school desegregation. On the other hand, advocates of the "tipping point" theory believe that whites will accept racial integration of their schools or communities until the racial minorities reach a significant proportion of the population. At the tipping point (which is defined differently by various advocates of this theory) whites will begin to protest desegregation and/or flee from the setting.

A logical extension of the tipping point theory would be that whites will react more negatively to the recent court orders to desegregate school systems than to the earlier court orders, because they indicate a future in which racial minorities will comprise substantial proportions of what they consider to be "their" schools. This hypothesis, of course, is the opposite of the one mentioned above. It will be possible to obtain evidence to determine which hypothesis is correct from the ten case studies that follow, because each had documented the historical precedents to the current school desegregation process. Cities that experienced symbolic school desegregation prior to actual desegregation will be compared with cities that implemented school desegregation plans following the *Green* case, to determine which cities had more conflict as a result of the court order.

LAW AND SOCIAL CHANGE

The relationship of law and social change has received much attention in sociological literature. For many years, sociologists accepted the theory set forth by William Graham Sumner that laws can be changed only after morals have changed. Recent social science evidence indicates that in fact the opposite may be closer to the truth. It appears that it is easier to change attitudes by first changing required behavior than vice versa. For example, a study by Deutsch and Collins (1958) indicates that residents of once-segregated public housing projects changed their attitudes to favor desegregation only after their housing projects had been desegregated. Similarly, Hyman and Sheatsley (1964) found that less than one-third the southern respondents favored racial integration prior to integration of their communities, but after integration took place the proportion favoring integration increased to more than half. According to Hyman and Sheatsley, people begin to change their attitudes when official actions bury the issue they had been fighting for. It is not known, however, at what point people decide that an issue is a lost cause. The *Brown* v. *Board of Education* U.S. Supreme Court ruling failed to convince people that segregation was a lost cause. It is important to document the processes that are able to convince people that they should accept what they had so long fought against.

Although the ability of the law to bring about attitudinal change has been documented in the studies described above, the relationship between law and social change in school desegregation is not quite so clear-cut. Although courts throughout the country have ruled that public schools must be desegregated racially, the courts have varied greatly in their interpretation of what comprises school desegregation. Furthermore, many courts have left the planning of school desegregation to court-appointed experts, local community leaders, and even school officials who were found to be the perpetrators of racial discrimination. Thus, a group of actors who interpret and enforce the law are juxtaposed between the law declaring that school desegregation must take place and the ability to actually desegregate schools.

Thomas Pettigrew (1971) has noted that our society provides many institutional supports for racism. In a sense, our study documents the institutional supports that either allow racism to fester or require that desegregation be implemented. Such institutional supports include the actions of the various leaders who are charged with interpreting and enforcing the law. Pettigrew (1971) has also noted that a violent reaction to desegregation has usually been rational in the sense that it occurred when leaders hinted that violence would be tolerated. According to Pettigrew:

A multiplicity of factors must be relevant, . . . but tentative early work seems to indicate that the violence occurring with desegregation so far has been surprisingly "rational." That is, violence has generally resulted in localities where at least some of the authorities give hints beforehand that they would gladly return to segregation if disturbances occurred; peaceful integration has generally followed from firm and forceful leadership (1971: 130).

This contention is in agreement with Williams and Ryan's (1954) finding that a clear definition of law by authorities will help to reinforce the willingness to conform to new situations. By studying the actions of mayors, legislators, the police, and other officials in a position to enforce the law of school desegregation, we hope to gather additional evidence to test this hypothesis in a time when it has become popular to question authority. We hope to discover specific patterns of behavior on the part of public leaders that have led to increased acceptance of the court order as well as those that tended to incite conflict among various segments of the community. Furthermore, we seek evidence that will shed light on which public leaders are the most effective in peacefully implementing school desegregation. Based on her study of Boston, Rossell (1977) contends that the mayor is the most effective leader in the peaceful implementation of school desegregation. According to Rossell, school superintendents and other professional administrators cannot be as effective as the mayor because they lack the political skills to bargain and co-opt groups; instead they espouse a professional ideology that fails to view controversial social policy issues as being within their domain. Our study of ten cities, including Boston, should provide additional data concerning the feasibility of actors other than the mayor to provide leadership in the desegregation controversy.

COMMUNITY PARTICIPATION IN THE DESEGREGATION PROCESS

Many investigators have studied the issue of how successful school desegregation has been in relation to who controls the decision-making process—elite community leaders or citizens' committees selected for this purpose. There is little agreement among the various investigators concerning which type of control leads to more peaceful desegregation. Williams and Ryan suggested that when the administration and board keep control of the situation, decision-making power can be successfully shared with an officially appointed citizens' committee (1954: 242–243).

Based on their study of eight cities confronting the issue of voluntary school desegregation, Inger and Stout (1968) concluded, "The less the public is asked for its opinion during the period of policy formation, the greater the likelihood that the public will accept the integration plan." According to Inger and Stout, when school officials presented the desegregation plan as a proper goal of the educational system, the desegregation process was successful.

It is important to remember that Inger and Stout's cities were dealing with attempts to voluntarily desegregate schools; even though the possibility of protest and conflict exists in a situation of court-ordered desegregation, the decision to desegregate has been made by the court and is not in the hands of the community. Furthermore, Inger and Stout's study was based on a time period when people were more likely to accept the legitimacy of governmental authority. With the mood of the country questioning governmental decisions more in recent years, it is possible that officials' decisions do not hold the same weight they once did.

Public officials themselves seem uncertain about the best course to take regarding the school desegregation issue. Rubin's (1972) study of the Richmond Unified School District in California, a case study of a school board under pressure to take some voluntary action to desegregate schools, documents the community processes that took place when school board members appointed citizens' committees to make recommendations and conduct public hearings on the issue. Their intent in using these mechanisms was to "cool out" the opposition to the desegregation plan. These mechanisms failed to achieve the board members' goals. Instead, the hearings served as a forum for expressing racial prejudice. Furthermore, allowing time to elapse before the board made its decision permitted opposition groups to organize their effort against the desegregation plan. Board members continually backed off from making a decision; they were afraid to make a decision because they thought they would lose their bids for reelection.

Rubin's conclusion is that "once an issue becomes salient to a significant sector of the public, the mechanisms with which political leaders generally palliate conflict and soothe discontent fail to work" (1972: 199). This conclusion contradicts the conclusions reached by Hyman and Sheatsley as well as Inger and Stout. However, the actions taken by political leaders must also be viewed within the context of the timing of their decisions. Perhaps a firm commitment to a controversial decision at the outset prevents opposition from organizing and having substantial impact. Once opposition organizes, it is possible that public leaders' commitments to an issue are not as effective as they would have been earlier.

The hypothesis discussed above suggesting that public participation in the implementation of school desegregation creates rather than prevents conflict is in direct opposition to many theories of planned social change. Theorists such as Rogers (1962) contend that allowing citizens to participate in the planning process will result in greater commitment to the change that will take place. Evidently in recognition of this theory, judges, court-appointed masters, and school administrators have appointed citizens' committees to participate in the planning process for school desegregation. Of course, specifics of the given situation must be taken into account, and if citizens are ideologically opposed to school desegregation at the outset, the mechanisms used to persuade them to change their ideological stance must necessarily be forceful. The types of mechanisms used, the amount of control that citizens are allowed in the decision-making process, and the chronological point at which citizens are allowed to participate may all affect the probability of success in the citizen participation process. In some instances, citizens' committees may be appointed with the intent of co-opting the members in order to stave off conflict. In these instances, citizens' committees rarely have any real decision-making power. These committees may also be appointed at a chronological point after the major decisions have been made. Such a tactic may serve to make the citizens hostile toward the system that appointed them.

The case studies will provide some additional data on what types of citizen participation, if any, are effective in preventing conflict as the major reaction to school desegregation.

THE PHENOMENOLOGICAL PERSPECTIVE
IN SCHOOL DESEGREGATION RESEARCH:
DATA, METHOD, AND ANALYSIS

The Perspective

The perspective of sociological ambivalence (Merton 1976) is particularly valuable in studying school desegregation. The social events in this process are connected with feelings and facts about race and politics, fears and frustrations about success and failure—the meaning of these for individuals and their consequence for communities. To see, describe, analyze, and understand racial desegregation in education, the social researcher should adopt a role of *detached concern*. Such a researcher is both impersonal and compassionate; one's orientation can be both objective and subjective about each situation.

Probably one of the best examples of this research role is manifested by Marilyn Gittell (1971: 134–163). Gittell's case study of the decentralization and community-control controversy in education in New York City during the 1960s is superb. As a New Yorker, she was able to place the trends of the period she was studying within a historical context. The demand for separatism by blacks was a final reaction to the past failures of the city and its white majority to desegregate public schools, hire minority teaching and administrative staff. The demand also served to embarrass decision makers in the central educational bureaucracy.

As a sympathetic observer, Gittell was able to see diversity within the ranks of the black community and overcome the stereotyped views that characterize many studies of race relations. Her own perspective of sociological ambivalence enabled her to understand the ambivalent behavior of the leader of the city coalition (an association of militant reform groups). This leader had sent a telegram to state legislators opposing a decentralization plan that the New York State Board of Regents had proposed as a compromise, but personally appeared in the state capital to lobby for the plan as it was the only one with a good chance of becoming law. Gittell subjectively understood the complex adaptations required of minorities to cope with contingency and survive within their own community and in the at-large society when there are limited options. Yet, her objective analysis was that "the net effect of the various ideological differences among black and white reform groups was to enfeeble their collective strength" (Gittell 1971: 150).

Gittell linked local strategies within the minority and majority communities and discussed them as symbiotic. She acknowledged the concern for job security among white teachers and the union that they dominated, and understood this fear as the basis of some of their reaction. She noted as a liability the lack of knowledge of state legislative politics by black community groups that, in part, contributed to their lack of success. She interpreted the whole community-control decentralization issue as one involving the distribution of power as well as quality education. And she linked the final outcome to national trends in politics and philanthropy: because the chief city officer who supported decentralization lost reelection, this experience confirmed the inclination of most urban mayors to remove themselves from the educational arena (Gittell 1971: 156).

Moreover, a major foundation that had been deeply involved in the battle retrenched on its direct ghetto aid policy (Gittell 1971: 161). Marilyn Gittell could see all of this because she was a social investigator with a stake in the community. Her orientation to these events was both subjective and objective. As an observer, she was ambivalent.

We knew that many of the same issues encountered in New York City were involved in the communities included in our study of court-ordered school desegregation. To locate investigators who could assume a research role similar to that exhibited by Marilyn Gittell was our goal. We wanted observers with a detached concern who had a stake in the community—social investigators who could unite an objective and subjective orientation and who could be both impersonal and compassionate. In addition, we wanted investigators who would examine community organization and school desegregation from a phenomeno-logical frame of reference that included an analysis of the significance of events to the minority community as well as to the majority community. Finally, wo wanted investigators who could see the association, if any, between local events and happenings at state and national levels.

Beyond the perspective of sociological ambivalence, we believe that the frame of reference of phenomenology is essential in the reconstruction and analysis of community organization and school desegregation in time and space. The phenomenological frame of reference enables the researcher to analyze complexes of characteristics rather than single variables. The analytical framework for any investigation should be chosen because it facilitates observation and understanding. The analytical framework used has a great deal to do with the success or failure of any research effort to contribute to knowledge and understanding.

Theodosius Dobzhansky (1951) said that many who studied hybridization before Mendel did not discover the laws that were revealed by him because "they treated as units the complexes of characteristics of individuals, races, and species and attempted to find rules governing inheritance of such complexes." According to Dobzhansky, this was an error. He said that Mendel was successful because he understood that "the inheritance of separate traits [and] not [the inheritance] of complexes of traits had to be studied" (Dobzhansky 1951: 117). With reference to the human community and social processes, maybe it is the other way around. It is possible that we may be able to understand the principles that govern various forms of community organization and school desegregation only by using a method that analyzes complexes of characteristics rather than single traits.

This may be because human social systems are different from other systems of existence. As mentioned elsewhere by one of us, "in the physical system, the parts are the foundation of the whole. In the human social system, the whole is the foundation of each part. . . . In the physical system, each part is significant only if it contributes to the whole. In the human social system, the whole is significant only if it contributes to each part. . . . In the physical system, defective parts are disposed of and done away with. They impair the well-functioning of the whole. In the human social system, people who are less able are given care and support. Their presence and the compassion they evoke contribute to a sense of community" (Willie 1977: 5–6). This analysis points toward fundamental differences in the nature and function of human social systems and other systems in our environment, and suggests the need for different conceptual approaches for the purpose of understanding the principles that govern interaction within human social systems.

The phenomenological frame of reference is an approach that may be particularly helpful in understanding community organization and school desegregation. It is an approach, according to Robert Bodgan and Steven Taylor (1975: 4), that "directs itself at settings and the individuals within those settings holistically; that is, the subject of the study, be it an organization or an individual, is not reduced to an isolated variable . . . but is viewed instead as part of a whole."

The phenomenological frame of reference is a "procedure of getting at the meaning of [an] . . . act or symbol or institution . . . for the participants" (Smart 1973: 20). As stated by Smart, "A science should correspond to its objects. That is, the human sciences need to take account of inner feelings precisely because human beings cannot be understood unless their sentiments and attitudes are understood" (1973: 3).

Phenomenology is a frame of reference, a perspective, a point of view rather than a method. It is a perspective that helps an investigator to organize data that may be obtained from the use of a number of different methods. One could characterize phenomenology as polymethodic. Regardless of which method is used, the phenomenological perspective is "related always to the particularities of historic traditions" (Smart 1973: 159). It helps one understand social organization as it is in terms of what has been and will be; both the past and the future are part of the present. Social organization as seen from this perspective is related always to both function and purpose. Purpose and function are connected in that goals (or purposes) can be fulfilled only by alternative sets of relationships (or functions).

Social relationships are neither irrational nor aimless. All reciprocal social relations are responsible, which is another way of saying that all reciprocal social relations are directed by purposes. Sometimes purpose or goal is forgotten and sometimes it is embedded in the unconscious. Even so, until replaced by a new purpose or goal, it gives guidance of function to actions and reactions that are reciprocal in a collectivity. Random activity by aimless individuals is uncharacteristic of human beings in groups and communities.

The phenomenological perspective enables us to understand community resistance to change. Anxiety and even conflict occur when a community is confronted with a new social arrangement. Despite the fact that a new social arrangement such as school desegregation has the possibility of fulfilling an agreed-upon constitutional goal of the community, the anxiety and conflict occur because the emerging social arrangement destroys the security of the existing arrangement among some participants and creates hope and expectation of security in the new arrangement among others. This, therefore, stimulates self-preservation anxiety among those who felt safe in the existing arrangement. Just as the passing of the old order is the end of security for some individuals, the emergence of the new order is the beginning of security for others. Persons who focus only on the old tend to deny that the new arrangement could offer any benefit to individuals or the collectivity, and vice versa.

Self-preservation anxiety stimulated by social change can be reduced when the present is defined as reality in terms of both the past and the future. When the phenomenological perspective is used, existence is seen as a continuous event; the future is always a hope and the past is never a hindrance. Useful methods and techniques of observation in terms of the phenomenological perspective are those that provide essential information for explaining continuities and discontinuities, symmetries and asymmetries in personal adaptations and social relations. From this perspective, no social arrangement—symmetrical or asymmetrical—is classified as deviant. Because all reciprocal social interaction is responsible, the phenomenological perspective leads one to study collectivities in terms of the choices that,people make, the purpose they hope to fulfill, the association between personal gain and public benefit, and the consequence of discrepancy, if any, between the two.

The Method and Data

This study is a comparative analysis of ten communities undergoing court-ordered school desegregation. Our approach draws upon the experience of past community studies in that we attempt to utilize their most helpful techniques and eliminate those found to be least beneficial. Thus, we are using what may properly be termed an eclectic approach, collecting historical, ecological, and structural data as well as studying variables that reveal decision-making processes and interactions of individual actors and community organizations. With reference to individuals, we are interested in their reciprocal relationships and the meaning of these to the participants.

Three variables were used in the selection of the ten communities. (1) Because previous studies have postulated a possible relationship between population size and successful school desegregation, we have selected communities that vary in size—three with populations of over 500,000, four with a population range of 250,000 to 499,999, and three with populations under 250,000. (2) Also, it has been suggested that the proportion of minority group members in the total population is related to the ease or difficulty of implementation of a desegregation plan. Thus, we have selected communities that have a range of minority group individuals from less than 5 percent to more than 40 percent of the total population (see table 2.1). (3) The communities selected also represent various geographical regions of the country. This variable should enable us to determine if regional subcultural differences and previous history of de jure segregation in the South and de facto segregation in the North have had any impact on the current school desegregation process. The communities in our study are located in the states of Massachusetts, Pennsylvania, Delaware, Texas, Alabama, Virginia, Wisconsin, Nebraska, and California (table 2.1).

Our investigators were selected in accordance with our earlier discussion about the social role of the researcher. We decided to recruit teams of two or three persons who were residents in the communities to be studied. In this way, we were able to obtain people who had a stake in the community but who also could look at it with detached concern. The team members' knowledge of the community and its sociological characteristics was invaluable and provided a phenomenological perspective for the complex characteristics of school desegregation events within a historical context.

Our phenomenological perspective caused us to realize that the questions asked, the research methods and techniques used, and the interpretation of data all reflect values learned from life experiences. In order to overcome biases and perspectives imposed by individual life experiences, we required that our

TABLE 2.1. Sites Selected for Study

Community	1970 Population	1970 Proportion Minority* (%)	Geographic Area Included in Desegregation Plan	Date Suit Was Initiated	Date Desegregation Was Implemented
Boston, Massachusetts	641,071	18.2	City	1972	1974
Corpus Christi, Texas	204,525	6.3†	Corpus Christi Independent School District (does not include entire city)	1970	1971—first court plan 1975
Dallas, Texas	844,401	25.8	Dallas Independent School District (does not include all of Dallas; does include parts of two other cities)	1970	1971—bused some blacks 1976
Erie, Pennsylvania	129,231	6.8	City	1968—PHRC requirement 1971—court case began	1975
Milwaukee, Wisconsin	717,099	15.6	City	1965	1976
Mobile, Alabama	190,026 city ___ 317,308 county	35.7 city ___ 32.5 county	County	1963	1963—token 1968—faculty 1970 1971

Location	Population	%	District	Year	Desegregation plan
Omaha, Nebraska	347,328	10.6	Omaha Public Schools (does not include entire city)	1973	1975—faculty + 10% students; 1976 remaining students
Richmond, Virginia	249,621	42.4	City	1962	1966—freedom of choice plan; 1970—interim plan; 1971—extensive busing
Stockton, California	107,6441	20.5‡	Stockton Unified School District (does not include entire city)	1974	1975—senior high; 1976—junior high; 1977—elementary
Wilmington/New Castle County, Delaware	80,386 city / 385,511 county	43.6 / 12.7	Metropolitan (one town in county eliminated)	1971	1978

*Does not include those who categorized themselves as Puerto Ricans or Mexican-Americans.

†The Mexican-American population was 40.6% in 1970.

‡The Mexican-American population is estimated at 20%.

research teams be diversified by race and academic discipline. In an attempt to approach the research problem from the perspectives of both the dominant and subdominant groups involved in the desegregation issue, individuals representing both majority and minority racial groups were recruited for each team when possible. Team members recruited in each community represented different disciplines such as sociology, political science, journalism, education, or law.

The team members selected were often individuals who had played an active role in the desegregation process in their communities. For example, Jeffrey Raffel was the director of the Delaware Committee for the School Decision, a group appointed by the governor to facilitate the court's decision. Albert Foley provided human relations sessions for school personnel in Mobile, Alabama. Joyce Grant headed the program that paired Harvard University and Roxbury High School in a court-ordered program of college-school pairings in Boston. Although such individuals would not ordinarily fit the criterion of scientific objectivity, their knowledge of the situation as well as their academic expertise indicated to us that they would embody the detached concern that is imperative to understanding the community processes.

Our requirement that the research teams in each community be diversified in terms of race and academic discipline is a significant aspect of this study. The perspective of social scientists (and others) is affected by what we have termed the ingroup/outgroup syndrome. Stated briefly, the ingroup/outgroup syndrome holds that the ingroup tends to study the strengths of its own members and the weaknesses of the members of the outgroup. In public policy studies, this syndrome is manifested by the ingroup's assessing the appropriateness of the actions of its own members on the basis of intentions, and the appropriateness of the actions of outgroup members on the basis of consequences. The racial and disciplinary diversity of our teams served as a self-corrective measure against these tendencies and ensured that attention was given to the full range of concerns, including those that are negative or positive for all populations in the community.

It was apparent to us that hiring individuals in dispersed communities without providing guidelines for the type of data we wanted to collect would result in case studies that would suffer from the same methodological problems from which the earlier community studies had suffered. We decided that it was imperative that the team members understand the need for studying a standardized set of variables. Thus, we arranged for a training conference at our Harvard University headquarters to instill in the team members the value of a study with a standardized set of variables in order to facilitate comparative analysis. At that time, the team members were presented with a data checklist, which indicated by categories the variables with which we were most concerned. We also noted that it was likely that individual communities might have undergone processes that were unique and that these should be mentioned in the completed case study.

The team members also were presented with a list of suggested sources of data. Team members were instructed to report on the court findings, the development and design of a plan to achieve a unitary school system, and the implementation of the desegregation plan. They were asked to analyze reports in daily newspapers and neighborhood weekly newspapers. In addition, they were advised to interview key figures in the desegregation process, including local officials and community leaders at large and those associated with neighborhood and particular cultural groups; school board members and the school superintendent; members of formal voluntary organizations; and state and federal officials. Team members were expected to analyze the role of formal voluntary organizations by studying official documents and minutes of meetings held by the organizations. They were to collect demographic data from reports of the U.S. Census Bureau, statistics from the school department, the local clerk for elections, and the chamber of commerce, using standardized categories and dates for each city.

We did not standardize the data collection process to the extent of telling the team members exactly what data should be collected from which sources. Instead, we decided to rely on the expertise of the team members who had had extensive training in the area of legal and social research or investigative reporting.

We made site visits in each of the ten communities to meet with team members, conduct selected interviews as a check on the reports prepared by each team, and familiarize ourselves with each community for our comparative analysis.

The Analysis

At the completion of the data collection process, team members from each of the communities were reassembled for a conference at Harvard University to present the drafts of their case histories. Consultants from the other communities criticized each case study, which was read in draft form. The writers of case studies also received criticism from members of the Harvard faculty and graduate students who attended the conference. Thus, if a team from one community appeared to have omitted information that other teams found important in understanding the school desegregation process, that team was questioned by the other teams. This approach resulted in an explanation of why some data were omitted, or the realization that the omission was an oversight that should be rectified. The team members utilized the criticisms from the conference participants and a written memorandum from us as guidelines for revisions in the case study.

We have designed an approach that is an attempt to overcome some of the inherent problems in case study analysis. It is imperative to conduct case studies that can be replicated in a variety of settings, and that use a standardized set of variables. This approach may be used for studies other than community studies. It is possible that many other areas of research can utilize the phenomenological perspective and the method and technique of a central research staff that designs a project for case analysis, develops hypotheses, establishes data collection guidelines, and does a comparative assessment.

Other methods may be more appropriate for studying social structures and the individuals, aggregates, specific traits, and characteristics associated with them. But the process of interaction in a community setting is appropriately investigated by way of the case study and the perspective used in this study.

Indicating the significance of social interaction as the basic datum in sociology, Martin Buber has said, "The question of what a person is cannot be answered by a consideration of existence or of self-being . . . but only by a consideration of the essential connexion of the human person and his relations with all being" (Buber 1955: 180). The case study is a method and phenomenology is a perspective that facilitate investigation and analysis of the essential connections between persons in society, as persons-in-action and not as abstractions.

It is possible that our understanding of the process of social interactions in school desegregation has been hampered in the past by an inappropriate method and a positivistic perspective that rely largely on the survey method and statistical techniques of analysis. This method and perspective, and these techniques, facilitate the observation and analysis of characteristics abstracted from individuals or aggregates. But the process of interaction among individuals or between individuals and aggregates, or between aggregates and aggregates, probably are more significant in gaining an understanding of how social change has come to pass. Thus, the case study method and the phenomenological perspective may help us understand the complexes of interaction patterns and the principles that govern these patterns because they accommodate sociological ambivalence and focus on all reciprocal social relationships as responsible in terms of the purpose of the participants.

BIBLIOGRAPHY

Bogdan, Robert, and Steven J. Taylor. 1975. *Introduction to Qualitative Research Methods.* New York: Wiley.

Buber, Martin. 1955. *Between Man and Man.* Boston: Beacon Press. First published in 1947.

Coleman, James. 1975. "Trends in School Desegregation, 1968–73." Unpublished paper, Washington, D.C.: The Urban Institute.

Crain, Robert. 1976. "Why Academic Research Fails to be Useful." *School Review* (May).

Crain, Robert et al. 1968. *The Politics of School Desegregation.* Chicago: Aldine.

Crain, Robert, Elihu Katz, and Donald Rosenthal. 1969. *The Politics of Community Conflict: The Fluoridation Decision.* Indianapolis: Bobbs-Merrill.

Dahl, Robert. 1961. *Who Governs?* New Haven: Yale University Press.

Deutsch, Morton, and Mary Evans Collins. 1958. "The Effects of Public Policy in Housing Projects upon Interracial Attitudes." In Eleanor Maccoby et al. (eds.), *Readings in Social Psychology.* New York: Holt, pp. 612–623.

Dobzhansky, Theodosius. 1951. *Genetics and the Origin of Species.* New York: Columbia University Press.

Gittell, Marilyn. 1971. "Education: The Decentralization-Community Control Controversy." In Jewel Bellush and Stephen M. David (eds.), *Race and Politics in New York City.* New York: Praeger.

Green v. *New Kent County School Board.* 1968. 391 U.S. 430.

Hunter, Floyd. 1953. *Community Power Structure.* Chapel Hill: University of North Carolina Press.

Hyman, Herbert, and Paul Sheatsley. 1964. "Attitudes Toward Desegregation." *Scientific American* 211(1) (July): 16–23.

Inger, Morton, and Robert Stout. 1968. "School Desegregation—The Need to Govern." *Urban Review* 3 (November): 35–38.

Kirby, David J. et al. 1973. *Political Strategies in Northern School Desegregation.* Lexington, Mass.: Heath.

Merton, Robert K. 1976. *Sociological Ambivalence.* New York: Free Press.

Pettigrew, Thomas. 1971. *Racially Separate or Together?* New York: McGraw-Hill.

Pettigrew, Thomas, and Robert Green. 1976. "School Desegregation in Large Cities: A Critique of the Coleman 'White Flight' Thesis." *Harvard Educational Review* 46 (February): 1–53.

Rogers, Everett M. 1962. *Diffusion of Innovation.* New York: Free Press.

Rossell, Christine. 1977. "The Mayor's Role in School Desegregation Implementation." *Urban Education* 12: 3 (October): 247–270.

Rothbart, Myron. 1976. "Achieving Racial Equality: An Analysis of Resistance to Social Reform." In Phyllis A. Katz (ed.), *Towards the Elimination of Racism.* New York: Pergamon, pp. 341–375.

Rubin, Lillian B. 1972. *Busing and Backlash.* Berkeley: University of California Press.

St. John, Nancy. 1975. *School Desegregation: Outcomes for Children.* New York: Wiley.

Smart, Ninian. 1973. *The Science of Religion and the Sociology of Knowledge.* Princeton, N.J.: Princeton University Press.

Taylor, D. Garth, Paul B. Sheatsley, and Andrew M. Greeley. 1978. "Attitudes toward Racial Integration." *Scientific American* 238 (June) 6: 42–49.

Warner, W. Lloyd, and Paul S. Lunt. 1941. *The Social Life of a Modern Community.* New Haven: Yale University Press.

Warren, Roland. 1969. "Toward a Reformulation of Community Theory." In Robert Mills French (ed.), *The Community.* Itasca, Ill.: Peacock, pp. 39–49.

Williams, Robin. 1965. "Social Change and Social Conflict: Race Relations in the U.S., 1944–64." *Sociological Inquiry* 35:1 (Winter): 8–25.

Williams, Robin, and Margaret Ryan. 1954. *Schools in Transition.* Chapel Hill: University of North Carolina Press.

Willie, Charles V. 1977. "When to Resist Authority." *The Witness* (December).

PART II : CASE STUDIES

3

The Northeast Boston, Massachusetts: Ethnic Resistance to a Comprehensive Plan

Pamela Bullard, Joyce Grant, and Judith Stoia

Segregated public schools in Boston have been an issue for almost two centuries. In 1787, a petition to open Boston public schools to blacks was denied. The city set up separate "colored" schools in 1820. In 1849, by taking his case to court, the father of Sarah Roberts attempted to gain admission for her at one of the five white schools she passed on her way to a "colored" school, but the Massachusetts Supreme Judicial Court upheld the system of racially segregated schools. In 1854, de jure school segregation in Boston was abolished by the legislature (Hillson 1977).

Although de jure segregation had been outlawed, residential segregation increased the probability that de facto segregation would occur. Earlier patterns of immigration had created strong residential pockets of white ethnic groups such as Irish, Italians, and Jews, and the post-World War II patterns brought increasing numbers of blacks to the city. As the blacks came to the central city, whites began moving to the suburbs. The white population of the city shrank 13 percent from 1950 to 1960 and 8.1 percent from 1960 to 1970 (U.S. Census 1970). Of the city's total population of 641,071 in 1970, 104,707 or 16 percent were blacks. The black population of the city had increased rapidly from 1960, when it was 63,165.

THREE NEIGHBORHOODS

The neighborhoods in Boston reflect the rapid population changes that took place. Many of the organized activities concerning the school desegregation process in Boston revolved around neighborhood coalitions, particularly those in Roxbury, South Boston, and Charlestown. A comparison of these three neighborhoods reveals some marked similarities regarding the socioeconomic characteristics of their respective residents.

Charlestown, an area that is geographically isolated from the rest of the city (see figure 3.1), was settled by the Irish at the turn of the century. In the late 1800s, 40,000 people crowded into Charlestown's narrow streets, many

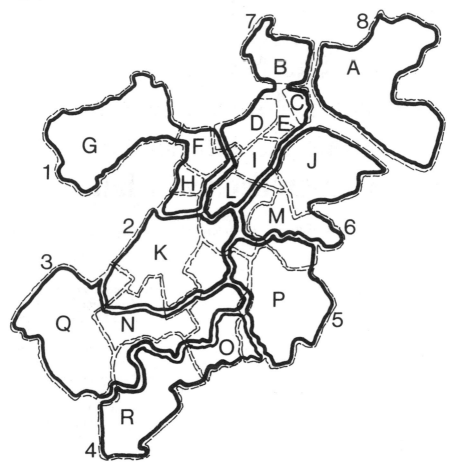

Figure 3.1. Boston, Massachusetts: Neighborhoods (dashed lines) and school districts (heavy lines). A. East Boston, B. Charlestown, C. North End/Waterfront, D. Back Bay/Beacon Hill; E. Chinatown, F. Fenway/Kenmore, G. Allston/Brighton, H. Mission Hill, I. South End, J. South Boston, K. Jamaica Plain, L. Roxbury, M. Dorchester/Uphams Corner, N. Roslindale, O. Mattapan/Franklin Field, P. Dorchester/Fields Corner, Q. West Roxbury, R. Hyde Park.

of them working at the nearby docks unloading freight or signing onto sea-bound vessels. But the dependence on the sea that brought Charlestown its boom years at the turn of the century spelled its decline in more recent times. Traffic through Boston Harbor gradually fell off from the early 1900s on, and with it went the jobs that had been the livelihood of so many Charlestown residents. Unemployment in Charlestown was accompanied by physical decay of the area. In 1970, Charlestown was composed of working-class whites and was predominantly Irish. The median family income was $8,828, and the median education was 11.5 years (U.S. Census 1970).

South Boston's predominantly white Irish population is also geographically isolated from the rest of the city. In 1970, only 388 persons out of 38,488 living in South Boston were black. City officials acknowledge that most of these blacks have since left South Boston, largely because of the tensions and hostility surrounding the school desegregation plan. A working-class community, the median family income in South Boston in 1970 was $8,704 and median school years completed was 11.2 (U.S. Census 1970).

Despite its working-class status, South Boston has produced many of the city's political leaders. The Irish have dominated the political forces in the city for many years, and South Boston has contributed to this phenomenon. With elected leaders from their neighborhood holding city-wide positions on both the city council and the school board, residents of South Boston have had access to channels of political control denied residents of other sections of the city.

Roxbury is the heart of Boston's black community. Of Roxbury's population, 75 percent is black and 24 percent is white. Although Roxbury includes more than 10 percent of the city's population, it counts more than half of Boston's black population. In 1970, it had the lowest median family income of any neighborhood in the city, $6,467, with a high percentage of its workers employed in clerical, service, and labor positions. Median school years completed was 11.0 (U.S. Census 1970).

These data indicate that Roxbury differs from Charlestown and South Boston greatly in terms of racial composition. However, the three areas are remarkably similar in the educational attainments of their populations. Although the economic status of all three areas is low, it is apparent that the black residents of Roxbury have had relatively less economic success than their white counterparts in Charlestown and South Boston.

The racially segregated neighborhoods of Boston did not lead to school segregation in and of themselves. Rather the federal court found in 1974 that the Boston School Committee had manipulated school district boundaries and utilized student attendance patterns that would reinforce the patterns of residential segregation. These and other deliberate actions comprised the court's finding that Boston had intentionally operated a dual school system—one for whites and one for blacks—over the years. Prior to this court finding, however, several important events in relation to the school system revealed the attitudes of both elected officials and citizens concerning the school desegregation issue.

The five members of the Boston School Committee are elected in a nonpartisan campaign and serve as at-large representatives. In the November 1961 election, Louise Day Hicks, a long-time resident of South Boston, was elected to the school committee with 38 percent of the vote. In 1963, she ran for reelection and received 69 percent of the vote, based on her advocacy of neighborhood schools (Ross et al. 1966). Often referred to as "the great white hope" or "Joe McCarthy dressed as Pollyanna," Hicks was the leader of Boston's antibusing forces. With Louise Day Hicks at the helm, Boston politicians would create, ride, and perpetuate the no-desegregation wave into office for the next fifteen years.

BLACK PROTEST

During the course of 1963, several events marked the black community's protest of inferior schooling for their children. In January black mothers protested, and in May a march on the state house was held. In both instances, protesters were demanding educational equality. The leader of the state house march, the Reverend James Reeb, urged blacks to boycott public schools to dramatize their cause.

As a response to these protests, the Boston School Committee met and negotiated with leaders of the National Association for the Advancement of Colored People (NAACP). But although the school committee did agree to study several of the NAACP's demands, it refused to acknowledge the fact that segregated schools existed. Therefore, the NAACP leaders also urged blacks to boycott the schools. A united black community organized a boycott that kept 8,000 black students away from the schools on June 18 (Hillson 1977: 53). Another successful black school boycott was held on 26 February 1964. At that time, school committee member William O'Connell was quoted as saying that the schools were not inferior but that the (black) students were (Hillson 1977: 54).

In April 1965, Melvin L. King led a march of 15,000 to the state house to protest de facto segregation (Hillson 1977: 55). In that same month, the governor's blue-ribbon advisory panel on Racial Imbalance and Education released a report entitled "Because it is Right Educationally." The key findings were that 45 of 200 Boston schools were "predominantly Negro" and that such imbalance was harmful to both white and black children. The report suggested transporting 5,000 white and black students to alleviate the situation.

On the same day the report was released, the Boston School Committee voted 3 to 2 to reject it. Committee member Joseph Lee said, "White children do not want to be transported into schools with a large portion of backward pupils from unprospering Negro families who will slow down their education. . . ." Committee Chairwoman Louise Day Hicks said the report was "un-American," and charged that a small band of racial agitators, not native to Boston, and a few college radicals were trying to tell the people of Boston how to run their affairs.

Despite the school committee's unfavorable response to the report, the state legislature acted on its findings. In August 1965, the Massachusetts Racial Imbalance Act was passed. It declared that any school with a nonwhite population in excess of 50 percent was racially imbalanced. The act required the city of Boston to submit plans to the state that would eliminate the city's predominantly black schools. Although state officials urged the committee to begin acting at once, a step at a time, the committee proposed the solution to "notify at least 11,958 Chinese and Negro pupils not to come back to Boston schools this autumn." In October 1965, the city census revealed that out of Boston's nonwhite school population of 21,097, 16,308 black students were in majority black schools. The student population system-wide was 91,800.

THE BATTLE JOINED

From 1965 until 1974, there was a steady cycle of plans submitted to the state, plans rejected, funds withheld, court battles, more promises, more plans. The school committee used one delaying tactic after another, and the state department of education was lax in its fight to uphold the law.

At the beginning of this cycle in 1965, Louise Day Hicks was reelected to her position on the school committee with an overwhelming 64 percent of the vote. However, it was not long before the black community began to gain some representation in the political arena. In 1967, Thomas Atkins was elected to the city council. Melvin King was elected as a state representative from Boston, and Paul Parks was appointed head of the Model Cities program. Ruth Batson, who had been involved with the education committee of the NAACP since 1960, helped to organize the Metropolitan Council for Educational Opportunities (METCO), a voluntary program to bus black children to schools in white suburbs.

In September 1965, a group of black parents led by Ellen Jackson organized Operation Exodus. A privately financed program, Exodus arranged to bus 400 black students from overcrowded ghetto schools to other parts of the city. One morning, with cameramen in tow, Hicks met the black students at a receiving school and demanded the yellow transfer slips of each pupil (Schrag 1967: 13). Despite such attempts to thwart Exodus, the program grew to 1,100 students in 1970. This same open enrollment policy that allowed the transfer of black pupils would be utilized by white parents and school officials to transfer white students out of integrated neighborhoods into all-white schools.

Another important event to occur during this period was the opening of the Lee School in Dorchester. When the school was designed in the 1960s, city officials had agreed that it would be racially balanced. Based on this agreement, the state provided 65 percent of the $8 million for the school's construction. By the time the school opened in 1971, the neighborhood in which the school was located had changed from predominantly white to predominantly black. Despite the fact that no busing was involved, both white and black students disobeyed the school assignments that sent them to Lee (in the case of the whites) or sent them to another school (in the case of the blacks). Bowing to parental pressure, the school committee voted to allow parents to decide where to send their children (*Boston Globe* 1975: 5/25).

State Commissioner of Education Neil Sullivan warned the Boston School Committee that if it wanted to receive its $21 million in state aid, it must change its "voluntary" school desegregation plan by changing the open enrollment transfer policy, developing new districts for junior and senior high schools, and adopting new district lines for the Lee and Marshall schools. Because the Boston School Committee refused to comply and continued to violate the 1965 Racial Imbalance Act, the state department of education withheld the money. The school committee responded by suing the state. The state in turn countersued, claiming that the Boston public schools violated the Fourteenth Amendment constitutional rights of black children.

A simultaneous development to the state case was a federal charge. In June 1972, the U.S. Department of Health, Education, and Welfare informed Boston of its intent to institute proceedings against the Boston School Committee on the grounds that it was operating a dual school system, a violation of the Civil Rights Act of 1964. In 1973, federal administrative law Judge Laurence King ruled that the school committee was guilty of the charge. Also in 1972, the state board of education directed Commissioner of Education Neil J. Sullivan to draft a desegregation plan for the city of Boston. Although Sullivan's plan excluded several large sections of the city and simply reassigned the students by race, the state board of education accepted the plan the same year.

In the fall of 1972, Suffolk Superior Court Judge Robert Sullivan rejected the state plan for not going far enough, ordered that $52 million in state aid to Boston be reinstated, and ordered the school committee to comply with the Racial Imbalance Act. The state board of education appealed the case to the state's Supreme Judicial Court, which ruled in 1973 that the state's desegregation plan be implemented at once.

Morgan v. Hennigan

In the meantime in 1972, the NAACP had hired J. Harold Flannery, a lawyer with much experience in school desegregation cases, as its attorney to file a suit against the Boston School Committee. The case was a class action suit filed in the name of Tallulah Morgan and other black parents of public school students on behalf of all black children in the Boston public school system against the Boston School Committee, the school superintendent, and the state commissioner of education. The case became known as *Morgan* v. *Hennigan* (1974). The complaint alleged that all black children had been denied equal protection of the laws through the intentional segregation of the schools by race. Additional charges in the federal suit that had not been included in the state suit were discrimination in the recruitment, hiring, assignment, and promotion of teachers and administrators; discrimination in curriculum, instructional materials, and resources; and discrimination in the amounts of money spent in white schools. The trial took place for fifteen days in May 1973, before Federal Judge W. Arthur Garrity.

In the interim, professional staff in the Boston school department were attempting to deal with the school desegregation issue on their own. In January 1973, Superintendent William Leary asked the school committee for authorization to appoint South Boston High School's headmaster, William J. Reid, as his full-time desegregation coordinator." The school committee refused ·the authorization, thereby thwarting Leary's effort to voluntarily deal with the desegregation issue.

On 3 April 1974, the Joint Legislative Committee on Education was holding hearings on the repeal of the Racial Imbalance Act, while 25,000 people demonstrated outside the state house. With Louise Day Hicks as their leader, the Save Boston Committee had garnered the large turnout using its system of block captains telephoning their neighbors (*Boston Globe* 1975: 5/25). The legislature was also being pressed to allow Boston to hold a referendum on the busing issue that June. The referendum, which was suggested by State Representative Raymond Flynn, occurred on 21 May. Although only 12 percent of the voters turned out, their vote was 31,000 to 2,000 against busing (*Boston Globe* 1975: 5/25).

On 10 May, Governor Francis Sargent vetoed a repeal of the Racial Imbalance Law but later proposed a substitute law allowing voluntary transfers by black students and a $500 reward for schools receiving black students. He admitted that a federal desegregation plan would make his suggestion irrelevant. Michael Dukakis, who was to run against Sargent in the November gubernatorial election, proposed an alternative community control of neighborhood schools act with racial integration at resource centers such as museums (*Boston Globe* 1974: 6/23).

On 21 June 1974, Judge Garrity handed down his decision: "The rights of the plaintiff class of black students and parents under the Fourteenth Amendment to the Constitution of the United States have been and are being violated by the defendants in their management and operation of the public schools of the City of Boston." Citing over 100 findings of fact, the judge ordered the discriminatory practices stopped. "It is ordered and adjudged that the defendants be permanently enjoined from discriminating upon the basis of race in the operation of the public schools. . . . Henceforth the defendants are under an 'affirmative obligation' to reverse the consequences of their unconstitutional conduct" (*Morgan* v. *Hennigan* 1974).

Judge Garrity found evidence of the school committee's intent to discriminate in the transcripts of its meetings as well as in virtually all of its attempts to avoid compliance with the Racial Imbalance Act. The result was racial segregation that "permeates schools in all areas of the city, all grade levels, and all types of schools" (*Morgan* v. *Hennigan* 1974). The judge ordered hearings to begin the following week on both the state desegregation plan and a general remedy for desegregation.

APPEAL

The night the decision was handed down, school committee member John J. Kerrigan appeared on television and announced that Judge Garrity's decision would be appealed. He also announced his intention to ask U.S. Senator Edward M. Kennedy to support antibusing legislation in the U.S. Congress. That same night Louise Day Hicks, who was then a city councillor, called a meeting of antibusing leaders at City Hall. Those present decided to call for a two-week school boycott in September. This was not an impromptu collection of individuals; their organization had been formed by Hicks in February and had held weekly meetings of invited antibusing leaders since that time. By June, when the court decision was handed down, they decided to expand their organization by inviting members of the Boston Home and School Association to join. This organization would soon become known by the acronym ROAR, which stood for Restore Our Alienated Rights.

On 26 June, at its first meeting after the decision was handed down, the school committee voted to ask the judge to either stay the plan until mid-October so that a city-wide plan could be designed, or to phase-in desegregation over a two-year period beginning with the middle and high schools. On 5 July, the school committee filed these motions. Judge Garrity held hearings on the motions and decided to allow the school committee to file its own two-year desegregation plan within two weeks. However, the school committee still refused to approve a plan that included busing the students in order to desegregate the schools. John Mirick, the school committee's attorney, announced the committee's decision to the judge, and on 30 July the judge ordered that the state's plan be implemented by September 1974.

In the spring, Mayor Kevin White started attending kaffeeklatsches in private homes in an attempt to gain peaceful compliance with the court order. Twenty to thirty individuals who were opposed to busing were invited to each of these gatherings. The kaffeeklatsches took place in every section of the city except South Boston. Mayor White specifically avoided South Boston because it was the heart of Louise Day Hicks' constituency.

Despite his own earlier attempts to prepare groups of citizens for desegregation, when the court order was handed down Mayor White immediately made a statement abdicating his own responsibility for providing leadership to the community in its implementation of the court order. He indicated that implementation of the court order was the school committee's responsibility and that his responsibility as mayor was to protect public safety (*Boston Globe* 1974: 6/24).

PLANNING FOR DESEGREGATION

During the summer of 1974, leaders of various groups in the community began meeting to plan their strategy for dealing with school desegregation. Leaders of the black community began to use their established organizations to prepare a coalition. The NAACP selected Thomas Atkins as president of what had recently been a leaderless organization. Freedom House, a social service agency in the black community since 1949, had established an Institute on Schools and Education in 1973 with Ellen Jackson as its head. After the desegregation order was handed down, the institute established a rumor center and neighborhood security teams that had the dual goals of protecting black children in white areas and white children in black areas. During the course of the summer, several hundred volunteers organized the teams and carried out office work.

Leaders of the Roman Catholic schools in the Boston archdiocese had announced in December 1973 that students would not be welcomed into the Catholic school system as a way of escaping desegregation. Humberto Cardinal Medeiros continued to stand by this decree verbally—although statistics would reveal that the decrease in Catholic school enrollments was beginning to slow down as desegregation took effect—and announced his support of the judge's order. The Roman Catholic church had also conducted in the spring of 1974 seminars for priests that emphasized the morality of integration and that helped to prepare priests to serve as monitors on school buses.

The City-wide Education Coalition (CWEC), a group composed of parents and teachers who had organized to pressure the school committee in its selection of a superintendent in 1972, also took an active role in the desegregation process. The CWEC set up an information center for parents in January 1974 and hired coordinators with strong ties to their neighborhoods, people who could explain the sometimes complex court language or school department policies in everyday terms, and who could bring their neighbors out to the bus stops during times of tension to act as monitors. The coalition also began a bimonthly newsletter, which had a circulation of about 10,000. It always drew the bulk of its membership from the white community, for it made organizing in troubled white neighborhoods its key thrust. It was here, the group felt, that the most difficulty was likely to occur.

Members of the press also met that summer. The Boston Community Media Council gathered to discuss the problem of how to approach the explosive busing issue without tarnishing its journalistic reputation. What its members decided collectively was to tell the truth but not to sensationalize. The two daily newspapers provided low-key coverage of the opening day of school. However, once problems erupted in the schools, the press changed its tactics and placed a great deal of emphasis on the negative aspects of the desegregation process.

The School Committee's Opposition

While these various community groups were making plans for implementation of the desegregation plan, the school committee was working to stop implementation of the plan. That same month the superintendent asked for a delay, saying that the school system was not ready. The judge denied this request. A pattern of uncooperative behavior on the part of the school department began to evolve. The court ordered the city to release funds, hire proper personnel, and sign bus contracts.

On 7 August 1974, the school committee voted to appeal three of the judge's orders: (1) his denial to stay the state order, (2) his refusal to exempt high school seniors, and (3) his requirement that blacks be hired as teachers on a one-to-one basis with whites until the faculty was desegregated. However, the law firm of Hale and Dorr, the school committee's attorneys, refused to prosecute these appeals.

Apparently Judge Garrity quickly became aware of the fact that the school committee had no intention of assisting with the implementation of the order. Therefore, in August he called on the Community Relations Service (CRS) of the U.S. Justice Department to help him monitor the implementation of the desegregation plan. The judge's formal order mandated that the CRS provide technical assistance, monitor parental involvement, disseminate information, and serve as the judge's liaison with the community.

Several weeks before the schools opened, the mayor, sports heroes, and politicians taped brief speeches for radio and television encouraging Boston citizens to protect the safety of their children. On 9 September, the mayor gave a speech on educational television in which he conveyed a double message to the public: "The order must and will be carried out. . . . I'm for integration but against forced busing. They are not mutually exclusive. . . . People who would boycott schools are asked to weigh the decision carefully, but it is their decision to make" (U.S. Commission on Civil Rights 1975: 30). A few days prior to schools' opening, on 9 September, ROAR mustered between 8,000 and 10,000 people for a demonstration on City Hall Plaza. Their wrath was so intense that they physically assaulted Senator Edward Kennedy, who had refused to endorse an antibusing movement, and they smashed windows in the John F. Kennedy Federal Building.

The first day of the school term was 12 September 1974. Of the students who had registered for school, 71 percent were present that day. The absentee rate was 15 percent higher than usual for the first day of school. The only schools where attendance was a problem were those involved in the desegregation plan.

SOUTH BOSTON HIGH: 1974

A handful of yellow school buses approached South Boston High School that first morning. They were met by reporters, camera crews, a few dozen police, and a crowd of several dozen protestors who jeered at the buses. As the black students left South Boston High School, hundreds of South Boston people jammed the sidewalks and clogged the streets. They hooted and gestured at the departing black students as police made little effort to keep them at a distance. The yellow school buses with the black students inside rolled down the hill.

As the last bus turned a corner and stopped for a red light, a blond teenager picked up a rock and heaved it through a bus window to the cheers of his companions. Soon other buses were also stoned, and several black students and a bus monitor sustained cuts. That the bus could have been caught in traffic, with no police escort of any kind when hostile crowds had been building all day, was an indication to many of how poorly prepared the city was to enforce this court order and, some would say, how the city's leading politicians refused from the outset to deal harshly with the protestors of South Boston.

The day's hostilities were not reserved for black students alone. A handful of white students had defied the antibusing movement's boycott of schools and had attended high school in South Boston that first day. As they left school, they became the immediate targets of jeers and threats from the crowd outside. After the first day, some white parents who continued to send their children to school in South Boston met them routinely at the end of each school day, disgusted that no one else in the school department or the city cared to support children who wanted to attend school. The much publicized boycott was effective in South Boston, but it had no noticeable impact elsewhere.

Each school day that first week, school buses in South Boston were stoned by an angry crowd that gathered each afternoon. NAACP president Thomas Atkins urged blacks not to attend school in South Boston, and many complied. Police Commissioner Robert diGrazia increased police force at the school substantially, with the number of police present reaching 200 by the week's end. Mayor Kevin White ordered police to disperse groups of three or more people near the high school, and groups of ten or more near schools anyplace in the city. The mayor promised in a press conference to ensure the safety of all schoolchildren in Boston.

The first day of school, both major Boston daily papers headlined their front pages with the news that all had gone well at the bulk of Boston's schools. This coverage infuriated antibusing people in South Boston and Charlestown, who charged that the press was covering up the violence in South Boston; although the stonings were reported, they were not the top of the news. It was the beginning of a long period of mistrust between the media and one segment of the public it covered.

If the press made a deliberate effort to remain restrained, it was not always clear that the press was not part of the story. For example, students would often comment that they would not be so boisterous leaving South Boston High School were they not assured of an audience from the press that waited daily outside. Sometimes it seemed like a self-fulfilling prophecy: the press waited anxiously for something to happen, and something always happened. But as many journalists are quick to point out, it is too simple a solution to blame the deep-seated emotions gripping Boston during its desegregation experience on the presence of a few cameras.

Following the first day of school, the mayor attended a meeting of black parents at Freedom House. Although the parents demanded that he call in the national guard and that he arrest those who had incited a riot in South Boston, he managed to quell them. They agreed to give him another chance of protecting their children.

Over the weekend city officials repeatedly assured black community leaders that the situation in South Boston was under control. On Sunday, Atkins told black parents to return their children to South Boston schools. On Monday morning, schools opened quietly in South Boston. A few hours later, three elected public officials from South Boston issued their "Declaration of Clarification," their purported analysis of why resistance to busing was justified. City Councillor Louise Day Hicks, State Senator William Bulger, and State Representative Michael Flaherty wrote that crime was so rampant in Roxbury that it was unsafe for whites to enter that community. If black leaders could halt the crime in their neighborhoods, the trio wrote, perhaps whites could consider going to school there.

In one passage, the declaration claimed that 100 black people who had killed whites in the previous two years were walking the streets of Roxbury. That the claim was entirely false was reported only in a few media outlets and generally stood unrebutted. The declaration ended with a note of commendation to the people of South Boston for the "restraint" they had shown.

State Representative Raymond Flynn, also an opponent of busing, refused to join the other three officials by signing their declaration. He viewed their statement as incendiary and irrelevant to the issue of neighborhood schools.

The situation in South Boston went from bad to worse. At night, bands of young men began roaming the streets of South Boston, smashing windows, setting trash can fires, overturning cars. There were few arrests, but many clashes between the gangs and the tactical police force. By day, public transit buses as well as school buses were being stoned. The crowds continued to swell each afternoon as classes ended, and buses in and out of South Boston traveled with police escort.

In an effort to counter the lawlessness now raging day and night in South Boston, city officials increased police patrols once again and closed tavern and liquor stores in South Boston until the evening. Planned marches through the neighborhood were canceled when city officials refused to issue parade permits. However, James Kelly, who established the South Boston Information Center to "preserve South Boston," had organized a parade through South Boston to protest busing. When he was told that he would not be granted a permit, he and 350 marchers decided to hold their march without a permit. Police attempts to break up the march resulted in assaults on black youths and on property, and in many arrests.

David Duke, Imperial Wizard of the Ku Klux Klan, paid a visit to Boston during that period. He got off a plane and went to South Boston, where a crowd gathered to hear him speak one night. The discussion was one that blatantly advocated racism (Hillson 1977: 3).

The trouble surrounding school desegregation was confined mainly to South Boston but occasionally spilled over to other parts of the city. At Hyde Park High School, the morning of 20 September was marked with fights in the classrooms and hallways. Finally, the situation became completely out of hand, with students rushing from their classrooms when the noise of a fight reached them. Superintendent Leary closed Hyde Park High School for two days, citing severe overcrowding as a key reason for the problems. Unlike South Boston, the problems in Hyde Park were limited to the school itself. There were no large crowds of community people gathered outside Hyde Park High School. Black leaders protested the closing, arguing that Leary was bowing to troublemakers.

Despite the violence in South Boston and Hyde Park, attendance throughout the system was inching upward daily. By the end of the first full week of school, 61,479 out of 81,772 students were attending school. Only at South Boston High did the boycott continue in force: 76 of 1,031 white students were attending high school, 143 out of 380 blacks. By the end of September, city-wide attendance was averaging nearly 80 percent, which is about normal (*Boston Globe* 1975: 5/25).

As the disturbances in the streets of South Boston continued during the first weeks of desegregation, various community leaders appealed to the court for a greater show of force. In the first month of school, 148 arrests were made, 129 persons were injured, and property damage amounted to $50,000. The judge said he had no plans to use federal marshals, state troopers, or national guardsmen.

In the meantime, the mayor made a public speech about the situation, indicating that the school department should be taking more responsibility for the situation. The school committee responded by requesting that the judge make the mayor a codefendant in the case. The judge agreed to make the mayor a codefendant so that he could monitor more closely the city agencies that were becoming involved.

At the invitation of City Councillor Hicks, about 300 antibusers continued meeting in the city council chambers in closed sessions to formally organize themselves. By the end of September, ROAR was publicly unveiled with the blessing and active participation of many of the city's most prominent politicians. ROAR routinely began holding its weekly meetings in City Hall, banning press and nonmembers alike from its sessions. One of ROAR's first events was a protest at the *Boston Globe* charging the newspaper with covering up black violence against whites.

COMMUNITY SUPPORT AND INCREASED TENSION

While all of these occurrences were commanding a great deal of media attention, Judge Garrity and the Community Relations Service were working on a plan to increase parental participation in the desegregation process. In his order of 4 October 1974, Judge Garrity established mechanisms for such parental participation. Each school would elect representatives to a Racial-Ethnic Parent Council (REPC). The mandated purposes of the REPCs would be to ensure adequate and impartial investigation and recommendations on racially and ethnically oriented school problems; to create communication among parents, students, teachers, and administrators regarding solution of such problems; and to promote understanding and common purpose among various elements of the community to offer the best education. Blacks, whites, Asians, and Hispanics were to be guaranteed representation on these councils.

These bodies would in turn elect representatives to a City-wide Parent Advisory Council (CPAC), which would meet regularly with the superintendent and the school committee. Separate student councils were structured in the same fashion as the parent councils at each of the city's schools.

Elections were in fact held at the schools in the fall; the most troubled school, South Boston High, was faced with the problem of most white parents' refusal to participate because they felt that participation would be symbolic of their acceptance of desegregation. Even though other schools managed to elect representatives, attendance at council meetings was not as high as anticipated, Hispanics and Asians failed to participate because of a language barrier, and the work of the councils got off to a very slow start.

In October, tensions in the city increased, and federal officials and the national media played a role in the events. On 2 and 3 October, South Boston High School was the scene of several interracial melees. The day of 4 October was planned for a school boycott by antibusers, to be accompanied by a peaceful rally in South Boston attended by 7,000 to 10,000 people.

On 7 October, a mob on the streets of South Boston dragged a black man from his car and attacked him. Black youths soon retaliated, and rioting spread to the vicinity of a black housing project. Mayor White responded by appealing to Judge Garrity to send in federal marshals. It was at this point that the judge asked the U.S. Department of Justice how many federal marshals were available. The crowded courtroom, much to the embarrassment of Mayor White and his staff, was told that there are only about fifty federal marshals in the entire country equipped for the type of work the mayor wanted accomplished.

White then changed his plea for help to an attack upon the federal court and sounded a theme he would repeat in coming years: "It's your federal court order, Your Honor, you enforce it." Mayor White then left the courtroom.

Lawyers for the plaintiff black parents in the case joined the mayor in asking for a show of force. But the court responded that "this is not a case that needs symbolism, this is a case that needs security." Citing the court's opinion in the Little Rock Arkansas case that neither public opposition nor public disorder could interfere with the protection of constitutional rights, Judge Garrity ordered additional security to be provided step by step.

On 9 October, President Gerald Ford held a press conference during which he was questioned about the situation in Boston. His reply was that he disagreed with the court order and with forced busing, although he did ask the people of Boston to reject violence. Ford was immediately criticized for inciting further resistance and violence.

The mayor responded to Ford's press conference vehemently with a press conference of his own. He stated that he would support Phase II of the desegregation plan only under four conditions: that (1) the federal government issue guidelines on committing federal force, (2) the federal government guarantee the safety of Boston's schoolchildren, (3) changes be made in the desegregation plan to eliminate inequities, and (4) more financial aid be forthcoming.

At about the same time, Mayor White invited five grass-roots whites who were antibusers and five grass-roots blacks to meet with him secretly at City Hall. He asked them to prepare a statement deploring violence and advocating safety for the students. Rita Graul, a leader of the antibusing movement and one of those attending the meeting, refused to endorse any statement without ROAR's approval. The debate became extremely heated and ended with no statement of consensus.

Then on 15 October, a white student at Hyde Park High School was stabbed. Everyone expected the stabbing to incite more violence, especially in South Boston. President Ford ordered the 82nd Airborne Division at Fort Bragg, North Carolina, to go on "increased readiness" in case they were needed in Boston. But the state police inside South Boston High were successful in defusing the situation. The national guard stayed in the armories for two weeks, then were sent home. The trouble in the streets of South Boston calmed, and police were withdrawn.

By 11 November 1974, South Boston High School attendance had reached a new high of 568, including 381 whites. However, whites had refused to elect representatives to a biracial student council, although blacks had elected representatives to the council.

Throughout all the chaos around South Boston High and Hyde Park High, the other 200 schools in the city were calm. Buses traveled daily through strange neighborhoods pulling students of all races together, many for the first time. There were no incidents, and attendance grew.

The quiet may have occurred because ROAR had turned its attention elsewhere. The November election included a referendum question, known throughout the city simply as Question 7, that if approved would have taken power from the school committee and given it to the mayor. Mayor White publicly endorsed Question 7 and cranked up his political machine to work for its passage, while ROAR opposed Question 7 and made it a battleground for the busing movement. The voters defeated the question, indicating that the present school committee's handling of the desegregation issue was what they wanted.

But if ROAR was satisfied with its electoral victory and its successful boycott of schools on 22 November, it was distressed over an inability to swell its ranks in communities outside of South Boston and Charlestown. For example, in Brighton, a community that is mainly white, but that has long had an integrated high school, parents rebuffed ROAR when antibusers tried to organize there. Brighton Home and School Association member Barbara Cosgrove said, "I didn't find them offering anything constructive, just a general atmosphere of fear."

CONTINUED TROUBLE AT SOUTH BOSTON HIGH

But events at South Boston High School were soon to overshadow any minor setbacks ROAR was experiencing elsewhere and to prove once and for all, antibusing leaders said, that forced desegregation could never succeed. Like so many other problems inside troubled schools, the biggest disaster of the 1974 school year was preceded by several days of small-scale violence at South Boston High: fights in the halls, pushing matches in the cafeteria. These events intensified during the beginning of December. On 4 December, an interracial scuffle between two youths broke out. The following day, a melee involving about sixty girls took place, and 125 white students left the building to protest. The following day, an assembly of white students called by the headmaster to encourage them to elect representatives to the student biracial council ended with a militant march through the school. Police eventually ejected the white students from the building.

On 6 December, the school committee held an informal meeting with ROAR leaders. Rita Graul encouraged the school committee not to apply for federal aid to assist desegregation and to refuse to submit a desegregation plan to Judge Garrity. School committee chairman John Kerrigan refused both requests. ROAR leaders also suggested that South Boston High School be closed.

On the morning of 11 December, a 17-year-old white student, a South Boston native and son of an active antibusing mother, was stabbed by a black student in the halls of South Boston High. Word of the stabbing spread through the school and through the streets. By midmorning, a crowd of several hundred angry whites had gathered outside the high school. White students already had been dismissed for the day, and inside waited several dozen black students. The crowd was angry, and even the appearance of their own Louise Day Hicks and State Senator William Bulger could not calm the mob. When Hicks announced that the student would be all right and urged the crowd to disperse, she received hoots of derision, perhaps for the first time in her political career.

It soon became clear that the police had a major tactical problem on their hands. The black students inside the building were being held virtual hostage by the mob outside. Even an immense number of police, officials felt, probably could not ensure a safe exit for the blacks. The police secretly led the black students to safety out the back door, while the crowd out front thought the blacks would be using the empty buses on that side of the building.

Superintendent William Leary decided to close the entire South Boston High School complex of nine buildings for the remainder of December. Its fate after the Christmas vacation remained in doubt. Some city leaders wanted the school closed permanently, arguing that desegregation could never come to South Boston. South Boston residents, on the other hand, anxiously pressed for the school to remain open. They wanted to keep their school, even if it meant keeping it under the unpopular terms of a court-imposed desegregation plan. To lose South Boston High School would be to lose an important part of their community.

The NAACP also wanted the school reopened. Some black leaders resented the notion that the antidesegregation groups could force them out of any public facility in Boston, especially a school and especially under these circumstances. Other black leaders thought the school should be closed permanently, because police were unable to control the violence. Mayor White also advocated closing the school permanently.

Judge Garrity refused to close the high school. Then he questioned the motives of a school committee that would let the violence and tension build to the point that injury was imminent. As this debate simmered, both sides marshaled their forces. On 4 December, 20,000 people joined a March Against Racism, called for by black State Senator William Owens. This event drew national civil rights leaders as well as a sizable number of white people. The very next day, ROAR rallied on the Boston Common, where 5,000 people cheered the call for a constitutional amendment to halt forced busing. Although Louise Day Hicks opposed it, the rally was endorsed by such political leaders as City Councillor Albert O'Neill, State Representative Raymond Flynn, and school committee member John Kerrigan (Hillson 1977: 97).

Superintendent Leary met with informal leaders of the South Boston and Roxbury communities as well as political leaders. One mother from South Boston agreed to organize mothers who would patrol South Boston High School to ensure the safety of the students. More than 100 South Boston mothers and several mothers from Roxbury volunteered for this assignment. And so Superintendent Leary decided to reopen the South Boston High School complex on 8 January. The reopening was peaceful, although the school was once more under heavy police protection.

Three hundred state troopers and 100 Metropolitan District Commission officers stationed at the school assumed many duties previously carried out by the Boston Police. Students and visitors alike began passing through a metal detector at the school door to guard against any weapons entering the building.

Roxbury High School, which had been closed along with its sister school, South Boston High, reopened as well. Roxbury High had been trouble free since its first day of school, although only a handful of whites attended. Because they were part of the same district, school officials closed Roxbury High when South Boston was shut down, a decision bitterly resented by the staff and students at Roxbury High.

MORE RESISTANCE FROM THE SCHOOL COMMITTTEE

While the violence at South Boston High School was causing repercussions in the rest of the city, the school committee, which was under court order to file a desegregation plan for the fall of 1975 on 16 December 1974, was refusing to obey the court. Staff at the school department had spent the fall working up an extensive proposal for the court. Because the plan included busing, the school committee voted three to two to defy the court order and not approve the plan for submission. School committee attorney John Mirick filed the plan on his own "as an officer of the court," without the school committee's approval.

The following day the lawyers for the plaintiff black parents asked for criminal contempt citations against the three committee members who would not approve the plan, John Kerrigan, John McDonough, and Paul Ellison. That same day, John Mirick and the prestigious Boston law firm that he represented, Hale and Dorr, announced their withdrawal from the case. They would no longer defend the Boston School Committee. The new attorney for the school committee was to be J. J. Sullivan, John McDonough's long-time friend.

In court the following day, 18 December, Judge Garrity denied the criminal contempt motion but ordered the three members to show cause why they were not in civil contempt of court. He set the hearing for 27 December.

Judge Garrity later found the school committee members in civil contempt. He ordered them fined and barred from participating in desegregation matters for defying his orders. They were given until 7 January to purge themselves of contempt. Meanwhile, the three who had defied the court became heroes to the antibusing forces. Their supporters rallied outside the courtroom and talked of defense funds. The two members who approved the plan, Kathleen Sullivan and Paul Tierney, were spat upon. Two of the three members who had defied the court were attorneys and were fearful that Judge Garrity would take some action preventing them from practicing law. They decided to purge themselves of contempt, filing the voluntary desegregation plan once again. Judge Garrity accepted this gesture and removed the contempt citations.

In the meantime, on 19 December, the U.S. Federal Court of Appeals for the First Circuit had unanimously upheld Judge Garrity's decision in the desegregation case. John Kerrigan immediately announced that the school committee would appeal to the U.S. Supreme Court. Mayor White said the city would fund the appeal, even though he believed that the chances for a reversal were slim.

PLANS FOR 1975

By 21 January, Judge Garrity had received sixteen proposals for the desegregation of schools in September 1975. By the end of the month, he had appointed two "court experts" to be his educational consultants. Dr. Robert

Dentler and Dr. Marvin Scott, dean and associate dean, respectively, of Boston University's School of Education, were to become major components in Boston's desegregation. Along with the experts, Judge Garrity named four "masters" to conduct hearings on further desegregation plans: Jacob Spiegel, a retired supreme judicial court justice; Edward McCormack, former state attorney general; Francis Keppel, former U.S. commissioner of education; and Charles Willie, professor at Harvard Graduate School of Education. Dr. Scott and Professor Willie were the only black members of the panel.

The masters visited schools and conducted eleven days of hearings, listening to school officials and desegregation experts from throughout the country. At the end of March, the masters and experts filed a desegregation plan of their own, which created nine community school districts and one city-wide magnet school; drew up contracts between school and museums, businesses, and universities; and created a city-wide education council. The plan called for the busing of 10,000 to 14,000 students.

The masters' plan was soon criticized, both for not going far enough because it left some districts 85 percent white and others 60 percent black, and for going too far because it included busing. The NAACP viewed the plan as a capitulation to the threats of violence. All major parties in the case attacked the masters' plan as "unconstitutional."

The court held hearings on the masters' plan and then proceeded on its own. The judge emphasized that he wanted not a plan of numbers, but one of educational quality. He continually stressed that no parent would refuse a bus ride for his or her children if at the end of it there was an excellent education. His emphasis was on the magnets—schools that would draw students from throughout the city and that would each specialize in a certain area of education. He personally met with college and business leaders in the Boston area, seeking their support and cooperation.

The school committee fought against university involvement, charging that the colleges would use Boston students for experimental purposes. Meanwhile, the antibusing movement was busy trying to spread its message and sign up converts. In Charlestown, ROAR found a ready-made following and soon was allied with the Powderkeg, a group of antibusers whose title suggested that that community would blow up any moment. But elsewhere, membership rolls remained about the same. Although membership figures never were published, many observers felt that ROAR reached its height during the first year of busing. The group was able to command public and media attention long after that, however, perhaps because many political leaders still championed its cause.

That same winter, ROAR made its bid to become a national organization. In March, 1,400 people mostly from Massachusetts, marched on Washington to support a constitutional amendment prohibiting busing. (That the amendment itself would have no effect on the Boston busing order was generally shrugged off by leaders of the Washington protest.) Louise Day Hicks led the protest in the hopes of shaping a national movement with herself as the head. But the march failed to attract the thousands of supporters the Massachusetts contingent hoped would follow their antibusing banner.

In the meantime, the mayor was buckling even more under the pressure. On 5 March 1975, Mayor White was quoted as saying that he was willing to talk about the possibility of providing city buildings and funds for persons interested in establishing alternatives to public schools. He did say it was illegal to do so as a way of circumventing desegregation and that any private schools established should enroll black students (*Boston Globe* 1975: 3/5). The mayor was not the only one who faltered in his support of the desegregation plan. That same month, although Cardinal Medeiros reaffirmed his belief in school integration, he denied any capability to help plan the process of integration.

In May, South Boston antibusing leader Mary Binda announced the antibusing movement's ultimate solution to the busing dilemma: South Boston's own private academy, South Boston Heights. Three private schools already had been incorporated by this time, South Boston Heights, Noddle Isle Academy in East Boston, and Hyde Park Academy, but none was actually functioning. Together they incorporated themselves as the Massachusetts Independent School Association. The academies never drew huge numbers of students, partly because of their tuition. Hyde Park Academy, for example, charged $576 a student. By January 1976, South Boston Heights had 400 students enrolled, Hyde Park counted 250, and Parkway Academy in West Roxbury reported 120 students.

DESEGREGATION: PHASE II

On 10 May 1975, Judge Garrity's order for Phase II was handed down. At its heart were twenty-two magnet schools that were to be paired with area colleges, businesses, and cultural institutions. The city was divided into eight community districts, the city-wide magnet district forming a ninth district. About 21,000 students would be bused (*Boston Globe* 1975: 5/11).

The plan closed thirty antiquated school buildings (the school committee had already closed ten), and established another district-wide level of parent councils (CDACs) as well as the City-wide Coordinating Council (CCC), a group of forty leaders of the Boston area, selected by the judge. This group would monitor the plan's implementation as well as supervise the CDACs (*Boston Globe* 1975: 5/11).

Phase II reached out into all sections of Boston, including areas such as Charlestown and West Roxbury that had been untouched by the state plan implemented under Phase I. Heeding the masters' plan, Judge Garrity did not immediately involve East Boston, that section of Boston separated from the rest of the city by water and accessible only by bridge or tunnel. A magnet school was set up in East Boston, but for the most part, desegregation in this predominantly Italian, and heavily antibusing, community remained voluntary.

The school committee immediately appealed the plan. It then asked the judge for a delay in its implementation. In the interim, on 12 May, the U.S. Supreme Court refused to hear the Boston case. Then on 24 May, Garrity refused the school committee's request for a delay.

May continued to witness events organized by groups on both sides of the issue. The NAACP organized a coalition of 10,000 marchers demanding quality education. The ROAR group held a national conference in Boston and elected Louise Day Hicks as president.

In June, the federal court delivered a lengthy memorandum spelling out the basis for the court's Phase II plan. Again, Garrity emphasized that the time was past when desegregation could be carried out by a "handful" of white and black students. He said that the nearest-school policy was inadequate because of segregated housing patterns that arose in part because of school segregation—a situation that could be corrected only by busing.

Community reaction to the Phase II order fell along predictable lines. Mayor Kevin White greeted the order with the warning that "Judge Garrity has virtually guaranteed a continuation of the present level of tension and hostility throughout the city" (*Boston Globe* 1975: 5/12). Louise Day Hicks called the plan "outrageous," "the product of a callous despotic mend," and predicted "chaos and disorder in the schools followed by a mass white exodus from Boston" (*Boston Globe* 1975: 5/11).

THE SUMMER OF 1975

During the summer of 1975, the court spent much time in preparing for the implementation of its plan. Court experts worked with school officials, but Judge Garrity consistently found cause to strike out against the school committee for "thwarting" Phase II by failing to appoint competent people, provide adequate funds, and plan teacher and administrative workshops. The school committee threw the blame back on the court.

Also during that summer, work continued on the court-ordered pairings, one of the most significant aspects of Phase II. Under the Phase II plan, twenty-three colleges and universities, fourteen cultural institutions, and twenty businesses collaborated with various schools in initiating educational programs. In the summer of 1975, institutions of higher education contracted with the Boston School Department to begin working with their pairing partners. Most pairings met for several weeks and emerged with a program to be implemented upon the opening of school. The planning efforts were supported by funding made available by the state department of education.

The universities, colleges, and cultural institutions developed various models for involvement depending on the availability of resources and staff. Many assigned faculty members as coordinators with release time from other responsibilities, while others hired new personnel. A school-by-school analysis shows that the pairing programs covered a wide spectrum of activities including classroom teaching assistance, staff development workshops, basic skills activities, college course work, and management assistance and training, to name a few. Each program was specifically designed to address the particular needs of the school or district in the pairing. Although reluctant to participate initially, all the college presidents committed their institutions to at least three years of involvement, a time period believed to coincide with judicial involvement.

Three years later the number of participating institutions had increased, but continuation was dependent largely upon outside sources of funding.

Like the universities, colleges, and cultural institutions, the business community was wary of entering a potentially violent situation. However, businesses joined with eighteen high schools to establish the Occupational Resource Center. Programs included such activities as exploring the world of work, business employees teaching courses in economics, and student internships in businesses.

In July, any hopes of an easy transition into Phase II were dashed when the school assignments suddenly were mailed to students with no prior warning. City and school department information centers were flooded with calls from anxious and confused and even angry parents. Also, 250 individuals blocked the entrance to South Boston High School to sabotage the election of white parents to the school's biracial council.

By August, many of the opponents of forced busing were beginning the agitation that would lead to a difficult school opening the next month. A handful of blacks trying to swim at Carson Beach in South Boston were met with angry gestures, words, and rocks. The disruptions soon spread to some housing projects in South Boston and Roxbury.

In Charlestown, which would be affected for the first time, Tom Johnson, president of the Home and School Association, urged a massive boycott. The strategy was announced at an antibusing march of several hundred people under the sponsorship of ROAR. Marching in the parade were State Representative Dennis Kearney, City Councillor Albert O'Neil, and Roberta Delaney, head of the Little City Hall in Charlestown. In Charlestown, as in South Boston the year before, resistance to busing seemed clearly to bear the official stamp of approval.

Parents working for a peaceful desegregation of the schools received neither the publicity nor the leadership of public officials accorded to the antibusers. South Boston's Diane Martin, of the Task Force for Positive Action, bemoaned the screamed insults and racial slurs, and the stoning of buses and demonstrations in front of schools. But her voice was faint compared to the opposition. Late in the month, parental turnout at open houses for parents was sparse, a fact blamed partly on apathy and partly on a lack of information from school officials.

If ROAR was relatively quiet over the summer months, the organization became highly visible a few days before the schools opened. An antibusing rally on City Hall Plaza heard Hicks warn that its participants were watching the demise of the great city. Other city officials as well as some union representatives joined her on the speakers' stand, once again lending credence to the hope that even at this late day, the federal busing order might be avoided.

Thirteen days before the opening of school, the City-wide Coordinating Council charged the school committee with foot-dragging and talked about a lack of readiness, mounting disarray, and problems with the transfer of power between the departing and entering superintendents, who were not on friendly terms to begin with.

Judge Garrity announced that he was considering a proposal by the U.S. Commission on Civil Rights to strip the school committee of its power because, according to the Civil Rights Commission report, its members were defaulting in their duty to desegregate Boston's schools. It was a threat that during an election year could not be ignored. Slowly, the school committee began approving funds and personnel. But the effort was, for many, too late. The buses rolled relatively peacefully under the increased security on the streets, but Garrity referred to key elements in the desegregation as "a horror show."

Mayor White was in an election year and faced a difficult race. Unlike the year before, White was highly visible, and he too took a hard line, insisting that those violating the law would not be violating local statutory laws, but federal laws.

THE SECOND YEAR: 1975

On 8 September 1975, 288 buses carried 25,653 students who were met coming and going by an extremely large show of police force. While helicopters circled overhead, on the streets there were over 1,000 Boston police, 350 state police,

250 MDC police, federal marshals, and 600 national guardsmen in armories in South Boston.

The police were as obvious in Charlestown on the opening day of school in 1975 as they had been subtle in South Boston the year before. The first morning, residents awoke to the whir of state police helicopters overhead. Sharpshooters with high-powered rifles stood on rooftops. Mounted police and motorcycle police alike guarded the high school, the expected scene of trouble.

There was no trouble that first day, inside any school in the city. Outside, there were brief skirmishes between police and youths in Charlestown, but no buses or black students were molested. The mayor termed it a "good day," and state Secretary of Education Paul Parks credited the calm to good planning.

Yet, like the year before, the emotions stirred during the day boiled over at night. In both Charlestown and South Boston roving bands of youths taunted police then ran away, started trash fires, and generally wreaked havoc in their neighborhoods. One night, the birthplace of John F. Kennedy in Brookline was firebombed with an antibusing slogan scrawled nearby. Four hundred Charlestown women began the first of several "mothers' marches" to protest busing, although they often distintegrated into shouting matches with the police, who refused to let them march near the schools. Yet none of the violence took place inside the schools. NAACP president Thomas Atkins speculated that the general calm was because "Phase II had an added sense of inevitability" that was lacking the previous year.

As attendance in the city's schools grew through the fall, the court concentrated more and more of its efforts in locating students who had left the system. The court found estimates that massive numbers of students had fled the system (estimated at 20,000 by antibusing forces) were far from the truth. The court discovered that Boston, like many big-city school systems, had for years inflated its enrollment figures to increase state and federal aid. Latest figures showed not 93,000 students, but 84,000 students. In the last two years the system had lost about 6,000 students from that 84,000 figure. How many losses were attributable to desegregation is unknown.

The show of force succeeded in scaling down the violence, but the weak link remained the Boston School Department. Superintendent of Schools William Leary had been replaced. His successor was Marion Fahey, a former teacher in the city's schools who had come up through the ranks of twenty-six years in the system. The shift of power and personnel and the implementation of a complex desegregation plan by an inexperienced administrative staff only increased the chaos.

By the end of two mainly peaceful weeks of busing, many community leaders outside of the antibusing strongholds were gradually becoming optimistic. Ellen Jackson of Freedom House in Roxbury remarked that developments seemed encouraging, especially when compared to the previous year. But she went on to caution that the increase of mothers' marches gave her the feeling that these marches were not spontaneous, but by design, and that they would increase still further in number and try to reach the schools.

Through the next several weeks a series of minor disruptions gave evidence of the smoldering tensions still inside some schools. On 8 October, black students refused to leave their buses outside South Boston High School to underscore their demands for more black teachers and aides. Another day 300 white students walked out of South Boston High School; they claimed blacks were "favored."

Also in October 1975, elections for Racial-Ethnic Parent Councils took place at all schools in the city. Although letters announcing the election were sent to 80,000 parents, fewer than 3,000 parents turned out to vote. Only 1,326 of the 2,000 council seats were filled (*Boston Globe* 1975: 10/26).

The majority of schools remained calm throughout the academic year Isolated disturbances occurred in Charlestown, which was included for the first time under Phase II. The situation at South Boston High School began deteriorating late in the fall.

Prior to the problems at South Boston High School, a city-wide election took place in November. As expected, all the prominent antibusing incumbents once again rode the issue into office with East Boston antibusing leader Pixie Palladino barely winning a spot on the school committee. Yet the highest vote-getter in the city was not a leader of the antibusing movement, but Kathleen Sullivan, a young, one-term member of the school committee who ran a campaign oriented to parental involvement in the schools and the importance of improving the quality of education. In a bitterly fought mayoral race, incumbent Kevin White won, though narrowly, in a contest in which both he and his challenger avoided the busing issue almost entirely. The success of the antibusing candidates may have encouraged the vehement antibusing forces in South Boston to continue their struggle.

SOUTH BOSTON HIGH: 1975

Although South Boston High School had witnessed numerous disturbances the previous year, in the 1975–1976 school year the situation became so intense that the judge took the management of the school out of the hands of the school committee and placed it in a federal receivership. This action served to further alienate the school committee and the residents of South Boston.

South Boston High School was the heart of the South Boston community. Over the years Boston teachers and administrators who did favors for school committee members were rewarded with positions at the school. The school was overstaffed; prior to the desegregation order, it had 100 teachers for less than 1,000 students. Yet this staffing pattern did not increase the educational quality of the school. South Boston High School students consistently scored below average on standardized reading tests, and less than 10 percent of the students went on to college.

The educational quality matched the physical condition of the school. It was one of the most rundown schools in the system. The paint in the building was peeling, graffiti were on the walls, toilets were broken and dirty, many lights did not work, and equipment was antiquated. The condition of the school could have been altered easily because of the special favor South Boston High School enjoyed with the school committee, but those with political power in South Boston did not view improving the high school as a priority.

The people of South Boston viewed desegregation as the end to South Boston High as they knew and loved it. It mattered little that no white high school student in South Boston was ordered bused out of South Boston High under Phase II. The only thing that mattered to the people of South Boston was that the high school was no longer exclusively theirs. Black students were in their high school, coming through their neighborhood. The center of their lives was under attack.

South Boston residents went to the defense of their high school. Before the buses rolled they led the marches, the motorcades, the rallies. When the motorcycles with their flashing lights followed by three yellow buses came up G Street, the major thoroughfare up to the school, they fought in the streets—with words, gestures, and eventually physical combat—with police who were protecting the black students. When the black students continued to come into South Boston, the white students went into the school and continued their fights. Those white students who wanted to fight to keep their school found a group of black students who, like themselves, were not interested in education, but in fighting. Every day the two groups would go at each other, often involving others who would have preferred to learn but found themselves dragged into the confrontations.

The school, which had always been open to white parents, remained open, and community residents held meetings in the school and goaded white students to fight to retain their school. The access enjoyed by whites was denied blacks. South Boston was not a place a black person could move through safely. Blacks were courting danger if they drove or walked through the community.

Black parents and leaders appealed to the school committee to take some action to improve the quality of education at South Boston High School. The school committee ignored the plea. The City-wide Coordinating Council asked to meet with the teachers to mediate the problems between whites and blacks at the school. The faculty flatly refused to meet with the CCC. The black community again turned to the court.

During the first year of desegregation school officials, white community leaders, and the mayor had wanted South Boston High School closed because of the violence. But for the black community, South Boston was a symbol of the desegregation fight. They were determined not to bow to the racism there.

In the second year, the white community changed its mind. It did not want to lose South Boston High School; it wanted the school kept open—but under its terms, and its terms were that South Boston High School be kept all white.

In November 1975, the NAACP took a surprising position in court. Attorneys said they wanted Judge Garrity to consider closing South Boston High School. They filed affidavits from black students citing harassment by white students and teachers, as well as unfair treatment by police. One affidavit told of a teacher who jumped up on his desk and made monkey gestures to black students in the class. Others referred to a football coach biased against blacks, who sent them into practice without proper equipment, and of a transitional aide who beat black students.

Additional affidavits told of antibusing meetings held inside the school auditorium by neighborhood parents who consistently yelled racial epithets and walked through the corridors singing "Bye Bye Blackbird." Between classes, according to the affidavits, white students would chant "Jump down, turn around, pick a bale of cotton," and "Two, four, six, eight, assassinate the nigger apes," with no reprimands from teachers or administrators.

The day after the NAACP filed its affidavit, the Boston School Committee and the Home and School Association asked Judge Garrity to delay for a month the NAACP's motion for a hearing on the problems at South Boston High School. Judge Garrity refused, saying the urgency of the situation and the serious nature of the affidavits dictated an immediate hearing. He asked his court staff and the CCC why he had been kept "completely unaware" of the deteriorating situation at South Boston High.

On 21 November, with a crowded courtroom and national press in attendance, Judge Garrity began hearing the testimony of black students. They detailed the charges in the affidavits, although there were some inconsistencies Defense attorneys attacked the credibility of the students and it soon became a matter of "whom do you believe—the students or the teachers, the police, the administrators?"

One of the most respected men in South Boston High was William Reid, headmaster of the school since 1965. Sixty-two years old and a resident of South Boston, Reid had been teaching history in the Boston public schools for thirty years, twenty-six of them in South Boston. He had welcomed the black students and tried to administer the school equitably. But the pressure from the community, the quality of his staff, and his own inexperience with desegregation made his task an impossible one. Since he had been at South Boston High he had given the community the kind of school it wanted. Now under court order, he could no longer provide that, nor could he provide the nondiscriminatory desegregated education the law demanded.

In the courtroom, Reid admitted that the black students' charges of racism in the school were "basically honest." He spoke of sagging teacher morale, and the lack of community support undermining desegregation. He said there was a growing white attendance but also an increasing number of fights between white and black students. But he did defend the education at the school. The following day Judge Garrity, unannounced, made his first visit to South Boston High School.

Hearings continued. In all, there were six days of testimony, with students, police, teachers, administrators. After the hearings, Judge Garrity returned to South Boston High for another look at the school. More extensive this time, his tour concluded by eating lunch in the cafeteria with students. Judge Garrity would remark later that he returned to South Boston High because he really could not believe what he saw there on his first visit.

On 9 December—a day known in South Boston as Black Friday—Judge Garrity handed down his ruling. South Boston High was put under total receivership of the court. The Boston School Committee was stripped of its power in all matters relating to South Boston High. The Office of School Security and the Office of [Desegregation] Implementation for the school department were also taken out of the hands of the school committee.

Expressing "enormous confidence" in Superintendent of Schools Marion Fahey, Garrity made her the immediate receiver, answerable only to the court, and Joseph McDonough, area superintendent of South Boston, was made supervisor of the high school (McDonough would later say he wished at the time he had said to the judge: "Thanks, but no thanks"). The court also ordered headmaster Reid and his staff, including the football coach, transferred to other schools.

As disturbing as the rulings were to the people of South Boston, it was Garrity's observations that alarmed people. The judge offered the first real glimpse of what was happening inside the school. The atmosphere outside the school—where sidewalks and lampposts were painted with "Resist," "Nigger Go Home," "Never"—was carried on inside the school. Black students all sat on one or the other side of the room or toward the rear, and at separate tables in the cafeteria. A black girl who took a seat at a cafeteria table at which some white girls were already seated was reprimanded by the building administrator for making a provocative move.

Garrity noted that of the 891 students enrolled (542 white, 315 black) average daily attendance was only about 340 pupils. The school, he said, was "identifiably white." Of the 100 teachers, 7 were black; of 45 support people, none was black, and of the 90 state troopers inside, only 2 were black. The atmosphere of the school was not that of racial or any other tension, but that of lassitude and emptiness. There was none of the youthful spontaneity characteristic of a high school. The students appeared to be the victims of constant cynical surveillance, unconcerned and uninvolved.

The sharpest attack was on the Boston School Committee. Garrity charged that the committee's principal tactic was to do no more than what the court ordered. The court therefore had to depend on the good faith and professionalism of various officials and employees of the school system to carry out the spirit as well as the letter of its orders to improve both desegregation and education at South Boston High School.

The night the ruling was handed down, the headquarters of the NAACP was firebombed. In South Boston, the order was met with anger and unrest. As school committee members made speeches condemning the court, tensions tightened inside the school. More police were called in, white students repeatedly walked out of class. The school committee appealed. Louise Day Hicks said Garrity's order "smacks of a totalitarian type of government. A police state exists" (*Boston Globe* 1975: 12/10). The judge became known in South Boston as "Hitler." Both the *Boston Globe* and the *New York Times,* however, editorially supported the judge's order.

While the community protested, the judge and Superintendent Fahey began plans for the revitalization of South Boston High School. Not having to deal with the school committee, special programs were instituted at the school, new equipment brought in, and over $100,000 worth of renovations were done inside the school, including a paint job.

The beginning of the year saw an interim headmaster running the school in relative peace while Garrity and Fahey began interviews of prospective headmasters. They decided on Jerome Winegar, an assistant principal at a St. Paul, Minnesota, junior high school. Although the school committee fought to reinstate Reid, Garrity finally ordered the school committee to appoint Winegar.

In April, Winegar made his first visit to South Boston High School. He was jeered and taunted. South Boston High School had prepared for his visit by writing in large neat letters across the street in front of the school, "Go Home Jerome" and "Winegar, We Don't Want You."

The violence that marked the first two years at South Boston High School had not returned with the same intensity. But as Winegar began to take over the helm of the school during the spring of 1976, and as he prepared for the next fall, he repeatedly told the press, "It's going to take a hell of a long time to turn this school around."

At the end of 1977, South Boston High School was still under receivership. In the fall of 1978, Judge Garrity removed the federal receivership from South Boston High School, which still had a higher than average suspension rate.

There were still disturbances inside the school. Millions of dollars had been put into additional programs, new teachers and staff had been hired, yet everyone agreed, South Boston High School still had a long way to go.

On 14 January 1976, the U.S. Court of Appeals for the First Circuit rejected a joint appeal by the mayor, the school committee, and the Home and School Association of the Phase II desegregation plan.

THE REST OF THE CITY

Also in January, students in East Boston walked out of school protesting the conversion of East Boston High School into a magnet school. Students at Charlestown High School began their daily marches to City Hall that same month. Leaving the school in the morning, several dozen students descended on City Hall to protest busing. There they were greeted warmly by Councillor Hicks and others, who arranged for them to wait comfortably in the council chamber munching on doughnuts and sipping coffee, while she organized a meeting with the mayor.

After this first warm reception, students from Charlestown High, and occasionally other schools as well, began marching out of their schools down to city offices fairly often. A smiling city official usually was on hand to congratulate their interest and placate them.

The resistance on the streets began to heat up around this time as well. In mid-February an antibusing march in South Boston erupted into a rock-throwing melee with police. South Boston leaders later accused police of overreacting to a peaceful march, even though seventy police were injured in the ruckus.

With the mayor's blessing, Police Commissioner diGrazia promised an all-out crackdown on future troublemakers, whether in the streets or at public meetings. Two weeks later, 250 people marched peacefully through South Boston, while police kept a low profile. The marchers clearly wished to demonstrate that they could parade for their cause without violence. Indeed, the march was heavily patrolled by men who called themselves the South Boston Marshals and who took it upon themselves to "police their own." However, the march ended in violence with attacks on blacks and battles with the police (Hillson 1977: 211).

ROAR continued to make free use of public buildings for private business until March, when public criticism and private rifts ended ROAR's weekly meetings in City Hall. The organization began to split in its own power struggle between Louise Day Hicks and Pixie Palladino, two women who had successfully shaped and ridden the antibusing movement into office. Although the organization was to continue its public posturing, its effectiveness clearly was on the decline. Palladino soon started a splinter group called ROAR United.

The City-wide Parents' Advisory Councils (CPACs) and the Community District Advisory Council (CDAC) were beginning to take their first public stands. In March, they appealed to diGrazia and White for a statement of support for those parents complying with Garrity's orders. And later they applauded the police commissioner's tough stand on troublemakers. Yet CPAC and CDAC never were to attract the strong support from public officials, state or local, so often enjoyed by those opposed to busing.

In March, the Massachusetts House of Representatives overwhelmingly passed a measure supporting a constitutional amendment prohibiting busing (Hillson 1977: 217). Also in March, the school committee intensified its conflict with Superintendent Fahey. Even though the superintendent had been cooperating with Judge Garrity and had been placed in charge of the South Boston High School receivership, the school committee had continuously evaded the judge's orders. Now the school committee was criticizing the superintendent for dragging in her desegregation effort. At the same time, the committee offered its own desegregation plan.

In April, the student marches to City Hall finally resulted in near disaster. A group of unruly white students from South Boston was enroute to City Hall to proclaim its opposition to forced busing when a black man crossed City Hall Plaza. Passersby stood stunned as the white youths beat the man with an American flag, breaking his nose and demonstrating to many once and for all that despite their protests that busing was the issue, the issue in fact was racial prejudice. Two weeks later, in possible retaliation, a group of black youths dragged a white man from his car and beat him so severely that he suffered extensive brain damage.

On April 23, 50,000 people joined on City Hall Plaza for a "Procession Against Violence." Billed as an event that took no position on busing but deplored violence, the procession finally brought together thousands of people in Boston who heretofore had quietly complied with the busing order while watching their neighbors riot in the streets, and all but the most virulent antibusing politicians.

On hand that afternoon were both U.S. senators, Edward Kennedy and Edward Brooke, Mayor Kevin White, Humberto Cardinal Medeiros, and many other prominent citizens. Prominent antibusers such as Louise Day Hicks and William Bulger refused to participate. It was the largest outpouring of public sentiment for peace, if not for busing.

In May 1976, Judge Garrity handed down his order for the third year of desegregation, known as Phase II B. The order included no district changes and no new educational programs. East Boston was still excluded from the plan. The basic emphasis in the third year was on refinement of the existing plan.

Negative reaction continued to be forthcoming from some of the antibusing leaders. State Senator William Bulger of South Boston declared that they would never quit.

Another controversy was stirred up in May by President Gerald Ford's suggestion that U.S. attorney General Edward Levi examine the Boston desegregation case for the possibility of filing a justice department brief in opposition to the desegregation plan. Leaders of the antibusing movement met with Levi to support this potential move. The NAACP and the Massachusetts Civil Liberties Union publicly denounced such an action as a "capitulation to violence." At the end of the month, Levi decided against appealing the case. Following his decision, much property damage took place in downtown Boston and at historic sites, presumably instigated by antibusing elements.

On 14 June, the U.S. Supreme Court once again rejected the appeal of the Boston case. The fire of the antibusing movement seemed to decrease over the summer; the huge antibusing marches of only a few years before seemed a thing of the past. When the U.S. Supreme Court decided not to review Judge

Garrity's findings, an air of resignation did settle into some parts of the more hostile communities.

It was at this time that Mayor White made one of his strongest appeals for cooperation in a speech that reflected the inevitability of desegregation.

While the most visible antibusing group, ROAR, was weakening, groups supporting peaceful desegregation were enjoying some growth and success. The parents' councils organized by the court floundered during the first two years of busing. In the third year, many began to operate as true voices of parental concern. For example, in August 1976 the CDAC for District 7 made a strong push for changes in the administration of the Blackstone School in the South End. It was one of many such actions to come out of the court-mandated groups.

During the year, the CDAC and the other court-mandated parents' group, the Community Parents Action Councils (CPACs) continued to press for changes in individual schools and to issue press statements. Although effective in many individual instances, the CDACs and CPACs never captured the attention of the press or the city's political leaders. Their strength and leadership remained grass roots. Seldom were their comments solicited by the press the way ROAR's had been following each disturbance in the previous two years. And no incumbent politician took the CDAC/CPAC cause on as his or her own. The organizations continued to operate without any leadership or endorsement from city officials.

During the school year, ROAR continued its decline. With the most peaceful school year yet, the incidents of antibusing marches and motorcades fell off sharply.

In June, reading scores for Boston schoolchildren indicated slight gains for minorities and no losses for whites (*Boston Globe* 1976: 6/22). Other measures of the success of the desegregation plan included private and parochial school enrollments. Only three private non-Roman Catholic schools had experienced enrollment increases of more than twenty during the first two years of desegregation. These three schools increased their enrollment by a total of 227 students during that period (Mass Research Center: n.d.). During the same period, Catholic schools, which had been facing a steady decline in enrollment, saw this decline slow down substantially. During the school years 1970–1971, 1971–1972, and 1972–1973, the Catholic schools had lost 8, 7, and 9 percent of their enrollment, respectively. In 1974–1975 the enrollment loss decreased to less than 4 percent and in 1975–1976 to 1.5 percent (Mass Research Center: n.d.). However, aggregate data such as these give no indication as to the causes of the slowdown of the enrollment decline. Even though it may have been caused by students transferring from public schools, other demographic changes may also have contributed.

In August, Judge Garrity reduced the size of the City-wide Coordinating Council (CCC). The original forty-two members had been appointed to reflect a broad range of opinion concerning the desegregation issue. As a result, the group spent most of its time debating the merits of desegregation. Therefore, Judge Garrity redefined the role of the CCC as well as appointing fourteen new members to the restructured fifteen-member body. Robert Wood, president of the University of Massachusetts, was retained as chairman of the body. The newly defined functions of the CCC were to be dissemination of information, monitoring of city-wide desegregation issues, serving as a liaison between the court and the community, and monitoring the Community District Advisory Councils (CDACs) (*Boston Globe* 1976: 8/25).

THE THIRD YEAR: 1976

September 1976 was peaceful compared to previous years. Police were on hand, but not with the show of force that had marked the previous year. There were some disturbances in South Boston, but Charlestown High and Hyde Park High were calm. Desegregation appeared to have settled in at those schools, and although the schools were not an oasis of brotherhood in a torn city, at least the fighting was over there.

The fighting did continue at South Boston High. Headmaster Jerome Winegar, importing staff from his native Minnesota, implemented heretofore unheard of vocational and educational programs. There was less violence but there were just as many suspensions, sometimes over a dozen a day. The South Boston community on the whole was still hostile to Winegar, although he did make a few friends. Toward the end of the year, Winegar came under heavy criticism from both black parents and other white administrators, who said he had failed to turn South Boston High School around.

School committee member Kathleen Sullivan began urging the court's withdrawal from South Boston High School. Throughout the year Judge Garrity refused, on the grounds that the school committee's affirmative duty to help desegregate the schools and improve education was still being ignored by the majority of the committee. Under these circumstances, how could the court believe that the letter and spirit of desegregation would be carried out?

On the political scene, the "great white hope" of Boston suffered one of her most serious political setbacks. Louise Day Hicks ran for Register of Deeds of Suffolk County, a relatively obscure, safe position where she could quietly gather a handsome salary for six years. She lost the election to school committeeman Paul Tierney, who did not base his campaign on the busing issue.

With the schools operating smoothly, the school committee began its drive to regain control. It first wanted South Boston High back. But after Judge Garrity held hearings on different motions, he said he found no reason to believe that the school committee would take over an affirmative desegregation role at the school. Garrity pointed out that the committee had not even met with headmaster Jerome Winegar to discover what was happening at the school. When the judge suggested they might want to do that, the committee tried but was prevented by Winegar's cautious attorney.

When the committee failed to regain control of South Boston High School, it filed a motion in court to have Garrity give it control of the entire system—for Garrity and the federal court to bow out. The committee's filings vowed to carry out all past and future mandates of the federal court. In lengthy committee meetings the members, with the exception of vehement antibusing member Pixie Palladino, promised to keep the schools running exactly as Garrity wanted, to keep all his appointments, to carry out all orders. In effect, if the committee kept its vows, it would have had control over the school system in word only, having promised to bow to the judge's wishes.

The school committee's motions to have the federal court relinquish control came in a court session that left no doubt that, for the sake of education, the court could not bow out. The March 1977 session was one of the most frustrating in the history of Boston's desegregation. The school committee attorney, inexperienced in education as well as law, fumbled for responses to the judge's questions. Plaintiff's attorneys themselves expressed a lack of knowledge of matters brought up by the bench. Attorneys for the other parties kept a self-conscious silence as the court began asking questions:

Why is a scientific magnet school in East Boston sitting with no books in its library, no maps, globes, or scientific equipment in its laboratories? With the school having opened the previous September, the court had repeatedly told the parties to have work completed for the students, yet that had not been done. Everyone blamed everyone else.

Why did the school committee and school department fail to inform parents of special testing for their children? Instead, one day the tests were just thrown at students throughout the system.

Why had not the necessary bilingual and special education equipment been delivered to receiving schools? It was sitting in storerooms while students went without services.

Why had no party acted on the complete failure of the school committee and school department to implement a vocational education plan? State education officials claimed that Boston had some of the worst vocational services in the state.

Garrity paid more than lip service to the school committee's and other city officials' cries that he step out of the case. But he once again said that the disengagement of the court was being delayed by the people who most wanted the court out—the Boston School Committee:

The school committee's lack of commitment to desegregation and consequent foot-dragging and obstruction is one factor of the equation that has obligated the court and its experts to remain intimately involved in the operation of the public schools. . . . In this respect the court must be mindful of the fact that the present school committee, despite occasional protestations of intentions to the contrary, continues to behave like the predecessor committees in that it refuses to assume its constitutional obligation to act affirmatively to implement and sustain desegregated education in the city of Boston (*Boston Globe* 1977: 5/7).

The example given by the judge this time was the school committee's failure to desegregate the kindergartens as called for in his original order of 1974. The court noted how, in fact, the school department had segregated kindergarten students, with black children forced to do most of the traveling to school. The judge ordered desegregation of kindergartens and a permanent department of implementation to replace the office of implementation, which he claimed had been rendered ineffective by the tampering of the committee. He hoped that the permanent department would take over many of the responsibilities now handled by the court. The school committee appealed.

At the end of 1977, there was some evidence that tensions were beginning to be resolved and that the antibusers were beginning to withdraw from their roles as leaders of the movement. Members of the media as well as of the school committee began to take some actions that indicated that they were aware of their responsibilities. Events indicating these trends included a conference called in May by the Freedom House Coalition for members of the media to discuss press coverage of the desegregation issue. Representatives of many major news outlets attended and agreed to investigate the coalition's charge that the media had conspired against the black community in its coverage of the school desegregation issue (*Boston Globe* 1977: 5/25).

The school committee approved the nomination of John Coakley as superintendent in charge of desegregation and head of the court-mandated Office of [Desegregation] Implementation, created as a permanent department within the school system to monitor desegregation (*Boston Globe* 1977: 6/1).

Several days after this appointment was announced, School Committee President Kathleen Sullivan and Superintendent Marion Fahey gave some indication that their conflict might be ending by jointly supporting a request that Judge Garrity release South Boston High School from its federal receivership and that the court withdraw from the Boston school desegregation case. This was the first time that the superintendent had added her support to the numerous similar requests made by Sullivan (*Boston Globe* 1977: 8/4).

Although controversies were cooling off in some areas, they were just beginning to erupt in other areas. For example, school officials began accusing the court experts of using the desegregation issue to build their own careers. The experts denied this and continued making student assignments until late August, when it was discovered that about 5,000 students had been incorrectly assigned. As parents and school officials alike protested, Judge Garrity stepped in and ordered the court experts to correct their original assignments.

THE FOURTH YEAR: 1977

Although there were no disruptions, boycotts, or violence, the first day of school in September 1977 proved to be one of the worst. The buses failed to show up. The bus companies said they did not receive assignments and bus routes in time; the school department blamed it on the bus companies and the court experts; the school committee blamed Judge Garrity; and the parents and students were bewildered. At 7:15 A.M., with literally thousands of students at bus stops or on their way to bus stops, the school department informed media outlets that most buses would not be showing up. Two weeks later, Superintendent Fahey announced that the opening of kindergarten would be delayed because of problems with assignments and bus routes. However, once the buses arrived, the school year began peacefully.

The situation in the Boston schools has remained calm, although the progress in education is still unknown and will be for years to come. Slight gains on standardized tests have been noted for some grades, but it is too early to measure the educational impact of desegregation. Statistics from the State Department of Education reveal that progress has been made toward desegregation of the schools (see table 3.1). According to these statistics, an estimated 16.7 percent of Boston's schools were racially imbalanced (defined as more than 50 percent nonwhite) in June 1977. However, newspaper reports indicate that a large proportion of schools are still racially imbalanced: the *Boston Globe* reported in December 1977 that 65 schools (43.3 percent) were still racially

TABLE 3.1. Racially Imbalanced Schools in Boston: 1967–1976, with 1977 Estimate

Year	Total Number of Racially Balanced Schools	Total Number of Racially Imbalanced Schools*	Total Number of Boston Schools	% Imbalanced Schools	
1967 Oct.	139	52	191	27.2	
1968 "	139	57	196	29.1	
1969 "	137	62	199	31.2	
1970 "	137	67	204	32.8	
1971 "	137	66†	203	32.5	
1972 "	140	62	202	30.7	
1973 "	135	65	200	32.5	
1974 "	128	61‡	189	32.3	Phase I
1975 Nov.	112	55	167	32.9	Phase II
1976 June	109	53	162	32.7	Phase II
1977 June	119	26§ 65**	155	16.7¶	Phase II

Source: State Department of Education, Annual Racial Census; Boston Public School Department, Attendance Unit; Ch. 636 Office.

(*) Defined by the Racial Imbalance Act (1965) as schools having more than 50% nonwhite student populations. (†) Of these schools, 39 had nonwhite populations in excess of 80% of student enrollment. Of the remaining 164 schools, 81 or 50% had white populations in excess of 90% of student enrollment. Certainly this may be termed operating a dual school system. (‡) The amelioration here results from the closing of some schools. (§) This figure represents a best estimate in the absence of official racial census. (¶) Overall decline in the number of racially imbalanced schools is actually from 46 in 1965 to 26 in 1977, an improvement of about 52%. As measured from 1974 (the first year of court-ordered desegregation) the improvement becomes 57%, from 61 schools in 1974 to drop to 26 students in 1977. Court-ordered closings of schools in 1976 and 1977 assist the improvement in this percentage figure. (**) State Bureau of Equal Education Opportunity. (From Clark Fisher 1977.)

imbalanced according to the most recent State Racial Census (*Boston Globe* 1977: 12/21).

Politicians who led the antibusing movement are beginning to fade from the scene. Louise Day Hicks, who had garnered 69 percent of the vote in 1963, lost her bid for reelection to the city council in 1977. Similarly, antibusing leader Pixie Palladino lost her seat on the school committee in the same election. However, Raymond Flynn, another antibuser and former state legislator, did win a seat on the Boston City Council for the first time in the November 1977 election.

Calm has returned to South Boston High School. The recently appointed headmaster and his staff have initiated many new educational programs at the school, and many white students have returned. Symbolic of this trend was the return to South Boston High School in September 1977 of the son of the founder of South Boston Heights Academy. Athletic teams at the school have become truly integrated. The state police troops were finally withdrawn from the school on 23 November 1977.

South Boston and Charlestown, the two communities that had been most racially isolated before busing, had the most racially motivated problems after busing. The resistance to busing was strongest in these areas, and the resulting inability of blacks to even enter the communities was largely confined to these two parts of the city.

Conversely, those neighborhoods that had had greater racial integration of one sort or another before busing had fewer, if any, problems. Brighton, for example, was not a very integrated area before busing, but many black students had attended Brighton High School for many years. There were virtually no problems with busing in Brighton. Communities such as Jamaica Plain and the South End had had integrated schools and neighborhoods before court-ordered desegregation. Busing had little impact there. And although Roxbury is residentially predominantly black, whites have long worked and commuted through it. It is not at all unusual to see white people in the heart of Roxbury. Throughout busing, the schools in Roxbury remained quiet, among the safest in the city.

The mechanisms established for parental participation have been recognized as one of the most positive changes that the desegregation plan has instituted. Although participation levels are not as high as had been expected, particularly in the Hispanic and Oriental communities, parents now have available to them a mechanism through which to air their grievances.

The situation should not be portrayed as ideal, however. The CCC recommended that the judge not step out of the case (*Boston Globe* 1977: 12/9). The judge evidently agreed with this assessment for he has not relinquished his control over the desegregation of Boston schools.

BIBLIOGRAPHY

Adkins, John F., James R. McHugh and Katherine Seay. 1975. *Desegregation: The Boston Orders and Their Origin*. Boston: Boston Bar Association.

Boston Globe. 1974: 6/23, 6/24; 1975: 5/25, 10/26; 1976: 6/22, 8/25, 8/27; 1977: 5/7, 6/1, 8/4, 12/9, 12/21 Supplement on School Desegregation.

Fischer, Clark. 1977. "A Case Study of the Boston Public Schools: The Development of University-School Pairings to Support Court-Ordered Desegregation 1975–77." Dublin: Unpublished master's thesis.

Hillson, Jon. 1977. *The Battle of Boston*. New York: Pathfinder Press.

Massachusetts Research Center. n.d. *Education and Enrollment; Boston Phase II*. Boston.

Morgan v. *Hennigan*. 1974. 379 F., Supp. 410 (D. Mass.).

Ross, J. Michael, Thomas Crawford, and Thomas Pettigrew. 1966. "Negro Neighbors—Banned in Boston." *Trans-Action* 3:6 (September-October): 13–18.

Schrag, Peter. 1967. *Village School Downtown*. Boston: Beacon Press.

U.S. Bureau of the Census. 1970. *Characteristics of the Population*. vol. 1. Washington, D.C: GPO.

U.S. Commission on Civil Rights. 1975. *Desegregating the Boston Public Schools: A Crisis in Civic Responsibility*. Washington, D.C.: GPO.

4

Erie, Pennsylvania: The Effect of State Initiative

Joyce Miller Iutcovich and Elaine Clyburn

Erie, the third largest city in Pennsylvania, is located in the northwest corner of the state. In 1976, the city had a population of approximately 120,000. As in many urban areas, Erie's population had declined by more than 18,000 between 1960 and 1976 (see table 4.1).

TABLE 4.1. Population of the City of Erie

1900	1920	1940	1960	1970	1976
52,733	93,372	116,147	138,440	129,188	120,000

Source: U.S. Census data.

BACKGROUND

Erie is often considered a "middling" kind of city (cf. Garvey 1978: 1): it is a medium-sized city, it is dominated politically by a large middle class, and it has neither a large social elite nor large numbers of urban poor. According to the 1970 census, the mean salary of Erie was approximately $10,330, which compares favorably with other urban communities of similar size in the northern part of the United States. However, it is significant to note that only 15 percent of the employed population earned more than $15,000 annually, and only 2,055 earned more than $25,000 per year.

In Erie, the population is characterized by an average educational level of twelve years, and only 10 percent of the population has a college education according to the 1970 census. Although there are five colleges within the area, Erie actually suffers from a "brain drain" because there are not adequate professional and managerial positions within the community to support the college-educated population. As a result, Erie has been labeled as a "beer and bowling" town (Garvey 1978: 14).

Economically, Erie is a manufacturing city with 40 percent of the labor market employed in one of its major industries. Erie's geographical location is ideal for increased economic development; it is close to the iron and steel mills of Pittsburgh, the petroleum of Oil Creek Valley, and the coal fields of middle Pennsylvania.

Erie is considered an ethnic city with a large population of Poles, Italians, and Germans (see table 4.2). Although the city was originally settled by Yankees, their percentage of the total population has greatly declined over the years. The black population of Erie, according to the 1970 census, is roughly 7 percent, although this percentage is considered to be somewhat low according to the local NAACP, which is currently conducting its own minority census. Adjusted figures place the black population at around 10 percent.

Historically, there has been no inner-city ghetto area for blacks; however, there are areas within the city where blacks are heavily concentrated, just as there are areas where other ethnic groups are concentrated (see figure 4.1). Low-income housing tends to be concentrated in the older sections of the central city, whereas middle- and upper-income housing tends to be located on the outer fringes of the east and west sides of the city. The outer fringes of the city contain populations that are more ethnically heterogeneous than that of the inner city.

The black population within Erie, for the most part, work in "the shop," which is how the factories are referred to, or for federally funded agencies. A small group of black professionals and a few small-business owners, generally those offering personal services such as barbers, beauticians, and a mortician, reside in the city.

Socially, blacks have been relatively isolated within the community. Blacks have generally reported that they felt that the majority of Erie residents do not accept them within the mainstream of activity, especially when it comes to the major institutions in the area. That is, there are relatively few blacks within the city and county government, few who have faculty positions within the local schools and colleges, and few who have jobs within the city's financial institutions. The few blacks who hold management-level positions have been recruited from outside the area. What results from this recruitment process is a minority population that is not "hometown" and not totally committed to remaining in the area. Even the blacks from the area who have achieved higher education do not remain in the community. Consequently, the community has been unable to retain a large number of qualified blacks who are capable of building a competitive power base. This is not to say that the Erie residents are openly hostile to the black community; rather it is a circumstance of "benign neglect." The general attitude of the rest of the community is that other ethnic groups have made it up the economic ladder and blacks can do the same.

TABLE 4.2. Historical Pattern of Ethnic Groups, City of Erie (%)

	1900	1920	1940	1960	1976
Yankee	39	36	32	27	21
German	41	36	31	28	25
Irish	10	8	10	8	7
Polish/Slovak	4	12	14	19	20
Italian	2	4	7	11	13
Black	1	1	2	5	10

Source: U.S. Census data.

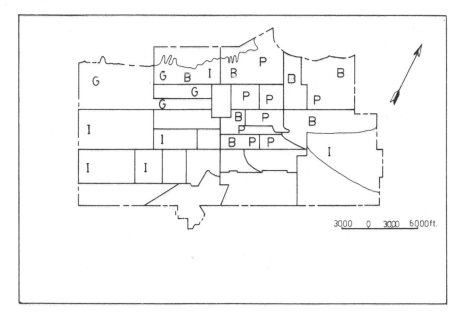

Figure 4.1. Census tracts in the Erie SMSA. Ethnic concentrations: G = German,
I = Italian, B = black, P = Polish. Adapted from U.S. Department of
Commerce, Bureau of the Census, 1970 Census of Population and
Housing Census Tracts.

The NAACP is the only viable national organization for blacks with a chapter in Erie, and it has maintained a biracial membership throughout the years. Its leadership positions have also been held by both blacks and whites. At present, its officers report that the local chapter is less active than it has been in former years. Blacks also have their own social organizations and ethnic activities. Just as there is a Polish Foresters Club, a Slovak Club, an Italian-American Day, there is also a black-sponsored Miss Tawny Beauty Contest. There are also forty-three black churches within Erie, but most are storefronts with pastors who have full-time employment elsewhere.

The religious affiliation of Erieites is also a very important factor along with ethnicity in determining the "flavor" of the community. A 1975 study conducted by a local college estimated that the city was composed of 55 percent Roman Catholics and 45 percent Protestants (Rosenthal 1975). The large Catholic population has resulted in a very strong Catholic school system. In fact, the student enrollment in the parochial schools over the past two decades has ranged between 60 and 70 percent of the public school enrollment. According to 1976–1977 school statistics, there were 6,647 students enrolled in twenty Roman Catholic grade schools compared to 9,944 students in nineteen public schools. Approximately 40 percent of the elementary school population and 26 percent of the secondary school population were enrolled in the parochial school system. The large Catholic school system has both positive and negative effects on the Erie School District. On one hand, there is a substantial savings to the district because its tax base may be used for fewer students than a city of its size might expect. On the other hand, the parents of the parochial school students are often indifferent to the public school system.

Regardless of the source of information, it has been repeatedly acknowledged that both religion and ethnicity are critical factors in the political system of Erie. The incoming immigrants have all started at the bottom of the ladder, and Italian and Polish groups have broken through into prominent political and economic positions, creating interethnic conflict in the process. The political arena also includes the school board. For over twenty years the board has been dominated by Catholic directors, many of whom never had any of their children enrolled in the public school system. Catholicism has provided one of the major coalescing factors for many of the ethnic groups—the Italians, Polish, Irish, and Germans. It is these groups, also, who have provided the backbone for the Democratic party, which has controlled Erie politics for over fifty years.

Consequently, from 1950 on, the school board has been the "stomping ground" for many Democratic faithfuls—especially those who share a view of politics as people-oriented and not issue-oriented. One Erie political scientist has stated that "under this kind of political climate, personal relationships and personal followings are often influential in Board decisions, particularly in the matter of personal appointments. This is not to suggest that school directors are any less interested in 'good education' but it does sometimes result in basic disagreement over *who* will execute policies" (Garvey and Cohen 1977: 12).

This attitude of the school board directors, however, became a very critical issue in the 1967 school board elections.* It was at this time that a nonpartisan group of parents formed the Committee for Better Schools and supported a slate of both Republican and Democratic candidates who were committed to the revitalization of the schools. This group of parents and other concerned citizens were dissatisfied with the existing board, which they viewed as unresponsive to the needs of the schools and the children. They charged that supplies and maintenance of the school buildings were inadequate (many were built in the late 1880s), and that most appointments in the system resulted from partisan political favors. It has been reported by many citizens and former members of the school board that, although there was never sufficient evidence for prosecution of graft or bribery, there were hints of self-aggrandizement by board members. For example, a school board member might get a new set of tires because a surplus showed up in the school district warehouse.

For a brief period (1970–1974) the board was composed of enough reform members that they were able to start developing new programs in the schools. This board also hired a reform superintendent who was to develop and implement these new programs. It was at this time that a new conflict between board members and the administration came into focus. The controversy can best be described as a conflict over philosophy as it affects curriculum and teaching methodology. The community perceived this problem as essentially a disagreement over conservative versus liberal, or progressive versus traditional education. For the most part, the ethnic Democrats were aligned to more traditional and less experimental education. The reform board, on the other hand, had Project Individual, a program that was characterized by an open classroom setting with emphasis on individual attention. Only a small number of teachers, half the board members, and the superintendent were dedicated

* The school board is composed of nine members who are elected at-large from the district to a six-year term on a rotating basis; three members are elected every two years. They serve without pay. The board in turn appoints a superintendent for a four-year term.

to developing this innovative educational system. The cry for "back to basics" became a rallying point for opposition groups and eventually all but one of the Project Individual programs were dismantled.

Moreover, starting in the late 1960s, a number of potentially volatile issues confronted the board. Racial tension and violence occurred in several schools, not only among students but also between students and faculty. Differentiated suspension and expulsion rates among blacks and whites resulted in intervention by the NAACP, which sought the establishment of a disciplinary code and standard grievance procedures. Public school teachers had gained the right to strike; they utilized this right twice.

Although this investigation is concerned with the desegregation of the public schools, it is important to realize that it was not this issue alone that created the difficulties within the district. Rather, the desegregation order occurred at a time when school officials already were occupied with issues that aroused public attention and reaction.

DEVELOPMENT AND IMPLEMENTATION
OF A DESEGREGATION PLAN

In February 1968, the chairman of the Pennsylvania Human Relations Commission (PHRC) and the state superintendent of public instruction directed the Erie School District, along with sixteen other Pennsylvania districts, to submit a desegregation plan and timetable that would eliminate racial imbalance in all the schools prior to 1 July 1968. The PHRC found de facto segregation in the Erie public school system, which was construed as a violation of the public accomodation section of the Pennsylvania Human Relations Act (1961), which states:

> It shall be unlawful discriminatory practice . . . (i) For any person being the owner, leasee, proprietor, manager, superintendent, agent, or employee of a place of public accommodation, resort, or amusement to (1) Refuse, withhold from, or deny to any person because of his race, color, religious creed, ancestry, or national origin, or to any person due to use of a guide dog because of the blindness of the user, either directly or indirectly, any of the accommodations, advantages, facilities, or privileges of such place of public accommodation, resort, or amusement" (Pennsylvania Human Relations Commission).

The determination was made by the PHRC on the basis of finding one or more schools within the district with a black student enrollment of more than 80 percent according to a census conducted in the fall of 1967. Prior to its identification of segregated school districts within the state, the PHRC had had its jurisdiction in such matters firmly established in a 1964 test case against the Chester School District. The PHRC's desegregation guidelines permitted a racial population variation of plus or minus 30 percent from the total percentage of minority students of the same grade span. In the Erie School District, which had a total of thirty-one schools at that time, there were sixteen schools that fell below the recommended percentage and six schools with greater than the allowed percentage (see table 4.3).

TABLE 4.3. Student Population by Race, 1968–1977

		Total Enrollment	Black Enrollment	% Black
1968	Secondary	9,992	1,075	10.75
	Elementary	11,714	1,814	15.48
	Total	21,706	2,889	13.31
1970	Secondary	9,090	1,183	11.5
	Elementary	10,060	1,990	16.5
	Total	19,149	3,173	14.2
1972	Secondary	9,672	1,273	13.2
	Middle	412	78	18.9
	Elementary	9,360	1,704	18.2
	P.I. School	538	67	12.5
	Total	19,982	3,122	15.6
1975	Secondary	6,484	945	14.6
	Middle	2,341	618	26.3
	Elementary	8,125	1,681	20.6
	Total	16,950	3,244	18.0
1977	Secondary	5,380	862	16.02
	Middle	3,550	806	22.70
	Elementary	7,075	1,645	23.25
	Total	16,005	3,313	20.69

Source: School district of the city of Erie.

In addition to the stipulation for racial balance within the student population, there were a number of other guidelines and recommendations jointly adopted and issued by the PHRC and the Pennsylvania Department of Education. Their first document, *Desegregation Guidelines for Public Schools*, adopted in March 1968, required that each school reflect in its enrollment a cross-section of the entire community, that all levels of school staff be racially integrated, and that school systems strive for quality education. School officials were required to rectify situations that resulted in segregation and to submit desegregation plans to the state. School boards were further encouraged to obtain citizen involvement in the development of the plan and to take preventive action to avoid segregation in the future.

The Erie School District responded to the state's directive on 28 June 1968, when it submitted its first desegregation plan to the PHRC. The commission, however, officially voted to disapprove the desegregation plan except for that part of the plan that dealt with the closing of one inner-city school (Marshall School) whose racial composition was predominantly black. The commission indicated that its disapproval was predicated on the fact that the plan did not include methods by which the remaining desegregation would be accomplished, or the timetable by which such racial imbalance would be corrected. As a result, the PHRC set a new deadline of 30 September 1968, for the submission of a supplementary plan and timetable. During this time, the Erie School District was unable to prepare a plan and requested an extension, which the commission granted. In December 1968, the superintendent submitted additional plans that were again disapproved by the commission for a lack of methods and timetable of desegregation. A new deadline of 1 July 1969 was then set for the submission of an acceptable plan.

In the summer of 1969, the PHRC met with school board members and advised that it was hiring an educational consulting firm, Peat, Marwick, & Mitchell, to propose a long-range plan for Erie that would include a desegregation plan. The date for submission of the desegregation plan was extended until 1 May 1970. In the fall of 1970, the long-range plan was completed and adopted by the Erie School Board. The PHRC once again rejected the plan because it would not take effect until September 1973, and because only black children were to be bused.

At that point, the school board opened the issue to public hearings. A voluntary group known as the Urban Coalition offered to devise a short-range plan. The school board accepted its offer.

In January 1971, the PHRC accepted a short-range desegregation plan that reorganized the school system so that the fifth and sixth grades became a part of middle schools. The plan was to go into effect that same year.

However, a group of antibusing parents, Concerned Parents and Taxpayers, took the school system to court at the state level, asking for a permanent injunction of the short-range plan. The permanent injunction was not ordered, but the judge did order that the school system reconsider the plan, keeping in mind the "best interest of the school children of the city of Erie." The board never complied with this order.

In June 1971, the PHRC conducted a public hearing and determined that the Erie School District was still in violation of the law. The PHRC ordered the school board to adopt a plan within thirty days. When the board failed to act, the PHRC petitioned the Commonwealth Court for enforcement of its order. The result of this court hearing was a consent decree on 3 May 1972, in which the two parties negotiated an agreement requiring the school district to develop an acceptable plan by 1 February 1974. The plan was to desegregate all schools by fall 1974 and to make an effort in good faith to achieve a desegregated professional and nonprofessional staff that reflected the population of Erie.

On 2 February 1974, the board again submitted a desegregation plan that the commission rejected because it did not comply with the court order of 3 May 1972. Again, the PHRC petitioned the Commonwealth Court for enforcement of its order. The court held the district was "technically in contempt" of the court order of 3 May 1972, and it ordered the PHRC to propose a desegregation plan.

On 7 August 1974, the PHRC filed its plan, and the Commonwealth Court held hearings on whether the court should order implementation of the commissioner's plan; instead, it ordered the district to submit a plan within forty-five days. At this time, the district petitioned the U.S. District Court for the Western District of Pennsylvania to order the PHRC to amend its desegregation plan to conform with the Education Amendments of 1974. The judge ruled that those prohibitions against ordering busing for the sole purpose of achieving racial balance apply to federal courts and officials, not to state agencies.

On 10 March 1975, the district submitted a plan authored principally by the superintendent, who indicated that he treated desegregation as "an ordinary educational program" (U.S. Commission on Civil Rights report 1975). Although the plan still failed to fulfill the consent decree of May 1972, it was accepted as a partial fulfillment by the PHRC.

The school district of the city of Erie had proposed a desegregation plan that it felt met the following basic objectives: (1) as little disruption of the student's educational environment as possible; (2) a minimum of busing and a maximum of walking within the existing state guidelines of one and one-half miles for elementary students; and (3) having available, if the parents so desire, transportation for any student who is moved from his or her original school.

The district's plan contained a number of methods through which it would achieve racial balance within its elementary schools. It was mutually agreed that the middle and senior high schools were already racially balanced. The district's plan contained the following provisions:

1. School system organization. The district reiterated its commitment to the implementation of the 4-4-4 plan when the appropriate facility would become available. Until that time, the alternate systems of 6-2-4 and 5-3-4 are being used.

2. Student reassignments. Entire grades could be reassigned to other schools (usually within walking distance) in order to effect racial balance.

3. School closings. It was recommended to close seven elementary schools in the old section of the city (not including Marshall School, which closed in 1968). Four of these seven schools were closed by 1978. A proposal was offered to use many of these buildings for community programs such as adult learning centers, Head Start programs, and health clinics.

4. Experimental schools. The Burton experimental school (K-4) would not be altered although it had a 50 percent black student population. Burton School served as a pilot school for the Urban Network Project, funded by the Department of Health, Education and Welfare. According to this district's administrators, "This is a unique experimental program that has strong community and extensive parental support. The program attempts to eliminate cultural deficiences by using strong supportive staff, reduced class size, personal counseling, home visitation, and increased rapport among home, school, and community. . . . It is feared that any alteration of the Urban Network Program could result in a significant loss to the entire Burton School community at a critical point in the program's development" (Erie Desegregation Plan 1975: D-Z). Harding School, still maintaining some of the Project Individual program, would remain an open enrollment school.

5. Transportation requirements. The transportation requirements of the district would remain basically the same with some modifications. Furthermore, it was emphasized in the district's desegregation document that "this proposal is fundamentally an attempt to avoid massive busing by reassigning students in dissolved attendance areas. *Thus, whenever feasible, this proposal employs walking rather than busing to balance schools racially.* The proposal will not significantly *increase* the need to bus students" (Erie Desegregation

Plan 1975: 12). Eleven percent of the students previously had been transported by bus; this proposal increased that by only 1 percent. The bused students receive passes for the public transit system and are subsidized by the school district. Only special education students ride the yellow school buses.

6. Supportive programs. Supportive programs in reading, math, and counseling were instituted and/or maintained in every elementary school because each school now had a significant number of culturally and educationally disadvantaged students.

On 29 April 1975, the Commonwealth Court amended its order to allow the desegregation of two schools to be delayed—one until fall 1975, the other until fall 1977. The achievement of black staff goals was also delayed until fall 1977. As late as spring of 1978, the delayed parts of the plan had not been implemented, but the PHRC took no further action against the school district.

The process of submission, disapproval, and extension of deadlines had begun in 1968 and continued through plan after plan, hearing after hearing, until March 1975, when the school district submitted a plan that was finally accepted by the commission. Indeed, the development and implementation of a desegregation plan for the Erie School District was a long-drawn-out process that was characterized by the news media as a "hot potato" being juggled from one hand to another. The Erie school directors and administrators were caught in a dilemma. On the one hand, there were taxpaying citizens within the city who opposed busing for the purposes of desegregation. On the other hand, if the district did not comply with the PHRC directive to integrate the schools, it faced the loss of substantial state and federal funds.

It is important to note here that the original directive to the Erie School District to desegregate its schools was not a court order directly monitored by the courts. It was only a request made by the PHRC and Pennsylvania Department of Education for the districts to submit a desegregation plan and timetable— a plan that would be locally designed and implemented. The PHRC left the specifics of the plan to school district officials. Only in 1974, six years after the original request and two years after the consent decree that the Erie School District had not fulfilled, did the commission propose a plan of its own. Even at that point, the court did not accept the PHRC plan because the district had not submitted its comments to the court regarding the plan. The court also considered it more desirable if the desegregation plan came from the district itself and not from a state agency.

COMMUNITY ACTION GROUPS

During the period of desegregation planning, there were many groups that vocalized their support of or opposition to the desegregation of the Erie School District. There were no community action groups that played a strong leadership role in advocating school desegregation. On the other hand, there was an organized coalition of parents and concerned citizens who maintained an antibusing stance and who fought a court battle over one of the desegregation plans submitted by the district.

Committee for Better Schools

During the 1967 election of school board members, a nonpartisan group of parents and teachers known as the Committee for Better Schools (CBS) decided to organize their support for candidates for the board who would "revitalize the schools." It was the general consensus among this parent-teacher group that Erie public schools were in deplorable shape and that in order to change this situation, it would be necessary to elect board directors whose first concern was the schoolchildren and not their own personal gain. It was not until 1970, however, that this group was able to elect a majority of reform board members. In that year, the reform members together with a new superintendent began designing and implementing what was known as Project Individual. Although the CBS did not have as its express purpose the desegregation of the schools, this group did consider racial desegregation of schools a necessary part of its educational program. Members of the CBS argued at school board meetings with opposing citizens' groups concerning their educational programs; in fact, board meetings became more heated than they had previously been. CBS members reported instances of threat and harassment; however, there were no indications that any threats were carried through.

Concerned Parents and Taxpayers (CPT)

The most vocal group in the desegregation issue was the CPT, which first came into existence in October 1970 after rumors had spread that busing would include white children as well as black children. The Peat, Marwick, and Mitchell long-range plan originally proposed the busing of black children from the inner city to effect racially balanced schools. When this plan was rejected by the PHRC and rumors were spreading about two-way busing, the group rapidly coalesced and expressed its concern over the busing issue. Initially, the leaders of this group presented to the board a petition of over 16,000 signatures of persons opposing the busing of any students. When the group formally organized and was at its peak, it had twenty-five to thirty members on the executive board and had distributed approximately 2,700 membership cards. There were four major goals of the group: (1) to stop the reassignment of K–6 students from neighborhood schools; (2) to suggest short-range and long-range plans for better education; (3) to make the public aware of the conditions within the school district; and (4) to see that every tax increase was used for better education.

This group held numerous meetings that were open to the public, staged demonstrations at school board meetings, and let their views be known by writing letters to the newspaper and appearing on radio and television. The CPT also filed suit in the Court of Common Pleas for a permanent injunction against the implementation of the January 1971 short-range plan, which would have desegregated the elementary schools by the fall of 1971. To raise money for this court suit, the group was able to organize approximately 500 volunteers to canvass the community. Although initially it was the intention of the CPT leaders to stay out of politics, the group soon realized the necessity of supporting candidates for the school board who would represent their views.

The CPT as a group, however, did not engage in violent activities; neither did it attempt to set up private academies. There was a time when the arguments became rather intense, especially when the Concerned Parents and Taxpayers confronted the Committee for Better Schools at school board meetings. These confrontations became a concern of the two groups, however, and through private meetings with representatives from both sides they attempted to resolve some of their differences.

The CPT soon branched out and became involved in other issues. One of its primary issues concerned its objection to the development of Project Individual; CPT argued that the schools should "get back to basics." Although the CPT did not really have much success with the desegregation issue, its opposition to Project Individual eventually resulted in the discontinuation of this program along with the firing of the reform superintendent and his staff. In 1978 the CPT was only loosely organized, but the leaders of the group were still very active in school district affairs and made every attempt to achieve the goals they originally formulated.

NAACP and Concerned Black Parents and Taxpayers

The largest minority organization involved in the desegregation of the Erie school system was the local chapter of the NAACP, but this organization maintained only a peripheral involvement in the issue. One of the major concerns of the NAACP's education committee, however, was the differential expulsion and suspension rates between black and white students, particularly at the high school level. Many black parents organized to demand the development of a code of discipline and grievance procedures to assure that all students be treated alike. The confrontation over the handling of discipline problems between the black community represented by the NAACP, and the Erie school district began prior to and continued after the original PHRC directive to desegregate in 1968. In the early part of 1968, several black parents had spoken out at school board meetings protesting what they felt was unequal treatment of their children, especially when there were discipline problems. When they failed to obtain satisfactory responses from school officials, these parents asked the NAACP to represent them in negotiations with the school system.

The controversy escalated when the school district established an alternative class for students under sixteen years of age who had "behavior problems." Black parents complained because the first such class, formed after a disturbance at one of the high schools, was composed of all black students and a white teacher. In addition, the class was temporarily housed in a school building that had been closed as unsafe for regular classes. A school board member undertook working with a broadly based committee to establish a district-wide discipline code with more opportunities for hearing appeals and more stringent procedures for suspension and expulsion of youngsters.

In the midst of this struggle, the PHRC was viewed by some citizens as doing something positive for black parents by insisting that the schools desegregate and that they employ more minority teachers. However, school board minutes indicate that most individuals who identified themselves as black parents of public school children continued to express concern for quality education. Desegregation, as such, did not appear to be their major concern.

A group called Concerned Black Parents and Taxpayers was formed as an ad hoc organization to deal with some of the issues presented by Concerned Parents and Taxpayers. This group shared some members with the NAACP education committee, who were primarily concerned about their children being bused or walking long distances. At school board meetings, they expressed concern about the small number of minority teachers and the lack of concern they felt many white teachers had for minority children. These parents maintained a commitment to the concept of neighborhood schools. They were opposed to the plan that required their children to walk up to a mile and a half across busy intersections. Most of these black parents preferred busing to walking long distances, across railroad tracks or busy streets. The concerns of the NAACP and the CBP appear to overlap. Throughout the desegregation controversy, both groups continued the same theme—quality education for black children "who are turned off by teachers in the schools of Erie" (School Board Minutes 4 March 1971).

Clergy

Church organizations, interfaith councils, and individual clergymen frequently voiced their opinions concerning public school issues and attempted to serve the school district by becoming a part of advisory committees, task forces and the like. With regard to the desegregation issue, the major religious organization to become involved was the Interfaith Clergy Association for Social Justice. This organization was composed of Roman Catholic, Protestant, and Jewish clergy who were young to middle-aged and liberal in their ideology. This group was supportive of the necessity to desegregate and they tried to influence other clergy; they spoke at board meetings and wrote letters to the newspaper.

A great many members of the clergy, particularly Catholics, did not feel that desegregation was an issue in which they should be involved. However, the Roman Catholic Bishop of Erie did prohibit transfers from public schools to the Catholic school system for one year. In a letter to all pastors of the parochial schools dated December 1970, the bishop stated, "Effective immediately, for one year no transfer students will be accepted from the public schools of the metropolitan Erie area to the Catholic elementary schools." Indeed there is no statistical evidence that the parochial schools greatly increased their expected enrollment by accepting transfer students. Overall, the enrollment of both the public and parochial schools has decreased over the past decade as a result of the decline in the school-age population.

Urban Coalition

The Urban Coalition in Erie was founded in 1968 with private and business funds for the purpose of bringing the total resources of the community to bear on solutions to urban problems by bringing together all segments of the population. It was modeled after the National Urban Coalition: a small group of men invited approximately 135 of Erie's leading citizens to become charter members. According to the bylaws of the Urban Coalition of Erie, its purposes were charitable, educational, and scientific. Membership was available to persons living in or regularly employed in Erie County who represented one or more components of the urban community: business, commerce, industry, communications, professions, education, religion, organized labor, local government, racial minorities, and the poor. There was a paid executive director but most of the activity of the coalition was handled by task forces in areas such as housing, employment, and education.

The Urban Coalition of Erie had first become involved in the school district's problems during the controversy over discipline within the schools. In the fall of 1970, after a number of the district's plans had been rejected by the PHRC, the Urban Coalition again offered its services in the development of a plan that would meet PHRC guidelines and gain a measure of community support. The district accepted this offer, and the project was turned over to a Citizen Task Force spearheaded by the Urban Coalition.

The task force had representatives from a wide range of community groups. The plan that this group finally submitted in October 1970, however, was basically the same one previously submitted by the superintendent. Essentially, the task force recommended that (1) all fifth and sixth graders would attend school in the seven inner-city elementary schools to be phased out in the long-range plan; (2) students in grades K–4 who would have attended any of those seven schools would be enrolled in other elementary schools in the district with a distribution procedure that would result "in the attainment of racial balance;" and (3) a substantial number of those students would have to be bused (*Erie Times News* 1970: 12/21).

Although the Citizen Task Force had represented a wide range of interests within the community, "essential and sizable groups either withdrew from the task force or approved none of the plans considered, including the PTA, the teachers organizations, and the major parents' groups" (*Erie Times News* 1970: 12/21). These groups were disgruntled because the task force, without question, operated under the assumptions that the elementary schools were in fact segregated, and that any plan to eliminate segregation would have to conform to PHRC guidelines.

Although this plan did not have any significant community support, it was adopted by the board and submitted to the PHRC for approval. The PHRC accepted the portions of the plan dealing with pupil desegregation; however, the plan was never implemented because the CPT filed suit in the Court of Common Pleas for a permanent injunction.

Building Task Force and Education Task Force

After the consent decree of 3 May 1972, when the court ordered the PHRC and the school district to work together, the district administrators formed a Building Task Force (BTF) and an Education Task Force (ETF). These task forces were in charge of the development of a desegregation plan that was to emphasize a new learning program and that was to be submitted for approval by 1 February 1974. The BTF had fifteen members who represented many interests in the Erie community: the city Department of Planning, school district administrators, the chief clerk's office, the Association of University Women, the local Community Action Agency, the Intermediate Unit of the State Department of Education, the Erie Education Association, the City Council of PTAs, Concerned Parents and Taxpayers, and Citizens for Better Schools. Two school board members served as cochairmen. Each major ethnic and racial group was also represented on the task force. The express purpose of the BTF was to decide which elementary school buildings were to be phased out and how to house a new 4-4-4 program. A major part of the overall program was to purchase the Sears building, which had recently closed in the downtown area, and to develop a K-4 learning center there.

The Education Task Force was composed primarily of educators who were concerned with the development of the learning program that was advocated by the reform superintendent, who saw learning as a "process whereby students inquire and experience in a flexible structure with a variety of materials" (*4-4-4 Plan* 1973: 12/12, 2). The five learning principles proposed by the ETF included individualized and personalized learning, active learning, balanced learning, learning through stated objectives, and diagnostic teaching. This 4-4-4 Plan was submitted to the PHRC, which disapproved because it did not comply with the consent decree of 1972. Moreover, at the time this plan was submitted, the superintendent had already been advised that the board had voted not to renew his contract, which expired the following spring. Thus the learning portion of the plan, Project Individual, which was the superintendent's initiative, was implemented without the presence of its prime supporter.

OTHER CONCERNED GROUPS

Teacher's Groups

Prior to the spring of 1971 there were two majoi teachers' organizations in the school district, the Erie Education Association and the Erie Federation of Teachers. From 1968 to 1971, representatives from both organizations attended school board meetings regularly in order to testify on behalf of their membership in areas such as classroom size, discipline, hiring, and retention.

Both teachers' groups were represented on the task force headed by the Urban Coalition that developed a desegregation plan for the district. By December 1970, the Erie Federation of Teachers had withdrawn from the Urban Coalition Task Force. Spokespersons for the federation indicated that the withdrawal resulted from the federations's opposition to following the PHRC guidelines and the federation's lack of influence in the group. The Erie Education Assocation remained affiliated with the task force.

In 1976, eleven white teachers filed suit in the U.S. District Court alleging that they had been dismissed before minority teachers with less seniority. The school district had contended that it had to retain minority employees in order to maintain racial balance. On 26 June 1978, Judge Gerald J. Weber ruled that the action of the Erie School District was illegal and a case of "purposeful racial discrimination" (*Erie Times News* 1978: 6/26).

The teacher organizations had little to say publicly about desegregation but were vocal about their own concerns related to it. If classroom size, attendance at seminars, work load, and so on, were involved in desegregation, then the organization spoke to those issues.

The Superintendents

From 1968 to 1978 there were three superintendents in the Erie School District. Six months prior to the expiration of a superintendent's contract, he or she must be advised in writing of the expiration date and may be advised that he or she and other candidates will be considered for the position. On 29 January, 1970 the superintendent, who had been in this position when the first desegregation order was issued, indicated in a letter to the school board that he would not be applying for renewal of his commission as superintendent because many problems and pressures had become associated with him personally (School Board Minutes 1970: 1/29).

A nationwide search was conducted by the board, and on 14 April 1970 the new reform superintendent was appointed for a four-year term. On 23 April 1974 he was relieved of his duties and appointed special adviser until 30 June 1974. The third superintendent was then promoted from within the system, having served as a teacher and building administrator.

In 1968, the board generally looked to the superintendent and his immediate assistants to direct the school system through the desegregation issue with a minimum of controversy and expense. Initially, the superintendent was able to provide information and expertise but ultimately he was not able to cope with the demands of the PHRC. The prodesegregation forces thought the pace was too slow; the antidesegregation forces thought the pace was too rapid as well as too costly and disruptive. The student-teacher conflicts and ensuing efforts over an often-amended discipline code came to rest at the superintendent's desk. The reform board was intent on hiring a new person from outside the city, presumably unaffected by previous events in Erie.

The new superintendent was greeted warmly by the board and advised to make sweeping changes. He was a strong person who began to take some initiative in developing Project Individual and his own plan for desegregation. Although the board initially seemed to approve, some board members began to complain as the first teachers' strike developed, the PHRC rejected still another plan, and the various citizens' groups argued at meetings. The superintendent offered to resign early, but by a close vote the board rejected his offer. However, it was only a few months later that it unanimously voted not to renew his contract. The major complaint about the incumbent superintendent was that his actions were not in concert with the board's policies.

Government Agencies

The role that the PHRC played in the desegregation of the Erie School District has already been outlined; it was the major force initiating the desegregation order. The other agency that coauthored the request was the Pennsylvania Department of Education. The primary purpose of the PDE was to evaluate the educational aspects of the plans submitted and make the recommendations to the PHRC. On several occasions, staff of the PDE offered technical assistance in the areas of curriculum development and human relations workshops to improve communication between blacks and whites.

The federal government aided in the Erie desegregation case by granting the district funds from the Emergency School Assistance Act (ESAA) in 1974 to facilitate the implementation of the desegregation plan. In Erie, the ESAA program enabled the district to develop counseling programs for children who had adjustment problems in their new schools, remedial reading programs, and a multicultural exposure project that helped students to understand each other's cultures.

The original grant proposal submitted by the district was for a sum of $430,671. The district received these funds and is still receiving ESAA money; however, the amount has been reduced each year. Currently, a controversy has arisen within the school district concerning charges that ESAA funds are being utilized at the discretion of the school principals rather than on those reassigned students who need special attention and remedial training.

Another federally funded organization that has aided the Erie School District in the implementation of its desegregation plan is the Center for Desegregation and Conflict at the University of Pittsburgh. This center has administered in-service training and workshops for the ESAA staff.

Political Leaders and Police

The majority of political leaders within the community tried to keep a low profile with regard to desegregation and particularly busing. However, a few prominent politicians did express their support for the "No Bus For Us Guys" campaign, which was sponsored by the Concerned Parents and Taxpayers. The mayor was persuaded by the CPT to publicly contribute $100 to the campaign. In a more recent attitudinal survey conducted by a former reform board member, it is significant to note that of the more than thirty-five persons who were interviewed, only one remembered that the mayor took the stand that he did (Snell 1978). The state legislator from Erie's second legislative district also publicly endorsed the CPT. City councilmen, for the most part, made no public commitments concerning desegregation.

The police had no major enforcement role to play during the implementation of the desegregation plans. They had, on occasion, been called out to calm disturbances within the schools, but this was prior to any reassignment of students. Once the students were reassigned and the limited amount of busing was implemented, the police were assigned to spotchecking some of the pick-up points. According to the police, there were no major incidents requiring their intervention.

CONCLUSIONS

Several features of the desegregation process in Erie stand out for the impact they had on achievement of racial desegregation. First, the school board directors vacillated over their intent to comply with the PHRC directive and subsequent court order, although they had made attempts to submit some type of plan for each deadline. Their delay in these matters resulted in the formation of the CPT and other groups that voiced their approval or opposition to desegregation and its related problems.

Second, the Commonwealth of Pennsylvania is unique in that it has been the department of education and the Human Relations Commission that have requested the school districts to desegregate. These two agencies have made all attempts to ensure that plans are locally designed and implemented. Only when necessary has the commission gone to court to obtain compliance with its guidelines. These state agencies have monitored the plans and assured their proper implementation. Indeed, there was a great deal of resentment by the community toward the PHRC because it did not like state officials "telling it what to do." Once the public realized the inevitability of the situation, it peacefully complied.

Third, the media, for the most part, did not sensationalize the desegregation issue or give rise to the expectation that violence would erupt. It has been reported that the editor of the *Morning News* was instrumental in establishing secret meetings among opposing factions at the height of their polarization. Consequently, attempts were made by group leaders themselves to check any violence before it erupted.

Fourth, although most elected officials remained noncommittal, two of the most prominent within the area—the mayor, and a state assemblyman—voiced their support for the antibusing groups. This undoubtedly helped in the group's campaign against the implementation of busing and was instrumental in gaining popular support.

It is important to keep in mind the residential segregation of blacks and whites in Erie. The segregation is underlined by the generally lower economic, political, and social resources available to the black population of the community. The situation is further complicated by the interethnic competition among Poles, Italians, and Germans, who usually do not band together but who in issues surrounding race have indeed banded together against minorities. The small number of recently arrived Vietnamese families and the growing Latino population are also beginning to seek their own places in Erie. The presence of these groups, which have already been residentially confined to one or two distinct neighborhoods, will have an effect on the relative power positions of ethnic and racial groups in the city.

The impetus for school desegregation came from outside the community and found some support, although the major issue for black parents was and continues to be quality education. The PHRC has not followed up the failure of the school board to comply with its final order. The hope that desegregation would somehow serve to increase racial harmony or increased opportunity for some segments of the population has not been realized. In most desegregated classrooms, observers report that there is still an atmosphere of "us" and "them," with children from another neighborhood being identified as outsiders. Black and white citizens alike still strive to improve the quality of education in Erie schools.

BIBLIOGRAPHY

Erie, Pennsylvania, School Board Minutes. 1970: 1/29.

Erie *Times-News*. 1970: 12/21; 1978: 6/26.

Garvey, William P. 1978. "The Anatomy of a City." Unpublished article, Mercy-hurst College.

Garvey, William P., and Norman Cohen. 1977. *The Effect of Erie History, Traditions and Geography on the Present and Future of the Erie School District.* Report prepared for the Long-Range Planning Committee of the Erie School District.

Pennsylvania Human Relations Act. 1961. Section 5 (i) (1) October 27, 1955 P.L. 744, as amended February 28, P.L. 47, 1.

Pennsylvania Human Relations Commission. 1968. *Desegregation Guidelines for Public Schools* (March), *Recommended Elements of a School Desegregation Plan* (May); 1976. *Laws Administered by the Pennsylvania Human Relations Committee* (March); 1978. *Chronology of Relationships of PHRC with the Erie School District Regarding Pupil Desegregation* (April).

Rosenthal, Audrey. 1975. "Influences on Religious Identity in Urban Politics: A Case Study of Erie, Pennsylvania." Unpublished senior thesis, Mercyhurst College.

School District of the City of Erie, Pennsylvania. 1970. *Peat, Marwick & Mitchell Long Range Plan* (June); 1973, 1974, 444-*Plan*, 1915. *Erie Desegregation Plan* (May): 1976 *A Brief Description of the Emergency School Aid Program, Proposal for Emergency School Aid Act* (both February).

Snell, Doris. 1978. "Response to Desegregation Orders in Two Pennsylvania Cities." Unpublished Ph.D. dissertation.

U.S. Commission on Civil Rights. 1975. *School Desegregation in Erie, Pennsylvania* (May). Washington, D.C.: GPO.

U.S. Department of Commerce, Bureau of the Census. *1970 Census of Population and Housing.* Washington, D.C.: GPO.

5

Wilmington, Delaware: Merging City and Suburban School Systems

Jeffrey A. Raffel and Barry R. Morstain

In 1787, Delaware became the first state to ratify the Constitution of the United States of America. This distinction is viewed with pride by many residents, for as a small state Delaware rarely has been the center of public attention. With a total area of about 2,400 square miles (ranking forty-ninth of all states) and a population just over half a million (ranking forty-sixth in 1970), Delawareans are not normally accustomed to being participants in big events that attract the attention of the national news media.

Yet in September 1978, such an event bestowed another distinction on Delaware—the Wilmington metropolitan area became the first community in the nation to undergo court-ordered, metropolitan, interdistrict school desegregation.[1] On 1 July 1978, the Wilmington Public Schools and ten surrounding suburban districts serving a total of about 80,000 students were reorganized by court order to form one district, the New Castle County Public Schools.

As a result, in the fall of 1978 over 14,000 suburban and 9,000 city children were reassigned and bused to achieve racial desegregation. What had been a public education environment of eleven differentiated school districts was altered—to a new, single-district form. This transformation brought to the forefront a variety of problems and issues facing public education in the county.

The school desegregation situation in New Castle County generated considerable legal, political, and ideological conflict in the courts and other public arenas. The history of the school desegregation case, *Evans* v. *Buchanan* (1974–1978) is complex, for it originated during the mid-1950s, when the state had laws authorizing de jure segregation in the public schools; the case has been in and out of the federal courts to the present time. During this period, laws and policies which promulgated de jure school segregation were eventually eliminated. However, with the rise of suburbanization and the development of independent suburban districts, the racial characteristics of children in the public schools have increasingly paralleled those of other metropolitan areas—

1. Voluntary city-suburban desegregation arrangements have occurred in areas such as Hartford, Milwaukee, and Boston (METCO). Within a single district, court-ordered metropolitan desegregation has previously occurred, e.g., Tampa-Hillsborough County, Louisville-Jefferson County, Miami-Dade County.

a city school district where the majority of students are black, surrounded by suburban districts where the majority of students are white.

The bases of the Wilmington-New Castle County school desegregation case can be traced to several key factors: the state of Delaware's former de jure segregation of races in the schools, the prominent role of the state in providing for public education, the large population growth of the suburbs that resulted in differentiated residential areas and independent school districts.

ORIGINS OF *EVANS* v. *BUCHANAN*

In *Simple Justice* (1975) Richard Kluger has written, "In spirit if not in law, Delaware was a southern state, though it took the Union's side in the Civil War." Two of three counties in the state, Kent and Sussex, are rural in their composition and interests, were formerly slaveholding territories, and have wielded major influence in shaping state laws. Thus, it is not surprising to note that one year after the 1896 *Plessy* v. *Ferguson* U.S. Supreme Court decision, which perpetuated racial segregation by law, the Delaware Constitution was enacted into law with a provision calling for separate school systems for Negroes and whites.

"Even the most liberal community in Delaware—Wilmington—remained a Jim Crow town in 1950," observed Kluger, who concludes that Delaware was a most inhospitable place for Negroes.

All the public schools were segregated, not just the grammar schools. There were no black nurses in the white hospitals, and not nearly enough hospital beds were available to Negroes, who made up 14 percent of the state's population. There were no black clerks in the banks or retail stores. Restaurants and movie theaters and hotels in downtown Wilmington were strictly segregated, and no black men served in the Delaware National Guard. The state college for colored people at Dover was not nationally accredited, and nothing approaching equal protection of the laws was practiced in any walk of life throughout the state, which functioned as a fossilized racist encampment on the traditionally white-supremacist Eastern Shore Peninsula. (Kluger 1975: 543–544)

Schools for Negroes were woefully underfinanced—supported initially by a tax on property owned by Negroes—resulting in a situation where whites could attend school for twice as many months as Negroes. Only a gift of $2.6 million from Pierre S. Du Pont in 1929–1931 provided funds for schooling for Negroes and altered somewhat this bleak picture. Educational opportunities and facilities were separate but distinctly unequal as Delaware approached the decades of the Warren U.S. Supreme Court.

Despite the massive gains of the black schools, there were still two racially separate systems of education in Delaware by 1950. In that year, there were over 50 black school districts, overwhelmingly one-room affairs. By 1950, a black could receive a twelfth grade education only at Wilmington's Howard High School and Dover's Delaware State College preparatory department. There was no four-year secondary school in Sussex County until 1952, when

William Jason High School opened. As late as 1953, the state provided no funds for black transportation, and blacks were not allowed to share white buses under any condition (Kluger 1975: 543–544).

Despite the southern heritage of Delaware, the state court (Delaware Court of Chancery) was the scene of a number of landmark decisions in the early 1950s. "The University of Delaware became the first southern coeducational institution of higher learning to be integrated at the undergraduate level" (Taggart 1976) after Vice Chancellor Collins Seitz ruled that education of Negroes at Delaware State College was inferior to that of whites at the university and thus ordered the admission of the Negro plaintiff to the university.

As chancellor, Seitz continued to support Negro claims for equal educational treatment in elementary and secondary education. Two lawsuits brought by black parents in the early 1950s, *Belton* v. *Gebhart* (1952) and *Bulah* v. *Gebhart* (1952), resulted in state court rulings requiring the admission of black children to schools that were closer to their homes and educationally superior to the schools they had previously attended, and that had been previously attended solely by white children. In both cases, the inferior quality of black schools and the lack of state-financed transportation for black pupils were critical factors in the court's rulings (Taggart 1976).

The Delaware Supreme Court upheld the lower court holdings, and the state appealed the rulings to the U.S. Supreme Court. The Delaware cases were consolidated with cases from Kansas, Virginia, South Carolina, and the District of Columbia to form the famous *Brown* v. *Board of Education* (1954) case, which overturned the "separate but equal" doctrine of *Plessy* v. *Ferguson*.

In light of *Brown*, the U.S. Supreme Court remanded the original Delaware lawsuits to the Delaware Supreme Court to effectuate the transition to a racially nondiscriminatory school system. In effect, the 1955 holding of *Brown* v. *Board* (II) required that those who were responsible for promoting racial segregation by law had the duty to develop plans for the elimination of the dual, separate school systems. Responsibility therefore rested with local authorities to undo the segregated schools, and in Delaware the state board of education was required by the courts to pursue this goal. In 1955, the Delaware Supreme Court approved a gradual grade-by-grade desegregation policy and also held that no school district could proceed with a desegregation plan unless it had been approved by the state board.

In Delaware the state board of education has been the entity usually responsible to the courts for developing and implementing desegregation plans. This is due to the fact that the state board, under authority delegated by the state's general assembly, has been involved with the establishment of school districts and attendance areas. Equally important, the state has traditionally been the major source of funding for public education. Currently, the state underwrites about 70 percent of local school operating costs, such as teacher and school personnel salaries, transportation costs, school construction, and capital expenditures. Moreover, the state board has had the responsibility for teacher certification requirements, and has developed special purpose programs (e.g., vocational education, learning disability-special education) that cut across school district lines.

From a policy standpoint, the Wilmington School Board in the period 1954–1957 established a desegregation plan that created "racially neutral" geographic attendance areas. The Wilmington board, however, continued to follow a free transfer policy by which students in a given attendance area could transfer to another school if space were available. Because many residential areas in Wilmington were differentiated by race, and particularly with the general trend of white movement to the suburbs (to be discussed subsequently), the joint effects of these factors yielded a situation where most schools in Wilmington that were predominantly black prior to *Brown* remained so after three years of the initial desegregation plan for Wilmington.

Desegregation of schools in the suburban areas of New Castle County tended to follow a precept outlined in *Brown*—to desegregate "with all deliberate speed." Like many other communities, the emphasis was on "deliberate," not "speed." In 1956, Brenda Evans, a black parent who lived in the suburban Claymont School District, filed suit in the federal district court charging that the Claymont District was not admitting students in a racially nondiscriminatory manner and that the district had not submitted a desegregation plan to the state board of education. This suit was filed naming the state board of education as defendants, because the state board was responsible for developing effective desegregation plans. Because Madelyn Buchanan was president of the state board at that time, the lawsuit eventually became known as *Evans* v. *Buchanan*.[2]

In 1957, the federal district court found that very little effort had been undertaken by the state board to provide for unitary, nondiscriminatory school systems. The court enjoined all local school districts from refusing to enroll black students and ordered the state board to develop a comprehensive plan for the desegregation of all public school districts for the fall 1957 term. This decision was subsequently affirmed by the Third Circuit Court of Appeals in 1958.

The plan submitted by the state board called for desegregation on a grade-by-grade basis over a span of twelve years. The court rejected this plan and the board was required to develop a revised plan that would desegregate all grade levels of the public schools commencing with the opening of schools in the fall 1961 term.

The modified plan eventually approved by the district court included two components. On a short-run basis, any black student desiring admission to a white or integrated school should be allowed to transfer through normal administrative procedures. Looking to the future, the court instructed the state board to plan for completely integrated, unitary school systems. Eliminating separate black school districts was the focus here, and the state board was required to recommend to the general assembly a new school code that would eliminate categorizations and enrollments in public schools based on race. Legislation was proposed but the general assembly failed to enact it on two occasions.

Resorting to administrative and agency prerogatives, in the period 1965–1967 the state board proceeded with a plan that closed many small districts in the state. The elimination of these districts had the effect of eliminating de jure segregation, principally in rural Kent and Sussex counties.

2. This suit was originally entered as *Evans* v. *Members of the State Board;* after the federal district court consolidated several related cases, the suit became *Evans* v. *Buchanan* (1957).

THE WILMINGTON/NEW CASTLE COUNTY CONTEXT

The rapid growth of the suburbs, attendant changes in school enrollments, and school district consolidations in New Castle County occurred in an area covering 435 square miles. Almost one-half of this area is a rural area in the southern portion of the county, and consists of one school district, the Appoquinimink Schools, which was not one of the original ten systems that merged to form the Wilmington-New Castle County system. The heart of the metropolitan area is the city of Wilmington, which is surrounded by suburban areas totaling about ten times the fifteen square miles that Wilmington occupies.

During the twenty-five-year period from 1950 to 1975, Wilmington's population decreased in absolute terms, and the percentage of black residents in the city's population rose from 7.6 to 55.5 percent (see table 5.1). In New Castle County, the population nearly doubled in this twenty-five-year period, whereas the proportion of black residents increased only slightly, from 11.8 to 13.9 percent. These demographic changes had a concomitant impact on the social characteristics of schools in the city and suburban areas.

When *Brown* was decided in 1954, the Wilmington Schools enrolled 12,875 students, of whom 28 percent were black. In 1964, the enrollments had risen to 15,527, of whom 57 percent were black. By 1973, the enrollments had decreased slightly to 14,688, and 83 percent of the students were black. In the suburban areas in 1954, there were 21,543 children enrolled in the public schools, of whom 4 percent were black and 96 percent were white. By 1973, enrollments had jumped to 73,308 with a black enrollment of approximately 6 percent.

In sum, whereas enrollments in Wilmington grew slowly, then declined slightly over this twenty-five-year period, the proportion of black children tripled (from 28 to 83 percent). By contrast, the growth in suburban school enrollments was considerable during this period, while the proportion of black children in the schools remained rather stable, averaging between 4 and 6 percent.

With the rise of suburban housing developments and the tremendous population growth, independent school districts proliferated in the suburbs. The ability of many of these districts to offer full, comprehensive educational programs varied considerably. To effectuate school district consolidation, the

TABLE 5.1. Population of Wilmington and New Castle County

	Wilmington Total Population	% Black	New Castle County (including Wilmington) Total Population	% Black
1950	110,356	7.6	218,879	11.8
1960	95,827	26.0	307,446	11.8
1970	80,386	43.6	385,511	12.7
1975	76,654	55.5	393,648	13.9

general assembly passed the Education Advancement Act (EAA) (1968), which for a period of one year, delegated the authority to reorganize school districts to the state board of education.

What resulted from this statewide reorganization was a vocational district in each county and twenty-six separate school districts, twelve of which were in New Castle County. Even though many small, inefficient districts were consolidated, it is important to note that a specific statute of the EAA permanently fixed the boundaries of the Wilmington School District so as to be coterminous with the city boundary lines, the EAA legislation passed by the general assembly precluded the state board from considering the consolidation of Wilmington schools with any suburban districts in New Castle County. The act was passed at a time when many city schools remained identifiably black (the overall black student enrollment was 66 percent in 1968), and most suburban school districts were predominantly white. The Educational Advancement Act was to become one of the major factors in the *Evans* v. *Buchanan* case when it was reopened in 1971.

The political governance characteristics of the Wilmington metropolitan area, like the demographic characteristics, are similar to other areas in the nation. The city of Wilmington has a mayor-council form of government. The mayor and the twelve council members are elected for four-year terms, the latter serving part time. Even though many politicians and community leaders have talked about the need to minimize government in Delaware, possibly through some type of metropolitan government, the city remains separated from the New Castle County government, and the county government continues to include almost a dozen small incorporated municipalities.

Most residents of New Castle County live not in Wilmington or in the incorporated municipalities but rather in unincorporated areas dependent on the county for services. As the population has grown in these areas, the structure of the county government has also changed. Today, the county executive serves in a position similar to a mayor with six county council members elected by district and a council president elected at large every four years. The tax rates set by the county reflect the level of services provided to the various incorporated municipalities and the unincorporated portion of the county.

The separation of the governance of the city and its suburbs is set within a state where metropolitan and rural representatives have clashed for decades. Like states such as Illinois and New York, Delaware has a downstate and upstate political culture. In Delaware, the downstate climate is influenced by the rural nature of the two southern counties and their historical isolation from the major eastern seaboard transportation routes. The political strength of the southern counties is also historically based, and reapportionment notwithstanding, the downstaters seem to wield more power than their approximately 30 percent of the population of the state would suggest. Attempts to keep education outside the political sphere were reflected in the statewide conflict over executive reorganization in 1970. According to Paul Dolan and James Soles, two observers of the Delaware political scene:

the administrative reorganization effected in 1970 did not place the Department of Public Instruction within the so-called governor's "cabinet." The basic reason for noninclusion was the strong feeling on the part of many articulate persons that school administration should remain "nonpolitical" and therefore outside the immediate reach of the executive. In order to bring about the administrative integration both the legislature and the executive in 1969 agreed not to press for bringing the schools within the cabinet form. Thus, the department has remained outside the regular authority of the state administration in spite of the fact that the portion of current operating costs of public education supplied by the state was approximately 25 percent of the state budget in 1975 (Dolan and Soles 1976: 167).

Thus the governance of public education in Delaware remains headed by the state board of education. The state board has seven members who serve without pay, appointed by the governor; the president of the board serves at the pleasure of the governor. The superintendent of public instruction is selected by the state board and serves as the chief administrative officer and director of the Department of Public Instruction (DPI).

Although the state funds about 70 percent of the costs associated with public schools, localism—not state control—dominates the state's public education system. In a recent study of the degree of decentralization of state educational policy, Wirt (1977) found that Delaware was the twelfth most decentralized state. The state board and the State Department of Public Instruction exert relatively little control over local school districts. Department of Public Instruction officials are highly deferential to local school boards and superintendents. In fact, the advisory council to the state board is composed entirely of local district superintendents.

There are a number of reasons for local domination of the state's public schools. First, local control has been a dominant theme of public education in the United States, and Delaware has not been immune from this tendency. Second, this tendency is greatly reinforced by the small size of the state; superintendents and local school board members as well as their constituents have no trouble reaching their local legislators. Third, many state DPI officials have previously held positions in local districts. The state superintendent is a former superintendent of a rural school district in Delaware, and the president of the state board was formerly head of the Newark board, the largest district in New Castle County. To further reinforce this orientation, the legislature recently required that at least four of the seven members of the state board be former or current local board members.

In New Castle County, DPI is often viewed as a minor annoyance; it is rarely viewed as a help or as a strong directing force. Major initiatives taken at the state level (e.g., educational assessment, competency-based education) tend to be modified and watered down by local forces. To some extent the view of DPI as having limited efficacy results from large districts thinking they can do sophisticated tasks on their own and smaller districts being unconcerned with elaborate programs.

The result (and perhaps a partial cause) of this local control was the great diversity of local school districts in the 1960s and early 1970s, and the great influence of local superintendents on the style of the local district (Bishop 1976). In almost all of the school districts in Delaware, the local school superintendent dominates the decision-making process. This, of course, is not unique to Delaware.

NEW CASTLE COUNTY SCHOOL DISTRICTS

With the massive growth of population in the suburbs, differentiated residential housing areas and school districts emerged in New Castle County. Of the various school districts that existed in the county, three served primarily upper-middle-class white families, three were principally middle-class white in their characteristics, and three served white working-class blue-collar families. Additionally, another suburban working-class district, situated in an area having considerable tax-exempt property, tended to have biracial school enrollments (approximately 55 percent black and 45 percent white in 1975–1976). Finally the Wilmington public schools, enrolling about 20 percent of the county's schoolchildren, served primarily minority children (approximately 85 percent black and 5 percent Hispanic) from low-income families (figure 5.1).

Delaware's most prestigious school districts were the three suburban districts on Wilmington's northern border—the Alexis I. Du Pont, Alfred I. Du Pont, and Mt. Pleasant school districts. In 1975–1976, approximately 20 percent of the public schoolchildren in the county attended these public schools (see table 5.2). About 95 percent of the enrollments were white children, and most came from middle-class to upper-middle-class families. Compared to children in other areas of the county, children in these three districts scored the highest on standardized achievement tests, and the vast majority go on to college (see table 5.2).

The three areas differ somewhat in character, although average costs of housing were not too dissimilar several years ago. Mt. Pleasant comprised a relatively old and well-preserved residential area and had a long history of excellent public schools; Alfred I. was composed almost entirely of suburban developments built in the last two decades along a major suburban road of shopping centers, the Concord Pike; Alexis I. was in the heart of "chateau country" with a sprinkling of nationally known historic sites like the Winterthur Museum.

To the west of Wilmington are the predominantly middle-class suburbs of Marshallton-McKean, Stanton, and Newark. These areas are composed primarily of suburban developments built in the 1960s. The Newark School District, prior to the 1978 court-ordered reorganization, was the state's largest in student enrollment; it served about 20 percent of the county's students. The city of Newark, where the University of Delaware is situated, served as the center of the school district, but only about one-third of the residents served by the district live within the city limits. Stanton (with 5,000 pupils) and Marshallton-McKean (with 3,500 pupils) were fairly proximate to the second major suburban shopping center road in the county, the Kirkwood Highway. All three areas have pockets of working-class families, but each district served predominantly middle-class students. Newark and Marshallton-McKean also have very small black communities within their boundaries, but neither had a black enrollment beyond 5 percent in 1975. Students in these three middle-class districts scored right below the three upper-middle-class districts on standardized test scores; in 1973, these students' average scores were above the mean for the county as measured by the Delaware Education Assessment Program's standardized tests.

About 20 percent of the public school students in the county attended schools in the working-class districts of New Castle-Gunning Bedford, Claymont,

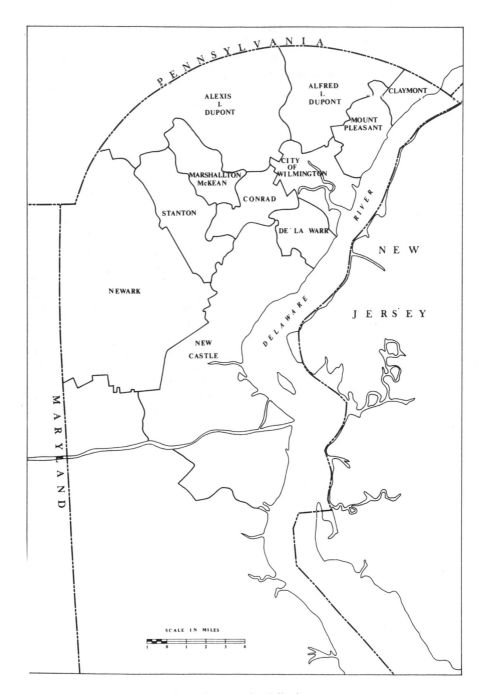

Figure 5.1. Wilmington/New Castle County school districts.

TABLE 5.2. Selected Background Information for New Castle County School Districts

Public School District	Total School Enrollment[1]	% Black	% White	DEAP Avg. Score[2]	% to College[3]	Avg. Housing Cost[4]
Upper Middle-Class Areas						
Alfred I. Du Pont	10,261	1.0	97.8	57.9	81.3	$33,531
Alexis I. Du Pont	3,258	3.9	93.8	57.1	71.0	37,150
Mt. Pleasant	4,868	2.7	96.0	55.6	71.4	36,361
Middle-Class Areas						
Marshallton-McKean	3,713	4.8	94.9	51.1	54.6	29,755
Newark	16,923	4.3	94.2	51.6	50.3	29,740
Stanton	5,237	.7	98.1	53.1	50.3	25,452
Working-Class Areas						
Claymont	3,306	4.3	94.9	52.3	57.9	29,755
Conrad	5,334	3.2	95.9	49.8	37.5	23,769
De La Warr	3,172	54.9	43.9	43.0	36.4	18,459
New Castle-Gunning Bedford	9,016	5.9	92.9	50.2	40.5	22,125
Urban Area						
Wilmington	13,852	84.7	9.8	40.4	32.6	15,801

1. School enrollments and racial percentages for 1975–1976 year.

2. Delaware Educational Assessment Program, Grade Eight Average Test Scores for 1973.

3,4. For the year 1970; see Julie Schmidt, "Wilmington School Desegregation: A Case Study in Non-Decisionmaking," Master's thesis, University of Delaware Department of Political Science.

and Conrad. Each of these areas had enrollments of less than 6 percent black in 1975–1976. These areas are a mixture of industrial areas, apartment buildings and townhouses, and modest homes. Although the Claymont students have on the average scored above the mean on the DEAP tests, the students in the other two working-class districts scored almost exactly at the average.

The De La Warr School District is the anomaly in the county; it is an area with a high percentage of blacks. Its enrollment has been about equally divided between black and white students for a few years. In 1975–1976 about 55 percent of the approximately 3,000 students were black. The overall population of this area is majority white.

De La Warr is situated adjacent to a poor area of Wilmington, isolated from the rest of Wilmington and divided by access roads to the Delaware Memorial Bridge linking Delaware to New Jersey. There is a good deal of tax-exempt property in De La Warr, including the Greater Wilmington Airport and the Wilmington Marine Terminal. Over the last several years, De La Warr has suffered from racial conflicts, lack of funds, and high administrative turnover. Students in this area generally fared lower on standardized test scores than did those in all the previously mentioned areas, and about one-third went on for further education after high school.

Finally, the Appoquinimink School District (serving 2,400 students) comprises the most rural and southernmost part of the county. Like the districts in Delaware's southern counties, schools in this area have anywhere from 23 to 31 percent black students. This, coupled with its distant geographic location, has allowed Appoquinimink to be the only K–12 district in the county that was not directly affected by the *Evans* v. *Buchanan* desegregation remedy.

Throughout the suburban school-districts, pupils were generally assigned to their neighborhood schools. Those elementary students living more than a mile from their assigned schools, as well as those secondary school students living more than two miles away, have been bused to school at state expense. A majority of suburban students ride the bus to school. In the small and compact Claymont area, only about 10 percent were bused in 1974–1975, but in the Alexis I. Du Pont area, almost every child rode a bus to school. The districts south of the city have used buses the most; few students in Wilmington (approximtely 15 percent) rode buses at public expense.

A small majority of the total population of Wilmington is black (55 percent), but the white age distribution and Wilmington children's attendance in private and parochial schools (approximately 4,000 students) helped lower the percentage white in the public schools. In 1975–1976 the almost 14,000 Wilmington pupils attended a total of three high schools, four middle schools, fourteen elementary schools, and one special school for handicapped students. Nine of these schools were almost 95 percent black, a major point brought out in the 1971 reopening of *Evans* v. *Buchanan*. The Drew, Elbert, Stubbs, Bancroft, and Howard facilities, for example, were almost entirely black from the *Brown* decision until the fall 1978 term. Whereas in 1957 about two-thirds of the students in these schools were black, by 1975 these schools became almost totally black.

The public schools in Wilmington have faced educational problems analogous to those of other cities in the nation. In March 1973 Mark Shedd, ex-superintendent of the Philadelphia public schools, and a field team from the Graduate School of Education at Harvard University, conducted a one-week needs assessment of the Wilmington public schools (Shedd 1973). The team's report presented a number of criticisms and recommendations regarding the Wilmington schools. For example:

> Eighty-six percent of Wilmington's children are reading below grade level by grade three. Subsequent to grade three, gains average only four to six months per school year, resulting in growing cumulative deficits for most children. By grade six, 80 percent of the children are reading more than one year behind grade level and 60 percent read two or more years behind. By grade ten, the mean reading achievement level is 6.5 citywide and three quarters of the students are reading more than two years behind grade level. Thus, the extent of the reading problem is all pervasive in the Wilmington schools. . . .
>
> Reading achievement was proclaimed the first priority of the Wilmington public schools in 1970. Since then a coordinator has been appointed, public announcement of test scores has been instituted and an excellent comprehensive program has been drawn up. Funding of the program has not yet taken place, however, and without materials and staff the reading effort has little chance of success. . . .
>
> Administrators, teachers, parents, and community residents agreed that there exists a lack of parental involvement in the operations of the schools; and, more specifically, a lack of attendance on their part in the school's various parent councils and boards. Although generally supportive of the school system, community residents felt frustrated with the available lines of communications and do not feel that they are informed or included in the decision-making mechanisms in the schools. As a result, schools tend to operate and plan in isolation from their surrounding communities (Shedd 1973: 30, 22).

The Wilmington School District also had its share of political conflict. First, it had been under pressure from the city administration to reveal more of its financial affairs. Because the city had limited control over the public schools' budget (through a tax commission which included the mayor and three council members) and because the city spent about 25 percent of its budget on education in 1975, the cost-conscious city administration demanded more fiscal accountability from the schools. Second, teacher union-school district relations had been a source of conflict. Wilmington teacher salaries were higher than those in suburban New Castle County and many city districts throughout the nation. The Wilmington Federation of Teachers, affiliated with the American Federation of Teachers, however, had pressed for better wages while the city administration fought to keep a lid on the school budget. A bitter strike resulted in 1975. Finally, the school board, appointed by the mayor and governor, had suffered from interracial conflict, in part resulting from the growing movement by blacks to have local control over school affairs.

Similar to the De La Warr area, students in Wilmington have tended to score lower on standardized tests than students in other county areas; about one-third of the high school graduates continue their education. Unlike urban school districts in other parts of the nation, Wilmington was not a poor but rather a relatively wealthy school district. Wilmington's assessed valuation per student in 1975–1976 was about at the mean for the county, ranking fourth overall. This relatively high valuation results from the heavy concentration of commercial property and corporate office buildings in the city. Under Delaware's school finance system, Wilmington did about as well as other districts in garnering state funds. Yet, the city spent more per pupil than any suburban district because its local property tax rate was more than 50 percent higher than other districts, and its federal funds and grants were far greater than virtually all other districts. Actually, it was the De La Warr School District that suffered from the usual problems of the central-city school district, an inadequate tax base. On the other hand, the wealthy Alexis I. Du Pont School District raised more local funds than Wilmington with half the tax rate because it had the highest per-pupil assessed valuation of all areas. Yet, Alexis I. Du Pont spent about that of Wilmington on the average for each of its students in 1975–1976.

It is against this backdrop that the original *Evans* v. *Buchanan* school desegregation suit, filed in 1956, was reopened in the federal courts in 1971. This signaled a new phase of the desegregation controversy and the start of many events that eventually led to the comprehensive metropolitan-wide remedy ordered by the courts.

In the second phase of the *Evans* v. *Buchanan* case, the local federal courts were extensively involved in attempts to resolve critical questions regarding the factors and causes of segregated schools in Wilmington and the county. Moreover, the courts played a major role in determining the general nature of what kinds of desegregation remedies would be appropriate, being influenced both by their findings of fact in the liability aspects of the local case and by the decisions of higher federal courts. In later stages, from 1975 on, the local court was a principal forum for debate regarding the legality and potential effectiveness of a wide variety of desegregation plans proposed by the plaintiffs and defendants. As subsequent court rulings began to suggest that a comprehensive interdistrict plan was more likely, the actions and positions of key actors and groups became more influenced by political and organizational interests and ideological conflicts. To better understand these latter events and actions, it is important to first highlight the second-phase legal developments of *Evans* v. *Buchanan.*

REOPENING OF *EVANS* V. *BUCHANAN*

In the summer of 1971, *Evans* was reopened in the U.S. District Court by five black parents who had children in the Wilmington public schools. These parents had been helped by the local ACLU and white liberals in Wilmington; the local NAACP did not support the suit at this time because of fears that blacks would bear the brunt of desegregation and the loss of newly won power in the schools (Schmidt, in process). As noted previously, by the earlier 1970s the public school enrollments in Wilmington were about 70 percent black; many schools that were solely or predominantly black prior to *Brown* remained so over fifteen years later. Conversely, almost all suburban districts continued to be over 90 percent white in their public school enrollments. As legal activity regarding the case heightened in the 1970s, the enrollment picture related to the racial characteristics of the schools was not at issue—schoolchildren in this area were by and large racially isolated from each other along city-suburban lines.

What was at issue, however, were the factors that contributed to or caused this situation. The black parents who reopened the suit argued that the state was violating their "equal protection" rights of the Fourteenth Amendment of the U.S. Constitution in that black children were still in racially identifiable and segregated schools as a result of state actions and inactions. In essence, the plaintiffs argued that the state had not followed the requirements of *Brown* to dismantle a racially discriminatory, dual public school system; moreover, the 1968 Educational Advancement Act tended to perpetuate the dual system by keeping black children inside the Wilmington city lines and schools.

The state board argued that the actions and effects described by the plaintiffs were not racially motivated and were not the result of state action. They claimed that blacks and Wilmington's representatives in the state legislature had not opposed the Educational Advancement Act in 1968 and that the exclusion of Wilmington from any future consolidation was based on history (the city boundaries were drawn in 1919) and principles of educational administration (a school district of 12,000 pupils was an adequate but not yet too large district). According to this reasoning, they contended that the act was the result of normal (not racial) considerations of quality education and political compromise.

The three-judge federal district court, in its 12 July 1974 decision on the reopened *Evans* v. *Buchanan* case, agreed with the plaintiffs that the Wilmington schools remained segregated. The presence and continuation of racially identifiable schools "is a clear indication that segregated schooling in Wilmington has never been eliminated and that there exists a dual system. . . . This court must conclude that a unitary school system has never been established" (*Evans* v. *Buchanan* 1974: 13–14). The court failed to rule on the constitutionality of the Educational Advancement Act, however.

The majority of the court declined to select or specify a remedy at this point, that is, to decide whether an intradistrict or interdistrict plan was necessary. This position was perhaps due to the uncertainty at the national level regarding the appropriateness and legality of city-suburban busing and desegregation plans. The Detroit case, *Milliken* v. *Bradley* (1974), had already been argued before the U.S. Supreme Court, and many critical issues and standards that might apply to the Wilmington case were yet to be ruled on by the U.S. Supreme Court.

Thus in the 12 July 1974 *Evans* ruling, the district court strongly reaffirmed the state board's responsibility to desegregate the public schools under the Supreme Court rulings of *Brown* and *Charlotte* v. *Mecklenburg Board* (1971). The state board was required to submit both a Wilmington-only plan and a metropolitan plan. The key question of what kind of plan would eventually be ordered by the court was left unanswered, and no specific guidelines or planning parameters were issued to the local educational authority, the state board.

Less than two weeks later, on 25 July 1974, the U.S. Supreme Court issued the *Milliken* v. *Bradley* decision, which vacated the pending city-suburban desegregation plan in Detroit, and which more generally outlined the kinds of conditions that could conceivably permit an interdistrict school desegregation remedy. Residents of New Castle County breathed a sigh of relief—apparently, Wilmington's segregated schools were to be dealt with within the confines of Wilmington.

After *Milliken*, the local district court vacated its own order issued pursuant to its 12 July 1974 decision. The court invited suburban districts to enter the case, and called on both the plaintiffs[3] and the defendants to prepare written and oral arguments on the applicability of the *Milliken* decision for Delaware. As expected, the suburban districts entered the case as intervening defendants and argued, with the state board, that the *Milliken* case controlled the question of remedy in the Wilmington case. Specifically, they contended the U.S. Supreme Court's decision that "the scope of the remedy is determined by the nature and extent of the constitutional violation" and that:

> Before the boundaries of separate and autonomous school districts may be set aside by consolidating the separate units for remedial purposes or by imposing a cross-district remedy, it must first be shown that there has been a constitutional violation within one district that produces a significant effect in another district. Specifically, it must be shown that racially discriminatory acts of the state or local school districts, or of a single school district have been a substantial cause of interdistrict segregation (*Milliken* v. *Bradley* 1974: 5258).

The state and suburban board attorneys argued that there had not been any constitutional violations, and in accord with *Milliken* there was no justification for an interdistrict remedy.

On 27 March 1975, the district court ruled that *Milliken* was indeed applicable to the Delaware case, but disagreed with the defendants' view that no constitutional violations had occurred. The court noted that the state or its entities engaged in actions that contributed to residential segregation of races. Moreover, the state also helped underwrite the costs of transporting children to private schools, an action that assisted white children to enroll in private or parochial schools. Third, the court ruled as unconstitutional those provisions of the EAA that prohibited Wilmington from being considered for consolidation with suburban districts (*Evans* v. *Buchanan* 1975a: 23-24, 20, 51). The court advanced that it did not find evidence to indicate that the EAA's passage and statutes were racially motivated; nevertheless, the effect of the prohibitive statutes was such that in 1968 the state board could not include Wilmington in any reorganization plan that could have reduced the racial disparities between city and suburban schools. This exclusion of Wilmington occurred at a time when the state had an affirmative obligation under *Brown* and succeeding decisions to dismantle dual, segregated school systems. The court required in its March 1975 ruling that the parties to the suit submit desegregation plans in accord with the 12 July 1974 ruling, specifically, Wilmington-only and metropolitan plans. The state appealed the decision to the U.S. Supreme Court, which on 27 November 1975 announced that "the judgement is affirmed" (*Evans* v. *Buchanan* 1975b).

The U.S. Supreme Court ruling came during federal district court hearings on the nature and appropriateness of various desegregation plans. Based on its earlier order, the district court had requested that the defendants and plaintiffs develop plans; anyone else who wished could also submit Wilmington-only and interdistrict plans to the state board for review, with the state board subsequently presenting its recommended plans to the court for consideration.

3. In 1972, the Wilmington School Board had entered the case as intervening plaintiffs in *Evans* v. *Buchanan*.

When the court turned to the various local educational authorities, and any other interested parties, a free-for-all ensued. Over twenty-five different plans were submitted for state board and/or court review, ranging from completely voluntary freedom-of-choice plans on the one hand to a country-wide single school district with pupil reassignments among four regional attendance areas. These myriad plans came from the Wilmington and suburban boards, citizens, and parents, several community groups, and DPI staff under the aegis of the state board. The major alternatives included plans to (1) transfer only students in the Wilmington public schools; (2) divide the Wilmington School District into five sections to be recombined and reorganized with suburban districts; (3) establish magnet schools and freedom-of-choice plans within transfer zones defined as in (2); (4) establish a county school district; (5) exchange pupils across school district lines in clusters of city and suburban schools (Delaware Department of Instruction 1975).

None of these plans, however, was acceptable to the court. The court rejected the Wilmington-only plan because Wilmington's high proportion of black enrollment could not result in desegregation of the city's schools. The pie-shaped plan and the county plans were rejected because the court believed that the state legislature should and could enact such plans that allowed local officials to determine the governance structure. The voluntary plans were rejected because they failed to promise to desegregate the schools. Finally, the pupil exchange plan was rejected because of its administrative infeasibility. Thus, in its 19 May 1976 ruling (*Evans* v. *Buchanan* 1976a), no plan submitted was found to satisfy constitutional and/or practical standards.

The court first ruled that all suburban districts would be involved in the remedy,[4] and that a single district would replace the current Wilmington and suburban districts. Second, the court directed the state board to appoint immediately a five-member Interim Board of Education, which would have responsibility for the development of a desegregation plan, and which would subsequently govern and operate the single, reorganized district no later than 1 September 1977 (about fifteen months away). Moreover, schools with anywhere from 10 to 35 percent black students would be considered prima facie desegregated. Intermediate and secondary schools were to be desegregated by September 1977, and the elementary schools by September 1978.

The court left specific details such as assignment plans, school personnel, salaries, and tax rates in the hands of the local authorities. Equally important, the court gave the state legislature the right to devise alternative plans for redistricting the area, as long as the alternative plan took into account the racial assignment ratios and implementation dates specified above. Thus, the legislature (or the state board, acting under delegated authority from the legislature) could create one or more districts in the affected area pursuant to existing Delaware law. If no such action transpired, the court's one-district plan would serve as the organizational framework for desegregation.

---

4. The Appoquinimink District was not included for reasons presented previously. The County Vocational District was also excluded. Judge Layton dissented in part by indicating that he did not view the findings of fact persuasive to warrant an interdistrict remedy.

SIGNIFICANCE OF THE MAY 1976 COURT DECISION

The May 1976 federal district court ruling—one which in modified form would eventually lead to city-suburban busing and district reorganization—was received in varying ways by residents of the area. Most citizens were not sure what the ruling meant. School desegregation, as an issue, had been around for a very long time, staying for the most part in the netherlands of the courts. And nothing had really changed in the schools over this extensive period of time.

Some residents knew what the decision meant—simply, some court had ordered that kids were going to be bused in and out of Wilmington, white kids and black kids were being ordered by a court to go to school together. Neither black parents nor white parents knew the specifics of this busing—where, what grades, and so on. No one knew the specifics; the court had laid out only some general pieces of the picture, leaving the details and critical issues in the hands of local people.

But one aspect of the court's ruling was noted by many, particularly state and local educational officials in charge of public education. Existing school districts in northern New Castle County were to be eliminated; in its place would be a single district and governance structure. Up to now, such a massive reorganization was viewed by participants in the legal battle as remote. In May 1976, however, the prospect of one district instead of many took on real form. The court had ruled that the state could modify the one-district arrangement, as long as other desegregation guidelines were met. Absent any action by the state, one district would come into being, and this was just a little over a year away.

One other feature of the court plan marked a significant departure from past practice. Up to 1976 and throughout the previous *Evans* litigation, the state board was the entity designated by the court for having the responsibility to develop a desegregation plan. Now the court had created a new structure to do this, a five-member interim board, a board that would also assume governance and operating control of the city and county schools after the separate districts were dissolved. The state board's new role in this, as directed by the court, was to review the plan and advise the court on its merits.

It may be argued that the court was taking a gamble, a new kind of approach for Delaware, in trying to resolve the school desegregation situation. *Evans* started in 1957 and was reopened in 1971, and five years after that the schools in Wilmington were still predominantly black and schools in the suburbs were predominantly white.

The first-step remedy approach typical of many other school desegregation suits across the country—going to the educational entity most directly responsible for public education and having that body develop a plan—had not produced satisfactory or effective results in Delaware, back in the late 1950s, the early 1960s, or now in the mid-1970s.[5] And the protracted, adversarial debates in court when various plans were presented in the October-December 1975 hearings were likely very frustrating to the court. So many plans had been submitted yet nothing met practical or constitutional criteria. Thus, the court turned

---

5. Compliance with court requests and deadlines was always present. The plans themselves, however, were judged not acceptable. As discussed subsequently, only in the last rounds of court hearings (late 1977) was a compromise plan proposed and endorsed by the court in January 1978.

to an entity it created, the interim board, in hopes that it could develop an acceptable desegregation plan. In so doing, the court also created a body that in theory could provide a forum for bargaining and compromise as plans were forged.

In a sense, all the ingredients were present to effectuate a resolution of the school desegregation issue. The interim board membership was to be drawn from the school boards now representing the affected areas—one member was to be from Wilmington, one from Newark (the largest suburban district in the state), and three others drawn from geographical "sets" of school districts.[6] The interim board had the designated task of developing the desegregation plan, and equally important, it was responsible to the court. And now there was latitude for that group to argue, negotiate, and compromise both within the interim board and between the interim board and other groups that had a stake in public education in New Castle County.

But what was possible, in terms of a pluralistic decision-making model leading to compromise and resolution, was more myth than reality (Peterson 1976). The interim board had a projected life of less than a year—from the summer of 1976 to early spring 1977—and during its tenure the board made some progress through its task forces on various technical and generally noncontroversial problems related to desegregation. Yet, the critical issues facing it—pupil assignment and district reorganization—could not be satisfactorily resolved.

There were many groups and organizations that influenced the Wilmington/ New Castle County desegregation planning, including the suburban and Wilmington boards of education, the new interim board, the state board, and the state legislature. Other players on the scene were superintendents of the local school districts, governmental and elected officials, and community groups—some supportive of peaceful implementation or court-ordered desegregation, and one visible antibusing group.

What resulted from this interplay of groups and influences were several major conflicts or issues—one tied to pupil reassignment, a second to the redistribution of power in relation to the control of schools and governance structures (involving individuals and organization); the third, and perhaps less debated conflict, was related to the nature and process of desegregation planning. These issues interacted with and were influenced by a backdrop of ideological tensions manifest along legal, political, class, and racial lines. This ideological backdrop is important for understanding the crucible in which school desegregation issues and plans were formulated. This backdrop in its own right was a result of historical patterns of race relations and the implications and meanings of court decisions related directly and indirectly to the *Evans* case.

LEGAL ISSUES

After the district court ruling in May 1976, the suburban boards and the state reacted in tandem—appeals were again submitted to the U.S. Supreme Court.[7]

6. One member was to come from either the Alfred I. Du Pont, Mt. Pleasant, or Claymont boards; one from either the New Castle-Gunning Bedford, De La Warr, or Conrad boards; and one from either the Stanton, Marshallton-McKean, or Alexis I. Du Pont boards.

7. The De La Warr District, which had expressed a preference for a county-wide district, did not join in the appeals.

This time, however, the U.S. Supreme Court did not consider the issue of unconstitutional actions by the state or its entities, nor did it deal with the question of the scope or extent of the remedy ordered by the district court in its May 1976 ruling. The proper arena, it intimated, was the Third Circuit Court of Appeals (*Evans* v. *Buchanan* 1976b), and the defendants did not hesitate to lodge appeals with this body.

Although recognizing that it is not at all unique for defendants in school desegregation cases to file appeals, it is important to note that there were many uncertainties and questions raised by court decisions that played a role in increasing the defendant's tenacity in fighting desegregation in the courts. Moreover, the political and ideological conflicts in New Castle County, discussed subsequently, were such that not fighting desegregation would be political suicide. There was also a pervasive aura among school boards and in the legislature, that the legal decisions of 1975 and 1976 could be overturned. This to some degree emanated from U.S. Supreme Court rulings in other cases and the implications these rulings had vis-à-vis *Evans*.

In July 1976, the U.S. Supreme Court ruled in *Washington* v. *Davis* (1976), a police applicant selection case alleging discrimination against blacks in hiring decisions, that if there were no discerned acts of intentional discrimination—that is, no motivation or intent to discriminate—that any adverse impacts along racial lines would not be a sufficient showing to invoke a court-ordered remedy to alleviate racial disparities in employment, or more generally to undo the effects of adverse impact alleged by minority plaintiffs.

This ruling added fuel to the desegregation-fighting fire in New Castle County. The state board had consistently argued that it had not engaged in discriminatory actions. The suburban boards, for the most part also adopted this view, because each local district was currently operating in unitary fashion—there were no dual, segregated systems of education operating in any suburban district; school assignments and enrollments, it was argued, were done in a context of a unitary system for each suburban district. Some suburban districts, particularly those not immediately contiguous with Wilmington, also argued that they were a bit removed from the city—that even if some form of consolidation of Wilmington and suburban districts had transpired in 1968, they would not have been involved. Other, more contiguous districts argued that even if there had been discriminatory actions, all districts should be involved in the remedy.

A key, too, was the test of intention referred to by the U.S. Supreme Court in *Washington* v. *Davis* and in other school desegregation cases.[8] The district court's March 1975 ruling indicated that the court did not find that the purpose of the Educational Advancement Act of 1968 had an intentionally discriminatory purpose. This was a keystone of many subsequent arguments made by state and suburban defendants before the courts (*Evans* v. *Buchanan* 1975a). Many believed that it was only a matter of time before the decision would be overturned.

The conflict over school reorganization was also part of a larger context shaped in significant fashion by ideological conflicts along city-suburban and racial lines. The nature of ideological differences and tensions had a relationship

8. School desegregation suits remanded by the U.S. Supreme Court in this period included the Austin, Indianapolis, and Dayton cases, all referencing the intent doctrine of *Washington* v. *Davis*.

to the more recent history of race relations in the Wilmington metropolitan area and to attempts to make parent opposition to busing a political issue. In April 1968, the state national guard was ordered into Wilmington by Governor Terry, who feared that racial tensions would develop on a large scale after the assassination of Martin Luther King, Jr. Whether civil disturbances in the city would have occurred without the national guard, or whether the guard's presence prevented disturbances is difficult to determine. The presence of armed national guard, jeeps, and military paraphenalia did produce tensions, however. City residents, particularly blacks, lived with the incursion until January 1969, when Russell Peterson was sworn in as the new governor.

Also, 1968 was the year that the Educational Advancement Act was passed by the state legislature. No legislator from Wilmington, white or black, voted against the EAA. At that time, blacks were beginning to have more local representative control of the school board. There well may have been a desire to maintain the boundaries and integrity of the Wilmington district. Parents had some influence on the educational environment for their children, and the district was not in dire financial straits; in fact, its financial picture was very good relative to many suburban districts. Moreover, given the general control by whites of elected and appointed positions in Wilmington, the school board was the only city-wide entity in which blacks had substantial representation and influence. Thus, the dilemma faced by the Wilmington Board over the loss of political control by blacks versus school desegregation may have been present when the implications of the EAA's provisions were discussed.

Another factor in concentrating blacks in increasing numbers in Wilmington was racial discrimination in housing. As noted previously, the district court's March 1975 ruling found that discriminatory actions by the state and by the real estate industry contributed to residential segregation. Moreover, when public housing for low-income families was proposed in suburban areas, a great deal of opposition was encountered and as a consequence, public housing was centered almost solely in Wilmington and did not exist to any noticeable degree in suburban areas.

Public sentiment was another factor in generating the ideological tensions that swirled around the school desegregation issue.[9] Parents in the suburbs, almost all of whom were white, were almost unanimously opposed to city-suburban busing (polls indicated 90 percent opposition). City parents, however, almost all of whom were black, were equally divided in their expressed support or opposition to busing (i.e., about 40 percent in favor, 40 percent opposed, and 20 percent undecided). Parents in the suburbs, and parents in Wilmington to a lesser extent, viewed suburban schools to be generally superior to city schools. For suburban parents, having their children bused to a school in the city was not viewed favorably. Suburban parents, to a noticeably higher degree than city parents, felt that desegregation would lower the quality of education, and would not lead to reduction in racial prejudices. For example, in a poll

9. Interviews regarding desegregation issues were conducted with city and suburban parents by the College of Urban Affairs and Public Policy, University of Delaware, in two periods—spring 1977 and winter 1978. The observations noted herein are derived from these interview findings. See the Wilmington *News-Journal*, May 15–18, 1977 editions, and reports by the College of Urban Affairs and Public Policy for more detailed information.

conducted in the spring of 1978, 72 percent of suburban parents and 38 percent of city parents rejected the statement that "desegregation will help reduce racial prejudice." Moreover, both city and suburban parents expressed concern about the safety and welfare of children if busing were to come about. In the winter 1978 poll, 41 percent of suburban and 34 percent of city parents thought that busing would generate "a lot of violence."

The emerging backdrop of parent opposition to desegregation and the concomitant dissolution of existing districts was fueled by the legal positions of nonculpability advanced by suburban boards and the state board. Another factor, too, was parents' strong identification with their local neighborhood schools. At this time, moreover, most school districts had not been active in communicating to parents about the antecedents of the court order or about plans and prospects for the future. Parents may have not been well informed on desegregation matters, but suburban parents in particular had very pronounced feelings about it. They were strongly opposed to busing children and to the "loss" of their own district and their ties to local schools. This feeling was shared by many city parents, who also had long-standing attachments; the Wilmington School Board administrators; and teachers.

Prior to 1975, most local elected officials generally steered clear of the desegregation controversy. Yet all the ingredients were present to turn busing into an ideological and political issue. All the situation lacked was a spark, a catalyst, and the rise of a visible antibusing group, the Positive Action Committee (PAC), provided just that spark, one that would make local school authorities and elected officials, particularly the state legislature, take note of the busing issue.

THE ANTIBUSING MOVEMENT

"It's time to wake up, folks" was the slogan of the antibusing Positive Action Committee. Begun in February 1975, the Positive Action Committee quickly became the largest and most vocal organization in Delaware to oppose involuntary busing for the purpose of racial desegregation. PAC generated a tremendous amount of local publicity in its efforts to stop busing. It claimed over 10,000 members (dues were set at $2.50 per person), spent over $15,000 in printing materials to distribute literature throughout the county, held well-attended public meetings, and was an active lobbying force in the state legislature.

The fortunes of PAC have been tied to James Venema, a leader in founding PAC and its president until early 1978. Venema had been a registered independent until recently,[10] but his political stances consistently were conservative Republican. In many ways, Venema's style was much like that of many elected officials—well dressed, attractive, and pursuant of publicity. But Venema and several other leaders of PAC differed from politicans in their frequent use of sarcasm, attacks on people and organizations, and extreme rhetoric. Circulars and flyers for the Positive Action Committee, for example, have displayed a school bus labeled "The Kidnap Express," and PAC leaders have made reference

10. Mr. Venema changed party affiliation, to Republican, and launched a campaign to win the Republican Party's nomination to challenge the Democratic party incumbent, U.S. Senator Joseph Biden.

to "brainwashing and propaganda attempts" by organizations or individuals who were "buckling under" the implementation of desegregation.

The Positive Action Committee's stance has been that forced busing is the last straw in the erosion of our freedoms. As one leader put it, "In slightly over 200 years we have regressed to the sort of tyranny and injustice the British government imposed on the people of that time . . . (the judiciary is extracting) yet another freedom from our already dwindling supply" (Oberle 1975). Forced busing, according to PAC, was a reprehensible loss of freedom because busing takes away parents' rights, harms the education of children, causes people to flee the public schools, and is very costly. The Positive Action Committee leaders argued that busing and the erosion of our freedoms must be stopped, even if this necessitated confrontation between local and federal officials or the public and those who govern them. Confrontation did not include violence, but it also disallowed cooptation and cooperation. According to Venema, PAC "won't cooperate in implementation of a forced busing plan" but it opposed "vandalism, racism, and violence" (Whitcomb 1975). Venema tried to prepare PAC followers to resist a "massive busing order" by saying: "Keep your cool. Stay calm. Don't start running, hooting and hollering and tipping over buses . . . I'm sure the opposition is just waiting for us to lose our cool" (*Evening Journal* 1975a).

The Positive Action Committee viewed the state legislature as the focus for a confrontation with the judiciary and the federal government over busing. According to Venema, "We're going to get this issue to the voting booth. The general assembly is the last line of defense between federal power running crazy and the citizens. We want them to stand up and fight for the people" (*Evening Journal* 1974). The Positive Action Committee's focus on the legislature was tied to several strategies, the most apparent one tied legislator stance on busing to PAC endorsement or opposition to particular candidates during election periods. To quote Venema, "The people out there don't want busing. If we get a large enough membership we can put in or take out any politician we want" (*Evening Journal* 1975b). Other strategies for the Positive Action Committee were concentrated on membership drives, mailings, mass meetings, letters to the editor, and pressure on public officials.

The large membership of PAC indicates that the organization reflected the philosophy of many whites in suburban New Castle County. A poll conducted in the spring of 1977 revealed that suburban public school parents who received their information from PAC newsletters or meetings (about half of the sample) did not differ from suburban parents who had no contact with the group. Comparisons on a variety of background characteristics and political and educational attitudinal items indicated no major differences between the two groups. However, PAC followers differed substantially in their antidesegregation attitudes and their willingness and experience in taking action against busing. For example, even though 54 percent of those active in PAC (i.e., those who received information from meetings and newsletters) reported writing a letter to an official or newspaper about busing, only 13 percent of those who had no PAC contact reported taking similar action.

Not only did PAC reach about half of the suburban parents and claim over 10,000 dues-paying members, it also had strength throughout all the suburban school districts with the exception of De La Warr. In the blue-collar school districts 20 percent were activists; in the middle-class districts 16 percent were activists; and even in the upper-middle-class suburban school districts, 12 percent of the sample were activists. In each type of suburban school district, at least 37 percent received information through newsletters or meetings from PAC.

The Positive Action Committee did have a major impact on the state legislature's posture and approach to desegregation. It helped make the desegregation issue quite visible to both legislators and the general public and was influential in affecting the policies and verbal statements of the state legislature. But PAC failed in its major goals—to stop forced busing and to evoke a major confrontation between state and federal officials.

Several factors contributed to this failure. First, the organization's strident and ideological tone narrowed its constituency. The New Castle County public was not as conservative or as receptive to rhetorical overkill as PAC leaders. Postive Action Committee leaders were not completely able to dismiss an image of extremism. Second, like other community groups, PAC found it difficult to overcome long-standing political forces like political party identification and, perhaps more importantly, the power of local school officials who tried to keep PAC at arm's length. An attack on the public school system was an attack on the livelihood of these officials and their organizations, and thus had to be rejected ultimately. Third, PAC abrasiveness disturbed key executives and government officials who were not accustomed to receiving threats made in the public arena. Finally, as the desegregation process dragged on, and court rulings pointed increasingly to implementation of desegregation, PAC was not able to stop busing, and its support lessened as implementation loomed on the horizon.

DESEGREGATION PLANNING—MAY 1976 TO MAY 1977

The state legislature and the interim board had each been assigned major roles in the desegregation planning process. These two groups did not interact formally, neither did they work in conjunction with each other to achieve the goal of effective desegregation. On the one hand, the legislature became embroiled in mostly symbolic actions; the other group, the interim board, attempted to deal with the substantive issues raised by the court's directive, but was so enmeshed in political-ideological conflicts that it too failed to develop an equitable or effective desegregation plan.

The state legislature, by virtue of being in the public eye, helped contribute to the emotionalism that surrounded the *Evans* case. The vast majority of legislators were personally and ideologically opposed to school desegregation and the possible changes that would affect the composition and control of the schools. Moreover, legislators knew quite well that suburban parents were strongly opposed to forced busing. Added to this combustible mixture were PAC campaigning and lobbying efforts. The result was that legislators were compelled to "do something" about busing. What the legislature did, perhaps predictably, was to rail against busing and to resist any attempts to exercise leadership in developing effective desegregation plans and attendant implementation strategies.

In response to PAC demands and general public sentiment against busing, the legislature had already established a special legislative committee in July 1975 to study the impact of proposed remedy options ordered by the U.S.

District Court in its 27 March 1975 ruling. Committee objectives were to seek a stay, to review proposed desegregation plans, and to seek legal advice. The legislature also asked the three-judge district court to delay the date by which plans were to be submitted in order to allow for legislative deliberation and action (Committee 1975). When the court responded that the legislature could finds ways to participate without the requested delay, an adversarial posture was taken by the legislature that underscored many subsequent actions on its part. In this instance, angry legislators wrote the judges to demand their appearance in the legislature to explain their actions.

The judges did not avail themselves of this unique opportunity, and the legislature embarked on considering and/or passing a spate of obstructive legislation related to desegregation planning.[11] Phillip Kurland, constitutional law professor and legal consultant to the state, advised the legislature to "be like Caesar's wife; be beyond reproach" (Committee 1975). Kurland noted that an explicit legislative act aimed at obstructing desegregation would add weight to the plaintiff's contention that the state had played a role in furthering school segregation.

The advice from Mr. Kurland and other counsel, throughout the more recent stages of *Evans*, cooled somewhat the fiery passions in the legislature, as did the efforts of a few of the more liberal members of that body. Yet, there were no members of the legislature who took an active, visible role toward taking steps to plan for effective and equitable desegregation. Busing was a hot issue, and anyone—particularly legislators from suburban areas—who talked about planning "with equity" could expect to incur the rifled focus of PAC.

This is not to say that the legislature did not consider or recommend any desegregation plans. In both 1976 and 1977, the legislature passed voluntary transfer plans that were variations on the "freedom of choice" plans adopted elsewhere in the mid- to late 1960s. Under these plans, black schoolchildren in the Wilmington and De La Warr districts could transfer to a majority white school in the suburban areas. After implementation, these plans did not substantially change the enrollment picture in most districts. Magnet schools were also considered but not actively pursued by the legislature, and a special form of voluntary transfer referred to locally as reverse volunteerism was proposed in the summer of 1977.

The plans that were passed or proposed to the court had two things in common: they tended to place the burden of desegregation on black children, and they were judged constitutionally unacceptable by the court as the sole means to desegregate the public schools. On the whole, the legislature did not offer any proactive leadership in preparing for the implementation of school desegregation. Indeed, the actions of this body tended to inflame the controversy

11. Over the more recent history of *Evans* (1975 on), the general assembly passed legislation (in one or both branches) that would require a public referendum or approval before school boundary changes could be implemented. Moreover, other resolutions were adopted that would (1) make inquiry into the actions of Federal Judge Gibbons; (2) appeal and disclaim the New Castle Planning Board of Education; (3) request of President Carter that he remove U.S. District Court Judge Murray M. Schwartz. Additional actions of this sort ranged from subpoenaing a federal judge through passing legislation to "fine not less than $20,000 nor more than $40,000, or imprison for not more than five years, or both" federal judges who exceeded their authority (House Bill no. 567, 29 July 1977).

and increased rather than reduced the uncertainties that faced parents and school authorites.

THE INTERIM BOARD

The interim board established by the court in May 1976 had the awesome task of dealing with several controversial issues that would radically restructure education in New Castle County. These issues were (1) designing a pupil re-assignment plan across eleven districts in accord with the court's 10-to-35 percent minority racial ratios; (2) developing a district reorganization-governance plan, either in cooperation or in confrontation with the legislature; and (3) structuring a teacher and staff reassignment plan, with a host of salary and personnel issues, arising from eleven separate districts being involved in the remedy. Although the court had expected that the interim board would provide a forum for compromise, negotiation, and bargaining that would result in an acceptable and effective plan, what actually resulted was a heightening of conflicts and a lessening of any opportunity to develop such a plan.

When the interim board members were sworn in by the state board in July 1976, thirteen members took their position in lieu of the five originally con-templated by the court. The legislature had enacted a bill less than a month earlier that gave representation to each suburban district; Wilmington and Newark each had two representatives.[12] Although differences existed and problems arose among the suburban district representatives, there was con-siderably more consensus among these members when they were dealing with Wilmington's position on key issues. That is, whites numerically dominated the interim board, and there was little need to "compromise and negotiate" a solution satisfactory to both suburban and city parties.

The basic positions of the board members generally were influenced by personal views, parent opposition to busing, PAC, and local school board posi-tions taken previously,[13] as well as the forays of the legislature into matters involving school desegregation.

The interim board developed an organizational structure that it thought would serve as the basis for decision making in a rational framework.[14] Task forces were established for sixteen areas central to desegregation planning,[15]

12. Each of the eleven school boards made their nominations to the state board, which in turn appointed these individuals to the interim board.

13. The plans adopted by suburban districts (except De La Warr) during the 1975 hearings were based on general positions that would minimize changes for their parent and student constituents: maintain suburban district lines and personnel, minimize in-creased taxes for desegregation costs, restrict or reduce the involuntary busing of white children, and minimize any inequities among whites if busing had to be man-datory. Wilmington's position, too, was geared to minimizing the impact—on children in the city and through maintaining control over city schools (i.e., not dividing up the Wilmington district).

14. The form of operation originally adopted by the board appeared to have much in common with Peterson's models of rational and organizational decision making (see Peterson 1976).

15. Task force areas included communications, administrations, curriculum, instruction,

and citizen's advisory committees were eventually established for each task force. Research for Better Schools, a federally sponsored education laboratory, was used as a consultant to help guide the work of the task forces.

But instead of developing a unified, administrative structure immediately under the board, the board recreated its own divisions in the operational structure supposedly subservient to it. Hiring an acting superintendent was too controversial—be it someone from one of the existing districts, which would threaten other districts; or someone external to the situation, which would threaten everyone. Thus, the interim board hired an "administrative director," and to the superintendents in northern New Castle County[16] was given the responsibility of reviewing all task force work and making recommendations to the board. The interim board, therefore, placed great power in the hands of the local superintendents. By recruiting the administrative director from a local district and giving this individual limited powers, the interim board limited its ability to break from local school district organizational values, routines, and interests.

The superintendents were under varying pressures and instructions from their own school boards. Some wanted to take action; others did not or felt that they could not; some did not believe that their cases were lost. Jockeying for leadership positions and conflicts across districts and among personalities limited the desire for a unitary structure. The most obvious barrier was between the city as plaintiff and the suburban districts as defendants. Also, there were legal battles between districts adjacent to and further from the city, individual ambitions and fears about losing one's position in any later school-district reorganization, and old rivalries among school districts. No governmental unit had existed to bring these representatives together before; the county had no educational arm and the state was neither aggressive enough nor viewed positively enough to force or encourage cooperative planning. The court's creation of an interim board did not overcome localism; localism and protectionary views were built into the organizational structure of the board.

These factors had a major, debilitating impact on the board, which had great difficulty in reaching decisions, particularly those that threatened local interests. Said board member May Di Virgilio, "I can't find the words to tell you how I disagree with (a particular) plan. We're just passing the buck. We are more political than the general assembly. We just don't want to face the issue" (Bloom 1977a). Even the head of the superintendents council, Carroll Biggs, said, "The pure raw politics of the situation has inhibited any decision. It's been very difficult for any district to give up its position and not protect its own interests" (Bloom 1977b).

The politics of decision making in this context made it impossible for the

---

in-service training, desegregation plan(s), buildings and grounds, transportation, finances, professional personnel, support personnel, reorganization plans, pupil personnel, intergovernmental and court relations, legal relationships, and governance.

16. The superintendents' council had been established a few months previously, at the initiation of the superintendents, to communicate about desegregation issues and positions. Although all superintendents were initially involved, it soon lacked the participation, by exclusion or self-choice, of the Wilmington superintendent and, at times, the De La Warr superintendent (whose board's early position was one of recommending a county-wide district to the court).

board to move beyond the perceived interests of old school districts to a collective interest of pupils and their parents. This led not only to a dismissal of plans that called for a true reorganization, but also to the failure to consider changing the current district lines in the formation of a new organization-governance structure.

A majority of the board recommended that the current school districts be maintained for two years, and that an Intermediate School Authority (analogous to the interim board) be created to oversee pupil assignments. When the state board indicated that this plan did not meet the court's directive to reorganize the districts, the interim board voted to establish six "reorganized" districts immediately rather than after court appeals were concluded. In this plan, Wilmington would be divided and recombined with sets of whole suburban districts.

Pupil assignment then had to be decided by the board. The majority voted to make the Wilmington and De La Warr schools into fifth and ninth "grade centers." Representatives of these districts objected, saying that this would "emasculate" the districts and that busing black children for ten of twelve years and whites for two of twelve was inequitable.

The board's major decisions, it appeared to many, were protectionary in nature—making the fewest changes possible to suburban student assignments and maintaining suburban school-district lines. The Wilmington district, however, was to be eliminated as a separate entity. Educational goals were not of direct concern. The board did not operate as if maximizing educational choices for students, maintaining the best educational facilities, or maintaining a continuum of curriculum were their key goals. Many vocal members of the public and educational leaders criticized the interim board for being too political and not being concerned with education.

The political nature of the board's activities, its emphasis on noneducational concerns, and its reluctance to make significant provisions to involve concerned parents, students, and teachers in the planning process had another impact as well. Groups in the community who were supportive of effective and peaceful desegregation were now even more concerned about the status of desegregation planning and the limited role of citizens in the process, especially because implementation was less than six months away. The interim board's political aura and resultant plans had yielded narrow solutions that served the interests of the suburban districts.

The focus on the interim board soon became academic, for oral arguments by the state and suburban boards in their appeal to the Third Circuit Court of Appeals had occurred in March 1977. As a result of that court's May 1977 ruling, the focus shifted from the interim board to the state board and legislature.

CIRCUIT COURT OF APPEALS DECISION OF MAY 1977

Oral and written arguments presented to the circuit court by the defendants centered on two important matters. (1) There was no indication of the causality or degree to which allegedly discriminatory acts by the state had affected school racial enrollments; moreover, the district court had observed that the EAA's purpose was not racially motivated (this was the "nonculpability" issue, enhanced by U.S. Supreme Court decisions in *Washington* and other cases). (2) Even assuming that there were unconstitutional actions by the state, the district court had exceeded its remedial powers by ordering an extensive massive busing and reorganization plan (judicial "overkill" as it was popularly known).

The circuit court, on a 4-to-3 vote, affirmed the lower court findings and almost all of the general features of the desegregation plan ordered by the lower three-judge panel. It was not the domain of the circuit court, the majority opinion advanced, to try to guess what were the bases of the Supreme Court's four-sentence affirmation of the district court's March 1975 ruling. If the Supreme Court felt that the intent doctrine elucidated in the *Washington* case applied to *Evans*, it was its prerogative to do something about it.

The circuit court's decision, however, was to have a substantial impact on desegregation planning events in New Castle County. That is, the circuit court modified the original planning parameter by eliminating the 10-to-35 percent minority racial ratio that had been included in the May 1976 district court ruling. Although the latter court did not say that each school or grade necessarily had to have between 10 and 35 percent minority enrollment, the circuit court feared that these figures would be treated as a quota. There was no basis for the 10-to-35 percent ratio, it argued. However, the circuit court did not specify what would be the elements of an "acceptable" desegregation plan, or what ratios, if any, would satisfy the court; it simply reemphasized that the school situation should be returned to what would have existed "but for" the constitutional violations.

Equally noteworthy, the circuit court bypassed the interim board and directed the state to file a plan for desegregation, in accord with the lower court parameters, as modified, within sixty days. The dissenting opinion of Judge Garth, endorsed by two other judges, was prophetic, if not cryptic, regarding the situation facing the state in developing a remedy: "Neither the modified order nor the majority opinion reveals what desegregation means in this case. . . . I must confess that if I were a Delaware official charged with desegregating the schools. . . . I would not know where to begin" (*Evans* v. *Buchanan* 1977a).

The ball was back in the state's hands, not the interim board's, and the emphasis was on "but for." Racial ratios had been eliminated from the new directive, and a plan had to be developed within sixty days that would rectify only the very generally described constitutional violations affirmed by the courts. "But for" these violations, what would be the racial ratios in the city and suburban schools? This was an almost impossible question to answer, and the state board and legislature were subject to previous predilections—minimizing the impact of desegregation on white children and suburban districts.

With the circuit court ruling, hope for some sort of voluntary plan germinated in many quarters during the late spring and early summer of 1977. The legislative committee on desegregation and the state board of education each developed "but for" plans. The heart of the state board plan called for busing all black children living in public housing in the city of Wilmington (about 1,800 students), because the court had said that some public housing would have been built in the suburbs "but for" the constitutional violation. The state board plan also called for an additional 3,650 students from the city to be assigned to suburban districts to remedy the two other violations that the state board judged to have had significant interdistrict effects. They assumed that even if the 1968 Educational Advancement Act had permitted Wilmington to be consolidated, the city school district lines would not have been altered.

The legislative committee, also seeking to develop a "but for" plan that would minimize the impact on the suburban school districts, proposed a plan based on the concept of reverse volunteerism. Wilmington students would be assigned to suburban school districts, and, if the parents decided to volunteer them to remain in Wilmington, they would stay in the city schools. In both plans suburban districts would remain intact, and the Wilmington district would serve only those children whose parents did not rescind the proposed mandatory reassignment to a suburban area.

The state board presented a combination of the two plans during district court hearings in July 1977. The reverse volunteerism plan was to affect the school assignments of black children in grades seven to twelve only. It was "voluntary" on the part of the parents of these children, and in a direct way the kinds of programs and numbers of children remaining in Wilmington was uncertain—a "let the chips fall where they may" orientation. The task and burden of desegregation again explicitly fell to black parents and children.

District Court Judge Murray M. Schwartz, to whom the federal court gave the job of overseeing the remedy process, within a month after the hearing ruled that the "take it or leave it" plan by the state board was quite insufficient: "In formulating a remedy for constitutional violations, this Court must exercise its equitable powers. One would find it difficult to create a more graphic paradigm of an inequitable remedy than one which assigns to those who have been wronged the responsibility of correcting those wrongs" (*Evans* v. *Buchanan* 1977b). Judge Schwartz's ruling on 5 August 1977 came less than one month before schools were to open. Because there was so little time left and because the state had appealed the circuit court's ruling to the U.S. Supreme Court, Judge Schwartz issued an indefinite stay of implementation of a yet-to-be-developed acceptable desegregation plan.

Judge Schwartz also ordered the state board to appoint a five-member "new board" known as the New Castle County Planning Board of Education, and required that the new board plan for the desegregation of the schools within a single-district framework. On 3 October 1977 the U.S. Supreme Court denied the state's petition for a write of certiorari. On 8 November 1977, Judge Schwartz concluded that "September 1978 is the earliest practicable date by which implementation of an effective desegregation plan may be achieved." Judge Schwartz ruled that this plan should be submitted by 30 September 1978 and that the new board should submit a progress report every two weeks until the final plan was submitted. The components of the plan were to include both faculty and student assignments, pertaining to grades one to eleven in all affected districts.

After some volatile beginnings, an initial plan that would prohibit secondary-level students from being assigned to city schools, and a claim by a humanistically oriented female member of the board that key decisions were being made in the men's restroom (Nagengast 1977 and Moyed 1977), a white majority of the board voted to submit to the court a 10-to-2 plan, that is, a plan where students in the city and De La Warr school districts would be assigned to the white suburban districts for ten years while the students in the white suburban districts would attend schools in these districts for two years. The Wilmington representative on the new board submitted a plan based on an 8-to-4 concept. The court ordered the Pupil Assignment Committee of the new board to develop a 9-to-3 plan, which the court placed at the center of its final order on 9 January 1978 (*Evans* v. *Buchanan* 1978).

Although many specifics were left to the new board, Judge Schwartz's order was extensive: establishing a maximum uniform tax rate to support the public schools in the single district, requiring a plan that would include a full one to twelve grade span in Wilmington, ordering a "comprehensive in-service training program for teachers, administrators, and other staff in order to prepare personnel for the desegregation process," and directing that a human relations program for students be implemented to help ameliorate racial myths and stereotypes during desegregation. Judge Schwartz also required that bilingual programs and services for Hispanic students be incorporated in the curriculum planning for the new district.[17]

Following the August 1977 court ruling, the new board appointed a local superintendent to direct the planning tasks. A variety of committees were formed, composed solely of local school personnel; key committees were those related to pupil assignment, finances, and personnel. Systematic procedures for public input to these deliberations, before and after the 9 January 1978 court order, have never come about, principally because of the earlier quick-paced time line (5 August to 30 September 1977) for critical decisions and the general feeling of school leaders that "opening up" the desegregation planning deliberations to the public would impede the implementation process. A complementary explanation, particularly salient after the U.S. Supreme Court's refusal to consider the state's appeal and the 9 January 1978 court order, was that it was the "bottom of the ninth inning" and the last thing that school officials wanted was prolonged debate and controversy regarding school personnel and administrator assignments, tax rates, curriculum matters, school closing,[18] and pupil assignments. After the 9 January order, however, the board did institute human relations training for students, staff, and administrators, held open houses (over 10,000 suburban parents visited the city schools), moved to establish citizen advisory councils, established students' rights and responsibilities guidelines, and generally adopted a positive program to achieve effective desegregation.

PUBLIC OFFICIALS AND BUSINESS, RELIGIOUS, COMMUNITY, AND MINORITY GROUP INVOLVEMENT

Public Officials

The positions of governor, mayor of Wilmington, and New Castle County executive all changed hands in the 1976 election. The positions taken by former and current officeholders, however, were generally similar, that is, no official was inclined to take a strong, visible leadership position in support of city-suburban desegregation. Busing, here as elsewhere, was a volatile issue, and most officials

17. The Spanish-speaking community had been accepted as an amicus and had argued for these decisions.

18. Not unlike other communities, there has been a decline in the number of public schoolchildren in New Castle County, resulting in a need to close schools in this area. School reorganization and desegregation have been the catalysts to come to grips with this problem.

at one time or another and to varying degrees expressed their disapproval of mandatory busing and the substance of the court orders. On the other hand, all officials said that they would "obey the law" and implement whatever the court had ordered.[19]

Even though these positions were considerably less than the active, political-bargaining "broker" that Rossell (1977) has argued is desirable to effectuate peaceful desegregation, many of the former and current officeholders worked in varying ways to promote compliance with the law and communication on the issue at hand. Former County Executive Melvin Slawik appointed a committee of twelve in May 1974 (later called the Delaware Committee on the School Decision or DCSD) to advise the county government on how to prepare for an impending court decision whatever its content.

Former Governor Sherman Tribbitt was against busing but nonetheless supported efforts for peaceful implementation. Tribbitt supported DCSD and made it a state-wide group in January 1975. Under great pressure from PAC to disband DCSD, Tribbitt stated that he had absolutely no intention of disbanding the group. Tribbitt also helped form the county's rumor control center and its first information center. Perhaps most importantly, Governor Tribbitt assigned the state police jurisdiction over desegregation-related police activity. Before the governor took this step, the situation was ambiguous, for the county or state police would have authority if they reached the scene of a problem first (outside the city of Wilmington, where city police had jurisdiction). State police accepted this responsibility in a totally professional manner. For example, the officer in charge of the planning effort took a relevant university course, traveled to a number of communities that have faced this problem (Boston, Louisville, Prince Georges County), and worked with a large number of community and other resource people to prepare for this task. Workshops with clergy and for police troopers were held. The state police played a key role in the establishment of the information center and directed the effort that led to the training of city, county, and state police for desegregation duty.

As mayor of Wilmington from 1972 to 1976, Thomas Maloney was caught in a political bind. He was cognizant of the potential advantages of a metropolitan desegregation plan. After the July 1974 decision, Maloney was reported as "pleased" with the decision; he said, "The benefits to the city in terms of education and property values are clear" (*Philadelphia Inquirer* 1974). But as a candidate for the U.S. Senate against Senator William Roth, who had solid antibusing credentials, Maloney had to look to a predominantly white and antibusing constituency. Within a year and a half after his "pleasure" at the initial court decision, Maloney called busing "our national nightmare." He did not reappoint a white advocate of metropolitan desegregation to the Wilmington School Board, and declared in a newspaper advertisement that "I have always been against forced busing" (*Evening Journal* 1976). He attempted to induce a negotiated settlement of the suit but failed. Maloney also failed by a large margin to unseat incumbent Senator Roth.

William McLaughlin, taking over as mayor of Wilmington in January 1977, tended to be very supportive of planning and implementation activities. Mc-Laughlin also worked diligently to support communication and dissemination

19. The current mayor of Wilmington, William McLaughlin, has been a more consistent supporter of desegregation as discussed in this section.

endeavors. Early on in his tenure, McLaughlin announced his lack of interest in seeking higher officer or reelection, perhaps freeing him to assume the stance noted above.

The current governor of Delaware, Pierre S. Du Pont IV, periodically made known his disfavor of busing and the content of several court orders, yet consistently made available various staff to help coordinate and plan for the implementation of a court order. As September 1978 approached, Governor Du Pont began to increase his public comments underscoring the importance of obeying the law and the need for peaceful desegregation.

Delaware's delegation to the U.S. Congress, Senators Roth and Biden and Congressman Evans, spoke out against the perils of busing. Biden's opposition to busing seemingly increased with time. James Venema, the principal leader of the antibusing group PAC, had been chastising Senator Biden for his positions on the busing issue.[20] It is not known to what degree this had an influence on Senator Biden, who recently said that "No one has done more to stop forced busing than Joe Biden" (Panyard 1977).

Neither Senators Roth nor Biden were able to stop "forced busing" in New Castle County. They did, however, introduce several pieces of legislation in congress aimed at halting or significantly reducing busing as a remedy tool in school desegregation matters and gave publicity to these efforts back in Delaware.

The most significant local legislatures, the New Castle County Council and Wilmington City Council, tried to stay out of the desegregation issue. The county council passed a resolution supporting a county school district in April 1975 and quickly found itself under strong antibusing pressure to reverse its stand. From that point on the council avoided the issue. The city council also kept a low profile on the issue, but it did pass resolutions favoring peaceful implementation and the merging of the Wilmington School District into a county school district.

The Federal Government: Executive Branch

Unlike its legislative counterparts at the local, state and federal levels, the executive branch of the federal government played a positive role in the Wilmington case. Although its technical efforts were of limited value prior to the start of busing, its efforts to meet the more political needs were significant.

During the preimplementation period, the primary source of federal aid in the Delaware situation was the Department of Justice. Because only two of eleven school districts in the desegregation area were eligible for Emergency School Assistance Act funds prior to actual implementation of the court order, federal funds had a limited impact. The Wilmington district utilized federal funds and the services of the Center for Desegregation and Conflict at the University of Pittsburgh, a federal general-assistance center, for numerous desegregation-related activities. The state Department of Public Instruction held two conferences a year primarily for educators, plus two others for students, with the center's assistance. Two DPI human relations specialists were

---

20. In early 1978, Venema announced his candidacy for the Republican nomination to challenge Biden, a Democrat, in the 1978 senatorial election.

also funded with federal assistance, but they served the whole state, and turn-over in these positions was high. In brief, the nine suburban, primarily white school districts were relatively unaided by this federal help.[21]

The justice department's community relations specialist, Jon Chace, played a number of significant roles in the planning process in Delaware, including providing support for community leaders, communications across city-suburban and racial lines, calming emotional flare-ups, and supplying information on everything from monitoring commissions through police planning (Holman 1977 and Leo 1977). Chace's success was due to his ability to play a brokerage role, for his talents lay in mediation, compromise, and problem solving. Chace entered the case officially at the request of the DCSD.

Teacher's Unions

The Wilmington metropolitan case presented public officials with a continuing dilemma concerning teachers and other personnel. Because the Wilmington School District salaries were substantially higher than those in suburbia, re-organization would mean a large budget increase if salaries and benefits were to be leveled up to those in Wilmington, the district with the highest salary scale. Although the public was concerned about the higher taxes that would inevitably be tied to the $23 million price tag for leveling up all personnel the first year (the average salary discrepancy was $2,200), school personnel and their spokesmen were concerned about salaries and benefits as well as job security.

Judge Schwartz's January 1978 order did not order leveling up and did set a limit on the local property-tax rate, making a total leveling up appear to be improbable if not impossible. In the spring of 1978 the New Castle County Educational Association, an affiliate of the National Education Association, won the right to be the teachers' bargaining agent over the Wilmington Chapter of the American Federation of Teachers. The former had about 2,800 members, primarily from the suburban districts, whereas the latter had begun with a base of about 400 teachers predominantly from Wilmington. Other school system personnel voted to have an AFT-affiliated union represent them.

No agreements between teachers and the administration had been reached by July 1978. School officials did agree that no one, including administrators, should lose a position as a direct result of desegregation. But given declining enrollments partially caused by desegregation, teachers were not secure with this policy. Spokespersons for the teachers argued that teachers were being ignored in the desegregation process, but teachers were not kept more at arm's length than parents, students, or many other community groups.

Business and Religious Groups

The groups that became most involved in activities supportive of school de-segregation viewed this issue as a natural outgrowth of their previous work.

21. Suburban school district officials were strongly critical of the University of Pittsburgh staff's ability to help in the Delaware situation.

To groups like the National Conference of Christians and Jews (NCCJ) and the Delmarva Ecumenical Conference, desegregation was part of a larger religious commitment to furthering intercultural harmony. To the Greater Wilmington Development Council (GWDC), an economic development council with strong Du Pont Corporation backing, desegregation was an issue threatening the stability of the community and large corporations' ability to attract and retain personnel in the area. These groups were also corporate elite groups not under close control by members of the general public. Thus the GWDC could take a role that the Chamber of Commerce or Retail Merchants Association could not, just as the NCCJ could take a position that a church in a working-class area would find untenable. That is, most civic or religious groups dependent on donations were wary of becoming embroiled in the desegregation issue, for their constituents and donors might threaten their coffers.

A characteristic pattern of involvement developed. Both business and religious leaders first sought guidance from others on the national scene who were experienced in desegregation implementation. Both then worked through their on-going umbrella organizations. Over time, both sectors developed new organizations to focus on the desegregation issue.

The religious community focused initially on the activities of the Delaware Equal Education Process (DEEP), and after this probusing group was abandoned, they formed the peaceful implementation-focused Interfaith Task Force. The Delaware Equal Education Process had grown out of a local Urban Coalition task force. The Urban Coalition, primarily supported through corporate funds, had joined early in the legal suit as intervening plaintiffs. By the completion of the suit much corporate support had withdrawn.

The business effort developed SANE out of the GWDC. A nonprofit corporation, SANE worked to achieve peaceful compliance with the law. Their activities were very limited in scope and duration. One visible SANE activity was to provide copies of court rulings to the public. Moreover, SANE worked mostly in the public relations arena, hiring a public relations-communications firm to study the local situation and recommend media and outreach efforts "to help keep the peace." A secondary purpose of SANE appeared to reflect a concern of limiting the pressures on the corporate community to commit funds, personnel, and reputation to the desegregation issue. They had a five-member board and an executive director, and for the most part SANE worked in a closed style behind the scenes.

The activities of these two groups also had similarities. In the religious sector, the first major task was to prepare, involve, and organize one's own members or counterparts. The Greater Wilmington Development Council did this as well, but to a lesser degree. After analyzing the desegregation situation, leaders in both sectors began to pressure school and governmental authorities to do "the correct thing"—again, more evident in the religious sector. Much time and effort was spent by these groups in making suggestions to local and state authorities on "how and when" to begin implementation preparation. As it became clear that the school and governmental officials were not as positive toward taking steps to prepare as were these community leaders, each group began to develop its own programming. Delaware Equal Education Process and NCCJ held conferences, SANE planned an information center, and NCCJ expanded its capability to conduct human relations training. Each group brought in national authorities to help motivate and inform local leaders. But even though both the business and the religious groups wanted to convince the public that peaceful implementation should be their goal, both sectors suffered from limited legitimacy and the particular limitations of their images. Religious leaders were expected by many to be prodesegregation because they were out of touch with the hard realities of school conflict. Business leaders could also be favorable, for their children went to private schools. With the exception of DEEP, both sectors took public stances on "peace" but not "pro" city-suburban busing.

The efforts of the religious community appeared to have been more successful than those of the business community. The former worked closely with governmental, school, and community leaders in relative harmony and mutual respect. The latter faced more conflict and suspicion. Part of the reason for the differences in success lies in the nature of the key people involved in each effort, and these personalities were not happenstance but natural outgrowths of the type of sector. Specifically, the key business leaders were perceived as being analytical, secretive, and calculating, characteristics valued in the business sector. The religious leaders were personally committed and people oriented, traits necessary to those who want to succeed in the voluntary organization-religious sector. Because desegregation soon evolved into a political rather than a rational or organizational issue, the religious leaders' skills were more helpful than the business leaders' skills.

The business groups had financial resources, but much of these resources went toward paying people to consult and work on the desegregation issue. The religious community was able to free up the time of several key leaders personally committed to desegregation and also was able to utilize its grassroots organizational network in churches and synagogues. Although money was important, this network was even more significant given the ideological nature of the issue. Face-to-face involvement at the grass-roots level was very necessary, and the business community was generally unable or unwilling to utilize its own networks in the various corporations to reach people. But despite these differing resources, groups in both sectors lacked the legitimacy to reach the vast public and to greatly influence public officials and school authorities.

The Mass Media

One of the unique characteristics of Delaware is that it lacks its own commercial television station. Although Philadelphia television stations occasionally cover a Delaware news story and Delaware's educational channel has a nightly news program, most residents of New Castle County must get their local news from radio or the Wilmington News Journal papers (the *Morning News* and *Evening Journal*). In point of fact, the spring 1978 poll indicated a great reliance on the newspapers for desegregation news among all kinds of New Castle County residents.

The *News Journal*'s editorial position was in favor of desegregation through busing and the establishment of a county school district. The paper never wavered from this stance. Its news coverage, however, gave much space to PAC and its activities as well as to those groups supporting a smooth desegregation process. The *News Journal* was like other papers in its emphasis on conflict and events. With only occasional lapses, the *News Journal* gave desegregation full coverage. With the initiation of busing approaching, the paper reported the details of the student assignment plan in a special supplement, passed along the telephone number of the county-wide desegregation information center, and provided information to answer each week's most frequently asked question.

Even though local radio stations provided easy access for those on all sides of the issue, especially through the talk show mechanism, radio news often suffered from factual inadequacies and an overdependency on official organizational spokesmen and newspaper sources. The local educational television station fully covered the issue and presented lucid analyses, but the percentage of Delawareans who watched the educational channel was not high. The Philadelphia television stations produced panel-type shows on this issue a few times a year, but more were shown at 6 A.M. than in prime time.

The Community

Community groups supportive of the school desegregation process were not able to appeal to the public on the grounds of the desirability of desegregation and busing. Individual groups had little success in convincing school officials to "open up" the desegregation planning process. Over time, community group leaders worked to form larger coalitions and groups (across school district, city-suburban, and racial lines) to deal with the interdistrict nature of the issue. Finally a need for a single large coalition was recognized, and the Citizens Alliance for Public Education (the Alliance) was formed. The Alliance had its antecedents in two other groups, the Delaware Committee on the School Decision (DCSD) and an informal "breakfast meeting" group that included representatives of major organizations and agencies involved with desegregation. In New Castle County, these three groups became the most visible supporters of peaceful implementation, although a large number of smaller groups or efforts were present as well.[22] This section highlights the development and major activities of the three more visible groups involved with desegregation.

In January 1975, Delaware Governor Sherman Tribbitt established the DCSD as a state-wide committee, asking it to "develop methods to assist the Governor, County Executive, Mayor, State Board of Education, and the people of the State of Delaware to accept and implement, if that should prove necessary, the decision of the court. . . ." By this order, the governor expanded the committee of twelve that county executive Melvin Slawik had established more than a year before (May 1974), "to seek ways to react constructively to the federal court decision whatever it may be." The fifty members of DCSD served without pay and were appointed by the governor, the county executive, and the mayor of Wilmington. The initial membership of DCSD represented a

22. The major efforts at this level were those of the Greater Wilmington League of Women Voters, which organized meetings, prepared fact sheets, and held city-suburban tours and coffee programs, and the University of Delaware, whose College of Education conducted summer and school-year in-service training institutes for school personnel in human relations training and communications-crisis intervention skills. The College of Urban Affairs and Public Policy supplied professional expertise to the DCSD and the interim board, conducted parent surveys on key desegregation-related issues, and assisted the New Castle County Planning Board in computerizing student records from eleven districts for pupil assignment purposes.

spectrum of views and groups—parents, religious leaders, governmental representatives, as well as groups who were probusing, antibusing, or simply peaceful implementation in outlook.[23]

The activities of DCSD focused on holding public meetings to inform the citizenry, making suggestions for the humanistic component of desegregation, and attempting to resolve conflicts. The DCSD existence was based upon a "pluralist" model (see Peterson 1971) and it is therefore not surprising that its successes were with those acting in accord with the pluralist model. The DCSD had little influence over school officials, who were greatly constrained by their intention of avoiding probusing groups. Nor did the ideological legislative committee appreciate a group "devoted to making busing work." Similarly, the general public remained unknowing and unmoved by DCSD exhortations.

The successes of DCSD were primarily in arousing and coordinating governmental and community leaders to act in support of peaceful implementation. The early resolution of a police jurisdictional issue, the establishment of an information center operated by a variety of groups, the convening of a community coordination group (the Alliance) and a coffee program that helped many organizations to begin dealing with desegregation were all significant contributions. The secondary effect of creating a cooperative, supportive, and friendly atmosphere among community leaders was an important by-product. But in many ways the success of DCSD could well be measured by the success or failure of two groups it helped to establish to overcome its own limitations, the breakfast group and the Citizen's Alliance for Public Education.

Recognizing the complexity of the Wilmington metropolitan situation a two-day visit to Louisville-Jefferson County, Kentucky, was arranged for several DCSD members, the state PTA president, and the chairperson of the state Human Relations Commission in January 1976 with the help of the U.S. Justice Department's community relations specialist. The interdistrict situation in Louisville was viewed as being salient, for the Jefferson County and Louisville school districts had merged just before implementing a metropolitan desegregation plan. The Delaware representatives, on their return, determined that a monthly or biweekly informal meeting could possibly assist in the communication and resolution of problems accruing to the diversity of organizations and ideologies in New Castle County. Up to this point, most interactions had occurred in hallways outside the federal district court.

In March 1976, the first meeting among key agency, school district, and community leaders was held over breakfast. Over time, this breakfast group met regularly, about every other week, to discuss issues and problems in planning for school desegregation. Over thirty agencies or groups regularly sent representatives to these informal "meet and discuss" meetings, which were viewed by most participants as being very helpful in establishing more informal, face-to-face exchanges among people and groups.[24]

23. Not long after its inception, the antibusing members (from PAC) resigned from the committee. The PAC claimed that DCSD was probusing, "greasing the wheels for a massive busing order."

24. The breakfast group had a number of problems. First, given the lack of formal rules and authority, decisions often were made (or appeared to be made) arbitrarily. Who should be invited? Who should be told about the existence of the breakfast? What should be the agenda? The chairperson often had to make decisions about such issues

A lack of coordination among local community groups, and the great variation in the information level, experience, and activities of the local school districts regarding desegregation preparation activities led to a suggestion made in the breakfast group to hold a meeting of representatives of all such local organizations. The president of the state PTA called and chaired the breakfast meeting, which was primarily devoted to a description of the history and activities of each group. The personal contacts proved to be valuable later. One participant in the breakfast group, a black elected official, persistently argued that desegregation was primarily a political process, and as such, there was a need for a group to serve as a counterforce to those working to disrupt the school desegregation process. Specifically, a group was needed with leaders to perform such services as acting as spokespersons for peaceful implementation, coordinating activities and statements of all existing groups, coordinating and focusing outside resources, and generating grass-roots support. The breakfast group invited leaders to the meeting personally.

As a result of this meeting, the Alliance was established in the late summer of 1976 to provide an umbrella for groups and individuals working for quality public schools, citizen involvement, and peaceful implementation of the court order. Committees were named for finances, legislative and public information, school liaison, membership, and services. Over fifty key organizations joined the Alliance in an effort to work together for effective and peaceful desegregation planning.

One of the key focal points of activity for the Alliance was that of being the public conscience of local school authorities, pressuring them to open up their generally closed policy and planning activities to responsible public input in desegregation matters. Despite the involvement of some school officials with the Alliance, their general reluctance to involve the public did not diminish greatly during the latter stages of *Evans*. However, the Alliance did have some limited success in opening up the process during the period of the interim board, and pressured the new board in August 1977 to remove decision making from the men's restroom.

What successes the Alliance and other supportive community groups had was principally on the administrative rather than on the political dimension. That is, they worked with school and governmental administrators to prepare for implementation but they could not win legislative battles or change public opinion. These groups lacked the resources for political victory—numbers, appealing ideas, money, and consensual unity. Several factors were in their favor, however. First, subsectors of the community had organized first, and thus the Alliance was a coalition built on other coalitions (e.g., DCSD, SANE, DEA). Second, several of the coalition's major supporters had professional staff willing and able to devote a large percentage of time to the joint effort. Furthermore, many of the leaders of the Alliance had worked together for years on this issue. Personal relationships and community contacts were excellent. Fourth, the Alliance had access to national help (e.g., Ford Foundation

without strong guidelines or much input from participants. Second, the Wilmington superintendent participated only twice, and the formal representative from that school district hardly said a word. The suburban school superintendent's representative was an active participant but he tended not to report back to the other educational leaders. This not only limited the impact of the breakfast group, it also caused resentment among the superintendents who felt excluded.

funds, Lamar Society consultants); in fact, the Alliance became the center of national attention in terms of the Wilmington desegregation process. Fifth, the Alliance had time to develop because of the stay in the summer of 1977.

On the negative side, the Alliance suffered from many of the same dilemmas faced by the other coalition, the DCSD. It was continually faced with the basic problem of whether to act before a consensus was reached. Second, it suffered from a shaky and uncertain relation with the business community. Third, antibusing leaders refused to join it and called it a "cape" behind which "probusers" lurked. This made school officials somewhat wary of becoming too closely tied to it.

Thus the supportive coalitions were hampered by the extent to which decision makers and the public did not follow the pluralist model in stressing compromise and bargaining. To the extent that the pluralist model was followed, the Alliance and DCSD lacked resources to be influential. But the DCSD, Alliance, and breakfast group did influence political executives, administrators, and school officials to some extent; more importantly, they were successful in fulfilling a number of communications and issue-raising functions in the school desegregation process.

Black and Minority Groups

The entrance of the majority black Wilmington School Board as an intervening plaintiff in 1972 preempted black organizational activity in the desegregation process. Wilmington School Board representatives presented a minority perspective on the court-established planning boards and in the courtroom itself.

The Wilmington branch of the NAACP had refused to become involved in the case when it was reopened in 1971. But under the new leadership of James H. Sills, who in the summer of 1978 became a member of the county school board, the local NAACP offered to support the case and entered the suit in 1974. The plaintiff's lawyer advised against its formally entering the case at that time to avoid further delaying the resolution of the suit. Although later leaders of the Wilmington NAACP occasionally complained of inequities tied to the desegregation process, their effect was minimal.

The Wilmington Home and School Council worked closely with parents, primarily through the federally funded Parent Educational Resource Center. Workshops for parents, and newsletters helped to bring needed information to parents. The information level of Wilmington parents remained very low throughout the process, however.

The strong feelings many blacks held against busing and their concern for the effects of the desegregation process on blacks led to the formation of a black group opposed to busing, the Committee to Improve Education (CIE). The CIE filed an amicus brief to argue against busing and for alternative techniques to improve black achievement. Leaders did not abandon coalition efforts to work for a peaceful transition.

A group of black community leaders met several times in an attempt to form a black political force focusing on school desegregation that would exist beyond the expected dissolution of the Wilmington School Board. A local black judge was named chairman, and a proposal for local foundation funds to hire staff for monitoring the desegregation process was developed but never submitted. The group never got off the ground. Thus, as the significant decisions about desegregation were being made in the courts and on the court-directed boards, the major minority spokesman remained the Wilmington board president, Wendell Howell. But in the spring of 1978, Howell was accused of having improvements done to his home by Wilmington public school employees, and he was forced to resign his school board position.

THE FIRST DAY OF SCHOOL: DESEGREGATION BEGINS

On 11 September 1978, after a last-ditch effort to obtain a stay was denied by U.S. Supreme Court Justice William Rehnquist, the court-ordered pupil assignment plan went into effect in New Castle County. Tranquility prevailed. The local newspaper captured the mood in a series of positive headlines:

School Opening Draws High Marks

Police "Happily Bored" with Deseg Implementation

Desegregation is Underway Quietly; School Openings Normal

Teachers, Students Delighted

First Day is Breeze, 4th R is for Routine

Busing: 3 Days' Practice Makes (Almost) Perfect

Desegregation Begins Quietly, Peacefully

The national and Philadelphia media were full of praise for the people of New Castle County. A KYW-TV (Channel 3, Philadelphia) editorial on 13 and 14 September stated:

The buses have been rolling since Monday, carrying out the court-ordered desegregation of public schools in Wilmington and ten suburban school districts. And so far, it's working smoothly; even though busing involves lots of kids and lots of parents who don't like it. In other cities that's been the formula for trouble. But not for Wilmington, and not for its suburban neighbors. And they deserve a lot of credit. Like it or not, the courts have ruled. And the good people of New Castle County are obeying the law. That's the way it's supposed to be in our country. And nobody can point a finger at Wilmington, the way they do at Boston and at other cities where there was so much trouble in other years. Sure there were some mixups. You don't bus 47,000 school kids without some confusion. But only 10 out of 600 buses were late—SEPTA should have such luck with its buses. And in spite of rumors of boycotts, attendance actually was better than normal. Parents and school kids were not passing up a chance for their kids to learn, because of an unpopular court order. The court-ordered desegregation may work after all. Or, it may turn out some years from now to have been a mistake. But the way everyone is pulling together is no mistake. It's one of the most valuable lessons the kids will ever learn.

The month of August and the first week in September had been full of last-minute preparation activities built upon previous efforts. On 22 August,

Governor Du Pont named ten leading citizens, including a former governor and U.S. senator, labor and business leaders, school board members, and a professional football player, to the Effective Transition Committee. The ETC was to oversee the entire implementation process. A trial run of emergency procedures tested the preparedness of the police, information center, and official communications system a week before school began. The media center was established by the executives' staff group to provide information to the press. It served over 250 media representatives during the first week of school. The information center had over 100 operators, mostly volunteers, prepared to answer calls from 7 to 14 September. Almost 3,000 calls were received. The Newark and Wilmington city councils voted to provide the Alliance with a modest amount of funds to work for a smooth desegregation process. The federal government, through the ESAA program, paid for programs mandated by Judge Schwartz and thus saved the state's taxpayers funds and protest. The county school district's Human Relations Advisory Committee, composed of many of the leaders of groups active in the Alliance and DCSD, interviewed a large number of school principals to assess preparedness for desegregation. The results indicated that the schools were ready. Citizen advisory councils at each school were planned and some begun before school officially opened. The teachers association halted bargaining and agreed to open schools without a contract.

The week before school opened was entirely devoted to in-service training capped by an open house for parents and students on Sunday. The governor and mayor visited the schools to reassure people that school was going to open peacefully and positively the next day. The night before school began, school officials participated in four ecumenical services to pray for a smooth desegregation process. The long hard work had paid off; the first week of school went smoothly. The buses rolled and the students learned, but this represented the end of one difficult process and the beginning of another.

The full impact of desegregation in Delaware will not be known for years. But at this juncture one can review the most recent episode in the long struggle and reach a number of conclusions about the desegregation process. The overriding conclusion must be that despite intense feelings against busing and the great political volatility of the busing issue, political conflict was confined primarily to conventional political battlefields and not the streets. Few protests or disruptions marred the transition from segregated local districts to a large, desegregated county school district.

PROTEST AND DISRUPTION

The only formal demonstrations were arranged by black leaders in the summer of 1977 to focus attention on a pupil reassignment plan that they considered inequitable. Fewer than 100 people participated. Spontaneous protests occurred at a junior high school in the Marshallton-McKean School District in 1976–1977, but it involved only about fifty students and did not last for an extended time. In the fall of 1978 a large number of voluntary transfer students met some transportation problems, white hostility, and inadequate school preparation, but incidents were short-lived.

Not until the spring of 1978, when a student-orientation plan was begun across the districts of the entire desegregation area, did a mass protest occur. Almost every suburban high school was the scene of protests over the orientation, with the primary protest activity being the cutting of classes (about 3,000 students were involved). After about 1,000 student suspensions and the release of the student assignment plan for the coming fall, the mood changed back to a more tranquil one. Two students received broken bones when crowds pushed them into the way of local automobile traffic, but no major violence occurred. The largest disruption occurred a month after school began. On 15 October 1978, the New Castle County Education Association voted to stop working without a contract. The strike lasted for over a month; it was finally agreed to level up salaries over a two-and-a-half-year period.

IDEOLOGICAL VS. PLURALIST POLITICS

The absence of major disruptions should not obscure the intense political conflicts that raged in Delaware. At the core of these conflicts was race. The busing controversy not only pitted whites against blacks, but the city against the suburbs. The nature of the political conflict was ideological as in the model described by Peterson where (1) participants in the policy-making process will include groups committed to broad objectives which become involved in a range of policy questions; (2) such groups will find similar allies and similar enemies across a range of policy questions; (3) enduring and significant linkages between inclusive social groups and important political factions will occur; and (4) groups will find defeat of opposition preferable to "reasonable" compromise (Peterson 1971). This model stands in contrast to the pluralist model, in which groups focus on narrow issues of self-interest, alliances shift according to the issue, and differences are compromised in reaching resolution.

If the ideological divisions had been reinforced and exploited by all politicians and community leaders, the transition in Delaware would have been very traumatic. But many key decision makers attempted to alter this ideological conflict with pluralistic tools. That is, they tried to transform an ideological battle into one where all advocates could sit down together and reach some agreement. The federal court tried to settle the *Evans* case through means of a pluralistic model, where bargaining, compromise, and negotiation would forge a desegregation plan acceptable to the plaintiffs, defendants, and the court. Such qualities had not been present in earlier court hearings on a spate of plans, none of which yielded a promise to work effectively and realistically at that juncture. But what took place within the interim board dynamics was not compromise or bargaining leading to an acceptable plan. A pluralistic, theoretical strategy came into the picture to confront the very real phenomena of ideology and political-organizational interests, and the latter elements won the first match hands down.

The odds on pluralism winning the battle against ideology and organizational interests, even with the former's stablemates of compromise and negotiation, now appear to have been quite low—not a good bet. Controversy, disagreement, and politics wracked the interim board, its members representing at all times their own personal ideologies and on many instances their organizational-district allegiances. And the interim board had relied on an administrative-planning substructure that was controlled by the superintendents of the districts that were purportedly to be dissolved at some point in the not-too-distant future.

But neither the superintendents nor their respective boards had a strong desire to see the districts dissolved and merged into one large district.[25] Constituents in the suburban areas almost to a person did not want forced busing. And PAC, the visible antibusing organization, provided the spark that just about guaranteed that the questions of racial equity and equality would pale in comparison to the increasingly politicized and symbolically enhanced issues of local control of schools and court-ordered busing. Communications from school or governmental authorities to parents about the background, nature. and rationale for the court's massive busing plan or alternatives to it were slight if nonexistent in most areas of the county. Nor did the state legislature proceed to accept the court's pluralist invitation to modify its May 1976 ruling. In fact, the legislature tended to inflame the issue with deliberations on "obstructive" pieces of legislation and strong, threatening verbal stances. When this body did enact plans for desegregation they were all voluntary in nature, and placed the burden of effectuating desegregation solely in the hands of "those who had been wronged," according to the federal district court judge.

In December 1977, only when it was a virtual certainty that Judge Schwartz would in short dispatch be ordering a one-district remedy and a 9-to-3 city-suburban busing plan, did the legislature consider legislation that would give the state board leave to create multiple reorganized districts in New Castle County. At this juncture, the conflict between pluralism-compromise and ideology was, to some, at its zenith—and it involved all key participants in *Evans*. Governor Du Pont, wanting to exercise leadership in the pluralistic arena of the legislature, pushed for the bill's enactment. Downstate legislators, although never pleased with the prospect of a large district in northern New Castle County that might at some future time affect the organizational status and funding of school districts in Kent and Sussex counties, as well as New Castle County legislators voted down the resolution that would have given the state board the latitude to reorganize the affected area into multiple districts. The PAC had lobbied with "let the judge pull the trigger," and the legislature heeded this ideological and catchy reminder—let it not be said that the legislature ever played along with, or was responsible for, the massive remedy ordered by the courts. Moreover, with some planning for a one-district remedy in hand, and with some inkling of how the reorganized school system would affect the positional status of school officials, the response of public educational authorities in New Castle County in an indirect way complemented the legislature's stance—the former now wanted one district and the latter did not want to be viewed as the culprits in a crime perpetrated on their constituents, the voters of New Castle County. The resolution went down to defeat, and less than a month later, on 9 January 1978, Judge Schwartz issued the one-district order and busing plan as expected.

Community groups supportive of peaceful implementation also used strategies based on the pluralist concepts. Groups like the Alliance and DCSD tried

---

25. De La Warr, the poorest district in the affected area, was an exception in that it had earlier proposed a county-wide district with four attendance areas.

to bring together working-class whites and other antibusing suburbanites, and blacks with the white, upper-middle-class propublic school leadership. But one of the prices that had to be paid to maintain this effort was an inability to divide the coalition through taking sides on the merits of busing in general or any particular plan. Despite this stated neutrality, the antibusing public never really accepted this stance. Nor were school officials anxious to encourage the involvement of a wide array of members of the public in the desegregation planning process. When attempts were made to open up the desegregation planning processes, local school officials, influenced by organization and self-interests, effectively maintained control in shaping the future design of public education in New Castle County.

Governmental executives had taken a number of other pluralist-based actions before the attempt to have the state legislature enact a four-district plan. Governor Tribbitt had established the DCSD with the county executive and mayor. Mayor Maloney tried to have the city and suburban school districts agree to a negotiated settlement. All sent representatives to the breakfast group and an intergovernmental task force on desegregation. Each of these actions helped somewhat to modify the ideological conflict across jurisdictional and racial lines.

Thus some forces (i.e., state legislature, PAC, school boards) pushed or maintained the ideological warfare. Other (i.e., governmental officials, supportive community groups, Community Relations Service, the federal courts) tried to use pluralist tactics. Although ideological conflict remained at the heart of the busing controversy, the pluralist initiatives served as a brake on the ideological conflict. Several other factors also helped to keep the Delaware situation fairly tranquil.

First, the major decision makers in Delaware never wavered from their position to emplement the law, even if it involved busing. Even though some state legislators raised questions about their willingness to obey a court order, the governmental executives and state and local school boards were not obstructionists. They were in favor of implementing the law.

Second, community groups like the DCSD substituted for governmental and school officials in taking responsibility to inform and prepare the public for school desegregation. As the process progressed, the mood of inevitability and the clarification of who held authority in this complex situation allowed officials to take more positive action. For example, a survey of city and suburban parents in early 1978 indicated that a large majority of parents in both residential areas believed that busing was inevitable, and about one-half of the suburban parents felt that public officials should accept, if not work for, peaceful implementation of the court order (Morstain 1978). This was a substantial shift from a year previously in the general posture and stance of parents with children in the public schools, and with the shift came a willingness to deal more realistically with desegregation preparation.

The third reason for the lack of violence and disruption was the relatively conventional politics of PAC. Not only had PAC preempted any other antibusing effort, PAC also channeled antibusing efforts into the mainstream of the political system. The state legislature, congress, and school boards were the targets of PAC, and PAC's leaders did not believe that protest activities would help them to reach their goals. In the spring of 1978, James Venema announced his candidacy for the U.S. Senate seat held by Joe Biden. In the summer of 1978, Venema faced off in a primary fight with an equally con-servative downstate Republican. Concurrently, several PAC leaders had become active in movements to start private schools. Thus the antibusing movement seemed to accept the immediate inevitability of the busing order.[26]

Each of these factors must be tied to the middle-class nature of much of New Castle County. The population was not a collection of ethnic enclaves or people struggling to keep their heads above water. The middle class would not support or participate in extremist actions. Even though working-class areas were certainly affected by the desegregation order, middle-class individuals dominated the state board of education, the local boards in middle-class dis-tricts, and even held major influence on boards in working-class areas.

A second factor that helped to shape the nature of the desegregation process in Delaware was the national mood. Although the situation was made more difficult by the uncertainty that surrounded the position of the U.S. Supreme Court, the situation was aided by the change in atmosphere in Washington emanating from the presidency. With President Carter's election and actions (e.g., sending his own daughter to a desegregated if also neighborhood school), Delawareans found it difficult to argue that relief was certain at some point.

It must be emphasized that the rhetoric of PAC and the state legislature, the complexity and uncertainty surrounding the case, the lack of many people supporting busing, and the strong feelings against the changes that would result were severe obstacles to overcome. Thus the final factor that helped to keep the calm was Judge Schwartz's decision to stay implementation from Septem-ber 1977 to September 1978. The added time greatly reduced uncertainty about the Supreme Court's position (it refused to hear the Delaware case in October 1977) on the nature of the desegregation plan, while it allowed the feeling of inevitability to mushroom. The many who viewed busing as a fate worse than death were able to come to terms with busing and prepare for it because of Judge Schwartz's decision.

Although school desegregation was the referent for the considerable legal, ideological-racial, and political conflicts that surfaced in New Castle County, the full range of consequences—in education and other arenas—are still un-known.[27] It will take some time, supplemented by the perspectives of different observers of this locale's desegregation attempts, to record the effects of metro-politan school desegregation and reorganization on the lives and welfare of students, parents, and school personnel, and the changes perhaps brought to businesses, political, and government-related institutions.

What is known now, however—at least from this country's experiences in coming to grips with school desegregation—is that metropolitan and local political processes, as Norton Long (1967) observed, are a mesh of conflicts played by a variety of rules, a variety of players, and for a variety of stakes.

26. In the spring of 1978 Concerned Parents for Childrens' Rights was formed as a result of the student demonstrations. Leaders promised that their group would be a more aggressive alternative to PAC, especially in the use of demonstrations. But although they have staged a few small protests, the group has plans to work within the school district citizens' committee systems now being planned.

27. In 1977, the *Newark Weekly Post* estimated the legal costs to date as over $200,000, but it is difficult to separate desegregation-based legal fees from regular school district legal expenses.

In the dynamics of the Wilmington metropolitan area, dynamics that may affect the entire state to some degree, the "school desegregation game" was really many games wrapped into one, by choice or design. The legislature's chess strategy was to play with style, the political and governmental executives played to avoid a loss, the courts wanted to end the game by mutual consent, and local school officials wanted to keep the chess set. The outcome of these interrelated games remains to be determined.

BIBLIOGRAPHY

Belton v. *Gebhart.* 1952. Del. Ch. 87 A. 2d., 137.

Bishop, Clyde. 1976. "An Analysis of the Delaware Educational Assessment Program." Unpublished dissertation, College of Urban Affairs and Public Policy, University of Delaware.

Bloom, Marlene Z. 1977a. "Desegregation Board Approaches a Nail-Biting Deadline." *News-Journal,* January 11.

Bloom, Marlene Z. 1977b. "Fighting, Rather than Planning, Is One View of Interim Board." *Morning News,* May 19.

Brown v. *Board of Education.* 1954. 347 U.S. 483.

Bulah v. *Gebhart.* 1952. Del. Ch. 87 A. 2d., 862.

Charlotte v. *Mecklenburg Board.* 1971. 402 U.S. 1, 15.

Committee, 1975. Special Legislative Committee on School Desegregation, Final Report, September 15.

Delaware Department of Instruction. 1975. "Desegregation Plans Submitted to the State Board of Education." August.

Dolan, Paul, and James Soles. 1976. *Delaware Government.* Newark: University of Delaware.

Educational Advancement Act, 1968. 56 Del. Laws, Ch. 292, S.6.

Evans v. *Buchanan.* 1957. 152 F. Supp. 886 (D. Del.). 1974. 379 F. Supp. 1218 (D. Del.). 1975a. 393 F. Supp. 428 (D. Del.). 1975b. 423 U.S. 963. 1976a. 424 F. Supp. 875 (D. Del.). 1976b. November 29, U.S. Supreme Court Decision. 1977a. 555 F. 2d. 373 (Third Circuit). 1977b. 435 F. Supp. 832 (D. Del.). 1978. January 9.

Evening Journal. 1974. "Antibusing Group Raps Legislature." August. 1975a. "Mr. Venema's Welcome Words." November. 1975b. "Group Urges Voluntary Pupil Shifts." June 12. 1976. Advertisement. October 28.

Holman, Ben. 1977. "Desegregation and the Community Relations Service." *Integrated Education.*

Kluger, Richard. 1975. *Simple Justice.* New York: Knopf, ch. 18.

Leo, Peter. 1977. "He Seeks Harmony on Civil Battlefields." *Evening Journal,* October 27.

Long, Norton E. 1967. "Political Science and the City." In Leo F. Schnore and Henry Fagin (eds.), *Urban Research and Policy Planning.* Beverly Hills, Calif.: Sage.

Milliken v. *Bradley.* 1974. 418 U.S. 717.

Morstain, Barry R. 1978. "Parent Views on School Desegregation and Related Educational Issues." College of Urban Affairs and Public Policy, University of Delaware, March.

Moyed, Ralph. 1977. "They're Doing Our Business in the Boys' Room." *Evening Journal,* September 1.

Nagengast, Larry. 1977. "Closed-Door Deseg Debate Opens Wounds." *Morning News,* August 31.

Oberle, William. 1975. Letter to the Editor. Wilmington *Evening Journal,* November.

Panyard, Jim. 1977. "Busing Cost Small, Biden Says." *Sunday Philadelphia Bulletin,* April 24.

Peterson, Paul E. 1976. *School Politics: Chicago Style.* Chicago: University of Chicago Press. Much of Peterson's work is based on Graham Allison, *Essence of Decision.* Boston: Little, Brown, 1971.

Philadelphia Inquirer. 1974. "Court Orders Desegregation of Wilmington Schools," July 13.

Rossell, Christine H. 1977. "The Mayor's Role in School Desegregation Implementation." *Urban Education* 12 (3) (October): 247–269.

Schmidt, Julie. In process. "Wilmington School Desegregation: A Case Study in Non-Decisionmaking." Master's thesis, University of Delaware Department of Political Science.

Shedd, Mark, et al. 1973. "The Wilmington Public Schools: A Preliminary Needs Assessment." Report to the Wilmington Board of Education, April.

Taggart, Robert J. 1976. "Desegregation in Delaware, 1950–1967." *UPDATE,* Delaware Committee on the School Decision, p. 2.

Washington v. *Davis.* 1976. 426 U.S. 229.

Whitcomb, Robert. 1975. "Desegregation Planning Looks Toward September," July 23.

Wirt, Frederick M. 1977. "School Policy Culture and State Decentralization." In Jay Scribner (ed.), *The Politics of Education.* Seventy-sixth yearbook of the National Society for the Study of Education, Part II, Chicago: University of Chicago Press.

6

The South and Southwest Corpus Christi, Texas A Tri-Ethnic Approach

Amelia Cirilo–Medina and Ross Purdy

HISTORICAL BACKGROUND

Corpus Christi has historically been the locus of long contacts and conflicts among groups of people who have occupied the land. Political domain has rested successfully in the hands of Native Americans, Spaniards, Mexicans, United States traders, Texans, and United States Anglo-Saxon citizens. Blacks alone have never controlled Corpus Christi throughout the history of the area.

The Mexicans first gained control of the land in 1791 with a settlement in the area. By 1820, the Corpus Christi Bay area was one of the busiest ports of Mexico (Linn 1883: 11–13). By 1835, Spain had deeded the total area of Nueces County to Mexican ranchers in the form of large land grants. That same year Texas won its independence and bordered the area just north of the Nueces River. The territory below the Nueces River still belonged to Mexico. Traders from the United States and an influx of Texas settlers established themselves in the area by 1839. Guerrilla warfare between Texas and Mexico extended into the area.

With the coming of Zachary Taylor and the U.S. Army, the Mexican War broke out. Taylor's army began advancing toward Mexico in 1846. By 1848, Mexico was forced to sign a treaty at Guadalupe Hidalgo near Mexico City and was forced to give up the land from the Nueces River to the Rio Grande along with territory from other states for a sum of $3 billion. Mexican citizens who lived in the area were given all the rights and privileges of United States citizens by the treaty, but during the war many had fled into Mexico. Others sold their lands voluntarily, by force, or by fraud (Haynes 1859: 25). Some Mexicans were killed and their lands confiscated. by 1859, all grants but one were out of Mexican-American hands.

Former Mexican citizens in the territory won through the Mexican War of 1846–1848 were granted all citizenship rights and privileges in accordance with the U.S. Constitution under the terms of the United States Treaty of Peace, Friendship, Limits, and Settlement with the Republic of Mexico (1857). Implicitly, the treaty secured for these new citizens a right to equal protection under the law as guaranteed by the Fourteenth Amendment.

As a consequence of the treaty, Mexican-Americans were enumerated as part of the white race beginning with the first United States census of 1850. The practice stopped with the census of 1930, when the white race was subdivided to account for the Hispanic or Spanish-surnamed population. After the 1954 *Brown* decision, it became a common practice in Texas to combine black with Mexican-American pupils to comply with the court ruling.

Although Texas did not enact statutes for segregation of Mexican-Americans, it did establish a provision for "taxation of Africans," for "African Schools" in the Texas Constitution of 1866 (Art. VII, Sec. 7). However, many school districts with small black populations provided no schools for black Americans. A revision in 1869 distributed state educational funds equally among both races but made no provisions for separate facilities; hence a third revision was made in 1876 to provide for separate facilities for "white" and "colored." In Corpus Christi, separate school facilities were provided for black American students in 1872, when their public school education began.

The Texas Constitution empowered public school officials at both state and local levels to establish public school policies subject to legislative mandates (Art. VII). State officials were given supervisory, policy formation, and planning powers and duties. The state board of education is made up of elected members from each of the twenty-four federal congressional districts. Board members serve for six years and one-third the board is elected every two years. The board appoints a commissioner of education as head of the Texas Education Agency (TEA).

Management and control of schools were delegated to elected local officials, either county boards or boards of trustees for "common" or "independent" school districts (Texas Education Code Ann. 17.21-31, 22.01-.12). Local agencies are considered agents of the state and have autonomous powers in matters of assignment of pupils, creation of school facilities, employment and retention of staff, school zoning, and other duties. The TEA must oversee, at regular intervals, that local education agencies (LEAs) carry out state policies and regulations. State accreditation of public schools is based on these reviews. That local school boards are autonomous is being used by the commissioner of education and TEA as a defense for its failure to enforce compliance of the Equal Opportunity Act of 1974 in a civil suit (U.S. Civil Suit 5281, 1977) brought against the state by the American G.I. Forum and the League of United American Citizens (LULAC).

Actual entrance of Mexican-Americans in local public schools dates to 1891 (Taylor 1934: 192). Evidence from widely separate parts of the state shows that public education was not originally provided for Mexicans (Taylor 1934: 192; Morrel 1936). When public education was finally offered, separate Mexican schools were established. As the practice spread, "tri-ethnic" school systems became prevalent. These systems were composed of dual ethnic systems within dual racial systems in communities. Mexican-Americans and Anglo-Americans had separate facilities. These systems were implicitly sanctioned by state officials, who provided funds for such systems after reviews of system operations (TEA, Public School Directory, 1923–1940). Shortly after the entry of Mexican-Americans into public schools, the *Corpus Christi Caller* (1892: 1/27) made the observation: "The Mexicans, whether immigrants or natives, maintain the characteristics of the people who dwell beyond the Rio Grande. . . . Since the Mexican children have been admitted to the City Schools, it remains to be seen what effect more direct contact with children of Americans will have upon them." However, a separate school was provided for Mexican-Americans. In

1896, the enrollment was 110; by 1929, it was 1,320. The first Mexican-Americans graduated from this grammar school in 1904.

In 1918 a statute was adopted by the state that required that public schools be conducted in English except in border towns with 5,000 or more inhabitants. Spanish could be used in elementary schools at those schools (Texas Acts 1918: 170). The law was revised in 1939 by the legislature (Education Code, Sec. 4.17) making violation of the "English-only rule" by school employees a misdemeanor subject to a fine and removal from office.

It was not until 1930 that the 1876 provision for separation of "whites" and "colored" was held not to authorize segregation of Mexican-Americans except for linguistic purposes (*Salvatierra* v. *Independent School District* 1971) thereafter, a Texas Attorney General's Opinion (1947: 128,39) that separate schools for Mexican-Americans could not be established, although students could be segregated for three years if the separation was based solely on language deficiency and in no part upon ethnic considerations. A suit alleging segregation of Mexican-Americans in four school districts was filed in 1948 (*Delgado* v. *Bastrop I.S.D.* 1948). Immediate integration was ordered with a proviso that permitted segregation in the first grade "solely for educational purposes" as "a result of scientific and standardized tests."

The Texas superintendent of instruction, L. A. Wood, issued regulations to comply (TEA Bulletin 248, 1948–1949: 45). In 1949, a complaint was filed against the public school system of Del Rio (*Salvatierra* v. *Independent School District* 1971). The Texas Superintendent of Instruction withdrew accreditation. Shortly thereafter, the powers of the superintendent of instruction, an elected official, were transferred to a newly created commissioner of education by the Texas legislature. They termed the regulations an "emergency measure" and rendered it effective on 7 July 1949. Del Rio appealed to the state board of education and the Woods decision was reversed. Accreditation was not removed.

DEMOGRAPHIC PROFILE

Corpus Christi is shaped like a seagull in flight between the Corpus Christi Bay and the Nueces Bay about 160 miles north of Matamoros, Mexico, on the Gulf of Mexico. It lies 210 miles southwest of Houston and 145 miles southeast of San Antonio. It is the center of activity for the Coastal Bend area of thirteen counties with a 1960 population of 419,778 and a 1970 population of 433,822.

Corpus Christi is also the hub of activity for the Corpus Christi Standard Metropolitan Statistical Area and the seat of Nueces County. It has a land area of 105 square miles; in 1970 the population was 204,525 representing a 22 percent increase over the 1960 population of 167,690. However, most of the population increase was due to annexation. Within the 1960 city limits, only a 6.8 percent increase occurred.

For statistical purposes, the city has combined census tracts having similar social and economic characteristics into four geographical areas (figure 6.1): Central, Flour Bluff, Northwest and Southwest. In 1970, according to city statistics (Community Renewal Program 1973: table 3.14) the Central census count was 70,298 or 34.4 percent of the population. In this area, the Anglo-American population is 6,850 or 9.7 percent of the area and 6.3 percent of the total city Anglo-American population. There are 53,005 Mexican-Americans

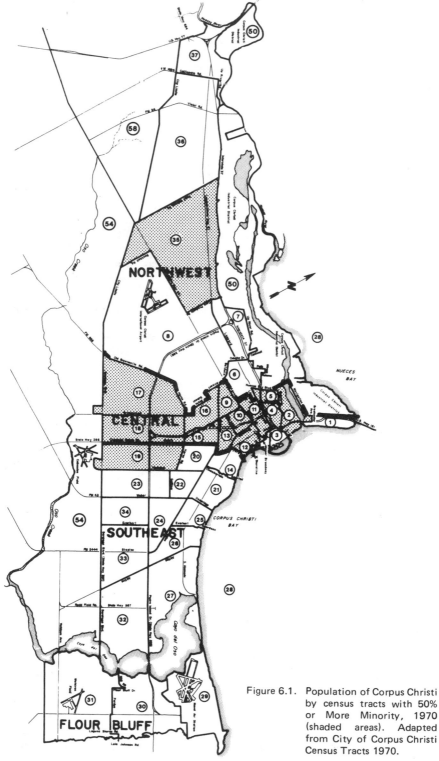

Figure 6.1. Population of Corpus Christi by census tracts with 50% or More Minority, 1970 (shaded areas). Adapted from City of Corpus Christi Census Tracts 1970.

who comprise 75.4 percent of the population of the area and 63.8 percent of the total city Mexican-American population. The number of black Americans in the area is 9,410 or 13.4 percent of the area, or 89.4 percent of the total city black population.

The most populated section is the Southeast area (see table 6.1) which contains 98,223 people or 48.0 percent of the population. This area is composed of 76.6 percent Anglo-Americans, 22.3 percent Mexican-Americans, and .2 percent black Americans. Of the city's Anglo-American population, 69.3 percent live in this area; 26.4 percent of the total Mexican-American population of the city live there; and 2.2 percent of the black population of the city reside in the Southeast.

The Northwest is much smaller, with a total population of 23,791 or 11.6 percent of the city's population. The population of the area is 69.6 percent Anglo, 28.2 percent Mexican-American, and 1.8 percent black. The city's 15.2 percent Anglo population reside in this area, compared with 8.1 percent of the city's Mexican-American population and 4.2 percent of the city's black population.

TABLE 6.1. Ethnic Population of Corpus Christi by Geographical Area, 1970

	Central	Flour Bluff	North-west	South-east	Corpus Christi
Total Population	70,298	12,213	23,791	98,223	204,525
% total city population	34.4	6.0	11.6	48.0	100.0
Anglo population	6,850	9,986	16,565	75,247	108,658
% total Area Population	9.7	81.8	69.6	76.6	53.1
% total city anglo population	6.3	9.3	15.2	69.3	100.0
Mexican-American population	53,005	1,429	6,709	21,904	83,037
% total area population	75.4	11.7	28.2	22.3	40.6
% total city Mexican-American population	63.8	1.7	8.1	26.4	100.0
Black population	9,410	444	439	233	10,526
% total area population	13.4	3.6	1.8	0.2	5.1
% total city black population	89.4	4.2	4.2	2.2	100.0

Source: City of Corpus Christi, Corpus Christi Community Renewal Program, *Economic Study*, March 1973, table 3.14.

The Flour Bluff area is the least populated section. It contains only 6.0 percent of the city's population. The ethnic breakdown is 81.8 percent Anglo, 11.7 percent Mexican-American, and 3.6 percent black. It contains 9.3 percent of the total Anglo population, 1.7 percent of the total Mexican-American population, and 4.2 percent of the total black population.

Thus, it can be seen that most of the black population (89.4 percent) lives in the Central area, commonly known as the Corridor, Hill, or Cut. Over one-half of the Mexican-American population live in the Central area with recent movement into the adjacent census tract of the Southwest.

Until recently, Anglo-Americans were numerically the largest group in Corpus Christi, whereas Mexican-Americans were a close second; black Americans constituted only a very small share of the total population. Mexican-Americans have been increasing numerically since 1960 and even more so since 1970. Anglo-Americans declined between 1960 and 1970; after 1970, their rate of decline appears to have accelerated. In the 1960s, the black American population remained just about 5 percent of the total population. Since 1970, however, the black American population has grown at a faster rate. By 1974, according to local estimates, Mexican-Americans had become a plurality of the population (47.4 percent), the Anglo-American population constituted a minority (43.7 percent), and the black American population was still quite small (8 percent) (table 6.2).

Residential segregation according to race or ethnic group exists in Corpus Christi. In many urban areas, "across the tracks" designates the resident separation; in Corpus Christi, it is "on the Hill" or "in the Corridor." Until the Fair Housing Act of 1954, real estate subdivisions in the city declared that no one "shall sell, convey, or lease the premises herein conveyed to a person or persons not of the Caucasian race, nor shall any firm or corporation composed of such. (County of Nueces, *Deed Records*, vols. 1, 2).

Segregating policies that did not specify restrictions to Mexican-Americans were carried out by informal means, such as simple refusal to sell. Segregation was more strictly enforced against dark-skinned Mexican-Americans or those who spoke English with an accent. In Corpus Christi, ethnic lines for residence were not originally held as firmly as in other towns. The rapid expansion of the city resulted in intermingling of the groups in many areas.

TABLE 6.2. Ethnic Population for the City of Corpus Christi, 1960–1977

Total	Population	Mexican-American		Black		Anglo	
		Number	%	Number	%	Number	%
1960	167,690	59,859	35.7	9,207	5.5	96,373	58.8
1970	204,525	83,037	40.6	10,526	5.1	110,962	54.3
1974	214,979	101,812	47.4	16,754	7.8	93,866	43.7
1975	217,365	—		—		—	
1976	219,933	—		—		—	
1977	222,500	—		—		—	

Source: U.S. Bureau of the Census, Census of Population 1960 and 1970. Figures for years after 1970 are estimates that appear in Corpus Christi Department of Planning and Urban Development, *Demographic Study* (no date), p. 22.

Regulations against black residents were more strictly enforced. As the black population spread out into other census tracts, the Anglo population would move out. One such case is in the Crossley Elementary Zoning Area. In 1954, Crossley was an all-white school. In 1955, 18 percent was black; in 1978 it had become the most segregated elementary school, with an enrollment of 99.2 percent black. It is still an unwritten policy among several real estate brokers not to show homes in certain neighborhoods to blacks or Mexican-Americans.

Analysis of racial and ethnic group residential segregation by census tracts reveals an interesting pattern. Whereas Mexican-Americans are moving in greater numbers into Anglo-American neighborhoods, they remain a significantly segregated minority. If one imagines Corpus Christi in 1970 to be shaped like a seagull, then the Mexican-American population is concentrated on the body of the seagull. The eight census tracts that are 70 percent or more Mexican-American are all contiguous, are all located in this central band, and all show an increase in proportion of Mexican-Americans between 1960 and 1970.

The black population of Corpus Christi has been and remains small and residentially quite concentrated. Most of the black population resides in four tracts. Two tracts, which were each about 75 percent black in 1970, contained 42 percent of the city's blacks. Another two tracts contained an additional 34 percent of the black population. Black Americans, however, make up only 22 percent of these two tracts. In those tracts with a large percentage of black residents, the remaining population is almost exclusively Mexican-American. The relatively small number of Anglo-Americans living in "black tracts" in 1960 dropped even more by 1970, thus heightening the degree of residential separation between blacks and Anglo-Americans.

The location of the black-populated areas of the city presents an interesting picture. The two areas with the highest percentage of blacks are located on the north end of the band of Mexican-American minorities that bisects the city. However, this black area is separated from the Mexican-American population by a freeway and is bounded on the other side by the river and industrial development. The other two tracts that contain significant numbers of blacks are also located in this minority corridor, but on its outer edge.

In summary, the general level of residential separation between Mexican-Americans and Anglo-Americans seems to be falling although segregation remains. Between black and Anglo, however, the level of residential segregation shows no sign of appreciable decline.

Information on the number and location of minorities, while important, does not indicate the social and economic conditions of the minority population of Corpus Christi. Table 6.3 shows income, housing, and educational characteristics for each ethnic group. Blacks and Mexican-Americans are less well off than is the total population. Several specifics here merit some mention. First, the black population of Corpus Christi is considerably better educated on the average than is the Mexican-American population, yet the black population's median income and proportion professionally employed is lower than that of the Mexican-Americans. This may be at least partly accounted for by the considerably higher proportion of black families that are headed by females. Another interesting pattern here is the relationship between income and public assistance. Mexican-Americans have lower incomes than the total population and a higher percentage of families below the poverty level. Yet, despite lower incomes, a smaller proportion of Mexican-American families receive public assistance than among the total population.

TABLE 6.3. Social and Economic Characteristics of the Total Population and Minority Groups of Corpus Christi, 1970

	Total Population	Mexican-Americans	Blacks	Anglos
Aged 5–24 years	85,107	39,241	4,451	41,415
% population aged 5–24 years	41.6	47.3	42.3	37.3
Persons per household	3.42	4.3	3.32	
Median years of education	12.1	8.4	10.3	
% high school graduates	51.7	29.0	32.7	
Median family income	$8,468	$6,225	$5,245	
% families below poverty level	15.5	28.1	32.9	
% families receiving public assistance	12.2	11.4	20.3	
% households with female head	10.2	11.3	20.6	
Mean value of owned house	$9,400	$6,900	$8,000	
Mean gross rent	$63	$55	$49	

Source: U.S. Bureau of the Sensus, Census of Population and Housing, 1970. Census Tracts. Final Report PHC(1)-51, Corpus Christi, Texas.

TABLE 6.4. Occupation by Ethnic Group Corpus Christi, 1970 (%)

Occupation	Total Population	Mexican-American	Anglo	Black
Professional and technical	15.3	8.1	20.2	7.5
Managerial and administrative	9.8	5.3	13.1	2.1
Sales	8.2	5.4	10.5	.9
Clerical and kindred	17.8	15.1	20.3	7.1
Crafts	16.2	17.2	16.1	10.1
Operatives	8.3	11.6	6.3	8.9
Transport	4.1	6.9	2.2	6.8
Laborers	5.4	9.6	2.6	9.3
Farm	.6	.8	.5	.1
Service	11.6	16.6	7.4	25.1
Private household	2.8	3.4	.7	21.3
Total	100	100	100	100

Source: U.S. census data.

One of the most basic factors affecting the context within which ethnic relations occur is the economic structure of the area. Table 6.4 presents 1970 data on the distribution of occupations among the three ethnic groups. The highest categories in the area, professional and managerial, are dominated by Anglo-Americans. From these broad data it appears that Mexican-Americans more likely occupy slightly higher-status occupations than do black Americans. Among the employed blacks in Corpus Christi, 56.4 percent are employed in either service or private household occupations. Only 20.0 percent of the Mexican-Americans and even a smaller proportion of Anglo-Americans (8.1 percent) are so employed. These figures become more significant when it is remembered that black Americans have a median level of education that exceeds Mexican-Americans by almost 2 years (table 6.4).

DESEGREGATION ATTEMPTS: 1938-1978

The city of Corpus Christi is divided into five independent school districts: Calallen, Corpus Christi, Flour Bluff, Tuloso-Midway, and West Oso (figure 6.2). In 1967, the total enrollment of the independent districts was 51,546. Corpus Christi Independent School District (CCISD) had the majority of students with a total of 43,464 or 84.3 percent. Calallen, Flour Bluff, and Tuloso-Midway each had 3.6 percent, and West Oso had 4.9 percent. Enrollment for the five districts by 1970 was 56,109. Although Corpus Christi increased to 46,270 pupils, this was only 82.5 percent of the total enrollment, 1.8 percent less than in 1967. But whereas Corpus Christi decreased in percentage, Calallen and Tuloso-Midway gained by 0.3 percent or 3.9 percent of the total enrollment; Flour Bluff gained 0.5 percent or 4.1 percent of total enrollment. West Oso gained seventy-nine students but lost 0.3 percent for 4.6 percent of the city's enrollment. The desegregation case deals only with the Corpus Christi Independent School District, which was the only district involved in the suit.

The Corpus Christi Independent School District adopted a Neighborhood Policy Concept on 6 September 1938. This meant that Mexican-American and Anglo-American children would have to attend schools within the boundary or zone in which they lived. A state statute provided separate schools for black students; hence these students continued to be bused to their own schools. A number of Anglo parents whose children attended Crossley and Freeman elementary schools protested the zoning because it would send their children to Southgate, which had 100 percent Mexican-American enrollment. Anglo parents circulated petitions demanding a new school building for their children or bus transportation out of the area. They even threatened a court suit. Their request for transfers out of the area was granted by the district.

In 1940, the League of United Latin-American Citizens (LULAC) established the Little School of 400, a program to teach 400 basic English vocabulary words to Spanish-speaking preschoolers, to help these children cope in an all-English environment in a school unresponsive to their language needs. In addition, in 1948, Dr. Hector Garcia organized the American G.I. Forum to combat discrimination in the educational system of Texas.

A study of school conditions by the local NAACP in July 1948 showed existence of inadequate facilities at three majority black schools. The school board assured the NAACP that they were doing everything possible to provide

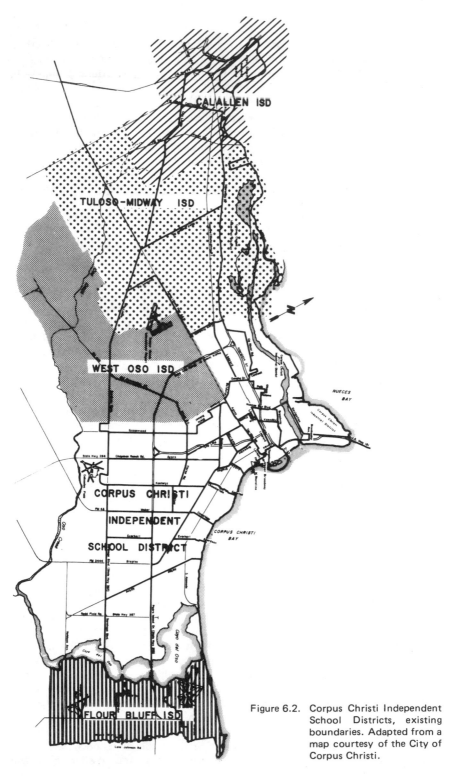

Figure 6.2. Corpus Christi Independent School Districts, existing boundaries. Adapted from a map courtesy of the City of Corpus Christi.

equal education for white and black children; yet conditions remained relatively unchanged.

One year after the *Brown* decision, the NAACP asked that the school be desegregated or else the board would be faced with a court suit. The school board announced that the schools would be desegregated that fall. All black students could attend their neighborhood schools. The school district continued busing black children from Calallen and Flour Bluff, two outlying school districts, into the city's all-black neighborhood schools. The all-black enrollment school buildings continued to deteriorate, as did all Mexican-American neighborhood schools.

Angered at a 20 percent drop in black teachers, NAACP in 1958 asked that faculties be integrated, and that teachers recruited be from black colleges. The board took no action. The same request was repeated by the NAACP in 1963. The superintendent of schools responded by saying that "since its inception, the district has operated under an unwritten policy of hiring Negro teachers for Negro schools." Only forty black teachers and two black principals were part of a faculty of 1,572 at that time.

Blatant examples of discrimination against Mexican-American students also continued. For example, the father of one Mexican girl attempted to have her transferred to a school that offered college-oriented courses. Although the father indicated his willingness to pay tuition and to provide transportation, the principal refused to admit the student to the school. He had previously admitted the girl's neighbor Anglo-American student under similar circumstances (Texas Advisory Committee Report 1975: 4–5).

Black students living outside predominantly black neighborhoods were permitted to attend their neighborhood schools. Most ended up in Mexican-American schools, whose physical or academic condition was no better than that of black schools. Some black students transferred to south side schools. However, black students from the Flour Bluff Independent School District continued being bused into the black neighborhood schools; thus the schools still had an almost 100 percent black student body.

The Corpus Christi Human Relations Commission (CCHRC), established by the mayor in 1963 to ease racial tensions in the city, was asked by minority group leaders to assist in solving problems that existed in the school system. In the early 1960s, the CCHRC investigated zoning patterns and school policies, conditions, and curriculum. After the investigation, the CCHRC attempted to meet with the school board in 1964, to no avail. They continued their attempts and finally a meeting was scheduled in April 1967. The school board insisted that no discrimination existed in the schools. At a second meeting held in August, the CCHRC formally charged the school system with de facto segregation. The Human Relations Commission also advised the board that a Citizen Advisory Committee should be formed. The school board rejected the recommendation. The city PTA became involved and wrote to the city Human Relations Commission (*Caller-Times* 1967: 8/17) stating that the PTA was quite capable of advising the school on school problems. Following this admonition, the Corpus Christi Human Relations Commission took a more passive role in school affairs.

Other individuals concerned with the school system did not remain so passive. In 1968, José Cisneros, a Mexican-American member of the United States Steel Workers of America Union Local 5022, found that he could not afford to continue sending his children to a Roman Catholic parochial school when his third child reached school age. He transferred them to a neighborhood public school, Prescott Elementary.

In an interview with Xavier Perez (1975), Mr. Cisneros said, "I noticed poor maintenance of the school, the bathroom was stopped up and dirty, the windows were broken, and the tiles were falling off the ceiling." Mr. Cisneros discussed his concerns with other parents of the predominantly Mexican-American neighborhood. Several fathers who were also members of the Steel Workers Union decided to take advantage of a vacation and visit the school. They were appalled at the conditions and asked for improvements. The principal refused, claiming that it would be too difficult and that he would get in trouble with the superintendent of schools. These men organized a group and continued an investigation into other aspects of the school. They found that the school had no teaching aids such as projectors or tape recorders, which were routinely distributed to south side schools. They met with the superintendent and demanded improvements. The superintendent ordered some of the improvements and replaced the Anglo principal of the school with a Mexican-American principal.

The group began attending school board meetings to request a new junior high school on the southwest part of town, as had been promised in the last bond election. That promised southwest school, Paul Haas, was built in Pharoah Valley, a south side neighborhood. The group met with the superintendent to complain about the site that had been chosen. The superintendent insisted that the school was on the west side. After proof of its location was presented, he said that the school was already built. His attitude, according to Cisneros, was, "What are you going to do about it? There's nothing you can do about it now."

Further investigation of the schools showed that children were tracked into ability groups. Children in the highest ability group in the west side fit into the second ability group in the south side. Curricula in west side schools were also limited; few college-oriented courses were offered and trade courses predominated. Parents were also concerned about the complete segregation of ethnic and racial groups and the stereotyped images that each group held of the other.

As a result of the refusal by the superintendent and the school board to desegregate, the group decided to resort to legal action. About that time, Paul Montemayor, a Mexican-American, was appointed to a national United Steel Workers of America nine-member Civil Rights Committee. Cisneros approached him about the possibility of the labor union's involvement in a civil suit. Montemayor agreed to present the possibility of the local union seeking relief through litigation to the organization's executive boards. The regional and national levels of the union approved the expenditure of funds for such litigation against the school board.

Thirty-two members of the local union of United Steel Workers of America who were parents of children in the schools signed the suit charging segregation of Mexican-American and black schoolchildren in the schools of Corpus Christi on 22 July 1968. The plaintiffs who signed included twenty-five Mexican-Americans and five black Americans from the local union of 400 members. The make-up of the union approximates that of the city: 46.3 percent Mexican-American, 7.4 percent black Americans, and 46.3 percent Anglo-Americans. Although there were Anglo-American union members and townspeople who offered to be part of the plaintiff's suit, the group decided to file with only Mexican and black Americans as plaintiffs.

In 1970, two years after *Cisneros et al.* v. *Corpus Christi Independent School District* (1970) was filed, the case finally went to trial. After eleven days of testimony and sixty pieces of evidence, Judge Woodrow Seals ruled that Mexican-Americans were an identifiable minority class, and that de jure and de facto segregation did exist in the school district. In June a partial final judgment ordered the district to employ more minority administrators and teachers and to submit a desegregation plan to be implemented in September 1970.

The school board attempted to appeal the decision, but Judge Seals was on vacation out of the country, and the case was temporarily transferred to Judge Owen Cox's docket. In an unprecedented move, Judge Cox, sitting temporarily for Judge Seals, granted a stay on July 1970 because of the school district's plea that it could not comply with the order within a month.

The plaintiffs appealed Judge Cox's decision to the Fifth U.S. Circuit Court of Appeals a week later. They asked that Judge Cox's stay be overruled and that a reinstatement of Seal's original plan be made. By 3 August, the Fifth Circuit Court of Appeals struck down the stay. The court refused to reconsider the stay again on 10 August 1970.

On the following day, 11 August, the school district appealed to the U.S. Supreme Court. The executive branch of the United States Justice Department filed a memorandum with the Supreme Court supporting the school board's stance. On 20 August, United States Supreme Court Justice Hugo L. Black granted a stay until the Fifth Circuit Court of Appeals or the full Supreme Court could file on the merits of the case concerning Mexican-Americans. The ruling would apply only to the legality of Mexican-Americans within the *Brown* decision, not to black Americans. However, on 23 August 1970, Judge Cox added the black students to the stay order after the black population petitioned to be part of that stay to avoid one-way busing of black American students.

Judge Seals issued a final ruling in July 1971 that called for busing of more than 15,000 students that fall. Parts of the ruling included Seals' requirement that the school district make periodic reports to him, listing the exact numbers of teachers and students by ethnic background for each school in the system. In an interview in August 1971, the superintendent stressed that even though up to 15,000 students were due to be reassigned in the fall, the Corpus Christi schools would not provide any bus transportation. The superintendent cited severe handicaps in complying with Seals' order, specifically, that buses, even if budgeted and ordered, could not be delivered to the district for six or eight months. Transportation was left up to parents. Opening of schools was delayed from 25 August until 1 September to allow student transportation plans to be made by parents.

Nonetheless, in July 1971, the Corpus Christi School District asked for an additional stay, which U.S. Supreme Court Justice Black granted. The school board continued a series of appeals to the Fifth Circuit Court of Appeals. The court upheld all findings of Judge Seals' original trial court, but indicated that the remedy as Judge Seals had outlined was too severe for the district to implement by September 1971. The district was ordered to investigate other alternatives and remedies to substitute for that original order.

The U.S. Fifth Circuit Court of Appeals delayed any decision in February 1972 until the Supreme Court could offer guidance. It also barred the school from any construction without court approval until after the court case was settled.

The U.S. Fifth Circuit Court of Appeals en banc (all judges present) again found the Corpus Christi Independent School District guilty of violating the civil rights of Mexican- and black American students under the Fourteenth Amendment of the U.S. Constitution. They agreed with Judge Seals' decision that unconstitutional segregation existed and ordered a desegregation plan.

Finally, on 23 August 1972, Judge Cox ordered the school district to produce a skeletal plan by 15 September 1972. The plan was submitted on the day of the deadline. The plaintiffs submitted a petition for rejection of that plan, which called for a reassignment of 3,665 pupils and closing Coles Elementary, the all-black school. Judge Cox rejected the plan, calling it "superficial," and ordered a new plan by 11 June 1973.

A petition was also submitted by the district to the U.S. Supreme Court for a review of the case concerning Mexican-Americans. The Supreme Court turned down the district's request.

Again on deadline for submission, the school district entered a new plan that called for immediate boundary changes with more changes for the 1974–1975 school year. This included the addition of ninth grade to high schools, the creation of a fifth high school, and the closing of several schools. The plaintiffs again objected to this plan. They claimed that the plan was not extensive enough to present a "dual neighborhood system." They also called for employment of a greater number of minority professionals.

The judge ruled to implement the plan on a temporary basis on 15 August 1973.

Cox's court issued a Memorandum in Order on 5 December 1973. Cox ordered the district to cease the implementation of the 11 June plan immediately. The Coles Elementary School changes were allowed to remain, but no other implementation could be undertaken. Cox ordered the district to initiate a new voluntary ethnic-transfer plan. The purpose was to see if enough students would transfer to other schools voluntarily to achieve desegregation. Voluntary transfers could be granted on January and September of 1974. Steelworker representative Paul Montemayor and John Cartwright, a plaintiff in the court case, objected to the voluntary transfer plan. On 1 August an article appeared on the *Caller-Times* (1974) outlining the disappointment with the plan including the district itself.

On September 1974, the school district began compiling the results of the voluntary-transfer policy; 1,300 students asked for transfers, all but thirty of whom were minority students. Numerous meetings occurred between attorneys for both sides and the court. A new plan was asked for by the plaintiffs.

Beginning in July 1974, numerous private citizens, as well as strong citizens' groups, publicly expressed their dissatisfaction with the lengthy processes of the court case. Paul Montemayor again complained (*Caller-Times* 1974: 7/5) that Judge Owen Cox is "not taking any steps to implement an integration plan other than the current voluntary-transfer approach." Montemayor urged citizens to voice their dissatisfaction with the slow process of the court case by picketing the school board building, as well as the homes of the superintendent and board members.

Dr. Hector P. Garcia issued a recommendation (*Caller-Times* 1974: 7/7) asking for Judge Cox's resignation from the case because Cox seemed "unable due to personal or philosophical reasons to carry out the orders of the Fifth Circuit Court of Appeals."

Some black leaders called a press conference on 1 November 1974 to emphasize their dissatisfaction with what they termed "one-way busing" of black children. These same leaders stated that they wanted to avoid the problems that Boston, Massachusetts, had faced in the wake of court-ordered busing, and emphasized their hope that black citizens in Corpus Christi would abide by any future court orders. They also pointed to a need for "positive action to prepare the community for integration" (*Caller-Times* 1974: 11/1).

The plaintiffs and the U.S. Justice Department asked that a plan following the U.S. Fifth Circuit Court of Appeal's specification be formulated. These briefs were submitted in November and December 1974. The justice department declared that the district's plan to use $7.89 million for construction would "merely perpetuate ethnic isolation" in some schools. In addition, the NAACP again contended that black students were carrying the burden of desegregation by one-way busing.

Judge Cox asked that a new plan be filed by the school district on or before 2 January 1975. The plan submitted by the board called for busing 13 to 14 percent of the elementary school students, closing two schools, and pairing seventeen elementary schools. The plaintiffs objected, requesting that all twenty-seven elementary schools be included.

During the following eight years, more than ten desegregation plans were submitted by the school district, the plaintiffs, the U.S. Department of Health, Education, and Welfare, private citizens, and the court itself through specially hired consultants.

The school district filed their two plans, for the elementary and for the junior and senior high schools, only under protest. Neither plan required busing. The elementary school plan changed boundaries of eleven schools, shifting fewer than 1,000 of 45,542 students. The change in minority attendance would be from about 1 percent in five schools, and to about 20.42 percent in one school only. Beach School would be closed and its 136 students (76 Mexican- and 60 Anglo-Americans) would be transferred to Washington Elementary, an almost all-black school. Boundaries would change in minority west side schools, but no boundaries would change in south side schools. This plan was declared unconstitutional.

A second plan dropped optional zoning at four junior high schools. It attempted to increase Anglo attendance at one school by 10.45 percent and to decrease black student attendance from 1.03 to 0.48 percent. Two other junior high schools remained with no black students. A fourth would increase its black population by less than 1 percent. The Mexican-American attendance at three schools would have increased by less than 1 percent. At the high school level, no schools would change by more than 5 percent in any of the three groups. This plan was also not acceptable to the court.

Another plan submitted required an equidistant approach to integration by drawing zones between two schools. The result was that some schools remained with no black students; and most of the other schools were predominantly one-race student bodies. This plan was not accepted by the court either.

The plaintiffs offered two plans. One was drawn by a desegregation expert, Gordon Foster. The Foster plan would have affected 69 percent of total grade level attendance in twenty-nine out of the forty-three elementary schools. It called for rezoned attendance districts including junior and senior high schools. Transportation involved 16,900 students including 7,000 from elementary schools. Four elementary schools would have been closed, including the three attended predominantly by black students. A second plan was formulated by Mrs. James Scott, a parent. The Scott plan paired schools and provided for children to go to their neighborhood schools for four years and to the paired school for two years. A third plan filed by the U.S. Department of Health, Education, and Welfare would have paired thirty-two elementary schools and would have required busing of about 15,000 students. Arturo Vasquez, a board member, also filed a plan.

Dr. Joseph Rupp, the county medical examiner and member of the antibusing group Concerned Neighbors, came up with a computer plan that Judge Cox accepted and ordered implemented for the 1975-1976 school year. The court requested that Dr. Rupp, two computer experts, two lay advisers, and the district's pupil-accounting administrators refine the plan. The computer plan called for a 25-75 majority-minority or minority-majority mix with walking grids of not more than two-mile radii around schools. This would result in no busing or minimal busing for areas outside grids. A map with fifty-two grids resulted. Each grid had approximately forty students from first through sixth grades. It took 22,000 computations to come up with the 25-75 mix for grids. The information became available to parents through the *Corpus Christi Caller-Times* three weeks before the 1975-1976 school year. The district developed an alphabetical dictionary to randomize the selection of students to be bused in each grid. No student was to be bused for more than one year. The plan called for the busing of 600 minority and 900 Anglo students from thirteen out of thirty-seven elementary schools (*Cisneros et al.* order of 7/26 1975: 5).

Finally, in August 1975, seven years after the suit was filed, buses began to roll, with 1,500 students selected by lottery system to pick letters for last names from grids, and 10,000 other students walking to schools within their 2-mile grids to other than their neighborhood schools. Four schools, Austin, Furman, Southgate, and Wilson were closed. As a consequence, the results included an occasional Anglo-American student going to a west side minority school, some schools having 100 percent of their student bodies moved, and many students of the same racial or ethnic groups passing each other on their way to the other student's neighborhood school. The 25-75 ratio was not achieved. A 20-80 ratio was applied for by the schools and granted by the judge, but that ratio was not achieved either.

The situation caused Dr. Rupp to proclaim that his "diamond" was left in the rough. The plaintiffs, plus a large proportion of the community, were so dissatisfied with the mere moving of bodies that the justice department decided to study the results. It concluded that a substantial reassignment of students from their neighborhood schools by walking long distances had apparently little desegregation effects and very disruptive results (Rich 1975: 4). Thirteen schools remained with 81 to 99 percent minority enrollment, though there was a great deal of movement among students from these schools.

Judge Cox ordered the grid plan continued during the 1976-1977 school year in spite of the dissatisfaction, but allowed for modifications of grid assignments, the opening of a school for the gifted, the closing of Wilson Elementary, and the addition of seven more elementary schools to the lottery (*Cisneros, et al.,* order 5/24/1976: 213). Great dissatisfaction with the plan finally convinced

Judge Cox to order the grid plan discarded at the end of the 1976–1977 school year.

The paired-school plan involving busing continued with third and fourth grades going to west side minority schools and fourth and fifth grades going to south side majority schools. Kindergarten, first, and second grades were not affected by the plan in the seventeen schools involved.

A series of antibusing rallies were held by the Concerned Neighbors in August 1976. The group staged a school boycott on 3 and 4 September. The absentee rate, according to school statistics, was only slightly higher than usual.

On 19 July 1976 a plan for the extension of integration into the junior high as required by the court, was submitted by the school board. It called for busing 1,356 students in five out of fourteen junior high schools with a 3–2 pairing of south side and west side schools. The plan also called for closing three minority junior high schools that needed extensive repairs (*Cisneros et al.* order 7/19/1976: 5, 6). The judge requested that consideration be given to integration of students in the high schools. The school board proposed boundary changes plus a reassignment of students on their first entrance into high school as sophomores. Although minorities had enrolled in south side schools, the west side schools still remained with a high percentage of minority schools.

On 22 May 1978 a compromise was reached by the plaintiffs, José Cisneros et al. and the Corpus Christi Independent School District. The compromise called for the addition of Allen and Travis, two west side elementary schools, to the pairing-busing list. The south side schools to be paired have as yet not been selected. Four west side elementary schools are to be rebuilt on their present sites, including Crossley. One west side minority school will be closed. No other existing plans have been changed. Inequities are still in evidence in personnel and pupil assignments and in facilities. Before renovating or building can be carried out, however, a school bond issue must be passed. Most west side schools are still over 80 and 90 percent minority. Renovations and rebuilding are at least two years away if a school bond issue passes. Otherwise, inequities will continue in the Corpus Christi Independent School District unless cooperation or compromise prior to presentation to the courts replace confrontation after plans are formulated and submitted by the district, plaintiffs, and other parties involved.

THE ROLE OF THE SCHOOL BOARD

School board members are elected at large for six years on a staggered basis of 2-2-3 on even-numbered years. In case of resignations, the remainder of the board selects a replacement until the nearest election. That position, too, becomes open for election for the remainder of the unexpired term. There is no compensation for serving. The at-large system, which does not provide for run-offs, has made it possible for special interest groups to capture seats. This makes it difficult, if not impossible, for racial or ethnic minority groups to gain representation of their own choosing.

No black had served on the board until February 1978, when Elliot Grant, a Baptist minister, was appointed by the board to serve on a four-year un-expired term. Two months later, Grant ran as an incumbent and won. Only two Mexican-Americans had served on the board, one of them briefly from 1935 to 1938. In 1976, Arturo Vasquez, who had served for twenty-four years as the only Mexican-American representative, lost his seat to Dale Hornsby, ex-president of Concerned Neighbors, an antibusing organization. This defeat resulted in an all-Anglo-American board for a school district with a 63.1 percent minority enrollment. In October 1977, Clemente Garcia, a Mexican-American pharmacist, was selected by the board to an unexpired term of two years. An all-male board resulted. In April 1978, in what was termed a fluke by many people, three minority members were elected—the two incumbents appointed by the board and Dr. Arturo Medina, professor of educational administration at a local university.

Only two women have served on the board since its inception, and both resigned before their first terms expired. In 1972, Marsha Darlington, the second woman to serve on the board, a housewife and a member of the board of Concerned Neighbors, won one of the two positions available. Concerned Neighbors scored a victory in that election when Dr. Cornell Barnard, who was running for a second term and who also had its endorsement, captured the second seat.

The makeup of the board has been almost completely conservative, professional, Anglo-American businessmen. Members tend to get elected for tenures that last as long as twenty-four years. They rarely verbalize a platform except for antibusing, antiunion, and proneighborhood school sentiments. Because of its makeup, the board did everything in its power to prevent court-ordered desegregation. Dr. J. Albright, a school board member, said in an interview with the Texas Advisory Committee of the U.S. Civil Rights Commission (Report, May 1977: 60), that the school board opposed desegregation that included massive busing because it felt that a majority of the community believed in neighborhood schools and that integration would eventually evolve through natural migration patterns.

From January until April 1972, board member Arturo Vasquez boycotted the school board meetings to protest the board's stance on desegregation. He called the board and superintendent "arrogant and having a lack of understanding" (*Caller-Times* 1972: 3/14). He called for an improved racial-ethnic balance on the board. As a general rule, incumbents who seek reelection are not defeated. New members are usually appointed by the other board members at the resignation of incumbents. They then run as incumbents and win. The defeat of Arturo Vasquez, the only Mexican-American trustee, was a rare occurrence.

A suit has been filed (*LULAC* v. *School Board,* Civ. Action 74–95) to change the school board to single-member districts. The Anglo-Americans as well as the black Americans oppose such a change. The black leaders feel that they have a better opportunity in an at-large system than they do competing within Mexican-American and black districts.

THE SUPERINTENDENT OF SCHOOLS

Since its inception in 1909, the Corpus Christi Independent School District has had eleven superintendents, all Anglo-Americans. The present superintendent and the school board have steadfastly denied the existence of any type of discrimination, segregation, or inequality of schools. Dr. Dana Williams, then superintendent (*The Weekly Current Magazine* 1970: 9/30), said that the district operated a unitary system and no favoritism had been shown to any one school or student groups. He also said, "From an economic stand point, this district would have to cut back on what it's doing for its young people now, if it were to do what Mr. Cisneros seems to believe the most important goal in education, that is to socialize young people. . . . If we start transporting students, and pairing and mixing just for racial balance, I think we will see a lot of white flight."

According to a former board member, Dr. Williams had a tremendous influence over the school board. Because of the large amount of planning that must be done by the board and the lack of pay, it is purported that the superintendent and his staff do most of the school board's planning. In May 1974, the superintendent established an advisory committee for advising the superintendent on methods of desegregation. The G.I. Forum refused to join, calling it a useless venture. One NAACP representative resigned two months after appointment. Other members who resigned included the representatives of the Mexican-American Chamber of Commerce, LULAC, and the Coastal Bend Labor Council. The committee is still functioning but its contribution is negligible. The superintendent has steadfastly refused to take any part in any of the community's efforts to deal with the desegregation process, either those that have resisted or those that want to follow the orders of the court. The superintendent refused to testify at the Texas Advisory Committee hearings to the Civil Rights Commission in May 1976. He refused, he said, because the school board was still under litigation. He testified under subpoena on 17 August 1976.

LOCAL ORGANIZATIONS

In June 1970, one of the first groups formed as a result of the desegregation case—Concerned Neighbors, Incorporated, whose main objective was to oppose forced busing of school children. The first president of the group said the organization favored "neighborhood schools, integration and freedom-of-choice schools" (*Caller-Times* 1970: 6/26). The group also announced that it favored positive methods to prevent "forced busing" and "equal educational opportunities" for all children regardless of race or ethnic origin. The group attempted to reach its goals through rallies, community meetings, petition drives, letters, telegrams, and trips to seek the influence of state and national legislators.

The group also made a study of the schools and court plans. It attempted to intervene in the case but its request was turned down by the judge. The group later unincorporated itself in order to become politically involved, feeling that de jure segregated schools did not exist in Corpus Christi and that the court case was unfairly conducted.

In 1975, Concerned Neighbors called for a boycott of the schools as a protest against busing. According to the school administration the absentee rate was only slightly above the normal absentee rate.

Another organization that became involved in the desegregation process was the Committee for Racial Justice, a subgroup of the Young Women's Christian Association. This group included members of all three major ethnic groups, and its objective was to secure equal educational opportunities for all groups. It sponsored several forums that featured school board members or school board candidates as speakers.

The League of Women Voters was the first group to hold a forum on desegregation efforts being carried out in other communities in their efforts to solve their own desegregation processes. The group reached the consensus that among the most important factors in successful integration were the attitudes of parents, teachers, and school officials.

Another group known as Citizens for a Positive Climate for School Integration and Education involved many business and religious leaders of the city as well as members of community service organizations. The group placed a full-page newspaper advertisement in August 1975 urging the adoption of a code for responsible citizenship. The code called for an adjustment to promote orderly and efficient opening of schools and the adoption of proper channels to report grievances.

The Cultural Awareness Committee of the Mental Health Association issued a formal statement outlining what it believed were the shortcomings of the computer plan. It considered the destruction of the parent-teacher associations in the elementary schools a negative result of busing. The group pointed to the overenrollment of some schools and underenrollment in others.

Another group which sought to influence the community and court-ordered busing plans was the City-wide Parent-Teachers Association of CCISD. This group conducted a survey in which they claimed an overwhelming majority (18,113 to 131) of those polled were against busing and for neighborhood schools. Parent-Teacher Associations from four west side schools voted not to take part in the poll.

Not all organizations formed with the purpose to oppose busing. In the summer of 1970, the Association for Educational Understanding (AEU) came to life. The organization included members from the three major groups—Mexican-American, black American, and Anglo-American. Its goal was to "build better community relations and a better school system." The organization set up a hot-line to answer inquiries concerning the desegregation case and school plans. It also urged that temporary mobile housing be used at schools to balance the ethnic makeup of all city schools.

Although LULAC sent representatives to different committees and seminars, the organization did not take any strong stand on the desegregation issue. One of the reasons for this failure was that some members had children going to south side (Anglo) schools whom they did not want transferred to west side (minority) schools. Attorney William Bonilla, former national president of LULAC, filed a petition in federal court to give temporary guardianship of his two sons to a west side couple to keep them on their school's football team. Others immediately followed suit for various reasons including avoiding busing. A temporary injunction against such guardianships was asked of Judge Cox. The students involved graduated before the case came to court.

POLITICAL AND RELIGIOUS LEADERS

Political Leaders

United States Senators John Tower and Lloyd Bentsen, and Representative John Young were visited by board members of Concerned Neighbors in order to gain their support (*Caller-Times* 1971: 10/13). Bentsen arranged a meeting with Dr. Richard Brannen, chief advisor to the secretary of the Department of Health, Education, and Welfare. Tower and Young appear to have been more active in obtaining the aid of the executive branch of the U.S. Justice Department.

The ex-mayor of Corpus Christi, Ronnie Sizemore, indicated that the city had virtually no involvement in the case. However, on 16 August 1971 (*Caller-Times*), the city council took an official stance against student reassignment, and Mayor Sizemore sent a telegram to President Nixon asking his help with "serious community problems" being caused by reassignment. Mayor Sizemore invited the superintendent (*Caller-Times* 1971: 9/1) to a retreat to "discuss serious community problems."

Texas Senator Mike McKinnon, a speaker at an antibusing rally in the coliseum, said, "I am against busing and will always be against busing" (*Caller-Times* 1976: August).

Religious Leaders

Carolyn and Fred Swearingen, creators of the Committee for a Positive Climate for Integration and Education, sought to bring about a change in attitudes in the summer of 1975 by inviting twelve influential clergymen representing all three racial/ethnic groups to meet and discuss what needed to be done. The committee was expanded to include businessmen, educators, city council members, and other community leaders. The clergy was urged to speak out for peaceful integration. The group addressed the school board and asked them for moral leadership and to take positive action in the responsibility of integration planning. The group also held a series of human relations' workshops in an effort to prepare the community. Although school officials were invited to take part in these activities, they never participated.

Black religious leaders have been very active before, during, and after the court suit. One minister who supported busing for the purpose of desegregation pleaded with the school system to prepare the students for their imminent transfer to a desegregated school. He was also a member of a group that requested the school district to apply for federal funds available for summer programs to prepare students and teachers for the change. The Reverend Harold Branch said in an interview, "We thought we had the ears of the Administration, and then all of a sudden the door was closed" (Civil Rights Commission Report, May 1976: 5). He went on to say, "Those children were troubled and disturbed, and they constituted the largest group of casualties of our school system probably in the history of our effort to prepare our kids for life."

The Mass Media

The local newspapers, the *Corpus Christi Caller* and *Times,* morning and evening issues of Hanke-Edwards Publishers, have played vital roles in dissemination of information on the Corpus Christi desegregation suit. Many times they were the only source of information concerning plans and activities available to parents of children in public schools. Their coverage of the case won the state

Associated Press Award in 1976 for excellent reporting. The newspapers also provided a forum to allow people to express their opinions and frustrations with the process and with each other through Letters to the Editor. It appears that the *Caller-Times* had a major part in the prevention of violence. The papers did editorialize about obedience to the law and peaceful implementation.

In January 1978 a new biweekly, *The Sun,* began publication. It developed a circulation of 35,000. Its editorials were very critical of the school board and school administration.

The city has nineteen radio stations, some of which disseminated information. Two radio and one television station are Spanish-language stations. The radio stations were very active in the dissemination of information to the Spanish-speaking population; the television station did not begin operation until 1976. No black-oriented news stations or papers exist on a city-wide basis. News coverage of black activities is very minimal.

THE POLICE

The Corpus Christi police department had no specific, overt plan dealing with the desegregation process. The department attempted to keep as low-key as possible. Nonetheless, officers revealed in an interview that special attention was given to the situation by asking patrol cars on their regular route to keep an eye out for any problems that might arise because of busing. Although the department was concerned, they anticipated no riots or any other violence. Patrolmen were asked to monitor the buses on their routes to school during the first few days of busing but were told to keep their distance. Patrolmen were cautioned to keep doing things as routinely as possible. Because no events out of the ordinary occurred the first few days, the police felt confident that no problems would arise.

Police were not sent to any schools as a preventative measure, although they did patrol certain schools with a history of incidences more carefully. No arrests and no incidences occurred that were attributed to court-ordered busing.

TRENDS IN STUDENT ENROLLMENT

A hypothesis that the drop in Anglo students represents white flight to escape busing and integration is questionable in light of the available evidence. A large decline in the Anglo-American student population began its downward trend before the implementation of busing. Between 1969 and 1974, Anglo elementary enrollment dropped 27.2 percent. Junior high schools experienced a decline of 44.5 percent in Anglo-American enrollment from 1969 to 1977, although no junior high school students were bused.

Increase in local private and parochial school enrollment has been minimal since the desegregation process began (*Caller-Times* 1976: 8/27). The annual increase in private school enrollment from 7 to 9.1 percent over a ten-year period does not account for the loss of students in the Corpus Christi Independent School District enrollment.

Suburbanization has been occurring for some time in the Corpus Christi metropolitan area and is reflected in the increase in enrollments of some suburban school districts. High-income Anglo-American families continue to move to new developments across the bay to Portland and northwest to Calallen. Evidence presented earlier showed a decline of Anglo population in the core census districts.

The drop in Anglo-American fertility rates is another possible explanation of a decline in student enrollment. Generally, fertility has been considerably lower in the Anglo-American population than in the Mexican-American population. According to the 1970 census, the number of children born per 1,000 couples aged thirty-five to forty-four years was 65 percent higher for Mexican-Americans compared to Anglo-Americans of the same age bracket. Incomplete data prepared by the Department of Planning and Urban Development (1977) suggest that rates of fertility in the 1970s are falling faster for Anglo-Americans than among Mexican-Americans. Thus a decline in Anglo student population is in part due to the processes of suburbanization and fertility decline.

UNUSUAL ASPECTS OF THE CASE

The desegregation case of *Cisneros et al.* v. *Corpus Christi Independent School District* (1971) includes a combination of factors that mark it as being quite different from other desegregation cases. Unlike other non-English-speaking groups seeking equal educational opportunities through bilingual education, the plaintiffs in *Cisneros et al.* sought to establish that Mexican-Americans are an identifiable group or class and thus fell under the *Brown* decision for immediate injunctive relief. Judge Woodrow Seals found that Mexican-Americans, by whatever name used to identify them, are legally an identifiable ethnic class sufficient to bring them under the protection of the Fourteenth Amendment of the United States Constitution as applied to *Brown* v. *Board of Education* (1954). This finding was based not only on the fact that Mexican-Americans are a numerical minority in the country if not in Corpus Christi, but also on the fact that the group has suffered discrimination in the schools. Their own political and economic impotence prevented Mexican-Americans from correcting the situation. The importance of the court finding was that it offered a new legal tool in the continuing struggle to improve the educational status of disadvantaged minorities.

The district court judge concluded that Corpus Christi constituted a dual system within a dual system (commonly referred to as tri-ethnic), because it involved segregation of Mexican-American students (a class within the white race), from the dominant group (all others in the white race not Mexican-American and commonly referred to as Anglo), and black American students from the dominant group.

Earlier precedents set on ethnic isolation of Mexican-Americans in Texas were by-passed and the district court relied upon *Brown* as an authority for its holding injunctive relief.

Although segregation of blacks had been mandated by state statute, Mexican-American segregation had come about from practice and policy, which are more subtle forms of discrimination.

The ruling in *Cisneros et al.* not only offered a new legal tool for the improvement of educational status of disadvantaged minorities, but it also made possible the use of the court system to end the practice of combining minority groups into all-minority schools.

The Corpus Christi case is also unusual in that a minority that had once been the dominant group and sole land owners of the area had become the subdominant minority and was forced to litigate for equal educational rights.

In addition, the *Cisneros et al.* case was the first desegregation case to be totally financed by a labor union for the plaintiffs.

CONCLUSION

After ten years of litigation, *Cisneros et al.* v. *Corpus Christi Independent School District* had by no means come to a favorable conclusion for either plaintiffs or defendants. Anne Dodson, school reporter for the *Caller* wrote:

> Like a wind stirring only distant trees, integration had little impact on Cross-ley Elementary School.
>
> Court orders have come and gone for the past five years, but the Black children remain in a cultural isolation which last week's ruling leaves unchanged. . . . Driscoll and Miller, predominantly ethnic minority schools (junior and senior high schools) are also untouched by any integration order (*Caller-Times* 1978: June).

Most west side schools still remain virtually minority, a condition that will not necesarily change as the Mexican-American population continues increasing and the Anglo-American population continues decreasing. In addition, economic and housing patterns in minority communities remain virtually unchanged.

BIBLIOGRAPHY

Books and Journals

Blanton, A. 1923. *A Handbook of Information, Education in Texas, 1918–1922.* Austin: Texas Education Agency.

Blinkley, W. C. 1925. "The Expansionist Movement in Texas." *Publications in History,* 3. Berkeley: University of California Press.

Bolston, H. E. 1915. *Texas in the Middle of the Eighteenth Century.* Berkeley: University of California Public History, 3.

Castaneda, C. E. 1924–1925. *Southern Historical Quarterly,* 28: 191. Translation from Almonte, "Statistical Report on Texas."

Corpus Christi Del Mar Library. 1973. *Hartsell, Virginia 17 Years Later.*

Davenport, H., and J. K. Wells. 1918. (Translation of *Historia General of Natural de Las Indias.* Madrid: 1853). *The First Europeans in Texas, 1528–1536.* Southwestern Historical Quarterly, 22.

Delgado v. *Bastrop I.S.D.* 1948. Project Report "De Jure Segregation of Chicanos in Texas Schools." *Harvard Civil Rights Civil Liberties Law Review,* 7(2) (March 1972): 334.

Ford, Col. J. S. 1852. *Memoirs of John S. Ford 1815–1874* (Ms. in University of Texas Library, 7 vol.).

Haynes, John L. 1859. Texas House Ex. Document 52. 36 Cong. 1 sess. p. 25.

Hodge, F. W. 1907-1910. *Handbook of America Indians.* Washington Part I.

Linn, J. 1883. *Reminiscences of Fifty Years in Corpus Christi.* New York.

Morrell, E. 1936. *The Rise and Growth of Public Education in El Paso.* Austin: University of Texas Press.

Olmstead, F. L. 1957. *A Journey Through Texas.* New York.

Perez, X. 1975. "Desegregation in Corpus Christi." Unpublished term paper, Corpus Christi State University.

Perez, X. 1976. "Update of Desegregation in Corpus Christi." Unpublished term paper, Corpus Christi State University.

Saavedra, A. 1976. *The Attitudes and Opinions of the People of Corpus Christi Toward Desegregation, Busing and Equal Educational Opportunity.* Unpublished Ph.D. dissertation, University of Michigan.

Southerland, Mary A. 1916. *The Story of Corpus Christi.* Houston.

Taylor, P. S. 1934. *An American Mexican Frontier.* New York: Russell and Russell, reissued 1971.

Wooten, D. G. 1898. *A Comprehensive History of Texas.* Dallas, 2 vol., vol. 1, p. 371.

Ybaken, H. K. 1856. *History of Texas.* New York, 2 vol., vol. 2, pp. 354-355.

Newspapers

Corpus Christi Caller and Times. 1927-1978.

Daily Corpus Christi Chronical. 1938: September.

The Dallas Morning News, Texas Almanac State Industrial Guide. 1977. A. H. Belo Corporation. Texas Almanac Communication Center.

Nueces Valley Weekly. 1958: 1/2.

The Sun. 1977-1978.

Weekly Current Magazine. 1970: 9/16, 9/30.

Public Documents

Cisneros et al. v. *Corpus Christi Independent School District* 324 F. Supp. 599, S.D. Texas 1970, appeal docketed no. 71-2397 (5th Cir. filed July 16, 1971); 324 F. Supp. 599 at 606, 608, 615, 616, 620; 330 F. Supp. 1377 at 1388; 427 F. 2d. 142 at 148 5th Cir. 1972; 427 F. 2d. 142 at 152, 1972. 467, F. 2d. 142, 1972. Orders: 19 July 1971; 10 Mar. 1975 at 7. 26 July 1975, 24 May 1976, 19 July 1976, 1977.

Corpus Christi, City of. Community Renewal Program. 1973. *Economic Study.* March. Department of Planning and Urban Development. *Demographic Study* (no date). *School Population by Ethnicity.* 1975.

Corpus Christi Independent School District. *School Board Minutes.* 1938-1977. *Pupil Accounting and Research.* 1960-1977.

County of Nueces. *Deed Records,* vol. A. 65 (p. 456), vol. 83 (p. 449), vol. 90 (p. 423), vol. 95 (p. 82).

Salvatierra v. *Independent School District.* 1971. 33, S.W. 2d. 790, Texas Cir. app. 4th District 1930, Cert. denied 284 U.S. 580, 1931.

State of Texas, Austin. *Texas Acts,* 4th Congressional Session. 1918. *Texas Attorney General Opinion.* Vol. 128, 39, 1947. *State Constitutions.* Article VII Section 1866, 1869, 1876, 1888. *Texas Law Review.* 337, 1971. *Lamar Papers:* House Ex. Doc. No. 53, 36 Cong. 1st Session (Sec. 10501), No. 2422, IV, No. 2081, III, No. 2079, III, No. 2421, IV, No. 2333.

TEA (Texas Education Agency). Bulletin 428: *Supplement to Standards and Activities of Supervision 1942–43,* No. 507, 1948-1949. *Education Annual Codes,* Section 11.2, 1928, 1930, 1939, 1971, 1977. *Public School Directory.* 1923-1940; no. 472, 1947: 13.

United States. *Brown* v. *Board of Education.* 1954. 347 U.S. 483. Bureau of the Census, *Census of Population, 1960-1970. General Social and Economic Characteristics, Final Report* PC(1)-C 45 (Texas), 1970. Texas Advisory Committee Report. 1975. *Commission on Civil Rights School Desegregation in Corpus Christi.* Commission Education Support Center, Office of Management, Washington, D.C. May 1977. Rich, J. D. 1975. United States Justice Department, Letter to School District Attorney. August 19, 1975. Civil Suit No. 5281. 1977. *LULAC and American G.I. Forum* v. *Texas,* U.S.E.D. Court, Tyler, Texas. Civil Suit No. 74–C95. 1974. *LULAC* v. *School Board.* S.D. Texas, August 14, 1974. *United States Treaty of Peace, Friendship, Limits, and Settlement with the Republic of Mexico.* 9 Stat. 922, I. S1 No. 207, 1857. (Commonly called Treaty of Guadalupe Hidalgo).

7

Dallas, Texas: The Intervention of Business Leaders

Geoffrey P. Alpert, H. Ron White, and Paul Geisel

The 1976–1977 school year marked the beginning of the Dallas Independent School District's (DISD) efforts to implement a desegregation plan accepted by the U.S. District Court (*Tasby* v. *Estes* 1976). The plan, an outgrowth of a judicial process, was developed under the leadership of the Dallas Alliance and is a substantial policy document attempting to deal with the complex issues of school desegregation and quality education. The plan supported by the court embodies the contributions of many different groups and attempts to balance the varying educational philosophies and attitudes held by the citizens of Dallas. As is frequently the case when a policy document attempts to address many different needs and viewpoints, complete satisfaction for any one group is seldom achieved. Despite the strong reservations held by some for the court-ordered plan, the first year of desegregation brought little of the conflict seemingly common when some other major cities have implemented school desegregation programs.

The goal of this study is not to evaluate the plan ordered by the court or the degree of compliance achieved by the DISD. Rather, the goal is to provide a data base and an analysis of the trends indicated after the plan had been in effect for one year. When the process of appeal and the adaptation to the many court orders have run their course, then a complete assessment will be possible. Essentially, this is the story of a community in transition that has not fully experienced desegregation in its schools.

DEMOGRAPHICS

The Dallas Independent School District includes 351 square miles in Dallas, 12 square miles in Rylie, and 20 square miles in Seagoville. Rylie was incorporated into the DISD in 1960, and Seagoville joined the DISD in 1964. It has been estimated by the DISD research department that prior to 1970, slightly more than 90 percent of the DISD was in Dallas. Even though this figure has declined since 1970, it has not done so appreciably. In 1970, the population from which the DISD drew its students was 787,151. The population eligible to be students was 193,428 and enrollment was 164,937 (85 percent). In 1976, the population from which the DISD drew its students was 795,111. The population eligible to be students was 176,400, and enrollment was 139,080 (79 percent).

Within the DISD there are 19 high schools (grades nine to twelve), twenty-two middle schools (grades four to eight), 135 elementary schools (grades Kindergarten to three). In addition, there are 5 alternative schools and 4 magnet schools (all grades nine to twelve) that emphasize business and management, creative arts, health professions, and transportation technology.

The racial composition of the DISD in 1969 was 61 percent white, 31 percent black, and 8 percent Spanish. In 1976, the percentages had changed to 38 percent white, 47 percent black, and 14 percent Spanish. In 1971, shortly after the school desegregation suit had been filed, 120 out of the 180 schools were of predominantly one race.

Information on private schools in Dallas is difficult to obtain. According to the North Central Texas Council of Governments, in 1969 there were 4,942 students enrolled in private schools compared to 9,120 in 1975, almost an 85 percent increase. According to the 18 April 1976 edition of the *Dallas Times Herald*, there are approximately eighty private schools in the Dallas area. Most of the schools are operated by the Roman Catholic Church, but many have been established recently in Protestant church buildings. Although consenting to house these schools, church leaders state that they should not be used to avoid desegregated public education. A few schools have enrolled a small number of students from black and brown populations. However, the proportion of minorities in the private schools is exceedingly small.

BACKGROUND AND HISTORY

The Texas Constitution of 1866 provided that income from the permanent school fund should be employed exclusively for the education of white children. This constitution also gave the legislature the power to levy a tax for educational purposes provided that all the tax money paid by blacks was to be used for the maintenance of a system of public schools for them exclusively (*Vernon's Constitution* 1866: II, 420).

The Reconstruction legislature of 1867 eliminated segregation, and the constitution of 1869 did not mention separate schools. However, the legislatures of 1873 and 1875 repealed most of the laws of the Reconstruction period. The present constitution reestablished separation of race but mandated impartial provision for each (*Vernon's Constitution* 1866: II, 470).

Maintenance of separate school systems was enforced on the state level by supplemental legislation known as the Gilmer-Aiken law or the School Program Act of 1949, which prohibited expenditure of public funds in integrated schools (*Vernon's Civil Statutes*).

The final decree of *Brown* v. *Board of Education* (*Brown* II) was handed down on 31 May 1955; it required that segregated education be ended "with all deliberate speed." In October of that year, *McKinney* v. *Blankenship* (1955) established that the state constitution and statutory provisions were unconstitutional to the extent that they required segregation for the allocation and expenditure of public school funds. However, the decision in this case did not force integration. It held only that segregation was unconstitutional.

SCHOOL DESEGREGATION IN DALLAS

The Dallas Independent School District, the seventh largest school system in the nation, first experienced litigation concerning school desegregation in 1955 immediately following *Brown* II. At that time, the NAACP filed suit against the school system. In 1957, the U.S. Fifth Circuit Court of Appeals ruled that Dallas schools must be desegregated "with all deliberate speed" but set no specific date for implementation. The same appellate court, in 1960, upheld a "stairstep" plan that was to integrate one grade a year. After a few years, it became apparent that this approach would produce no significant results in eliminating racially separate schools. Finally, in 1965, the appeals court threw out the stair-step plan and ordered that all grades be integrated by September 1967. The extent to which that order was implemented was still of relatively little impact. In October 1970, the Dallas legal services office of the Office of Economic Opportunity filed suit in behalf of twenty-one blacks and Mexican-American plaintiffs asking U.S. District Judge William M. Taylor, Jr. to develop a comprehensive plan to effectively desegregate the "tri-ethnic school system." A major change resulted in that faculties were finally integrated on a 75-to-25 ratio of white to black in each of the 180 schools from elementary through the secondary levels.

In August 1971, Judge Taylor approved a plan that proposed a design to effect a "confluence of cultures" program, incorporating, among other things, closed circuit television exchanges among elementary schools wherein many features of instruction and interethnic exposure could be facilitated. Plaintiffs appealed to halt the plan, pending the awaited ruling in the overall suit.

School opened in the fall of 1971 without major incident after a fairly substantial student reassignment was established. Few white students responded when scheduled for busing to previously all-black schools. Whites leaving the school system and accelerated private school enrollments were the predictable results, whereas the number of blacks transported to previously all-white schools increased significantly.

Almost four years passed while the plaintiffs waited for a ruling from the circuit court that would once and for all require that the current plan be discarded in favor of one that would meet what they considered to be adequate constitutional standards. Finally, on 23 July 1975 that decision came: the dual system was to be dismantled by January 1976. Judge Taylor's order was vacated in a thirty-seven-page opinion providing for the formulation of a new plan and for periodic progress reports by the district court until implementation was achieved.

After a series of last-minute evasion efforts by DISD authorites, including seeking a stay order from the U.S. Supreme Court, which was denied, a new plan was formulated and announced by the school board. Concurrently, anti-busing forces mobilized and there quickly emerged a highly vocal and politically forceful movement to oppose student reassignment by means of forced busing. At the same time business, religious, and civic leaders responded to the order by offering their support. The media responded in a way that provided informative coverage. Both broadcast and print news outlets gave in-depth attention to sound, well-balanced features that called for the rational, law-abiding inclinations of countless organizations and centers of influence.

The DISD plan, submitted to Judge Taylor on 10 September 1975, called for busing about 18,000 students—6,000 Anglo, 10,000 black, and 2,000 Mexican-American; forty-six schools were to remain all-minority in composition. Given saturated media coverage (including an unprecedented all-network television "simulcast" during prime time), an impressive selling job was done to provide detailed information and to gain public acceptance—all to no avail. Judge Taylor, within a week, rejected the DISD proposal and ordered plaintiffs and defendants to produce yet another plan. There were "46 reasons," he said, why the proposal plan was not acceptable—the number of schools that would remain as one-race enrollment.

All schools within the DISD were included in the 1975 court order except East Oak Cliff and Seagoville; the latter area was isolated geographically on the periphery of the city and the former is a predominantly black section of the city. Consideration was given to including other school systems that were adjacent to the DISD. The suburban school systems that surrounded the city of Dallas were named in the suit. All but Highland Park, one of the most affluent areas, were dropped. The decision in *Tasby* v. *Highland Park Independent School District* (1975) was based on the Milliken standard, which held that cross-district desegregation could be implemented only when there was evidence that the school districts or the state had contributed to segregation. This suburban school district was not included in the school desegregation order for Dallas because there was no evidence that it had contributed to school segregation in Dallas. Another district that shares a common boundary with the city of Dallas is the Richardson Independent School District. It too was excluded from the court order. The Richardson Independent School District extends into a small portion of the city of Dallas. Highland Park and University Park are incorporated cities within Dallas city limits that also have independent school districts.

INSTITUTIONAL DISCRIMINATION AND PAST COMMUNITY ACTION

The Greater Dallas Human Relations Commission was established in 1969. For the past two years, it was funded privately and locally by the Zales and Hobitzzelle foundations, and had an annual budget of $50,000. The commission is currently funded by the United Way and has a budget of $90,000 per year.

There are twenty-four members on the commission. The racial composition is Anglo eleven, black eight, Mexican-American four, and Native American one. Members are elected by community-wide nominations (there were 450 nominations for the last election) and serve a two-year term. A member may succeed himself or herself for one additional term. The staff of the commission consists of a director and three professional workers.

In 1971, the commission received some federal funds over a two-to-three-year period from the Emergency School Aid Program and later from the Emergency School Aid Act. With the funds, student human relations programs were initiated in the schools to help all children as well as many parents with the problems concerning school desegregation.

The commission relies heavily on conciliation because it is an unofficial organization with no subpoena power. Prior to implementation of the school desegregation plan, the commission researched areas of the country that were experiencing difficulty in undergoing court-ordered desegregation. At the invitation of the commission, a leader from the city of Louisville came to Dallas to discuss with the community network problems that could have been avoided in that city. Although the commission has been of some help largely in conciliating complaints of employment discrimination, it is fair to conclude that community organization and school desegregation has not been an area of strong contribution. The other institutional systems in Dallas that could deal with discrimination are like the commission: weak, inert, or outright adversaries of the racial minorities.

In January 1971, a survey conducted by the Greater Dallas Housing Opportunity Center for the federal Department of Housing and Urban Development revealed incidences of undisguised discrimination, particularly in apartment rentals (Rencher 1974). A report was issued that named Dallas as one of the most segregated cities in the United States (Rencher 1977). These data indicate that Dallas has begun to deal with the racial discrimination but has a long way to go in completing the job.

Involvement of religious institutions was indirect and passive; religious leaders attempted to influence the values of the business leaders who participated in negotiations with the minorities. At the same time, the churches were establishing private schools, which could be called private alternatives to desegregated public education. Most church-sponsored schools proclaimed to be open institutions, however, and a few enrolled some black and brown students as token evidence.

Dallas is a business-controlled community that has been referred to as a business oligarchy. The political structure, the educational system, voluntary health and welfare associations, and even the churches and synagogues all are controlled by business. Because business power is so pervasive in the community, its leaders of necessity must become involved in nonbusiness issues such as school desegregation.

Through the years of dependency on business, the other systems in the community have failed to develop the skill and capacity to rally together segments of the community outside their control. Thus an educational issue such as school desegregation that involves public opinion and political, economic, racial, and educational components for successful implementation could not be handled by the school system alone. The only system in Dallas capable of marshaling a joint effort in the community is the business sector.

Despite its pervasive control, there are sectors of the community beyond the immediate influence of the business oligarchy. These are the racial and ethnic communities whose residents have been treated largely as invisible people in the past and excluded from participation in public affairs. The past practice of a few top business leaders arriving at a decision that they believed to be appropriate and then assigning some of their colleagues the responsibility of carrying it out did not work for the school desegregation issue. The top business leaders did not know the real desires and complaints of the plaintiffs and the populations they represented. There had been limited contact in the past.

Moreover, the school desegregation issue clearly was a national issue that transcended the limits of the local community. Dallas business leaders said they had to become involved after they read about problems with school desegregation caused in Boston and Louisville. Dallas business leaders did not want their community to experience similar disruptions. Also they wanted to avoid situations that would result in whites leaving the city, as they had in Atlanta and in Washington. Finally, they were quite anxious to maintain a good business climate in the region. The business leaders considered community turbulence associated with school desegregation to be incompatible with a good business climate, which clearly ranked as their highest priority.

The Dallas Citizens Council, consisting of the heads of the 200 largest businesses in the area, stood at the top of the decision-making hierarchy. It had not taken proper cognizance of the school desegregation issue, largely because its members were not in contact with and had no mechanism for promoting dialogue between its members and racial minorities. There is evidence that this group had lost some of its contacts with other sectors of the community as well. For example, a professional mass media specialist was elected mayor. He was not the candidate endorsed by the citizens council, as most mayors had been in the past. Although the insurgent political movement was short lived and lasted for only five years (a regular with good business connections succeeded him), the fact that a more or less independent mayor could get elected shocked the business establishment, which largely had had its way in politics in the past.

The election of a nonestablishment mayor and the court cases brought by blacks and Mexican-Americans demanding a fair share of educational services upset the equilibrium and threatened the profitable business climate that had been in existence. This tranquility had been maintained at great expense to the aspirations and interests of racial and ethnic minorities in Dallas. When these minorities began to protest the top business leaders in Dallas were concerned, but they did not know how to deal with the situation.

Younger business leaders who wanted a role in the decision-making process, and some of the older business leaders who had maintained lines of communication with other sectors of the community through community service organizations in both white and minority sectors, realized that solutions to the impending school desegregation issue depended as much on the responses of the minorities as on the initiatives of the majority. Some of the younger business leaders connected with national firms that had outlets in other cities that had experienced court-ordered school desegregation alerted their Dallas employees of the need to deal affirmatively with desegregation.

The Urban League became involved at an early stage too. At one of its meetings, an attorney advised its board that the school desegregation issue was too complicated to be handled by politicians and lawyers alone, that chaos would occur if the community did not get involved. This prediction was to spur some well-respected business leaders into action.

The Dallas Citizens Council and the Greater Dallas Planning Council—top business and political groups—were informed of the need to develop a unified urban planning strategy that could tackle governmental, educational, housing, and other community problems in addition to those more specifically concerned with business. The top business leadership in the community acknowledged that a structure different from that which currently existed was needed to implement such a strategy. The Chamber of Commerce had already been experimenting with obtaining a broader base of community input by utilizing Chicano administrators and staff in its Urban Affairs Department and was asked to refine the proposal for a new comprehensive planning structure in the community.

The structure that came into being was the Dallas Alliance. The forty-member Dallas Alliance Board of Trustees was black, brown, and white; members were affiliated with a range of community organizations, including the Dallas Community Council and the Dallas Black Chamber of Commerce. It was one of the first decision-making forums in the community to include community leaders representing a wide range of social groups. The Alliance was financed largely by the Chamber of Commerce.

The Dallas Alliance was conceived as an organization that would serve as a catalyst to stimulate and encourage combined efforts of community groups in seeking resolution to urban problems affecting Dallas. The purposes of the Dallas Alliance are to provide leadership, to help solve urban problems, to stimulate joint action by governmental and private concerns, and to generate citizen involvement in the community development process.

The Dallas Alliance is governed by a board of trustees comprised of eight ex-officio members, eight elected or appointed governmental officials, and twenty-four members from the business sector and the community at large. The racial composition of the board reflects the racial ratio of the city's population.

During the month of October 1975, the Dallas Alliance became involved in the Dallas desegregation issue when the board of trustees approved the formation of an education task force. Prior to that time, the Alliance had presented its posture on quality public education in a public statement published in Dallas newspapers in July 1975. The statement called for community acceptance and support for whatever plan emerged as the district court's order. In addition, representatives of the Alliance convened meetings with the various lawyers involved in the litigation, in an effort to effect a resolution that would be agreeable to all parties, including the court. For several months Alliance trustees and staff diligently communicated with members of the various factions in the community. Past experiences and the lack of trust and confidence that the parties had in each other prevented the success of these efforts.

It soon became apparent that there was a stalemate. Increased tensions in the community prompted several Alliance trustees to consider the feasibility of forming a group to address the education issue and possibly to develop a plan for desegregation to present to the court. Consequently, the Education Task Force of the Dallas Alliance was formed, and held its first meeting in early October 1975, when it identified its mission as the development of a school desegregation plan and presented a proposal to the board of trustees for approval. It was the general opinion of Alliance trustees that a consensus plan developed by a racially mixed community group could provide a stimulus for community support.

The Alliance task force was a twenty-one-member group consisting of seven Anglos, seven Mexican-Americans, six blacks, and one American Indian. Task force members represented a variety of community elements, including businessmen, lawyers, blue-collar workers, civic leaders, clergy, housewives, governmental professionals, and educators. Each member of the task force brought the needs and concerns of his or her respective community or group to the attention of others.

The objective of the task force was to develop a plan representing a consensus of the various groups involved. In the original challenge to the task force, Chairman Jack Lowe, Sr., acknowledged and emphasized the difficulty of the task force mission. He stated that the chance for successful completion of this task was perhaps one in a thousand and that the group would have to dedicate and commit itself to an extraordinary effort and openness. Mr. Lowe further acknowledged, at the outset, that the lack of intergroup trust characteristic of the participants in the suit also existed for the task force, and that all white, black, and brown members would have to develop sensitivity to this issue.

Paul Geisel, a specialist in urban affairs, was engaged in the role of executive director. Geisel himself is white, and was the minority group candidate for the position. Geisel had received his Ph.D. from Vanderbilt University and was professor of urban affairs at the University of Texas in Arlington. A black law firm headed by H. Ron White was retained as one set of attorneys for the Dallas Alliance and the education task force when the appeal process began. Walter Javin, a black attorney, and Dan Solis, a Mexican-American attorney, associated with White on the case.

Several resource persons were invited to Dallas to discuss concepts of school desegregation. Additionally, local representatives from the city manager's office, the county government, and the DISD met with the task force to provide data and statistics on the county transportation networks, county resources, city population, migration patterns, demographics, and school system.

By mid-December 1975, the task force had received an enormous amount of input from educators, specialists, and consultants, and had evaluated various education models employed in other communities. Task force members articulated to Geisel the types of programming and concepts that they considered appropriate for the Dallas community. Geisel then met with DISD staff to enlist their assistance in creating a tentative plan based on the recommendations of the task force. The completed material, submitted to the task force by DISD staff on 6 January 1976 essentially served as a working document. Task force members, equipped with a wealth of information and a number of alternatives, revised, modified, and negotiated each concept of the plan until a consensus was reached.

The importance of the work of the task force became apparent to the community on 18 December 1975. Judge Taylor called a meeting to discuss the case with all litigants, including the plaintiffs, members of the school board, members of the city council, and the attorneys. It was clear on that date that the plaintiffs, defendants, and intervenors' attorneys had not been able to agree on a joint plan. Additionally, the district court had been apprised that the education task force of the Dallas Alliance was attempting to prepare a plan to be submitted. The chairman of the Education task force presented a statement regarding the composition of the task force, its concerns, and its objectives. The district court made it clear that the efforts of the task force in attempting to develop educationally sound and constitutionally viable desegregation concepts were appreciated. The district court encouraged the task force to continue its efforts. The task force continued to work for a period of approximately five months.

A major stumbling block in the path to a consensus plan was the student racial ratio for each school. Even though the overall racial makeup in the DISD was 44 percent Anglo, 44 percent black, and 12 percent brown, the racial ratio in the first grade was approximately 75 percent minority and 25 percent Anglo. It was clear that an Anglo majority in every school in the DISD was impossible. Each ethnic group had different priorities, needs, and motivations for developing a workable desegregation plan. The plan that evolved from the task force was based on these objectives: to ensure that the system was sensitive and responsive to the educational needs of each child, to provide equal educational opportunity and thus remove all vestiges of a dual school system, and to establish a strong accountability system to assure quality education for all. The primary intent was to provide educational programs appropriate and beneficial to each student regardless of age, sex, or ethnicity.

The concepts presented to the district court were designed to erase, insofar as possible, the importance of locality and racial identification of schools through the creation of magnet schools, vanguards, and academies. This approach, in addition to its educational merit, was intended to minimize any imagined or real stigma associated with race.

THE DESEGREGATION PLAN

To monitor implementation of the final order, which was filed on 7 April 1976, the Dallas division of the United States District Court required internal accountability of the DISD and external accountability through independent audit. Additionally, a court-appointed citizens' group, the Tri-Ethnic Committee, monitors the DISD and submits reports to the court on implementation of the order.

The Tri-Ethnic Committee had been established by the 1971 court order. Fifteen new members were appointed by the court for staggered two-year terms beginning 1 July 1976. The group has no legal authority but functions as a liaison between the community and the court to monitor the implementation of the plan. It acts in an advisory capacity only to the district court. Enforcement is a function of the court.

The desegregation order of 1971 proposed to involve 7,000 students, but it was rejected by the appeals court because it had no effect on most of the district's one-race schools. The 1976 desegregation plan included busing 17,000 students in grades four to eight (out of a total enrollment of approximately 140,000) within their own subdistricts. In addition, 10,000 students volunteered to ride buses to attend magnet schools. The court order required six subdistricts, each having approximately the same racial makeup plus or minus 5 percent of the DISD as a whole. Crosstown busing of students was not part of the 1976 plan.

The Student Transportation Report from the External Audit of the court order shows a total of 9,156 students in grades four to six and 3,760 in grades seven to eight or, 12,916 students, being bused for desegregation purposes. Of the total bused in grades four to six, 31.1 percent are Anglo, 54.4 percent black, and 15.5 percent Mexican-American. In grades seven and eight, 25.9 percent are Anglo, 64.7 percent are black, and 9.4 percent are Mexican-American (U.S. District Court 1976). Transportation is provided to facilitate desegregation only for students assigned under the court order and for students who choose to attend a magnet school. When twenty or more students are traveling to a single destination under court order, transportation is provided; otherwise cards are given to each student to ride public buses at no charge. Special arrangements for transportation are made if the one-way combined distance from home to the Dallas Transit System route to an assigned school is greater than two miles. The involvement in the DISD in providing transportation for students is minimal.

Four senior-high magnet schools established by the court order were opened in September 1976 (see table 7.1). An additional three were opened by 1979. The current magnets are Business and Management, Creative Arts, Health Professions, and Transportation. Student stations are reserved for all groups so that the number of black, Mexican-American, and Anglo students equals the total student capacity of the school times the ratio of each group of students in the grades nine to twelve student population in the DISD as of 1 December 1975 plus or minus 10 percent.

Students in the DISD, according to the plan, may choose to attend any magnet school, transfer majority to minority (within specified guidelines), or attend a regular school in a designated attendance zone. The Dallas plan does not provide for pairing of schools. Where possible, the plan recommends that students who live in naturally integrated areas should not be reassigned to achieve desegregation elsewhere. Parent advisory groups are recommended for the early childhood and intermediate school centers within each attendance zone. The school district is allowed to adjust attendance zones and reassign students to conform with building space requirements, and to promote further desegregation.

The court order further provides for construction of new schools and renovation of existing facilities. Additionally, a central core of high schools is to be established within a two-mile distance of the inner-city highway loop.

The plan further mandates that bilingual education in Dallas be expanded and that it be based on the state board of education plan. In June 1977, the program was operational in twenty-nine schools. Funding is through the Texas Education Agency, from the federal Elementary and Secondary Education Act, and also from local district funds. Multicultural courses are to be established at all grade levels and in November 1976 already existed in twelve kindergarten to grade three centers.

Desegregation of school personnel is another feature of the plan. Teachers, principals, and other certified professional personnel are to include 31 percent blacks and 8 percent Mexican-Americans. Beginning in 1977, the school system implemented an administrative structure of 44 percent Anglos, 44 percent blacks, and 12 percent Mexican-Americans. Anglo and black percentages remain equal but if the Mexican-American enrollment increases to 14 percent, for

TABLE 7.1. Enrollment Figures for Senior High Magnet Schools for November 1976

School	Enrollment	White (%)	Black (%)	Mexican-American (%)
Business	1,482	14.7	69.5	15.8
Arts	708	40.8	51.4	7.8
Health	875	29.8	58.4	11.3
Transportation	623	29.3	50.2	20.5

Source: Dallas Independent School District, Dallas, Texas.

example, then both black and Anglo percentages would decrease to 43 percent each, according to the court order. School assignments for teachers and principals are made in accordance with *Singleton* v. *Jackson Municipal Separate School District* (1970), but if need occurs in special programs, DISD may vary the ratio with respective percentages established by Singleton.

THE SCHOOL BOARD AND THE SUPERINTENDENT

Two methods of selecting school board members have been employed during the period of the desegregation controversy. Prior to 1974, all nine members ran at large, that is, the entire DISD voting population voted on all nine members. Even then, there was a local area component to the election. The DISD was divided into six districts and a school board member was chosen from each district. To be chosen as a district candidate, one had to live in that district. The remaining candidates could stand for election regardless of where they resided within the DISD. Each member served a three-year term, but the terms were staggered so that all nine were never elected at the same time.

Beginning in 1974, the DISD held its first single-member district election as set up by the Texas legislature (Texas House 1973). The geographic area served by the school system was divided into nine districts, each with a total population of 89,500 or more. Voters in each district vote only for the candidate running in that district. The districts were formed according to 1970 federal census information.

In 1974, all school board members were elected for a three-year term. In 1977, all nine ran again. Five would serve two-year terms and four would serve four-year terms, the length of service being determined by drawing lots. In 1979, two-year members would come up for reelection. In 1981, all nine members would come up for reelection. This system is used because DISD districts are reappointed every ten years according to U.S. census population figures. Each time all nine members run, they draw lots to see who will serve two years or four years.

Since the 1974 elections by single-member districts, there have been a total of sixteen different members. Since 1974, the board composition has been two blacks, one Mexican-American, and six Anglos.

On the issue of desegregation, the school board has clearly split into two distinct factions—the Anglos versus the minorities. Though the whites do not overtly oppose desegregation, it seems clear that the Anglo and minority concepts of integration differ considerably. The whites cling to phrases like "neighborhood schools" and "naturally integrated schools." They seem to prefer equalizing facilities and often stress in their platforms that they oppose forced busing. The three minority members usually favor whatever promotes desegregation in the schools, though there have been exceptions.

The school board members are usually cautious in their public remarks to constituents on desegregation issues. The board was careful at all times to state that it would support the law. However, both the minority and the Anglo factions were equally persistent in assuring their constituents that they would do everything within the law to bring about popular and practical results. As one white board member noted on 15 June 1974, in reference to an out-of-court settlement, "I don't see any reason to back down and give away the ball game. In the time we've been given we've already made great strides" (Interview 1974). The board acquiesced as time passed and by the time the final order was issued in April 1976, the Anglo faction was supporting full compliance with the law and a smooth transition to desegregation.

Though the board was quite willing to fight the matter out in court, it did not encourage civil disobedience—at least not overtly. On 20 June 1975 the *Times-Herald* reported that the board members were in fact cautioned by their attorneys not to make public statements on topics related to Dallas school desegregation during the following thirty days. When the court made rulings, the board members would sometimes express approval or disappointment but that was usually as far as they would go.

The general rule seemed to be "do all you can within the limits of the law" to avoid desegregation. This sentiment was perhaps best revealed in a statement released by the board after they voted to seek a stay of the appeals court ruling through the U.S. Supreme Court: "We recognize unless and until a stay is granted, the fifth circuit order remains in effect and accordingly the board has scheduled immediate follow-up sessions with its attorneys to begin work for complying with the order" (School Board 1975).

The board's statement called for the community to respond with "dignity, honor, reason, understanding, and calm." The vote on the appeal exemplifies the racial factionalism that exists on the board: five whites voted for the appeal while three of the minority-group members voted against it.

It appears that the Anglo members wanted to maintain the court struggle in hopes of avoiding or minimizing busing, whereas the minority members would have welcomed an out-of-court settlement. As one black board member noted, "I would like to see a settlement in the best interests of the children. The trouble is the board doesn't want a unitary system" (Interview 1974). In contrast was the statement of a white board member given on the same day, "Any settlement would mean more busing of children than at present. That would only result in an acceleration of the Anglo exodus from the city (Interview 1974).

Despite the conservative orientation of a majority of the school board, there was apparently little or no conflict between it and Superintendent Nolan Estes, who seemed to have little involvement with the school board's politics. Estes appeared to be more interested in implementing the court's rulings and keeping the district's school system running smoothly and efficiently during this period of transition.

The *Times-Herald* reported on 13 March 1976 that Estes, in a confidential memo issued to the board, said, "It is our responsibility to make the court order work and certainly the staff is ready and willing to do so.

"As I told the business and civic leaders . . . the Alliance plan is a concept and now it is up to the board to spell out the details. The plan has optimum flexibility."

When the final order of April 1976 finally came down, the board seemed fairly resigned to comply. There never was a question about violating the court order. There was, however, a good deal of vacillating back and forth on whether to cross-appeal. But the incentive to appeal seemed to have diminished considerably after so many years of court battles.

Subsequent to the 1976 court order to desegregate the DISD, the superintendent resigned. Although there does not appear to be any direct correlation between desegregation and the resignation, the turbulence of protracted litigation and the inevitable court order that requires school desegregation is an exhausting experience for any chief school administrator. Moreover, the new educational arrangements ordered by the court are radically different from what existed before and require a great deal of energy to implement them in good faith.

Estes' priority was abiding by the law and ensuring a smooth and peaceful implementation of the court order. Because he was named in the suit, *Eddie Mitchell Tasby et al.* v. *Dr. Nolan Estes et al.,* Superintendent Estes did not wait for the board's approval to begin seeking support for the April 1976 court-ordered desegregation plan. In a private meeting with school principals, he praised the plan and urged moving forward with it in a positive manner (*Times-Herald,* 1976: 3/8). The superintendent supported both the Dallas Alliance plan and the school board's negative interpretation of that plan; in this way, he took a position that aimed to please those on both sides of the issue. Thus, when the board adopted a resolution one month before the court order was handed down requesting that the court not meddle with administrative and educational aspects of the Dallas schools, the superintendent supported their resolution as well as the plan, which included many administrative and educational changes.

There never seemed to be any question about whether the superintendent would continue in his post. His job at all times seemed secure. But in addition to the exhaustion that the period of extensive litigation heaped upon him, quite possibly the superintendent had attempted to please both sides too many times and was unable to act with legitimacy once the final court order was handed down.

OTHER COMMUNITY GROUP INVOLVEMENT

In a 12 September 1976 nationally syndicated article, Bryan Wooley, a *Times-Herald* editorial writer, stated: "Except for the minor logistical errors—students failing to find the right bus, or drivers losing their way along unfamiliar routes—the first week under the desegregation order has been unspectacular as the beginning of any school year. The reaction of some was disbelief that such a smooth transition was occurring in Dallas, which has the largest public school system in Texas" (Wooley 1976).

The article continues to make other observations that should not be overlooked: "More specifically, though, the success so far of the new Dallas busing plan is attributable to two facts: the Judge's Order was written almost entirely by representatives of the community itself; and the city's leaders are determined to make it work" (Wooley 1976).

Of what did this leadership and new community support consist? The political and business leaders promoted a policy of peaceful and smooth transition toward desegregation after the court order had been issued. They became a very positive force in encouraging nonviolent acceptance of the court's order. These leaders seemed content to let the case run its course in the courts. The *Times-Herald* reported on 15 June 1974, "a sampling of the Dallas leadership would seem to indicate there has been no public pressure brought to force settlement of the suit. It appears, instead, the city is resigned to an eventual decision by the U.S. Fifth Circuit Court of Appeals. Charles Roper, board chairman of the Dallas Chamber of Commerce, stated that 'By and large, I feel the city leadership, including the school district, has resigned itself to the fact we're going to have to wait and do what the Court orders.'"

Just as leaders were slow to support an out-of-court settlement, they were, in general, hesitant to make overt statements or moves that might indicate antidesegregation sentiments. A middle-of-the-road stance appeared to be the rule.

There were exceptions, however. For example, the city council told the city attorney in December 1975 to meet with the U.S. District Court judge to discuss the judge's attitude toward the possibility of the city of Dallas withdrawing from the desegregation case. Some believed this to be a tactic to avoid desegregation. According to this reasoning, if a city-wide busing order were issued, the court could not order the city to use Dallas Transit System buses to transport students unless the city was a party to the suit (*Times-Herald* 1975. 12/30).

After Judge Taylor issued his April 1976 ruling, the leaders moved from general passivity to a positive approach of support for the court order. Patience and understanding by the citizens were encouraged by Dallas leaders, and violence was discouraged. A statement issued by the Greater Dallas Community Relations Commission read as follows: "Cooperation can only be derived from individuals, pro and con, who follow orderly and peaceful guidelines to whatever they feel must be done in reaction to the court's decision" (*Times-Herald* 1976: 3/11). Most black community leaders favored desegregation but opposed the specific plan that was selected. On 10 March 1976, a group of black community leaders met at the Martin Luther King Community Center and expressed disappointment with the court's selection of the Alliance plan. However, they agreed not to take action until the plan was further explored (*Times-Herald* 1976: 3/11).

In general city leaders, including majority and minority representatives, were organized in their approach to achieving peaceful implementation of the plan. On the day the final order by the court was filed, Mayor Wes Wise stated, "A decision from the court now appears imminent and we must deal with it." He called a special meeting of the Dallas City Council to prepare a contingency plan to prevent disturbances that might occur as a reaction to the court order. The council met with the city attorney and the city manager to develop a course of action to follow once the school board was notified by the court. Wise noted, "We need the leadership to convey to citizens that regardless of what the order is, it must be obeyed" (*Times-Herald* 1975: 7/17).

A cooperative effort between the Dallas Chamber of Commerce and DISD was launched to implement the magnet school concept that was part of the court order. The chamber of commerce established several committees to help in the implementation of the concept. The persons heading these committees were some of Dallas' leading businessmen. The business leaders together with civic and political leaders set the mood and the pace for other sectors of the Dallas community. Their participation in school desegregation helped contribute to a more or less smooth transition.

Before the ink was barely dry on the court order, the Committee for Smooth Transition, a racially mixed group composed largely of members of the League of Women Voters and the Dallas City Council of PTAs, had begun to solicit public support. Concurrently, community organizations and community leaders diligently met with parent and community groups to explain the substance of the court order not only in terms of the impact on the students in the public school system, but also in terms of the potential benefits to be derived by various segments of the community under the plan.

The Dallas Council of Churches, in cooperation with other racially mixed organizations, sponsored a Community-wide Forum on Quality Public Education that was attended by over 500 community representatives, leaders, DISD officials, and staff. Again, the purpose was to generate excitement for, and peaceful acceptance of, the new Dallas plan for school segregation.

Numerous youth services agencies in Dallas met to jointly discuss and plan for cooperative after-school programming with their respective agencies and DISD.

The DISD and various community groups sponsored a number of training, orientation, and action programs for staff, parents, and others. For example, in one week in March 1976, the superintendent broadcast an address over television to school district employees, a briefing was held for representatives of key parent and community groups, a briefing was held for key business and government leaders, and a meeting was held for all principals. The school board held a meeting to discuss educational aspects of the plan, and each school principal held meetings with community representatives. In addition, clergymen held meetings on their own to discuss their role in the implementation.

In April 1976, following the issuance of Judge Taylor's final order, school officials began a series of television broadcasts and meetings designed to explain the order. School employees were addressed again, as were city-wide and neighborhood leaders. Each school in the district held a meeting to explain the order and student assignments to parents. Television stations aired a film explaining the desegregation plan, and school board members personally answered phone calls concerning the order.

Representatives of the teachers in Dallas had been involved in the issue since 1969, when the Dallas Classroom Teachers (a National Education Association affiliate) first issued public statements and passed a resolution supporting integration of the schools. In 1971, when a token number of students were bused, an appeals panel was established to hear teacher grievances from teachers who also were reassigned. Many problems arose then, and the DISD encouraged teachers to seek legal redress. Trouble shooters or ombudsmen, who were teachers were used to arbitrate conflicts.

Further evidence of community support for the spirit and intent of the court's order was demonstrated on 11 December 1976 by approval of an $80 million School Improvement Bond Package. Included in the bond package were specific allocations for new schools required by the court order. It has been reported that from the precincts identified as predominately black, over 75 percent of all votes cast in those precincts voted in favor of the School Improvement Program. It is difficult to assess the meaning of this vote. Did it represent acceptance of the desegregation plan or acceptance of that portion of the plan that mandated new facilities?

EFFECTS OF DESEGREGATION

As stated earlier, the U.S. Fifth Circuit Court of Appeals ordered the Dallas Independent School District to utilize six subdistricts for student assignment purposes with each having approximately the racial makeup plus or minus 5 percent of the DISD as a whole, with the exception of East Oak Cliff and Seagoville.

The court found the DISD student population for grades kindergarten through twelve to be 141,122 and the racial and ethnic composition of that student population to be 41.4 percent Anglo, 44.5 percent black, and 13.4 percent Mexican-American, and 1.0 percent other. The court ordered the student assignment plan that adopted the concepts embodied in the desegregation plan of the Educational Task Force of the Dallas Alliance "for removal of all vestiges of a dual system in the Dallas Independent School District." Yet, the U.S. District Court for the Northern District of Texas ordered a student assignment plan that isolated one almost all-black subdistrict.

East Oak Cliff has a racial and ethnic student population of 27,932, of which 95.0 percent is black, 3.1 percent is Mexican-American, and 1.9 percent is Anglo. The racial and ethnic population percentages in the East Oak Cliff subdistrict vary significantly from the city-wide percentages of Anglo, black, and Mexican-American students and are so far beyond the "plus or minus 5 percent" range of variability acceptable to the court for other subdistricts (except Seagoville) that this subdistrict cannot be construed as anything but a racially segregated subdistrict. As such, the presence of the racially segregated East Oak Cliff subdistrict violates the court's own standard for a student assignment plan and does not achieve the greatest practicable actual desegregation as required by the Supreme Court.

So that the educational experience in the Oak Cliff schools may be tailored to the unique cultural needs of the students, an assistant superintendent was appointed to oversee this subdistrict. This administrative officer is a black woman and is the only assistant superintendent based in a subdistrict. In general, the administrative structure of the Dallas Independent School District is centralized. The Oak Cliff subdistrict is the only one that is administered with decentralized authority.

What may have appeared at the outset to be an asset in which minorities might handle their own educational affairs is rapidly becoming a liability. It is said that black leaders in East Oak Cliff have been expending energy on "their" subdistrict instead of focusing on the total educational system. This should really be a plus for a heretofore neglected area. But not only is the remainder of the Dallas Independent School District not receiving the beneficial input and surveillance of blacks, but the issue of segregating blacks in East Oak Cliff has generated some philosophical differences within the black community. It is possible that the isolation of East Oak Cliff and the assignment of an on-site assistant superintendent for that district was planned in order to generate conflict within the black community and to deflect pressure exerted by blacks on the central school administration.

The controversial aspect of the nearly all-black subdistrict therefore may give rise not only to the racial isolation that it perpetuates but also may generate racial friction. Such internal bickering did not surface so clearly in the past, when segregation could be attributed to racial discrimination and external sources could be pointed to as the reason for the separation from the community at large. A sense of "we are in this together against a common enemy" prevailed then. Now the element of social-class conflict among blacks may emerge as a reality in this issue. Thus blacks in Dallas are faced with an internal conflict that is much different from the earlier conflicts they experienced when whites kept them a segregated minority.

Meanwhile, the white segregationists in the community, or those who grudgingly accepted integration, can use the nearly all-black subdistrict as a scapegoat by oversimplifying the internal struggle among blacks and defining it as an example of the fact that blacks are incapable of self-government and controlling their own affairs. The nearly all-black subdistrict in the Dallas plan is indeed controversial, and it does not yet appear what the ultimate outcome will be.

The Mexican-American community has insisted that it be dealt with as a separate entity. At times it forms a coalition with blacks such as on the school board. At other times it negotiates directly with the white establishment in terms of its own concerns. At times it appears to side with whites such as in its concern for neighborhood schools, although Mexican-American neighborhood schools may be a way of promoting local ethnic control. By maintaining a separate identity and refusing to be consolidated into a general minority category, the Mexican-American population has gained power. For example, the court-appointed Tri-Ethnic Committee has on it an equal number of blacks, browns, and whites.

The black and brown communities are aware of the fact that the white community can attempt to play one racial group off against the other. One way this was accomplished in the past was by identifying Mexican-Americans as whites. The DISD plan that was rejected by the court desegregated proportionately more Mexican-Americans than blacks. These and other kinds of differential treatment mean that the Mexican-American population must be on guard against being used by blacks or whites in ways that do not fulfill its own interests.

The Mexican-American population is approaching the critical mass that will enable it to have a political impact on the educational system as well as on other institutions in Dallas. Beyond its growing numerical strength, the Mexican-American population is now sufficiently differentiated to provide within it a leadership class that can negotiate with the establishment. There are members of this population who are trained and who have obtained experience in business administration, public administration, community organization, social work, education, the law, and other professions. Moreover, Mexican-Americans recently have gained elected and appointed positions in city government and in government-related organizations as well as in voluntary associations.

Media coverage of Dallas has lauded the success of the city in dealing with school desegregation. Success has been defined in terms of the lack of violence or school boycotts. Many local leaders attribute the successful desegregation to the fact that community leaders took the initiative and designed their own desegregation plan which the court accepted. Yet it is reasonable to question whether desegregation has actually occurred, given the exclusion of an East Oak Cliff. This question will likely have to be answered by the U.S. Supreme Court. If violence is avoided by maintaining segregation, the definition of success does not comply with traditional judicial rulings.

POSTSCRIPT: APPEAL OF THE PLAN

The Dallas branch of the NAACP appealed the court order that left half or more of the black students in racially segregated schools (U.S. Court of Appeals 1978). The entire plan was not rejected by the U.S. Fifth Court of Appeals, but the student-assignment section of the Dallas school desegregation plan was found not acceptable because of the number of one-race schools remaining. That part of the court-ordered plan that was rejected by the appeals court left 27,000 students of the 136,000 total in all-black schools.

According to the *New York Times,* "The court's main objection was to the district plan's creation of an all-black subdistrict in the East Oak Cliff section south of downtown Dallas. School officials contended that it provided a 'separate but superior education.' They said that the plan was the only feasible one in light of natural boundaries and white flight" (*New York Times* 1978: 4/26). The appeals court did not agree.

The appeals court said in its 1978 ruling: "We remand the case to the district court for the formulation of a new student-assignment plan and for findings to justify the maintenance of any one-race schools that may be a part of that plan. The district court is directed to include in its plan a majority-minority transfer option with adequate transportation" (*New York Times* 1978: 4/26). The direction has been set. The Dallas Independent School District is in its final approach to devising a plan to comply with the requirement of the U.S. Constitution. It has few options now. Thus far, the community has adapted to the desegregation of whites in a nonviolent way, but it has not fully experienced desegregation of blacks in public education.

In October 1977, the Dallas Independent School District wrote in *Up-Date,* its network newsletter, that the "'unparalleled' community support it received" contributed to the first year's successes. The newsletter indicated that its new goal was "to go even above and beyond the court order to achieve a first-class education for the sake of all our children." With continued help from the business community, Dallas may be able to desegregate all of its schools, and provide a quality education, too, if the definition for a desegregated school system is amended by the U.S. Supreme Court to extend from individual schools to districts.

BIBLIOGRAPHY

Brown v. *Board of Education* 1955. 349 U.S. 294 75 S. Ct. 753 (*Brown* II).

Beck, William W., and Glenn M. Linden. 1979. "Anglo and Minority Perceptions of Success in Dallas School Desegregation." *Phi Beta Kappan.* January.

Dallas Chamber of Commerce, Career Education, 1977. *The Dallas Story: Business Community Involvement in the Public Schools.* August.

DISD Staff 1976. Working document of desegregation plan submitted to Dallas Alliance Task Force on January 6.

Interview 1974. Interviews with school committee members June 15.

McKinney v. *Blankenship* 1955. 154 Tex 632, 282 SW 2d. 691.

New York Times 1978: 4/26.

Rencher, Rick, 1974. Speech at the Fair Housing Office.

Rencher, Rick, 1977. "City of Dallas Fair Housing: For Housing Plan." Report, Greatei Dallas Housing Opportunity Center, May, p. 1.

School Board 1975. Press statement released July 24.

Singleton v. *Jackson Municipal Separate School District.* 1970. *Federal Reporter* 419 F 2d. 1211.

Tasby v. *Estes* 1976. *Eddie Mitchell Tasby et al.* v. *Dr. Nolan Estes et al.* 412 F. Supp. 1192 (N.D. Tex.).

Tasby v. *Highland Park Independent School District.* 1976. No. 76–184. Second Amended Complaint *Tasby* v. *Estes,* 517 F. 2d.

Texas 1866. Article X, Section II, Constitution of 1866.

Texas House 1973. House Bill 206, Texas Legislature.

Times-Herald, Dallas, 1954: 6/15; 1975: 6/20, 7/17, 12/30; 1976· 3/8, 3/11, 3/13, 4/18.

U.S. District Court 1976. Dallas Division, Final Order by Judge William M. Taylor, Jr. CA3–4211–C (April 7); 1978. 572 F. 2d. 1010.

Vernon's Civil Statutes. Article 2922, II et seg., *Vernon's Texas Civil Statutes.*

Vernon's Constitution. Article VII, Section VII, *Vernon's Constitution of the State of Texas,* annotated, vol. 2, p. 420.

Wooley, Brian, 1976. Nationally syndicated newspaper article, September 12.

8

Mobile, Alabama: The Demise of State Sanctioned Resistance

Albert S. Foley

In 1954, when the *Brown* v. *Board of Education* decision was handed down by the U.S. Supreme Court, Mobile, Alabama was an almost totally segregated community with a totally segregated county-wide school system operated by an all-white, all-male, conservative five-member school board elected at large for staggered terms.

The chamber of commerce proclaimed that the city was a progressive, expanding center of trade as the nation's seventh largest port, with the world's largest concentration of paper-making machinery, the largest air force base located within the city limits of any city east of the Mississippi, and the most rapidly expanding growth rate in Alabama (table 8.1).

Mobile had grown from 65,000 before World War II to 252,000 during the four years of the war owing to the expansion of port and military activity and the huge shipbuilding operations up and down the Mobile River. There was some token desegregation at the huge federal Brookley Air Force Base and in the federal Corps of Engineers and post office employment patterns. The 124-

TABLE 8.1. Population of Mobile County, by Race, 1950–1970

	1950		1960		1970	
	No.	%	No.	%	No.	%
Total Mobile County	231,105	100.0	314,301	100.0	317,308	100.0
White	153,006	66.2	212,873	67.7	214,070	67.5
Non-white*	77,999	33.8	101,428	32.3	103,238	32.5

Source: *U.S. Census of Population.* Washington, D.C.: Government Printing Office.
*Includes less than one-half of 1 percent "other" than black.

year-old Roman Catholic institution of higher education, Spring Hill College, had partially desegregated in 1947 and had opened all departments to blacks by 1954.

Mobile generally adopted a "wait and see" policy at Alabama's official resistance to the 1954 U.S. Supreme Court decision. The governor, Gordon Persons, had officially declared it to be state policy to offer massive resistance to the Supreme Court's wide-ranging desegregation decisions. The state legislature passed resolutions of nullification and interposition to indicate its protest of racial desegregation. When the initial acts of massive resistance perpetrated by Alabama and other southern state legislatures were invalidated by the Supreme Court in 1955, it became evident that school boards would be faced with the necessity of complying with the *Brown* v. *Board of Education* decision.

In early August 1955, the Mobile County School Board issued a statement of policy that affirmed its intention to continue its segregation of the races in the schools under its jurisdiction. At a special meeting, it declared, "Any integration now is impossible without a disruption of our school system to such an extent as to impair its efficiency for an indefinite period . . ." (*Mobile Register* 1955: 8/16).

> It must be recognized that integration is not acceptable to the major proportion of our people. This is a factor that cannot be ignored, that is recognized by the Supreme Court in its decree implementing its decisions. The accomplishment of a complete and full result which the bulk of our people feel is imposed upon them by a superior power that as they see it was without adequate appreciation of the sociological, factual, and psychological conditions of our people may not be had at one blow. The traditions of two centuries can be altered by degrees only. This Board recognizes that these traditions must be altered under the law as decided by the Supreme Court; and that Court recognized by its decree that such alternation will require time (*Mobile Register* 1955: 8/16).

While affirming that the board's purpose was to attempt in good faith to perform its important public function of educating Mobile County youth, in the face of conflicting directives from the Alabama state constitution and decisions of the U.S. Supreme Court it did declare that it would comply with the provisions of applicable constitutional and statutory law of the state of Alabama, and with the decisions of the U.S. Supreme Court.

The board, to protect itself from possible action for contempt, stated:

> It should be understood that this Board does not seek either to defy or to ignore the decision of the Supreme Court; but it does intend within the law to exercise the judgment and discretion reposed in it by the people and recognized in the Supreme Court's decree so to perform its functions as at the same time to comply with the law and to achieve the best results in the education of the youth of Mobile County, maintaining scholastic standards and harmony with a minimum of potential for violence, disorder or friction that would greatly lessen the efficiency of public education in the county and would be of detriment alike to both races (*Mobile Register* 1955: 8/16).

FIRST ATTEMPTS

In August 1956, the voters of Alabama adopted a constitutional amendment that (1) empowered the state legislature to abolish public schools if necessary to prevent their integration; (2) authorized state aid in creating private segregated schools; (3) provided that counties and cities may sell or give away public facilities to private owners who could operate them on a segregated basis; and (4) gave parents the freedom of choice to send their children to schools attended only by members of their own race (see figure 8.1).

The amendment was the work of the state legislature committee headed by Senator Sam Englehardt of Macon and Bullock counties. Englehardt, who maintained his political power by the total suppression of the black vote in the two black belt counties he represented, was the state chairman of the White Citizens Council of Alabama. Senator Sam, whose constituency was more than 80 percent black, was an archconservative white supremacist. He took his cues from Virginia's massive resistance plan, from South Carolina's former Senator Jimmie Byrnes, and from the Mississippi State White Citizens Council, which were fashioning these patterns of legal resistance to desegregation.

The amendment had the overwhelming support of the state voters, who were overwhemingly white. The political powerlessness of the 40 to 45 percent black minority of the state population was obvious in the all-white state legislature, the all-white city and county governments across the state, and in the nearly all-white law enforcement agencies of the state.

The voters regarded the amendment as a stand-by empowerment, as they waited for the NAACP to attempt to bring desegregation into the Deep South. The last provision of the amendment encouraged one liberal, white upper-class lady, Dorothy Danner DaPonte, to exercise her freedom of choice in an attempt to desegregate one school. On 3 September, Mrs. DaPonte wrote a letter to the Mobile County School Board requesting the admission of her adopted black daughter, Carrie Mae McCants, into the all-white neighborhood school near their upper-class home in the Dog River area. Mrs. DaPonte acted without legal advice and without coordinating her efforts with those of the local NAACP black leaders. Unknown to her, they were in the process of preparing a group of thirty black parents to file a class action suit on behalf of their children, who were likewise kept out of nearby white schools within their residential neighborhoods.

On 13 September, the school board sent Mrs. DaPonte a letter officially denying her petition. It reaffirmed the official policy of evasion of the Supreme Court decision decided upon in the previous year. The local paper played up the school board's rejection of Mrs. DaPonte's petition with page-one importance. This led to a major community crisis in a pattern that would become all too familiar through constant reenactment.

The Ku Klux Klan, which had been revived in the local area as the Gulf Klans Inc., and other local antiblack zealots, embarked on a campaign of terror and intimidation aimed at this new target. Within a few days they organized a motorcade of a dozen and a half cars and trucks that journeyed out to the fashionable suburb and burned a cross at the entrance to Mrs. DaPonte's riverfront home. They initiated a telephone harassment marathon against Mrs. DaPonte and her relatives. Her uncle was harassed so severely that he had a heart attack on 19 September and died.

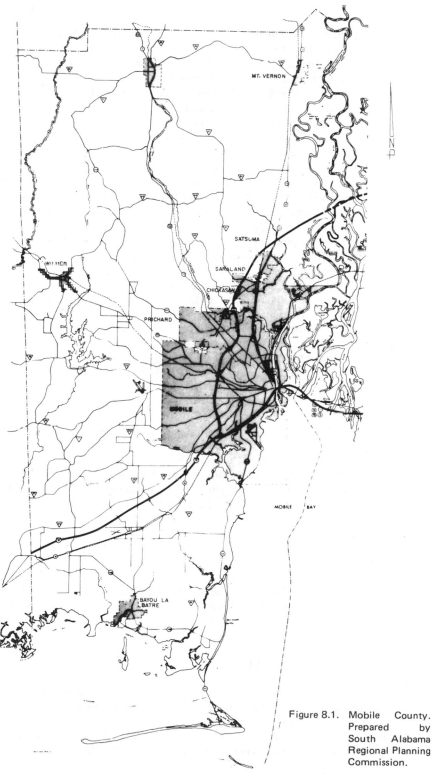

Figure 8.1. Mobile County.
Prepared by
South Alabama
Regional Planning
Commission.

The cross burnings were featured in the local press and on television and radio. They were also featured in the *New York Post* and in *Ebony* magazine, all of which added fuel to the Klan's fires of dozens of crosses in the city. The maraudings of the Klan were accompanied by the bombing of black homes, night parades in full regalia down the main street of the city, and ads in the newspaper. This series of violent events and the ensuing publicity turned attention from school desegregation to containment of the Klan.

The newly organized Mobile Council of Human Relations, the local unit of the Alabama Council on Human Relations and of the Southern Regional Council, petitioned the city commission to pass ordinances curbing the violence and intimidation by the Klan. This led to further disorders and more widespread efforts at intimidation of the white liberals who were sympathetic with the cause of school desegregation. It also resulted in decreased black parent involvement in the school desegregation cases.

Later that year the governor took action against the NAACP on a statewide basis. He secured a state court order prohibiting its operations in the state. This deprived the blacks of the vigorous leadership that the NAACP exerted from its New York and Washington offices.

Attention was further diverted from the school desegregation problem to the bus desegregation issue in December 1956, when Rosa Parks refused to yield her seat to a white passenger in Montgomery. For the rest of the year all eyes were focused on the courageous battle of the Montgomery Improvement Association led by Martin Luther King, Jr., that culminated a year later in the U.S. Supreme Court decision outlawing bus segregation in Montgomery.

In 1957, the state legislature amended its 1955 Pupil Placement Law, which had been enacted when the legislature abolished statutory requirement of segregated schools. The law stipulated seventeen standards for the assignment, transfer, and continuance of pupils in schools. Among these standards were availability of space and transportation, suitability of curriculum for the pupils, pupils' prior academic preparation, scholastic aptitude, psychological qualifications, effects upon other pupils' academic performance, and possibility of friction or disorder among pupils. The law was challenged by Birmingham black plaintiffs as incompatible with the Supreme Court's decision.

However, because the law did not mention race as one of the seventeen standards for pupil placement, the U.S. Fifth Circuit Court of Appeals and the U.S. Supreme Court both declared that the school placement law was not unconstitutional on its face even though the plaintiffs had insisted that its whole intent was to continue a system of separate schools for black and white in the state of Alabama. Under this pupil placement law, not even one black student was judged sufficiently qualified to be admitted to any all-white school in the Mobile area in the period 1958-1963.

LEGAL ACTION

After the black community had repeatedly petitioned the school board to desegregate the school system and received no positive response, a court case was initiated. Entitled *Birdie Mae Davis et al.* v. *Board of School Commissioners of Mobile County*, the initial complaint was filed on behalf of twenty students including Birdie Mae Davis and Henry Hobdy on 27 March 1963 in the federal

District Court of Southern Alabama in Mobile. The case was in litigation for fifteen years and was appealed to the U.S. Supreme Court.

Black lawyers representing the plaintiffs were Vernon Z. Crawford and Clarence Moses, of a Mobile law firm, and Constance Motley and Derrick Bell, from the NAACP Legal Defense Fund in New York. Crawford's life was later threatened for his presentation of this case. His home was bombed and the lives of his wife and children were endangered as well.

The timing of the case was in part responsible for the initial delays and postponements it encountered. It was filed just one week before Martin Luther King, Jr., began his historic and widely publicized demonstrations and marches in Birmingham at the other end of the state. The dramatic confrontations between the nonviolent demonstrators led by the Southern Christian Leadership Conference team and the ultraviolent Police Commissioner Eugene "Bull" Connor, with his electric cattle prods, his vicious police dogs, and his devastatingly effective fire hoses completely overshadowed other racial news in Alabama for the next half year. It also paralyzed peaceful efforts by testing the effectiveness of violent confrontation methods.

Nevertheless, on 6 June, three months after the filing of the *Birdie Mae Davis* suit, the Mobile School Board responded to the petition of the plaintiffs. It filed a brief opposing a preliminary injunction to compel immediate preparation of plans for desegregating the Mobile County Public Schools. The brief was accompanied by affidavits indicating that the schools' physical facilities had been taxed far beyond capacity by the 40 percent expansion of Mobile's school population that had occurred since the beginning of World War II. The brief also claimed that any desegregation plan calling for substantial and wholesale reshuffling of students for the 1963–1964 school year would result in chaotic conditions jeopardizing the education of all pupils.

The three-month delay in action by the district court had been facilitated when the U.S. Fifth Circuit Court of Appeals denied the plaintiffs' request that it compel Judge Daniel Thomas to make an immediate ruling. The Fifth Circuit Court decided that the Mobile judge was within his power of discretion in refusing an immediate order. However, he also failed to grant the school board's motion for dismissal of the plaintiffs' petitions.

DESEGREGATION IN ALABAMA

Five days after the school board's brief and accompanying affidavits were filed, the state of Alabama went through the ordeal of the desegregation of the University of Alabama in Tuscaloosa. A Mobile woman, Vivian Malone, had applied for admission to the university. After a lengthy litigation process, the University had been ordered by the federal district court in Birmingham to admit her. When the date for the execution of that order arrived on 11 June, Governor George C. Wallace, who had pledged that he would stand in the schoolhouse door to prevent desegregation, delivered on his campaign promise.

On 11 June, Governor Wallace mobilized more than 2,000 national guardsmen for emergency duty at the state university and flanked himself with a personal bodyguard of state troopers. Wallace then confronted and blocked federal officials Nicholas B. Katzenback (assistant attorney general), Macon

Weaver (U.S. district attorney), and Peyton Norville (U.S. marshall), who accompanied Miss Malone and James A. Hood of East Gadsden he stated that they violated the Tenth Amendment.

On the same night of the confrontation, President John F. Kennedy federalized the Alabama national guard and went on national television and radio to address the nation. He used the full power of his office to urge the nation to fullfill its promise of equality of opportunity. He called for the necessary legislation that Congress had been prevented from passing because of powerful southern filibusters.

On 19 June, President Kennedy asked Congress to enact the necessary legislation authorizing the attorney general to initiate desegregation suits and to give the federal government power to withhold federal aid from racially segregated programs. These were, later in the summer, incorporated into the omnibus Civil Rights Bill that was sent to Congress. The bill was enacted only after the death of the president on 22 November 1963.

Meanwhile, on 24 June Judge Thomas denied the motion of the plaintiffs for a preliminary injunction and set the case for trial on 14 November 1963. Two days later, the plaintiffs' attorney filed notice of appeal of this ruling to the U.S. Fifth Circuit Court of Appeals in New Orleans. Within two weeks, the judgment and order of the Fifth Circuit Court, dated 9 July 1963, was entered restraining the school board from requiring segregation of the races and requiring that it submit a plan for the immediate desegregation of Mobile County schools no later than 1 August 1963. The Fifth Circuit Court linked the Mobile case with the Birmingham case in its decision, overriding Judge Thomas granting of a year's delay.

It was in this context that the governor attempted to intervene in the case by issuing an executive order against the desegregation in the Mobile schools and specifically of Murphy High School, the largest all-white school in the system. He also mobilized the national guard to prevent the entry of black children into the high school.

On 9 September, the five Alabama federal judges issued a temporary restraining order enjoining Governor Wallace from interfering with the desegregation of Murphy High School or any other school in the state. Governor Wallace had assigned state troopers to bar the door of Murphy High School as he had at the University of Alabama. It was necessary for President Kennedy to federalize the Alabama national guard for the second time in three months in order to prevent Governor Wallace from using the guard to bar the access of Birdie Mae Davis and Henry Hobdy to Murphy High School (SSN 1964: May: 12B–13B).

The local White Citizens Council, which had been meeting during the summer to plan for the blocking of desegregation at Murphy High School, had urged parents either to keep their children home in protest against the desegregation of the school, or to instruct their children to make things unpleasant for black students who were admitted to Murphy. These parents were assured that the citizens council would pay all court costs in any cases that arose out of their vigorous protests.

The council did precipitate some incidents at Murphy. Almost 300 white students participated in noisy demonstrations. They paraded up and down outside the school windows trying to urge the other students to join them in boycotting the school; fifty-four of -them were arrested for truancy in this protest. The White Citizens Council put up the bonds to secure their release.

The White Citizens Council also urged the promotion of white private schools in order to keep white children from associating with blacks. At its September meetings the most recent private segregation academy set up in the state was praised. This was the Macon County Academy, a hastily organized secondary school attended by all of the white students who withdrew from Tuskegee High School when thirteen blacks were admitted earlier in the month. The academy had received the support of the governor and the promise of state funds. Tuskegee High School was thereby transformed into an all-black school.

Mobile citizens who organized to support desegregation experienced threats and harassments. One group that was singled out for White Citizen Council wrath was called Alabamians Behind Local Education (ABLE), an upper-middle-class integrated, liberal, white-led organization of about 210 members. This group had been organized in 1963 to counteract the forces in favor of shutting down the public schools and financing and promoting private schools with state funds. Alabamians Behind Local Education billed itself as a rallying point of common sense in the school crisis.

During the summer ABLE had sponsored a two-day workshop at the prestigious Central Presbyterian Church. It published flyers featuring its slogan, Keep Mobile's Schools Open, and distributed fact sheets about court decisions and the Alabama Pupil Placement Law, which was being used as the basis for the transfer of black students from formerly segregated schools to all-white schools. It also produced a thirty-minute television report on Mobile's schools and presented speakers to open assemblies for the discussion of the issues. Alabamians Behind Local Education supported public officials who were working to continue free public education and preserve the peace. The White Citizens Council undertook a campaign of harassment and intimidation aimed at silencing the opposition. Alabamians Behind Local Education officers were attacked in the press by Governor Wallace at the instigation of the White Citizens Council.

Other civic groups involved in the desegregation process, such as the Non-Partisan Voters League (successor to the banned NAACP chapter), the Mobile Council on Human Relations (affiliated with the Ford Foundation-funded Alabama Council on Human Relations and the Southern Regional Council), the U.S. Commission on Civil Rights Advisory Committee, and the American Friends Service Committee, all cooperated in the effort to facilitate the peaceful desegregation of Murphy. But progress in the desegregation of Murphy and of other schools was painstakingly slow during the next four years.

THE CONSERVATIVE MAJORITY

The presidential campaign in 1964 brought out a strong conservative majority in the county. Emma Lathrop-Smith's *The Radical Right in Mobile* (1964) showed the emergence of an extremely powerful, upper-class John Birch Society that, with its strong financial backing and its identification of the prointegrationist movement as a Communist movement, was able to stir up a great amount of community opposition to the further desegregation of the schools. Under the sponsorship of the local John Birch Society, the *On Guard* organization, the Christian Laymen's Association, and FOCUS (Freedom Over Communism in the United States) recruited substantial and influential membership in the Mobile area. These groups and the White Citizens Council presented speakers such as Governor Ross Barnett of Mississippi, Eugene "Bull" Connor from Birmingham, and Myers G. Lowman, the right-wing Methodist Circuit Riders agitator, who spoke to a large assembly on the subject "Fiddling While Church and Schoolhouse Burn."

The National States Rights Party sponsored speeches by Dr. Edward Fields, their national chairman, and by lawyer Matt Murphy, who was identified as the Birmingham lawyer for the Ku Klux Klan in the Viola Liuzzo murder trial. The *On Guard* group sponsored a round-the-clock telephone message that could be dialed to learn the current conservative ideology and the current target of conservative wrath. The recently organized Women for Constitutional Government advocated the repeal of the Sixteenth Amendment and the divesting of the federal government of all operations in competition with private business.

In the primary elections in May and in the presidential and congressional elections in November the county voted overwhelmingly for Republican candidates and their conservative platforms. It was alleged that the upper-class John Birch group and the middle-class White Citizens Council (which became infiltrated with former Klansmen and which split up over that and other issues) were mainly responsible for the community's turn to the right.

COUNTERVAILING FORCES

One of the countervailing forces to the conservative surge in Mobile was Title IV of the 1964 Civil Rights Act, which authorized the U.S. Commissioner of Education to support educational institutes in communities that were experiencing problems occasioned by school desegregation. Spring Hill College was represented at the planning conference for setting up the HEW Equal Educational Opportunities Program under Title IV. The college submitted a proposal for a series of summer training programs to run for three years, and follow-up year-round institutes in Mobile and in Birmingham. These institutes were designed to provide training in the handling of the problems of school desegregation.

At the first institute, held in June and July 1965, thirty school officials and teachers were enrolled. All were bona fide employees of the Board of School Commissioners; eighteen were white and twelve black; fourteen were males and sixteen females. The institute provided more than a dozen and a half nationally known and southern guest lecturers and consultants in the course of the six-week program. These sessions presented a view of desegregation that had not been presented by the local media or the school board.

Because of the community climate and the activity of right-wing moderates and radicals, including the Ku Klux Klan, these institutes had to be conducted without much public fanfare and media involvement. The Ku Klux Klan had burned two crosses on the college campus. It had threatened to dynamite the college buildings because of the integration of the school and its involvement in the prointegration and civil rights activities of the Alabama Council on Human Relations and the U.S. Commission on Civil Rights. Moreover, the school board had issued instructions that its personnel were not to participate in the activities of groups that favored desegregation. Consequently, it was at great risk and with great fear of reprisal in the form of dismissal that both black and white teachers and principals enrolled in these institutes. A number of in-service training, short-term institutes were conducted for the faculties of the area high schools and middle schools. The institute program continued for three years with increasingly wider impact on the school personnel. In the second summer, more than forty public school personnel enrolled in the 1966 summer school; an equal number signed up for the 1967 session.

In 1967, the *Birdie Mae Davis* case was revived by the formal entry of the U.S. Department of Justice in the role of plaintiff intervenor. On 14 June 1967 the attorneys from the U.S. Department of Justice filed a motion and a supporting memorandum, plus a motion for the supplemental relief on behalf of the plaintiffs. This action had been authorized by the Civil Rights Act of 1964.

The U.S. attorneys filed a motion to require the board of school commissioners to produce documents in open court dealing with the attendance areas, the feeder patterns, and the plans for school construction, school closings, and school consolidations. These documents, dating back to 1964, had previously been withheld from plaintiffs even though they were public documents. On the basis of this documentation, the justice department lawyers within three weeks produced a 110-page brief that contended that "the defendants are operating the public schools of Mobile County as a dual system, with one set of schools for white children staffed by white faculties and the other set of schools for black children staffed by black faculties."

The brief claimed that the evidence showed a perpetuation of this dual system in many ways: (1) by adopting a "school attendance plan" that failed to alter the preexisting dual structure; (2) by making administrative reassignments of students and reallocation of school facilities so as to preserve racial segregation in the schools; and (3) by planning and constructing new facilities and additions to old facilities so as to preserve racial segregation in the schools.

The department of justice contended that the limited desegregation steps taken by the school board had not resulted in a unified school system. They had simply permitted a very few black students to attend previously all-white schools, still identified as white. Of the 75,504 students attending public schools in 1967, 44,352 were attending white schools and 31,152 were attending black schools. Only 668 black students were estimated to be enrolled in thirty-one of the sixty-five white schools. The rest were attending thirty-four all-black schools.

This situation led to a motion by the U.S. Department of Justice seeking an order of the court that would require the defendants to discontinue operating the public schools of Mobile County as two separate school systems. To achieve this goal, it was requested that the defendants be required to survey the educational needs of the student population and the resources available to the school board to meet these needs without regard to the race of the students to be educated. It was also moved that they be compelled to adopt a long-range program of pupil assignment, school facility allocation, and new facility construction consistent with sound educational standards and their affirmative duty to eliminate the effects of the dual school system based on race. The motion further requested that the school board be required to transfer students administratively from overcrowded black elementary schools to underpopulated white elementary schools.

Though the opening of school was less than a month away, the department of justice asked that the school board be required (1) to provide students an additional opportunity to transfer under the Alabama Pupil Placement Law before the start of the 1967–1968 school year; (2) to make faculty and staff assignments on a desegregated basis; and (3) to take other steps designed to eliminate the dual school system.

In the long and meticulously detailed brief, the evidence from the school board's own records were spelled out for the court. It was shown that the school board had deliberately perpetuated racial segregation by converting at least five all-white schools into all-black schools during the last four years. From their own documents, the plaintiff intervenors were able to show the perpetuation of racial segregation by administrative reassignments of students, especially in the transfer of white students from areas adjacent to schools that had become 100 percent black.

Notwithstanding the very strong case made by the U.S. attorneys, the interim order issued by Judge Thomas relative to changes in attendance-area boundary lines set only three days for the special transfer period instead of the requested thirty days. During that time application for transfer was allowed to students whose residences had been changed from one elementary attendance area to another. They were authorized to transfer to the school serving the attendance area in which they were now living. This decision was appealed.

On 13 October the judge issued a final decree on the plaintiffs' motion for further relief and the plaintiff intervenors' motion for a more extensive supplemental program of relief based on freer student transfers; prohibition of perpetuation of the dual system, especially by new construction in segregated areas; modification of the bus transportation plan; and faculty desegregation. The court denied these motions and instead approved the defendants' desegregation plan for the year 1967–1968, which had been submitted on 19 October 1966. Four days later this decree was also appealed to the Fifth Circuit Court.

Most of the school year was taken up with the handling of this appeal in New Orleans. Only on 6 May 1968 was a judgment rendered by the Fifth Circuit Court reversing the district court and remanding the case for entry of the appellate court's decree. This decree was actually dated 12 March 1968 but was not received until May because of the delay in printing the text.

The court took note that the inflated figures stating that a total of 2,008, or 6.5 percent, of blacks were experiencing desegregation was reached by counting 1,316 blacks in formerly all-black schools that were attended by only four white students. The court found that the only blacks really experiencing desegregation education were the 668 attending schools with predominantly white enrollments. The court noted that although this was 511 more than the number of blacks who attended predominantly white schools the previous year, the percentage of blacks experiencing desegregated education was still too low.

The court mandated that attendance zones in the urban areas of Mobile County be devised to create a unitary, racially nondiscriminatory system. Faculty desegregation of all schools and prohibition of further construction were also decreed as mandatory minimum requirements for the school board. The court also added a strong order stating that no student shall be segregated or discriminated against on account of race or color in any service, facility, activity, or program including transportation, athletics, or other extracurricular activities that may be conducted or sponsored by the school in which he or she is enrolled. A student attending school for the first time on a desegregated basis, the court said, may not be subject to any disqualifications or waiting period for participating in these programs. This decree was entered by Judge Thomas on 3 May.

Further recourse to the federal courts on the appeal route was blocked by the U.S. Supreme Court in three more landmark cases decided on 27 May 1968. In these cases, the Supreme Court ruled that various freedom-of-choice plans allowing a pupil to choose his own public school were ineffective in desegregating the school system for compliance with the *Brown* decisions. Unitary nonracially identifiable schools were demanded as evidence of compliance.

The Mobile County School Board had made its first reluctant step in this direction earlier that month when on 16 May it made public the recommended attendance areas required by the U.S. Circuit Court of Appeals to promote complete desegregation of the local public schools, drawing the attendance zones on the basis of population and available facilities rather than on the basis of race. In July, a trial was held that resulted in a final decree that permanently enjoined the defendants from discriminating on the basis of race or color in the operation of the school system and required them to take affirmative action to disestablish all school segregation and to eliminate the effects of the dual school system as to desegregation, exercise of choice, transfers, and prospective students.

The only effective desegregation emerging from this decree was that involving the desegregation of each of the faculties at the elementary, junior, and senior schools. The court ordered that the ratio of white to black faculty members should be 60 percent to 40 percent, matching the proportions of the majority and minority populations in the city.

This decree had an ironic twist to it. At that point in time, only 52 percent of the faculty members were white and 48 percent were black. A new decree establishing the 60 to 40 percent ratio meant that the number of white faculty members would be increased by 8 percent and the number of slots available to blacks would presumably be reduced by 8 percent. This worked a great hardship on the black professional class, for whom the jobs available in the public school system were among the most lucrative and advantageous in the area. Nevertheless, because the court required it, faculty desegregation in accordance with the decrees of the Fifth Circuit Court was demanded. A report from the public school administration was required shortly after the opening of the new school year.

New white teachers employed in September 1968 were obliged to sign contracts for teaching posts in the all-black schools. This eliminated a large number of job openings at all three levels of the school system for black candidates that year.

BLACK LEADERSHIP

On 4 April 1968, Martin Luther King, Jr., was assassinated in Memphis. The reaction to this in Mobile led to the radicalization of some black organizations and the emergence of a new radical black leadership. The memorial march, the first large-scale demonstration of its kind in Mobile, was held on Sunday 6 April. It was hastily organized under the leadership of the Black Power Neighborhood Organized Workers (NOW). Both black and white community leaders, including many prominent white churchmen, participated in the march through the heart of the north side black ghetto, along Davis Avenue, down to the business district and to the Municipal Auditorium for a mass demonstration of mourning and sympathy for the slain civil rights' leader.

In the wake of this success the NOW organization began to adopt the ways of the more militant and radicalized black groups. Neighborhood Organized Workers had been organized in 1966 and incorporated as an educational organization with a nonviolent ideology. Upon incorporation it had named a public school teacher, David L. Jacobs, as president. Its purpose was to promote a grass-roots political education, voter registration, and a civil rights educational movement.

In 1968, however, the group was reorganized. A local black nightclub operator, Noble Beasley, was elected president. In the long hot summer of 1968, the group invited the Black Panther leaders to come to town for public meetings and demonstrations. By 15 May the Neighborhood Organized Workers had scheduled and carried through a march from the black neighborhood to the City Hall-County Courthouse complex. The march protested job discrimination as well as school desegregation. Neighborhood Organized Workers continued its meetings and demonstrations during the summer, culminating with a 26 July mass meeting addressed by Stokely Carmichael, who stated that the only way blacks would achive status in the United States is through armed insurrection.

The NOW leaders gained new confidence in their militant ideology. The NOW members appeared before the school board with more demands for desegregation and better conditions in the all-black schools. In April 1969, NOW began systematic picketing of all the all-black schools. The picketing followed the same general pattern at all schools. The pickets carried signs saying, "Mobile County School Board is racist," "Give us better schools or else," "Black students demand black history," "Black schools are junk yards, cheap ragged prisons for black students," "We want more teacher respect," "School Board says it's alright to use 'nigger'."

On 8 May the school board filed a petition asking for a temporary and permanent injunction against NOW and cooperating organizations such as the American Friends Service Committee. The allegation of the school board claimed that the picketing was distracting pupils' attention, drawing them off campus and into picket lines, and causing large numbers of students to absent themselves from classes. As many as 300 to 500 students were truant from the picketed schools, far above normal absentee expectations.

Both NOW and the American Friends Service Committee filed motions to dismiss the school board's charges on the grounds of First Amendment freedom of speech. They took this occasion to deny that they were engaged in a campaign to disrupt the operation of the schools in Mobile County or to advocate truancy. They insisted that NOW protested the denial of equal educational opportunities to black students in Mobile County. They criticized the inferiority of black schools, the lack of meaningful black education, token integration, and the refusal of the board of school commissioners to hire black central administrative personnel. They stressed that they were publicizing these and other racist policies through speeches, mass meetings, leaflets, and picketing in order to seek redress of grievances as guaranteed by the Constitution.

Investigation by the justice department and the FBI confirmed the peacefulness of the picketing process, but the district court nevertheless issued a preliminary injunction against the American Friends Service Committee and the NOW organization.

On 22 May, the American Friends Service Committee, which had greater resources at its disposal than did NOW, appealed the case to the U.S. Fifth Circuit Court in New Orleans and asked for it to grant a stay of the preliminary injunctions issued by Judge Thomas on 16 May. The case was finally decided six months later. The Fifth Circuit Court ruled in favor of the American Friends Service Committee and NOW. The injunction order of the district court was vacated.

In June the Fifth Circuit Court had reversed its own and Judge Thomas' decisions formulating attendance zone lines for grades one to eight in the city schools, adopting freedom of choice in the high schools, and permitting liberal transfers of white students from zones containing a predominantly black school. The court also disapproved the construction of a new expanded Howard Elementary School in the northside black ghetto and Toulminville High School because construction of these schools would perpetuate segregation.

The court stated that the school board's literal interpretation of the school attendance zones, apparently drawn on a nonracial basis, was now clearly not aiding the desegregation process or eliminating past segregation. It stated that the liberal permits to transfer issued wholesale to whites was tantamount to authorization of immediate resegregation of schools in mixed neighborhoods and was therefore not permissible under either the *Brown* or the *Holmes* decisions, which stated that desegregation could no longer be put off. It remanded the case to the district court ordering the judge to give it the highest priority on his calendar. The court also ordered that the federal Department of Health, Education, and Welfare Office of Education experts be asked to draw up an affirmative desegregation plan for all public schools as well as a plan for locating and designing new schools. The district court was also instructed to compel the school board to make all necessary information available to the HEW team.

The Fifth Circuit Court required the district court to demand that the school board develop an acceptable plan to conform with the constitutional rights of black students within thirty days. This plan would be approved by the court within ten days if the plaintiffs did not object to it. If the school board did not produce a plan within thirty days, the court was instructed to empower the HEW team to develop the plan. Within ten days after its filing the parties would have time to file objections and amendments. This new plan was to be set in motion at the beginning of the 1969–1970 term.

Anticipating the habitual delays and dilatory procedures used by the lawyers in the case, the Fifth Circuit Court said that there would be no stay of this order for petitions, appeals, rehearing, or certiorari motions. No extension of time would be granted because the Supreme Court had called a halt to all "deliberate speed" delays and had set the coming year as the deadline for compliance. The school board, in its familiar resistance pattern, refused to develop a plan.

THE HEW PLANS

A team of HEW experts headed by former Miami superintendent Joseph Hall and Jesse Jordan of the Region IV Office of Education in Atlanta came to Mobile to devise this fifth version of a desegregation plan, which was submitted on 10 July 1969 with a motion demanding immediate implementation. The HEW plan called for the pairing of schools in the inner city with schools in the western and suburban areas. Black children, who previously had been locked into the segregated schools of the inner city, were to be bused to the all-white schools in the western area in significantly large numbers. The plan also called for the elimination of the freedom-of-choice attendance plan and the liberal transfer policy that had nullified previous desegregation plans. The plan also called for the closing of Howard Elementary School instead of building a large, all-black facility there, and the abandonment of at least six other all-black schools.

In the Baker High School area in the western suburbs, construction of a new integrated facility was recommended. Black students living near this school had been bused thirty-eight miles to and from St. Elmo School instead of being admitted to their neighborhood school.

Within ten days after the plan had been submitted, the school board filed a motion to dismiss it. When the court rejected this motion, the board filed another motion to amend the plan; this motion was also denied. The plan also called for more extensive desegregation of faculties and staffs working with the children as well as professional and administrative staff in the central office. The basis for the school board's appeal was the principle of neighborhood schools and the parents' freedom of choice as to the race of the teachers of.their children.

The state legislature had recently passed a law empowering the governor to withhold state funds from any local school system in which parents were denied the free choice of the race of the teachers of their children. The law was promptly challenged in the federal court, which entered a temporary restraining order prohibiting enforcement of the new statute until its constitutionality was settled.

Meanwhile, the school board was severely hurt by a whirlwind from a different direction. In the summer of 1968, Hurricane Camille had filled the Gulf of Mexico with its record-making power. It had slammed ashore close enough to Mobile County to cause widespread damage to school buildings. Contracts for their repair were hastily drawn up based on somewhat inflated estimates of damage and of the windfall of disaster relief money made available to the stricken communites along the Gulf Coast.

The temptation to loot some of the fast-flowing funds was too great for some lower-level officials in the school board administration. The scandal unfolded during the course of the next twelve months in the headlines and the courts. Some third-level officials were indicted by a grand jury, prosecuted, and convicted. The board and the superintendent came under a cloud because all of this scandal occurred under their jurisdiction. The superintendent resigned and took another job elsewhere at the end of the 1969–1970 school year.

Meanwhile legal maneuvers had successfully delayed the adoption of the HEW plan. By December the school board had submitted an alternate plan, which in turn led to the filing on 15 January 1970 of a modified HEW plan. By the end of January the district court ordered this modified plan to go into effect on 1 February 1970. This decision was appealed by the plaintiffs and cross-appealed by the defendants, notwithstanding the Fifth Circuit Court's prohibition against dilatory appeals.

On 16 March Judge Thomas ordered the school board to follow his order of 31 January within three days or be fined $1,000 per day per member. This decision was also appealed, but the appeal and delay were denied in New Orleans.

A flurry of other appeals and motions kept up the pace of litigation both in Mobile and in New Orleans until June 1970, when the final decision of the Fifth Circuit Court was handed down. Noting that under the present plan 60 percent of the black students in the ninety-six-school systems were assigned to segregated schools, the court indicated that it favored the implementation of the department of justice plan submitted on 27 January 1970, which not only required the pairing of schools but the recasting of all grades. In place of the senior high school, junior high school, and elementary school concepts, the justice department plan required the pairing and designation of schools as elementary (grades one to five); middle (grades six to nine), and high (grades ten to twelve).

The justice department plan would thus make it possible for every black child in the Mobile school system to attend a desegregated school during the course of his education on at least one of these three levels. It affirmed the necessity of busing school children across the dividing line between the eastern and western sections of the city, which was the newly completed north-south Interstate highway I-65.

It also demanded further desegregation of faculty and staff, stating that the Mobile County school system had almost totally failed to comply with the faculty ratio requirement though ordered to do so by the district court on 1 August 1969. Only a few schools, one year later, were approaching the 60-to-40 percent faculty ratio.

Equality of access to bus transportation to all school facilities and to extra-curricular activities was also required in the district court order. This decree was followed by a supplemental order that allowed certain modifications in the 8 June plan altering the attendance zones of thirty-two separate schools on the basis of more efficient school administration in the absence of clearly discriminatory racial purposes.

The court also turned down the special request by twenty parents of school-children who would presumably be obliged to attend schools where a majority of the students were black. It stated that students who refused to attend the schools to which they were assigned by the school board under the order of the district court would not be permitted to participate in any school activities including examinations and receiving grades or credits. These nonconformers, as they were called, were thus faced with the alternative of withdrawing from the public school system and enrolling in private schools.

The school board lawyers filed a notice of appeal from the Fifth Circuit Court to the U.S. Supreme Court. This move did not buy another year's delay in the implementation of this more extensive desegregation plan. The board was ordered to proceed with its desegregation pending appeal.

Meanwhile the public schools prepared for a delayed opening of the school year. On 7 September, Governor Wallace, who had been reelected to a second term, was the main speaker in the Mobile area at the Princhard Park Labor Day celebration. Speaking to a crowd of approximately 6,000 people flanked by his lieutenant governor, Jere Beasley, and by Senate nominee Pierre Pelham, local leader of the White Citizens' Council, and by House of Representatives nominee John Tyson, Wallace continued his defiance of federal court desegregation orders by insisting on the neighborhood school attendance concept. He also urged the people to stand behind the provisions of the Alabama School Placement Law, which authorized parents to exercise freedom of choice in sending their children to the neighborhood schools. He told the audience, "If

I were you, I'd exercise my freedom of choice," which was in obvious support of the area-wide campaign by predominantly white parent organizations urging them to ignore the school attendance zones drawn up by the federal courts and to send their children to the schools of their choice.

At the Wallace rally and at many other right-wing rallies and meetings of parent-teacher groups in the area, the Concerned Parents and Citizens of Mobile County, a new umbrella organization headed by Melvin Himes, passed out detailed instructions on parent behavior for the opening day of school. One such flyer showed the picture of a parent and child approaching a principal with the parent saying, "This is the school of my choice. I demand classes, books, and teachers for my child. I will not leave until my demands are met!"

The day before school opened, the U.S. Justice Department was quoted in the public media as stating that it would take "those steps necessary to see to it that the federal district court orders are complied with." Other organizations such as the Mobile District Labor Council appealed to the citizens in the county to exercise sound judgment and reasonable action when the schools began their fall session. The labor council called on federal, state, and local officials to work diligently to "eliminate the present confusion and inconsistencies." The League of Women Voters also issued an appeal to all parents to send their children to their assigned schools on Wednesday, pointing out that the school board would lose approximately $1.37 per day per child in state funds if the pupil failed to attend his assigned school.

NONCONFORMANCE

Meanwhile, the schools opened up for the 1970–1971 school year under the court of appeals plan, which was a modified version of the plan submitted by the department of justice. This plan reduced the number of all-black elementary schools from twelve to six, projected to serve 5,310 students or about 50 percent of the black elementary school students in the metropolitan area (figure 8.2).

Enrollment figures for the 1970–1971 school year showed that the projection on which the court of appeals had based its plan were inaccurate. Instead of only six all-black elementary schools, nine surfaced as more than 90 percent by 21 September. These housed 64 percent of all black elementary school pupils in the metropolitan area, 7,651. The enrollment figures further indicated that of 6,747 black junior and senior high school students, more than 50 percent, were in all-black or nearly all-black schools rather than in none as projected by the court of appeals.

Because of the refusal of nonconformers to attend the schools to which they were assigned by the court-ordered plan, the projected desegregation did not come about. The total number of nonconformers overall was 1,102 on 9 September; 1,185 on 10 September; 976 on 14 September; 623 on 17 September; 572 on 18 September; 471 on 21 September. The vast majority of these were whites who refused to go to the formerly all-black elementary or middle schools in the inner city to which they had been assigned by the court-ordered plan.

This defiance indicated not only the extent of the intransigence of the parents but also the powerlessness of the school board to enforce its orders.

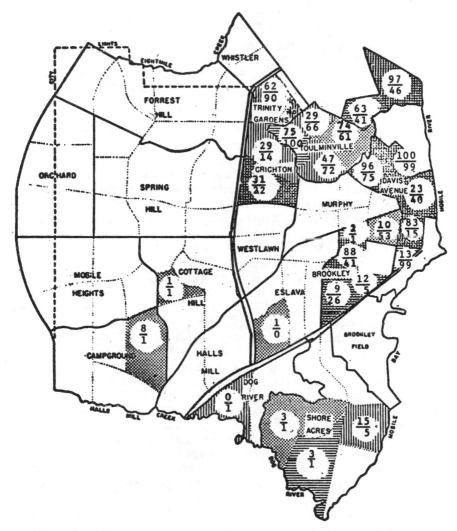

Figure 8.2. Nonwhite Population Percentage for Metropolitan Mobile: $\dfrac{1960\ \%\ \text{nonwhite}}{1970\ \%\ \text{nonwhite}}$.

Vertical shading: neighborhoods with extensive low-quality housing; horizontal shading: neighborhoods with a high number of welfare cases; dots; neighborhoods with a high rate of juvenile delinquency.

It also indicated the powerlessness of the court to achieve conformity to its orders when faced with wholesale defiance. The largest number of nonconformers were not even officially identified as nonconformers. More than 1,000 high school students assigned by the court-ordered plan to attend high schools east of Interstate 65 showed up instead at schools located west of Interstate 65, Davidson High School on Azalea Road and Shaw High School on Zeigler Boulevard. At Davidson, where the capacity was 1,800, 2,900 students showed up, all except ninety of them white. The vast majority of these students claimed legitimate residences within the official zone designated for

Davidson. This seems to have been done by using addresses of relatives who lived in the western part of the city.

The overcrowding at Davidson was matched by the underregistration of students at Murphy High School, where the black enrollment outnumbered the white enrollment, and at Williamson High School, a formerly all-black school where twice as many whites were assigned as blacks, but which turned out to be a predominantly black school in a predominantly black neighborhood as it had been previously.

The overcrowding at Davidson led to some serious concerns on the part of the fire marshal, the health department, and the principal of the school. All of this overcrowding was further evidence of white parents' determination to not conform to the court order and to continue the defiance which Governor Wallace had urged them to show. One further evidence of this defiance occurred on the junior high school level. More than 725 white students had been assigned to formerly all-back Booker T. Washington School in the Toulminville area. On registration day only about fifty of these students showed up. Most of them immediately requested transfer forms and withdrew.

At Murphy High School a new problem emerged with the new preponderance of black students in the student body. Where in previous years the blacks had been a beleaguered minority, their newly emerging black power consciousness caused a reversal of the direction of complaints. About forty white students and their parents met with U.S. District Judge Thomas to protest alleged violations of their civil rights by black students at Murphy High School. The complaints cited the presence of militant black groups, which were disrupting the school with the hope of being sent back to their former all-black schools, Central High and Toulminville High. The white students requested police protection in the hallways of the school as well as outside on the playground. They complained of harassment, intimidation, extortion, and physical violence at the hands of black students at Murphy.

The faculty at Murphy, alarmed at this new militancy and the racial turmoil it spawned, requested that federal marshals and armed guards be stationed at the school for their protection and that of the students. The faculty resolution, approved by both the principal and the assistant principals, asked for federal protection because the petitioners felt that the added protection should be at federal expense. This request was supported by Mobile Police Commissioner, Robert B. Doyle, who said that the federal government should have the expense of enforcing law and order at Murphy High School. Doyle's practice was to have police patrols on duty at the entrance and around the school grounds but not within the school buildings.

The September 1970 experience showed once more that each of the desegregation plans had a set of built-in self-destruct mechanisms. Parental defiance and lack of an effective strategy for dealing with it surfaced as one of the self-destruct mechanisms. A second self-sabotaging element in the 1970 plan was the school board's refusal to expand the bus transportation services available to children who were expected to attend schools far away from their homes. Black parents in the Trinity Gardens area organized their own Concerned Parents of Trinity Gardens. They requested the school board to provide their children with bus service to attend the schools to which they were assigned. They wrote a letter to the school superintendent on behalf of their own children as well as the children in the Whistler and the Toulminville areas asking for relief in the form of bus transportation.

On 11 September, the lawyers in the *Birdie Mae Davis* case filed a motion in the U.S. District Court to require the Mobile County School Board to provide transportation for any student in the system living more than two miles from the school to which he or she was assigned. The motion contended that the school board's arbitrary policy violated the constitutional rights of both black and white students who were assigned to distant schools in the reorganization plan.

The motion by the plaintiffs' lawyers was not acted on by the court, nor was the petition of the parents for bus transportation answered by the school board. This became the core issue before the U.S. Supreme Court in the plaintiffs' appeal to the highest tribunal.

The school board in its 9 September meeting received from Assistant Superintendent John Montgomery a report that stated that it was not practical to attempt to increase the transportation above and beyond the 225 school buses supplied the previous year. Only those students who had received transportation in the previous year were again provided with transportation. The school board adopted this policy even though it was assured of state funds for the transportation of any student who lived more than two miles from his or her designated school.

BIRDIE MAE DAVIS RESOLVED

On 20 April 1971 the U.S. Supreme Court rendered its final decision on the *Birdie Mae Davis* v. *the Board of School Commissioners of Mobile County* case. The writ of certiorari to the U.S. Court of Appeals for the Fifth Circuit had brought the case before the court in the fall of 1970 along with the *Swann* v. *Charlotte-Mecklenburg Board of Education* and the *McDaniel* v. *Barresi* cases. The cases were consolidated by the Supreme Court because they all occurred in states that had a long history of maintaining two sets of schools operated by a single school board deliberately separating students by race.

The constitutional issue placed before the Supreme Court was whether the unitary school system plan replacing the dual system could still provide for the operation of one or more all-white or all-black schools, apparently thus perpetuating racial segregation in those schools. The extensive and elaborate briefs filed on behalf of the school boards in all of those cases maintained that the surviving racial segregation of the schools was not owing to governmental or school board action but to conditions beyond the control of public officials, namely, long-standing housing segregation patterns set up by private home owners and/or by agencies not controlled by the school board.

On the constitutional issue, elaborate briefs were filed both by the school board and by the Mobile County Council of Parent-Teachers Associations supporting the school board. The lawyers maintained that the Constitution of the United States does not require the assignment of either students or teachers to the schools of the system in such a manner as to achieve racial balance in each school or some arbitrary mathematical ratio of black and white in each school. It was strongly maintained that the mere existence of one to five schools with a uniracial student body in an otherwise completely integrated and unitary system does not render that system constitutionally deficient.

The school board brief further maintained that it is constitutionally sufficient for a public school system to assign students to schools on the basis of attendance zones that are fairly drawn to normal standards of educational soundness and on the basis of nonracial criteria such as residential location. Insisting that the vital essential purpose of public education and of a public school system is education and not integration, it pleaded with the U.S. Supreme Court that public education be no longer used as a vehicle to promote the philosophy of association by compulsion.

> The quest for racial balance on the one hand and quality education for all children black and white on the other are on a deadly collision course. One will not survive their ultimate meeting. For those who demand racial balance, busing for the sake of busing, vindication of one constitutional right at the expense of the other it is pertinent to inquire as to where their motivation may lie. Are they interested in quality education or are they interested in revenge and retribution?
>   We respectfully urge this court to approve as a general principle the Constitutional validity of the neighborhood school concept and the Constitutional invalidity of arbitrary assignment of public school students and teachers on the basis of a ratio or quota, or in pursuit of racial balance" (U.S. Supreme Court, *Brief for the Board of School Commissioners of Mobile County* 1971: 99).

The brief filed by the Mobile County Council of Parent-Teachers Associations likewise made an elaborate plea for the sufficiency of the present desegregation plan. Extensive claims were made for the effectiveness of the current plan in achieving school desegregation. A detailed statistical table indicating the students assigned and the faculty assigned and the administrators assigned at each of the schools in the system for the 1970–1971 school year was presented. These figures, based on the estimates and not on the actual working out of the plan as affected by the defiance of the nonconforming students and teachers, were utilized in what was obviously an effort to make the ineffective desegregation plan appear to be effective in achieving a unitary system.

The brief claimed that the present unitary school system did not deny black children the equal protection of the law. It stated that no person is effectively excluded from any school because of race or color. It attacked the Fifth Circuit Court's 60-to-40 percent white-to-black faculty and staff ratio as a rigid and inflexible norm not hitherto sanctioned by the Supreme Court. It maintained that the transportation facilities and extracurricular activities were fully desegregated and in compliance with the *Singleton* v. *Jackson* ruling. It even cited the existence of the biracial committee as evidence of compliance with the previous requirements of the Supreme Court orders.

The issue of requiring the busing of children to desegregate each school within a unitary system was thus laid before the U.S. Supreme Court. The brief for the petitioners, prepared by lawyers from the NAACP Legal Defense Fund and Stanford University as well as by two lawyers from Mobile, took the opposite view of the validity of the neighborhood school concept and the legitimacy of the definition of a unitary school system in which segregated schools still existed. The brief urged the Supreme Court to declare that the general principle for bringing dual systems into compliance with the Constitution should be that every black child should be free from assignment to a black school—an identifiable racial minority school—at every grade of his education. This would define racially identifiable minority schools as those schools that by reason of a very considerable racial concentration or racial disproportion are conceived and designed to receive black children only.

It maintained that the assignment of black children to black schools cannot be justified on the basis of (1) transportation inconveniences and costs, (2) rigid theories about the maintaining of grade structure, (3) neighborhood associational values such as the facilitation of PTA meetings, or (4) concerns that children not be sent to a school in a "strange or hostile" neighborhood. The brief discussed the expensive use of busing by southern school systems to achieve segregation, often requiring a 100-mile round trip per day for a black student from the neighborhood of an all-white school to his black school fifty miles away. The brief urged the Supreme Court to approve the alternative plan number B-1, which would integrate all schools in Mobile County by the use of transportation facilities and techniques of the same kind used by the Mobile board in previous years to keep the system rigidly segregated.

The brief also urged the Supreme Court to approve the pairing of schools and the busing of children between these schools regardless of previous patterns of grade structure. It stated that the Mobile School Board "has used a great variety of differing grade structures and organizing the schools to keep them segregated." It also attacked the so-called neighborhood schools as a mask for the preservation of racial homogeneity. "The only sense in which such neighborhood values have been honored in Mobile is that where neighborhoods have been racially homogeneous, the racial lines have coincided with the school lines."

Concerning the busing of children to a different neighborhood that may be "strange or hostile," the brief maintained that this kind of hostility can no more be used to justify preserving segregation than any other form of opposition to integration. Any obstacles presented by hostility or strangeness could be overcome in order to give equal protection of the law.

The brief called upon the U.S. Supreme Court for a decision that would indicate whether the promise of *Brown* will be kept for thousands upon thousands of black children. "That promise is broken by the current approach of the Fifth Circuit which leaves segregation intact in the main institutions of the dual system—the all-black schools. The current approach of the lower courts represents a new kind of gradualism which functions in much the same manner as the doctrine of deliberate speed, now repudiated by *Alexander* and *Carter*. This Court should require that school districts maintaining the dual systems desegregate the schools now and maintain them in a desegregated status without separate racially identifiable minority schools," it concluded (pp. 84–85).

These arguments and those presented by NAACP lawyers and Anthony Amsterdam on behalf of *Swann* v. *Charlotte-Mecklenberg* carried the case. The U.S. Department of Justice added its weight to their arguments by filing a brief as an amicus curiae, or friend of the court. These reinforced the obligations of both Charlotte and Mobile to eliminate the last vestiges of the formerly segregated dual system by eradicating the racial identifiability of all schools within their jurisdiction.

In its decree on 20 April 1971, the opinion of the U.S. Supreme Court was delivered by Chief Justice Warren Burger. After reviewing the facts of the case and the principles it had invoked in deciding against the Charlotte Board of Education, the Supreme Court affirmed the Fifth Circuit Court of Appeals decision requiring faculty and staff desegregation on a 60 to 40 percent basis in all schools of the Mobile system. It reversed the Fifth Circuit Court of Appeals decision to treat the eastern part of metropolitan Mobile in isolation from the rest of the school system. It stated that the Fifth Circuit Court had erred in not adequately considering the possible use of all available techniques to achieve the maximum amount of practicable desegregation.

Even though not requiring a specific percentage of black-white or a 60 to 40 percent black-white ratio in the student bodies of each school, it did insist that the case be remanded to the district court to consider the use of all available techniques including the restructuring of attendance zones and both contiguous and noncontinguous attendance zones as well as bus transportation and split zoning.

The Supreme Court decision of 20 April did not create a big wave of reaction in the Mobile area. The general public realized that it was a lost cause from the start. Most of the strategists involved in the case realized that it was a last ditch, rearguard delaying action at best. Since the case had been argued on 13 and 14 October 1970, the school board had undergone a significant change. Conservative Sidney Phillips withdrew before the November elections. A new climate descended upon the board with his departure and that of the other defeated members.

The new chairman and president, Charles McNeil, came into the position as the most influential member of the board. McNeil decided to fulfill his responsibilities to the U.S. Supreme Court. He and his superintendent, Harold Collins, traveled to Atlanta for a preargument conference with Judge Griffin Bell, the Fifth Circuit Court chief implementer for the desegregation cases. Judge Bell frankly said that it would be ño use remanding the Supreme Court decision to Judge Thomas because that would lead only to a new appeal and another year's delay. He directed the parties to attempt to negotiate an acceptable plan for the 1971–1972 school year. Bell set a deadline for late June, at the end of which he said the case would be remanded to Judge Thomas if there were no further progress.

Collins returned to Mobile to step-up the development of a plan that would be the first offered voluntarily by the school board. He called in representatives of thirty interested organizations, showed them the dot-spot map of the distribution of the white and black students in all three educational levels, and the proposed lines that would desegregate every school within the metropolitan area.

Initial plans submitted to the lawyers for the plaintiffs were unsatisfactory. One of the plaintiffs' attorneys decided that negotiations would not work and prepared to ask Judge Bell to remand the case. Almost at the last moment before the deadline, the school board presented its preliminary plan, which appeared satisfactory to the lawyers for the plaintiffs.

The NAACP lawyers from New York came to Mobile to evaluate the proposals. Using the total desegregation standard of HEW's plan B-1 as a basis of comparison, they agreed that the school board probably did not have necessary bus resources to put the total desegregation plan into effect in September 1971. They agreed that a reasonable timetable could be a point of concession. They made some specific proposals for changes, such as specific schools that should be closed. Days of round-the-clock negotiating followed. Black community groups were brought into concurrence, and agreement in principle was reached by both sides.

To the NAACP lawyers the language of the plan was still much too vague to represent a final plan. At this point it was agreed that the plaintiffs would go into court and accept the plan with a three-year provision such as that agreed upon in the settlement of the Jackson, Mississippi case. This would allow them to file for relief after three years if the plan did not work out to effectuate desegregation.

THE COMPREHENSIVE PLAN

This comprehensive plan was submitted to the district court on 8 July 1971. It led to the consent decree the next day in which the district court adopted the plan and issued a decree concurred in by the plaintiffs. The decree directed that the plaintiffs could not challenge the plan for a period of three years. The school board would be given those three years to achieve a unitary system and the pupil enrollments projected by the plan.

In addition the judge decreed that the jurisdiction over the case would be retained by the court to assure that future school construction and abandonment would not be used to perpetuate or reestablish the dual system. The school board was required to file semiannual reports during the school year.

The rest of the summer was dedicated to the detailed plans for the upcoming school year. This would be the first school year in which the school board had abandoned its resistance to desegregation and had committed itself to a plan that would promise realistically to work now to achieve a unitary system in accordance with the U.S. Supreme Court decision.

The board admitted that the desegregation plans in Mobile County since 1964 had not effectively achieved the objectives for which they were designed. It noted that over the years mobility of segments of the population in an effort to escape integrated schools under these plans had resulted in the reduction of the white public school population and led to the resultant majority of black students in the schools in the inner metropolitan area. Though the overall school population under the jurisdiction of the board of school commissioners still had a majority of whites, this resulted from the predominance of the white population in the county rural area outside of the urbanized area.

The board instructed the administrative staff to prepare a plan that would provide equal educational opportunities and maximize integration to the degree that the population would remain stable.

The new superintendent was charged with the public relations program to communicate the plan to all segments of the population and to invite their suggested solutions to the problems that had to be solved. Many conferences were held with elected state, county, and city officials, the executive board of the chamber of commerce, PTA groups, concerned parents, NAACP leaders, principals' groups, teachers' groups, and the court-appointed biracial committee. The superintendent gave more than 200 talks to civic groups interpreting the plan and asking for citizen input and acceptance. The plan represented major concessions by both parties in the eight-year-long suit.

The key new feature of the plan was the busing of students to achieve the maximum amount of permanent integration in all the schools of the system. The intent of the plan was to provide every child in the Mobile County public school system with an integrated educational experience at every grade level to the maximum extent possible. The plan was also designed to relieve existing overcrowded conditions and to assure accreditation.

Three nearly all-black substandard elementary schools were to be closed. The middle school portion of the plan involved the use of twelve of the best and most educationally desirable facilities available to serve grades six to eight. It restructured all previously established middle school zones and created five new contiguous zones. It also required the closing of Central High School (which had been used as a junior high school) in the black community. Central had been the rallying point for the black community, especially with its record in the field of athletics, its championship football teams, and its major league baseball and basketball graduates.

The middle school plan anticipated at least 30 percent black enrollment in all of the middle schools. Three of these schools, however, had black ratios of 94 to 99 percent, indicating that they might be all-black and might be contested in the future as perpetuating the all-black dual-school arrangement.

On the high school level the plan called for the utilization of eight of the best and most educationally desirable facilities for students in grades nine to twelve. Two unsolved problems still remained in the retention of Blount High School as a virtually all-black institution with only 2 percent whites enrolled in a population of 2,089, and Toulminville High School with 9 percent whites in a population of 1,133. The court gave the school system three years to work out these problems.

The plan also contained detailed provisions for the desegregation of the faculties and of the central office staff at school board headquarters. A special contract with the University of Alabama was let for the purpose of studying in depth all departments of the school system to bring into focus staff accountability, performance, merit promotions, and desegregation. The board committed itself to the appointment of a black assistant superintendent on the same level as other assistant superintendents. It pledged that it would not fill any vacancy until an exhaustive search had been made for a professional of the opposite race from the previous incumbent.

The major concession made by the new board in its 1971 plan was the agreement to bus black students across Interstate 65 from east to west as well as to bus white students west to east. It agreed to a significant increase in the number of buses and to the nondiscriminatory hiring of bus drivers. It also issued wide-ranging and detailed policy guidelines for all aspects of school life, for special orientation programs, and for the instruction of students in the desegregation plan and their responsibilities in the matter. It also called upon each principal to assume leadership in the implementation of the plan and to establish student-faculty human relations committees and to see that all staff members and students exerted extra effort to ensure full participation by students of both races in extracurricular programs.

On the crucial matter of transfers, the board abolished its previous almost automatic granting of transfer requests. It stated that transfers would be granted to students only in cases of extreme hardship or where the student wished to transfer from a school in which his race was in a majority to one where his race was in a minority. It established a professional staff development program that emphasized the training of staff and student leaders for handling problems occasioned by school desegregation. Its program called for the intensive training of forty-five seminar leaders and supervisory personnel in a three-week workshop. These individuals would then in turn train 500 teachers and ultimately reach approximately 1,400 teachers with the program and through them over 33,000 students. Other provisions for compensatory education for disadvantaged and handicapped children were also included in the plan.

On paper once more it seemed as though the long and complicated battle for school desegregation was finally completed. When time came for the opening of school in September 1971 and the implementation of the plan, everyone expected disaster to strike once more. No outbreaks of violence like those during the previous year's opening weeks erupted in the schools. The neighborhoods of the newly integrated schools passed through the opening day's crisis unruffled by an overt resistance to desegregation. Two national television networks sent camera crews into Mobile to cover the anticipated "action." They were surprised to find that the busing of more than 26,000 children for the purposes of desegregation did not create a major furor in the city. They were obliged simply to concentrate on covering some of the factors that contributed to the peaceful desegregation.

PEACEFUL DESEGREGATION

Principal among these factors was the active campaign mounted by the prestigious League of Women Voters. Not long after the 22 April Supreme Court decision, the leaders of the league appeared before the school board and took a strong stand for quality education and stability in the schools. To this end they pledged their support for the U.S. Supreme Court decision and its implementation. They voiced their hope that no further court procedures would be necessary because these left students and parents in a state of confusion and were costly to the taxpayers.

These leaders urged both the board and the superintendent to take a positive attitude and to issue positive statements to assure the public that everything possible would be done to promote racial harmony. They felt that full integration could succeed, especially if the board would set up a biracial advisory committee composed of students, parents, teachers, and school officials. They called for the setting up of mandatory summer workshops to get teachers and nonteaching personnel to understand the problems of the integrated classroom and to learn ways to promote harmony. They also urged the establishment of biracial advisory councils in each school.

The main impetus for the league's involvement in the desegregation controversy came from Geraldine Koffler, who conceived the idea of a Make It Work campaign. Mrs. Koffler wrote the statement made by the League of Women Voters before the school board on 26 May. She sent more than 150 letters to leading civic and business organizations enclosing the statement and urging their support for the Make It Work campaign. She sent circulars to all elected officials from Governor Wallace on down, announcing the Make It Work campaign. With the help of a coalition including the American Friends Service Committee, the ACT education project, and the newly funded ESAA program, she staged a number of workshops and public meetings to galvanize support for the Make

It Work program. She and her fellow league members made many public appearances in support of the program, securing wide media coverage for the campaign. She designed a Make It Work lapel button and other publicity devices that counteracted the destructive influences of the White Citizens Council.

Other forces that also contributed to the relatively peaceful community scene in September 1971 were the Human Relations and Community Mental Health programs operated at the Spring Hill College Human Relations Center under a grant from the National Institute of Mental Health. The programs consisted of a year-round series of intensive institutes for school personnel, law enforcement officials, social workers, key clergymen, and community organization leaders. During the fall of 1970 and the spring and summer of 1971 approximately 160 community people enrolled in an intensive training program about the understanding of racial conflicts. They secured practical skills in the methods of mounting community programs to counteract the overt manifestations of racial psychoses in the Mobile area.

Formed at this time also was the Mobile Committee for the Support of Public Education. Under an ESAA grant, this nonprofit organization mounted an intensive mass media campaign aimed at the reduction of school conflicts.

A public relations firm was hired to produce a sixty-second spot showing scenes of peaceful and orderly operation of local desegregated school groups in classrooms, halls, laboratories, and school grounds situations. Against the background of a popular guitar musical number the message was delivered to the viewers and listeners: "School years should be good years, a time to learn, a time to enjoy, not a time of conflict. Mobile County has good schools with highly qualified teachers. They are handicapped by racial strife. They need help from all of us . . . students and parents, and citizens who know how conflict cripples a community. We can help by encouraging racial harmony in our schools. Only a few people of both races are causing the turmoil. It's time we said to them: 'Please stop. Let our children learn.'"

This message was aired on afternoon and evening prime time shows on both television stations for nearly two months. It was scheduled on the evening news and the late news. It was featured on the shows popular with teenagers. It was also run on all the popular teenage radio programs. More than 100 billboards viewed by 98 percent of the automobile public each week carried the message. It was also featured in newspaper ads and in widely distributed handbills and posters.

During the intensive saturation program no violence, fights, or disorders were reported in the schools. The superintendent declared that the program was the most effective single factor in the lessening of racial conflict in the schools. Even after the experimental period, whenever there was a threat of violence or a report of rumbles, the television and radio stations immediately began running the spots as public service programs.

BACKLASH

The puzzling upsurge of the violence in the schools after a peaceful and orderly opening up of the school year 1971 and its continuance into the school year of 1972–1973 was partly traceable to the upsurge of the Ku Klux Klan in a new and somewhat different form.

On Saturday, 28 August 1971, the press reported the incorporation of a new organization, the Assembly of Christian Soldiers Church. Their listed purpose was "to assemble for worship in Christian faith, minister to the members of the church society and to the world in propagation of the faith and to all needs of the members of the church society in daily life" (*Mobile Press Register* 1971: 8/28).

Some of the names listed were avowed, long-time Ku Klux Klan members. They had been secretly organizing during the previous six months as a state-wide group called The Southerners. In their bimonthly meetings at the American Legion hall, they seemed to be just another group of concerned citizens exercising their right to assemble freely and to seek redress of grievances. The leaders of the group were Asa Carter, coeditor of the paper called *The Southerner*, and Jesse Mayberry, who had both been leaders of the Original Knights of the Ku Klux Klan of the Confederacy.

At one of their Birmingham Klan meetings, Asa Carter had shot two of his fellow Klansmen who had raised questions about his management of the organization's funds. He was arrested and identified publicly in the court proceeding as the Imperial Wizard of the Ku Klux Klan. He came to Mobile to help in the organization of both the church and its lay arm, the Southerners, a paramilitary cadre of aggressive elite who conducted their close-order military drills and target practices in the woods near the University of South Alabama. They were linked with outbursts of violence against blacks on the university campus.

Carter proposed setting up a state-wide system of private schools that would not cost the white people anything extra if they joined and supported the church and if they shopped at the commissary that the Christian Soldiers were erecting alongside the church. He said that the brotherhood would donate the profits of the church and the commissary to the operation of the school in order to spare the white children the indignity of attending schools with blacks in the public system.

Enough money was raised to begin the construction of the school. Classes were set up and the commissary organized in a big building along with space reserved for the "church." A medical doctor gave the group a loan of more than $35,000 to stock their commissary with supplies. Meanwhile, however, their efforts at securing the loan of upwards of a million dollars from the local banks were thwarted when it was learned that the group was dominated by hard-bitten, bomb-throwing, violence-prone Klansmen. Their meetings, which originally drew 300 to 400 rural and urban malcontents attracted fewer and fewer people as their identity was revealed and their incitement to violence in the public schools was proclaimed.

The woman who had leased them the large building secured an eviction order when they failed to pay the rent. The doctor went to court and attached their unsold canned goods because of their failure to meet their notes on his loan. The school was moved to a small frame building and gradually died from lack of financial support.

But even though this private school with its few dozen students came to an early demise, other private schools were organized and continued to thrive in the post-1971 period because of the massive desegregation of the public schools. In 1970 the local lawyer for the plaintiffs in the *Birdie Mae Davis* case, A. J. Cooper, Jr., and David Jacobs, director of the American Friends Service Committee, together with John L. LeFlore, directed a letter to President

Richard M. Nixon, HEW Secretary Elliot Richardson, Commissioner Randolph Thrower of the Internal Revenue Service, Attorney General John Mitchell, and Secretary of Defense Melvin Laird. They asked the federal officials to use their executive authority to order all appropriate government agencies to withhold federal funds from private schools that were havens for nonconformers and that were blocking meaningful implementation of court-ordered desegregation.

The Internal Revenue Service was also asked to withdraw federal income-tax exemption privileges from these schools. The letter listed nineteen Mobile county schools in its request, including some long-established private and military schools and some church schools that had just recently expanded with the demand for segregated education for whites only. Most of these "seg" academies were small (fewer than 200 students on the average) and were housed in Sunday school classrooms in fundamentalist churches.

One final series of events in 1972 was an unsuccessful attempt to liberalize the composition of the school board. In the wake of her whirlwind activities spearheading the League of Women Voters' efforts to secure community acceptance of the Supreme Court decision of 1971, Geraldine Koffler filed as a candidate for the school board in the Democratic primary of May 1972. She based her campaign on an appeal for quality education and on the need for having a parent of schoolchildren on the board, whose current members had no children in the public schools.

In the three-way primary the incumbent, Homer Sessions, and the White Citizens Council candidate, William Westbrook, campaigned vigorously against Geraldine Koffler. Nevertheless, Mrs. Koffler emerged as the leading candidate in the primary. The White Citizens Council candidate was eliminated, and a runoff was scheduled May 30. The White Citizens Council candidate cast his support in favor of the incumbent. He launched a typical smear campaign, endeavored to frame Mrs. Koffler by devious methods, "accused" her of attending the human relations program at Spring Hill College (which Homer Sessions also attended), and put out anonymous misrepresentations of her campaign. He stated that she had signed an agreement with the NAACP to achieve total integration through total busing; had been very active in NOW, the Non-Partisan Voters League, ACT, and the League of Women Voters; had entertained blacks in her home; had been seen and photographed in company with black males; and had polled 92 percent of the black vote in the primary. The campaign was successful in reelecting the conservative incumbent.

The solid Democratic front had been breached by the Republicans in the Eisenhower administration only to make the county more conservative. The county had voted for Nixon in 1960, for Goldwater in 1964, and it went for Nixon again in 1968 and 1972.

Both the city and county commissions were elected as conservative segregationist candidates. The voters in general sided with the conservatives in their opposition and resistance to the efforts of the blacks to secure equal educational opportunity.

BIRDIE MAE DAVIS REOPENED

The three-year moratorium on further motions in the *Birdie Mae Davis* case ended in July 1974. The court had ruled that if the enrollment projections put forth in the 1971 plan were not achieved by the end of the 1973–1974 school year, then the plaintiffs could again legally challenge the school board.

The case was reopened by the plaintiffs in the summer of 1974. A special consultant in desegregation school plans from the South Florida School Desegregation Center at the University of Miami was brought to Mobile. This consultant, William Feild, wrote a report on the effectiveness of the 1971 desegregation plan for Mobile County. The report addressed itself to two questions: (1) Has the plan been substantially implemented? (2) Has the plan achieved maximum desegregation and a unitary school system? Dr. Feild's study of the semiannual reports filed with the court on the racial composition of students and faculty in all of the schools in Mobile County led him to answer both of these questions in the negative.

The initial plan submitted in 1971 directly affected fifty-five of the eighty-one schools in the county. The remaining schools were presumably to be desegregated in the course of the next three years in accordance with the U.S. Supreme Court orders to maximize desegregation as fast as humanly possible. By 1974, two of the original fifty-five schools had been closed. Of the remaining fifty-three schools, only twenty-three, or 43 percent, came within five percentage points of the racial composition specified in the original 1971 plan. According to Dr. Feild's calculations only 20 percent of the county schools were assisted in moving toward desegregation under the 1971 plan. Dr. Feild's conclusion was that the county school board was in fact still operating two systems, one rural and one urban-metropolitan.

The rural school population was 81 percent white and 19 percent black. The urban-metropolitan schools were 59 percent black and 41 percent white. In the urban-metropolitan area there were still fourteen schools that were all-black or nearly all-black, with only a scattered handful of whites in attendance. There were 10,900 black students in these schools, comprising 41 percent of all blacks in the metropolitan area.

The Supreme Court had ordered that a unitary school system should be achieved in which no schools would be racially identified as either all-white or all-black. The 1971 plan obviously failed to achieve this because 41 percent of the black metropolitan students were still in all-black or nearly all-black schools.

The school administration had achieved more desegregation of the faculty in accordance with the court decree. Virtually all of the schools were within a few percentage points of the 60 to 40 ratio required by the court order. However, the report showed a racial bias in the placement of principals in the integrated schools. Of the twenty-three black principals surviving the cut, nineteen were at all-black schools, only three at white schools, and one at an integrated school. Of the fifty-eight white principals, forty-nine were at white or integrated schools. Not one was assigned as head of an all-black or nearly all-black school.

On the strength of this report, the plaintiffs went back into the federal district court with a motion for additional relief on 20 March 1975. By this time a new federal judge had inherited the *Birdie Mae Davis* case, Judge Brevard Hand, who was not too different from his predecessor in his attitude toward the nettlesome case.

The motion for the plaintiffs summarized the conditions for the 1974–1975 school year as reported by Superintendent Harold R. Collins on 2 December 1974. It noted that the two historically black high schools, Blount and Toulminville, still had all-black enrollments containing 41 percent (3,512) of all black high school students enrolled in the metropolitan schools.

It also noted that three historically black middle schools (Dunbar, Mobile County Training School, and Booker T. Washington) still had 99 to 100 percent all-black enrollments and registered 32 percent of all black middle-school students (2,228). It reported that nine elementary schools in the eastern section of the city, containing 56 percent of all black elementary school students (5,508) still had substantially all-black enrollments—90 to 100 percent black; six of them were historically black schools.

The complaint summarized the situation by saying that eleven historically black schools had never been desegregated and 44 percent of black school students were still attending substantially all-black schools.

The plaintiffs asked the judge to declare the current student attendance plan for Mobile County to be a constitutionally inadequate remedy for the ongoing effects of the prior dual school system. They maintained that as a matter of law the defendants have the burden of proving that the continued existence of these all-black schools is not the result of present or past discriminatory action on their parts.

The petition requested that the court grant additional relief to the plaintiffs by ordering the defendants to develop alternative plans of desegregation and to set hearings on these plans. It asked the court to order the defendants to use a wide variety of remedial methods in desegregating the all-black and all-white schools still surviving in the county sytem; these methods included realignment of attendance zones, pairing or grouping of contiguous and noncontiguous school zones, altering the grade structure to maximize desegregation, and re-routing school bus transportation. The complaint also asked for the reassignment of principals on a more random basis rather than having white principals at all-white schools and most black principals at all-black schools.

The judge was understandably reluctant to expedite this case. He had been brought before the U.S. Supreme Court by the plaintiffs in a parallel case consolidated with theirs in which the lawyers had asked the judge to disqualify himself because of personal bias and prejudice. Upon appeal, the U.S. Supreme Court had denied the plaintiffs' charge that the judge had erred in not disqualifying himself. The whole case, however, left the judge in a less than favorable disposition toward the plaintiffs.

After a two-year unexplained delay, the judge finally set a hearing on 3 February 1977 to consider the motion of 21 March 1975, asking for additional relief. The lawyers for the plaintiffs had at the same time asked for an order to compel the defendants to respond to their interrogatories. The judge set a hearing on this for 7 January 1977, having issued his order to the defendants only a few weeks before, compelling them to file the desired reports. The answers to the interrogatories were delayed for months more in 1977. No further relief was granted to the plaintiffs during the year.

Meanwhile, the NAACP Legal Defense Fund turned its attention away from this litigation on the desegregation issue and directed it toward an attack on the all-white composition of the school board itself. This was done by filing companion suits in the federal court before a more sympathetic judge, Vergil Pitman, as voting rights cases for the representation of blacks on the city commission, the county commission, and the school board.

All three governing bodies were elected at large in a voting pattern that diluted the black vote. According to the plaintiffs, this nullified the effect of the Supreme Court's one-man, one-vote principle that had been applied to the redistricting of the Alabama state legislature and to others across the country. The plaintiffs requested that elections be held by district to allow black representation.

These cases were argued and won both before the district court and before the Fifth Circuit Court within the next three years. As of late 1979, they were still on appeal to the U.S. Supreme Court.

CONCLUSIONS

A study of the Mobile school system published in the *Christian Science Monitor* in Boston for Monday, 19 January 1976 characterizes Mobile as a beautiful old-South town with an industrial new-South look about it because of the recent oil and gas discoveries and the booming business in the port. Its school desegregation was characterized as a yes-and-no proposition. Many children (26,000) were bused daily from one neighborhood to another to comply with the court order. Still, some schools were not yet desegregated at all, and others had just a token few whites or blacks.

Faculty desegregation was characterized as "completed on paper," but faculty communication across racial lines and friendly cooperation of white and black teachers at the same school were seen as still a matter for future agenda.

White flight from the school system was deemed to be responsible for the loss of 20 percent of the public school population since 1970. The forty-six private schools with about 10,000 pupils were the main recipients of the white flight from the public schools. Episcopal, Methodist, Baptist, and even Lutheran schools were predominantly one-race schools.

Approximately 6,000 students were reported as attending Roman Catholic parochial schools that had been desegregated since the 1960s. Nothwithstanding the stern prohibition issued by the local bishop against allowing the Catholic schools to become havens for white segregationists, the Catholic schools were still enrolling a large percentage of non-Catholic students. Some of the Catholic schools were all-white or had only a few token black students in attendance.

The prospects for the future are not too favorable for any further desegregation, unless the school board changes its composition. A major blow was dealt the desegregation effort when the federal judge refused to assess the court costs and the lawyers' fees against the defendant school board. The lawyers claimed that they had incurred more than $225,000 worth of costs required for the long, tedious, and complicated litigation. The Fifth Circuit Court of Appeals upheld the district judge on the denial.

A recent statement by Judge Brevard Hand to the effect that Mobile County schools have been desegregated in accordance with the Supreme Court mandate seems to indicate that as long as he has jurisdiction over the case no further desegregation will be ordered.

BIBLIOGRAPHY

ABLE. 1963, 1964. Alabamians Behind Local Education, Organization Records Files. Unpublished.

ACT Educational Program. 1973. *An Analysis of the Maysville Community Schools* by Henry Rembert. Unpublished survey report, (August 6) p. 5.

Anderson, Robert E. 1971. "Mobile, Alabama: The Essence of Survival." In *The South and Her Children: School Desegregation, 1970–1971.* Atlanta, Southern Regional Council, pp. 38–49.

Dickerson, Donald B. 1971. *The Effects of Desegregation on Black Personnel and Black Schools in the Mobile County Public School System in the 1970–1971 School Year.* Unpublished survey report, pp. 33.

Federal Reporter
  Birdie Mae Davis v. *Board of School Commissioners of Mobile County,* 1963. 318 F. 2d. 63, 322 F. 2d. 356, 322 F. 2d. 359; 1964. 333 F. 2d. 53; 1966. 364 F. 2d. 896; 1968. 393 F. 2d. 690; 1969. 414 F. 2d. 609, 419 F. 2d. 883; 1970. 422 F. 2d. 1139; 1971. 430 F. 2d. 883, 889–891, Supreme Court Decision, April 20; all 5th Cir.

  National Education Association v. *Board of School Commissioners of Mobile County,* 483 F. 2d. 1022–1024 (5th Cir. 1973).

  Singleton v. *Jackson Municipal Separate School District,* 419 F. 2d. 1211–1218, 348 F. 2d. 729.

Federal Reporter Supplement
  Birdie Mae Davis et al. v. *Board of School Commissioners of Mobile County. Alabama,* 219 F. Supp. 542 (1963).

Feild, William B. *Report on Effectiveness of 1971 Desegregation Plan for Mobile County, Alabama.* Unpublished report.

Foley, Albert S. 1956. "The K.K.K. in Mobile, Alabama." *America,* 95(19) (December 8): 298–299.

Foley, Albert S. 1972. "New Church, Old Klan." *America* 127(12) (October 21): 321–322.

Graves, William. 1968. "Mobile: Alabama's City in Motion." *National Geographic* 133 (March): 368–397.

Lathrop-Smith, Emma. 1964. *The Radical Right in Mobile, 1963–1964.* Mobile, Citizens Committee for Constitutional Freedom, private mimeo publication.

League of Women Voters of Mobile, Organizational Files.

Mobile Committee for the Support of Public Education. *Organizational Files.*

Mobile Press (afternoon edition). Clippings of almost daily coverage of the school desegregation crisis.

Mobile Register (morning edition).

Parsons, Cynthia. 1976. "Report from 'Old South' Mobile, Alabama." *Christian Science Monitor* (January 19): B8.

Race Relations Law Reporter
  Birdie Mae Davis v. *Board of School Commissioners of Mobile County,* 1963. 8 Race Rel. L. Rep. 480, 901, 907; 1964. 9 Race Rel. L. Rep. 1179; 1965. 10 Race Rel. L. Rep. 1016; 1967. 12 Race Rel. L. Rep. 1820; all S.D. Ala.

Southern School News (SSN) 1963. "Court Tells Mobile to Present Plan for 1964–1965 Term." 10 (1) (July): 5–6; 1963. "Five U.S. Judges Enjoin

Wallace." 10 (4) (October): 10; 1964. "Public Protests and Violence Accompany Desegregation Moves" by Hoyt Purvis, 10 (11) (May): 12B–13B.

Supreme Court of the United States, October Term 1970
Birdie Mae Davis et al. v. *Board of School Commissioners of Mobile County.* On Writ of Certiorari to the United States Court of Appeals for the Fifth Circuit.

Brief for Petitioners by Jack Greenberg, et al. of New York, Vernon Z. Crawford and Algernon J. Cooper of Mobile; Anthony G. Amsterdam of Stanford, California. New York: Meilan Press, 1971, 85 pp.

Brief for the Board of School Commissioners, Abram L. Philips, Jr., Palmer Pillans, George F. Wood of Mobile. St. Louis: St. Louis Law Printing Co., 1971, 100 pp.

McDaniel, Superintendent of Schools, et al. v. *Barresi et al.* No. 420, October Term 1970 (April 20, 1971).

Swan v. *Charlotte-Mecklenberg Board of Education et al.* Nos. 281 and 349, October Term 1970 (April 20, 1971).

Thomason, Michael, and Melton McLaurin. 1975. *Mobile: American River City.* Mobile: Easter, 141 pp.

U.S. District Court for the Southern District of Alabama.
Birdie Mae Davis et al. v. *Board of School Commissioners of Mobile County.* Court Records, Clerk of Court Office, Mobile. Assorted and selected files.

United States News and World Report
1956. "The South Digs in to Fight Mixed Schools." 7 September pp. 25–27.

1958. "The Alabama Plan: New Answer to Mixed Schools." 5 December pp. 47–49.

University of South Alabama: Title IV CRA Center for Intercultural Education. Reports, records, files.

9

Richmond, Virginia: Massive Resistance Without Violence

James A. Sartain and Rutledge M. Dennis

The city of Richmond, Virginia, the former capital of the Confederacy, is located about 100 miles south of Washington, D.C., at the fall line of the James River. The river flows through the center of Richmond and forms the boundary between the surrounding counties of Henrico and Chesterfield. The city lies about halfway between the Atlantic Coast and the foothills of the Appalachian Mountains. Many view Richmond as special in that it serves as a geographical, political, and cultural link between the North and the South, plus potentially providing its citizens with what some may view as the best of both worlds. As someone once noted: "Richmond harbors few of the excesses of the North or of the Deep South. . . . [It is] more courtly southern than that usually associated with other regions of the South, yet remaining relatively untouched by the cold austerity of the North."

CITY AND COUNTY: POLITICS AND POPULATION

Independent cities in Virginia are not part of the county or counties in which they are located. This presents special problems in matters of cooperation between local governmental units and in annexation. Since the middle of the eighteenth century, Richmond has grown in size and in area through annexation, but because of the rapid urbanization of the surrounding counties within the last two decades, the option of annexation has become increasingly difficult. Annexation in Virginia is quite complex. The city desiring to annex a portion of an adjoining county must bring a civil suit before a special three-judge court and must present economic evidence as to why this annexation is essential to the well-being of the city. The county, in turn, offers reasons why the area should not be annexed. If the annexation is granted to the city, it must pay a court-determined sum to the county based upon the value of publicly owned buildings and land, streets, sewer systems, and other improvements, as well as for the anticipated loss of tax revenue over a period of years. This system guarantees hostility between the residents and between the governments of the two areas. The constant threat of annexation acts as a barrier to cooperation between the city and the counties. The counties fear that too much cooperation would weaken their position in an annexation suit.

The 1968 annexation of twenty-three square miles of Chesterfield County added 45,707 white residents and 555 nonwhite residents. Without this annexation the population would have been 52 percent nonwhite in 1970 (see table 9.1). The city experienced its first significant population decline (4.5 percent) between 1950 and 1960. One of the major reasons for this decline was the movement of many whites into the surrounding suburban counties. During this decade the white population declined by 18.8 percent, whereas the nonwhite population increased by 26 percent. With annexation of part of a suburban county, whites in Richmond were 58 percent in 1960 and 1970. This exodus of whites from the city is reflected in the sharp population increases in the counties that enabled the population to double. The extent of this increase in the counties is illustrated in Henrico County, where a nearly three-fold increase occurred in total population from 52,000 to 144,000 from 1950 to 1970 (see table 9.2).

The doubling of population results mainly from the flight of Richmond residents to the surrounding counties. According to data supplied by the Richmond Regional Planning Commission, between 1955 and 1960 Richmond contributed 35 percent of the families acquiring homes in the counties. The counties, however, contributed only 5.6 percent of the families moving into the city. A special census conducted in Henrico County found that of those indicating a prior place of residence, 38.5 percent cited Henrico County and 40.8 percent cited Richmond.

While white residents were moving into the counties, black residents were experiencing a sizable intracity migration. The black population has traditionally resided chiefly in the Church Hill section in the east, Jackson Ward in the inner

TABLE 9.1. Population of Richmond, Virginia, 1930–1970, by Race

Year	White	%	Black	%	Total
1930	129,871	71	53,058	29	182,929
1940	131,706	68	61,336	32	193,042
1950	157,228	68	73,082	32	230,310
1960	127,627	58	92,331	42	219,958
1970*	143,857	58	105,764	42	249,621

Source: U.S. Bureau of the Census.

*Reflects annexation of portion of Chesterfield County in 1968.

TABLE 9.2. Population of Henrico and Chesterfield Counties, 1950–1970

Year	Henrico	Chesterfield
1950	51,650	31,970
1960	111,269	61,762
1970	143,812	68,012*

Source: U.S. Bureau of the Census.

*Reflects loss of population through annexation by Richmond in 1968.

city, and the Randolph area in the near west end. Thus residential segregation has been very pronounced. A small percentage of the increase in the black population has resulted from births, but a much larger percentage has been due to inmigration. Richmond was therefore faced with the prospects of a steadily increasing black population and a rapidly decreasing white population.

The annexation of part of Chesterfield County in 1965 has been viewed as racially motivated, for without this annexation the city would have had a black majority. Following the annexation a civil suit was filed by Curtis Holt, a black civil rights worker, requesting the deannexation of this area on the grounds that it violated the civil rights of blacks by diluting the black vote in the city. This suit had a great deal of support in the annexed area, perhaps even financial support. From 1970 until 1977, Richmond was prohibited from holding municipal elections. In 1977, the U.S. Supreme Court decided that one of the results of the annexation would indeed be the dilution of the black vote. The Supreme Court agreed to accept the annexation results only if the city would restructure its voting procedure from an at-large to a ward system. With the approval of the court the city was divided into nine wards—four with a clearly white majority, four with a clearly black majority, and one "swing" ward about equally divided between black and white. By the time the first election was held, however, demographic changes had turned the "swing" ward into a majority black ward.

Richmond is currently governed by a city manager-council form of government. For several decades prior to the late 1940s, Richmond had a twenty-two member city council elected by wards, and an elected mayor. No blacks had served on the city council during the twentieth century. As a result of a reform movement in 1947, the voters approved a referendum that called for a nine-member council elected at large on a nonpartisan basis. The council was to select one of its members to serve as mayor and to employ a city manager (Dabney 1976: 334).

In 1948, Oliver W. Hill, a black lawyer, was elected to the city council. He was later to become one of the plaintiffs' lawyers in the first Richmond desegregation case. Since that time the number of blacks on the city council has varied from none to three under the at-large system. After the return to the ward system in 1977, the council became majority black (five blacks and four whites), and Richmond now has a black mayor. It is interesting to note that the current mayor, Henry Marsh, III, was the other attorney for the plaintiffs in the 1962 school desegregation suit. All the city managers had been white, until the city council membership became majority black. The changeover in race of the city manager was a major struggle.

Richmond is a city with a diverse economic base. It has a balance of production and service industries that has prevented some of the high unemployment prevalent in other cities, especially for whites unemployed. According to data supplied by the Richmond Manpower Program, the total unemployment rate for the city in 1970 was 3.5 percent. For blacks the rate was 4.2 percent and for whites, 1.9 percent. Thus the black rate of unemployment was more than double that of the white rate. A 1970 estimate placed the total unemployment rate for Richmond at 4.2 percent. According to the Richmond Manpower Program the black rate has traditionally been double the white rate. The rule-of-thumb guidelines used by the Manpower Program would place the rate of black unemployment in 1978 at about 6.6 percent and the white rate at about 3.1 percent.

The city is a major center for the production of tobacco products, metals, pharmaceuticals, paints, food products, fertilizer, and wood products. It is a regional center for banking and insurance; a number of large companies have their regional, national or international headquarters here. In the labor market, government employs 19.5 percent of the labor force; transportation, communications, and public utilities, 8.6 percent; finance, insurance, and real estate, 8.6 percent; and farming, mining, construction, and other, 7.0 percent. A higher percentage of whites is employed in the professional, managerial, and administrative areas. There is, conversely, a heavy concentration of blacks in categories such as service workers, operatives, and clerical and private household workers. Employment opportunities for blacks are skewed in the direction of low-prestige jobs. This is rather clearly shown by the 65 percent of employed whites who are in white-collar jobs and the 27 percent of employed blacks who work in professional, managerial, sales, and clerical jobs.

EDUCATION IN VIRGINIA: MASSIVE RESISTANCE

Virginia has been considered by some to be a border state and by others to be a part of the Deep South. Geographically there are many states further south, but ideologically none is farther south in culture and tradition than Virginia. Richmond is a major focal point for the spirit of the Old South. Here are located the Museum of the Confederacy and other reminders of the days of Richmond's greatest era of fame, such as the Robert E. Lee House and the headquarters of the United Daughters of the Confederacy. In or near Richmond there are nine Civil War (locally, "The War Between the States") battlefield parks and five Civil War cemeteries. All five of the monuments on Monument Avenue are of Confederate heroes. History is not a dead issue in Richmond. During the summer of 1978, a topic of considerable interest was whether the U.S. Congress would restore the citizenship of Jefferson Davis, the president of the Confederacy.

Even though racial segregation has been the rule of law and of custom in Virginia, the state has been generally free of violence and bloodshed experienced by much of the South. The Ku Klux Klan has not in recent decades been an important factor in most sections of Virginia. Even when racial problems have arisen, the leaders of both races seem to have exhibited a high degree of ritualistic politeness and decorum, a behavioral pattern that contrasts with the lack of such in other areas of the South. What appears to undergird this sense of politeness and decorum is the idea held by many whites that leadership roles should be played only by those who have attained a high social status, those who can qualify as gentlemen, and those who will preserve the status quo. Virginia has a long tradition of electing to high public office the courtly gentleman rather than the demagogue common to some other sections of the region.

V. O. Key, Jr., the noted political scientist, observed the consequences of Virginia's ideas on black-white relationships: "Rabble-rousing and Negro baiting capacities, which in Georgia or Mississippi would be a great political asset, simply mark a person as one not to the manner born. A public attitude favorable to this type of leadership combined with organization discipline represses most of the crudities commonly thought to be characteristic of southern politics. Virginia leadership is ingenious in stratagems to maintain political decorum" (Key 1949: 26). And, "Southern Negro voters generally align themselves with candidates and factions opposing the status quo. This tendency is less marked in Virginia and Tennessee where Negroes have voted longer and in larger numbers than farther south. In the cities, where Negroes vote in highest proportions, they have often been allied with the local arms of the Byrd organization, which in turn has protected their right to the suffrage. Virginia's white citizens in and out of the machine have demonstrated a relatively acute sense of responsibility toward the Negro—an attitude that may account in part for the fact that its race relations are perhaps the most harmonious in the South" (Key 1949: 32).

The post-1954 years have shown that blacks were becoming less willing to follow the dictates of white political leadership, and much less willing to preserve the "racial etiquette" that would ensure a continual monopoly in the political and economic arenas. But a sense of politeness and decorum seems to have persisted in spite of that assertiveness by blacks in the post-1954 era. As one Richmond black noted, when blacks and whites in leadership roles sit down to discuss racial matters there is a surface politeness. The white leadership "smiles and tries to charm you to death, but in the end nothing happens." The "sense of responsibility toward the Negro," as cited by Key, can be said to represent a paternalism that comes from the knowledge that one has overwhelming political and economic power, and therefore one can, in small ways, be generous in areas that are rather unimportant and inconsequential to one's continual power monopoly. Thus, affection and responsibility for blacks as claimed by whites must be viewed within the contexts of the particular and peculiar definition of affection where black-white relations are concerned.

In the years just before the U.S. Supreme Court's *Brown* decision, individual blacks were allowed in spheres heretofore prohibited. As previously noted, a black lawyer had been elected to serve on the Richmond City Council in 1948, and in the early spring of 1954 the Roman Catholic diocese announced that desegregation of its schools would take place that fall. There are indications that blacks in Virginia have not remained totally passive in the face of discrimination. When a 1904 Virginia law permitted common carriers to segregate, street car operators in Richmond chose to segregate blacks. John Mitchell, then editor of a black newspaper, *The Richmond Planet,* organized a boycott and picketed the lines for a year. The boycott was a success and later in the year the *Planet* exclaimed: "The street car company is busted: three cheers for the Richmond Negroes" (Dabney 1976: 271).

It also appears that the first direct public action by blacks toward the school system occurred in 1938, when the predominantly black Virginia Teachers Association and the NAACP formed a joint committee to end the salary inequality between black and white teachers. When the NAACP filed its "equalization of salary" petition in 1940, black teachers were being paid from $700 to $1,000 a year less than white teachers.

The U.S. Supreme Court decision to outlaw segregated public schools did not come as a surprise to most of the leaders of Virginia. The response was of course mixed, but most religious and political leaders called for moderation and for working out a solution to Virginia's problems within the law. At that time there was little hint of the passions soon to arise. Most of the people in the state evidently failed to see the significance of the decision or else were sure that it would not apply to Virginia—at least not in their lifetimes.

During the first few months after the *Brown* decision the strongest statements of support in Virginia came from church groups. Both the Southern Presbyterian Synod of Virginia and the Baptist General Association of Virginia called upon the people to recognize that the decision was in keeping with Christian theology and principle. A statement attacking segregation was also published by the Richmond Ministerial Association. It must be noted, however, that few white churches took an activist position on the desegregation issue. The church communities, Protestant, Roman Catholic, and Jewish, remained silent and provided virtually no moral or spiritual leadership during the school crisis.

A black attorney who worked with the NAACP on the school case in Richmond remarked on the "shameful role of the churches in their almost total silence on this great moral issue." The churches did not view the school issue as a moral issue, a view supported by the Reverend Theodore F. Adams, retired pastor of the white First Baptist Church. Dr. Adams recently stated, "Each [Baptist] church could take its own stand; the school issue was not viewed as a matter for the churches to decide." Thus, congregations were not up in arms regarding desegregation, because ministers were not pushing for an open church declaration of support for school desegregation. In either case, the school issue did not result in the splitting of churches in Richmond or in the firing of ministers. Church leaders and members seemed to have decided that school desegregation was a school issue and hence secular, rather than a church issue and therefore moral and spiritual.

No comments on the impact of the *Brown* decision on Virginia can ignore the importance of U.S. Senator Harry F. Byrd, the head of the "Byrd machine" and the most powerful political leader of his generation in Virginia. An archconservative in matters of politics, economics, and race, and a strong advocate of the rights of individual states, he was bitterly opposed to the encroachment on private and local public matters of the federal government (see Wilkinson 1968 for an excellent summary of Byrd's philosophy and career).

Harry Byrd was born in 1887, the son of Richard E. Byrd. His family had long been active in Virginia politics, and his father had served as speaker of the Virginia House of Delegates. His father was also a trusted member of the political organization of Thomas S. Martin. Harry Byrd dropped out of school at the age of fifteen years to attempt to salvage the faltering family-owned newspaper, the Winchester *Evening Star*. Within five years the paper was in sound financial position and was beginning to take strong positions on political issues in Virginia.

Byrd was later elected to the state senate, and in 1925 when he was thirty-eight years old he was elected governor. He was a strong governor and gradually assumed the leadership of the Democratic party in Virginia. Because the Republicans frequently did not even nominate candidates for office, Byrd was the head of virtually all political activity in the state. As governor he reorganized the state bureaucracy and "consolidated one hundred bureaus, boards, and departments, previously independent of the governor, into fourteen departments directly subject to the governor's control" (Wilkinson 1968: 7). He also reduced the number of elected officials from seven to three and pushed an antilynching law through a reluctant Virginia General Assembly.

In 1933, Byrd was elected to the U.S. Senate and served until his retirement in 1965. During these thirty-two years, he remained in close contact with every detail of the Virginia political scene. He exercised almost complete control over the general assembly, and his support was almost essential for any candidate to receive the nomination of the Democratic party in Virginia at any level of government. His political power was based upon the personal loyalty of the members of the Byrd organization. The "court house crowd" in the rural areas of Virginia was his major source of support, and those who were loyal received their political and economic rewards. Aside from the informal influence in securing the election of members of the machine to the general assembly, the governorship, and to hundreds of local offices, the power of the organization was manifest in some formal ways. The state Board of Compensation, appointed by the governor, set the salaries for almost all of the state employees on an individual basis. The general assembly selected all of the state circuit court judges in Virginia. These circuit court judges then appointed a wide variety of local boards, commissions, and individual office holders. These, in turn, controlled such important local matters as schools, elections, and property assessments (Wilkinson 1968: 33). The governor also had the responsibility of appointing the members of all of the state boards and committees. This highly centralized power assured the control of Virginia politics by Byrd and his friends for over forty years.

From the moment of the announcement of the U.S. Supreme Court decision on school segregation, Senator Byrd spoke out strongly against the right of the court to interfere in the internal affairs of the states. Byrd called the decision "the most serious blow that has been struck against the rights of the states" (Muse 1961: 5). Governor Thomas B. Stanley, however, issued a moderate statement at the time of the court decision, and it appeared for many months that the other Virginia leaders and the newspapers would follow his lead. However, Byrd objected to Stanley's position and helped to push Virginia into a position of defiance of the court decision (Wilkinson 1968: 152).

This dramatic shift over a period of months has been explained by Wilkinson (1968) as the result of the Byrd machine's struggles to hold onto its power. It narrowly escaped defeat in several primary elections and general elections between 1949 and 1954 and needed an issue to divert the attention of the people from the internal problems of the machine. It was also an issue that could be used to unite the citizens of Virginia around a common enemy (Wilkinson 1968: 152–154). Gradually other political leaders began to fall in line with Byrd's position, and Virginia's policy of "massive resistance" began to take shape (see Muse 1961, Ely 1976, Wilhoit 1973, and Bartley 1969).

If Senator Harry F. Byrd was the political force behind Virginia's massive resistance movement, then James Jackson Kilpatrick, editor of the *Richmond News Leader,* was its leading spokesman to the people. Kilpatrick was reared in Oklahoma and had strong ties in New Orleans. He became editor of the *News Leader* in 1951. Day after day his editorials called upon the people of Virginia to stand firm against desegregation of the schools. In part, he was strongly opposed to the U.S. Supreme Court's intervention in what he considered to be a matter of states' rights; and, in part he was an advocate of white supremacy (Kilpatrick 1962: 26–43). Even though he bitterly opposed the *Brown* decision and considered the U.S. Supreme Court had made a glaring constitutional error, he never advocated violence. He did, however, admonish Virginia's politicians and public to come up with a position that would be in "contemptuous defiance of Federal Court enrollment orders."

As the months passed, public opposition to school desegregation hardened. Even though the Ku Klux Klan and the White Citizens Council made little impact on Virginia, a local organization, The Defenders of State Sovereignty and Individual Liberties, did. It emerged as the spokesman for the segregationist viewpoint. The members were white, mostly middle class, and from the small towns and rural areas. Some of the leaders were minor officeholders in the Byrd organization. They published a newsletter, conducted letter-writing campaigns to state and national officials, and held numerous public meetings. The Defenders were "a major force in mobilizing segregationist opinion" (Ely 1976: 31).

Not all of Virginia's leaders were such strict segregationists. Some who called themselves moderates were not integrationists, but they favored obeying the law. They felt that a token amount of desegregation might satisfy the federal courts and give Virginia time to work out acceptable plans. Among these were state Senator Armistead Boothe, delegate Robert Whitehead, and Francis P. Miller. All of these men were Democrats, but they were not in the inner circle of the Byrd machine. Miller, in fact, was the leader of the anti-Byrd Democrats in Virginia. Even though these men had some followers outside of the Byrd organization, they made little impact during the early days of massive resistance.

During the summer of 1954, Governor Stanley appointed state Senator Garland Gray chairman of a legislative commission to investigate the possible courses of action for the state. For over a year the commission held hearings and floated trial balloons in the press. Finally, in November 1955, the commission made public its plan. There were three basic recommendations: (1) a system of tuition grants to be made to individual children in order that they might attend private schools if the schools were ordered desegregated; (2) a locally administered pupil assignment plan. Local school boards could assign pupils to a specific school. Although based on criteria other than race, its purpose was to keep desegregation to a minimum; and (3) to amend the Virginia constitution so as to eliminate the provision for compulsory attendance of schools. This amendment would provide that no child could be required to attend an integrated school (Muse 1961: 15).

The Gray plan pleased very few people in Virginia. The local option of pupil assignment displeased the supporters of massive resistance. The moderates and many parents feared that the plan would eventually destroy public education in order to prevent even a minimum of integration. The moderates, in fact, under Boothe's leadership had presented a local option plan under which "outstanding Negro students" would enter white schools. As Boothe outlines his program, "It does not mean that a predominately white school will have a large number of Negro pupils or that a predominantly Negro school will have a large number of white pupils. It does mean that a predominantly white school may have a limited number of qualified Negro students who want to go there" (Ely 1976: 114).

In spite of widespread misgivings, the movement to amend the Virginia constitution began. The general assembly quickly passed a resolution calling for a referendum of the matter of calling a constitutional convention. Led by Senator Byrd, who expressed some reservations about the Gray plan, the Byrd organization led the fight for the convention. A collection of anti-Byrd politicians, churchmen, and public-spirited citizens formed the Society for the Preservation of Public Schools. After a heated campaign the referendum passed and the results of the convention were a foregone conclusion. By the time the main features of the Gray plan had been enacted into law, however, it had been undermined by those seeking stronger measures. According to the hard-line segregationists any integration was too much, and the Gray plan did not now seem to go far enough.

In November 1955, Kilpatrick raised anew the old ideas of nullification and of interposition. His editorials in the Richmond *News Leader* set forth in strong language the idea that a state could place itself between the federal government and the people of the state, and that the general assembly could pass a resolution making the *Brown* decision null and void in Virginia. Senator Byrd supported Kilpatrick's ideas, and many of the political leaders joined him. Most of the lawyers in the state, however, felt that this was an unworkable maneuver. Later Kilpatrick admitted that interposition would not stand up in the courts but was a means of stalling for time (Dabney 1976: 345). Regardless of its legal value, the general assembly passed a resolution protesting this encroachment upon the reserved powers of the state and pledged to resist the U.S. Supreme Court on this issue. It called upon other states to do the same.

If it accomplished nothing else, the idea of nullification raised the massive resisters to new heights of influence and power. The people of Virginia responded to the political oratory and to the editorials. In response to this aroused mood, Governor Stanley called for the general assembly to meet in a special session in August 1956. The Gray plan was forgotten, along with local option and limited desegregation. In this short session of the general assembly twenty-three acts were passed. These acts can be divided into two major categories: acts aimed at curbing the activities of the NAACP, and acts related to keeping the schools segregated. The NAACP had been active in attempting to get black parents to file suits on behalf of their children. The general assembly now made it against the law and a criminal offense to counsel anyone who was challenging segregation. Attempts were also made to seize the records and membership lists of the NAACP. In several cases black parents were fired from their jobs if it was learned that they had petitioned for their children to attend integrated schools. Persons affected were mainly domestic workers. In a few cases, however, even grandparents were fired if their grandchildren's names appeared in the newspaper in a petition request. Black public school teachers and administrators were especially warned not to get involved in the issue. Further intimidation was used by calling those who opposed segregation before various legislative commissions.

Three major acts dealt with countering possible court decisions requiring local school systems to begin the desegregation process and were the legal underpinnings of massive resistance: (1) The general assembly created the state Pupil Placement Board. This board had the authority to handle all the cases of pupil assignment and of transfer, taking away the local option of the Gray plan. Its major function seems to have been to take the pressure off the local school authorities. (2) The governor was given a mandate to close any school ordered to desegregate, and to close all other schools on that level in the local system. He was to attempt to reopen the school on a segregated basis. If this failed and the local school board decided to operate on an integrated basis, the governor was to order all state funds to be withheld from all schools on that level in the entire system. (3) A system of state-supported tuition grants was established to make grants to any children in public school systems closed to prevent integration (Ely 1976: 45-46).

The general assembly also created two committees to investigate the enforcement of these laws and the activities of organizations that encouraged racial litigation. These committees were the Committee on Law Reform and Racial Activities and the Committee on Offenses Against the Administration of Justice (Ely 1976: 46–47).

This 1956 session of the Virginia General Assembly marked the legal beginning of massive resistance. The next two years did not bring significant changes in the laws of Virginia, but they did mark the crisis of public schools in the state. In 1957, the Byrd candidate for governor, J. Lindsay Almond, defeated the moderate Republican Ted Dalton. Almond pledged to carry out the fight for segregation, whereas Dalton argued for local option and local pupil assignment. Dalton was by no means an integrationist, but he believed that total defiance of the U.S. Supreme Court would lead eventually to a loss of control over the local schools. The campaign was more heated between the supporters of the two men than between the candidates themselves. Dalton carried out an effective campaign, but court decisions in other states and the federal troops in Little Rock doomed his chances of election.

In his inaugural address Almond repeated his strong stand against integration and for the preservation of states' rights. During his first few months in office he warned the people of Virginia that the time would soon come when they must face the choice between some desegregation in the schools or no schools at all. The two Richmond newspapers, the *News Leader* and the *Times Dispatch*, continued to urge the people to stand firm and resist the pressures from the courts and from the media outside of the state.

The story of the closing of some of the schools in Virginia is beyond the scope of this brief description of the massive resistance years. Warren County, Norfolk, Charlottesville, and Prince Edward County all had their schools closed for varying periods of time. Most of the white children in these areas were enrolled in existing private schools or in newly created white private schools. Some of the black students remained in all-black public schools and a few enrolled in private schools, but most, especially in Prince Edward County, were without schools for long periods of time.

The closing of some schools and the threats of more closings caused more and more moderates to speak out in favor of public education. The Virginia Committee for the Public Schools called for the preservation of the public schools even at the cost of some desegregation. Business leaders in a number of areas began to apply pressure on Governor Almond to find a solution. At first Almond continued to insist that he would never allow any integration in the state, but he began to waver when it became apparent that the state's legal position was weakening. Byrd and Almond had almost reached a parting of the ways. Byrd, with no direct responsibility for carrying out the laws of the state and the orders of the courts, could remain adamant about continued segregation. Almond, however, had to deal with these matters on a daily basis and had no desire to spend time in jail on a contempt of court charge as some suggested he should do.

On 19 January 1959, both the Virginia Supreme Court of Appeals and a panel of federal judges declared the laws directly related to schools to be unconstitutional. The end of the massive resistance movement was in sight, though Governor Almond continued to search for legal means of evading the court orders, and the state Pupil Placement Board remained in operation. It took lawsuit after lawsuit in almost every city and county to bring about the gradual end to segregated schools in Virginia, but the major battles were over. These lawsuits were sometimes filed by individual black citizens, but the majority were filed by the NAACP in behalf of parents and individual students.

EDUCATION IN RICHMOND: THE PUBLIC SCHOOLS

The Richmond Public Schools are controlled by a school board appointed by the city council. The members serve a five-year term and may be reappointed. From the early 1950s until 1968, the racial composition of the board was four whites and one black. During the massive resistance era a black, Booker T. Bradshaw, served as vice-chairman of the board. During this time Lewis F. Powell, who later became a justice on the U.S. Supreme Court, served as chairman. Dr. H. I. Willett served as the superintendent of education. Most of the members of the board were upper-middle class or upper class, few of whom had children in the public schools. There were traditional "slots" on the school board. For example, there was a lawyer slot, a black slot, a female slot, and a businessman slot. When a person was replaced on the board, the replacement usually filled the same slot. There was some effort made to have different geographic areas of the city represented on the school board. During the decades prior to 1960, serving on the school board was considered to be a civic duty. The members were usually content to let the school administrators handle the day-to-day operation of the schools.

During the legal battles over desegregation of the public schools in the late 1960s and early 1970s, several members of the board resigned or declined to be reappointed at the end of their terms. Over the past decade the composition of the board has changed. More blacks, more parents with children in the public schools, and more persons from the middle class were appointed. At the present time there are four whites and three blacks on the board. The chairman, Miles Jones, is black, as is the superintendent, Dr. Richard C. Hunter. In the past few years the board has become more aggressive and has occasionally taken action opposed by the city council. For example in 1970, the council requested that the board withdraw its legal suit to force a merger of the city schools with those of the two surrounding counties. The board refused to withdraw the suit.

For many years the public schools in Richmond enjoyed the local reputation of being among the finest in the South. It was widely believed that one of the white high schools, Thomas Jefferson High School, was "among the finest high schools in the Southeast" (Dabney 1976: 339), and it was claimed that this same school sent as large a portion of its graduating classes to college as any high school on the East Coast (Doherty 1972: 82). This reputation for excellence in public education in Richmond was based chiefly upon local evaluation of the white schools, though several black schools, notably Armstrong High School, had acquired a reputation for high academic achievement. This is in contrast with the other black high school, Maggie Walker, which was basically a trade school with a vocational education foundation. It should be noted that the Armstrong reputation may only be a comparison with Maggie Walker, and only in the black community. Black parents did not believe that Armstrong was a strong school when compared to other white high schools.

White school officials were generally indifferent toward black schools, as were the newspapers and the white community. All schools were segregated by race until two black students were admitted to a white middle school in 1960. It was not until 1963 that a white teacher taught in a black school. In 1965, seven black teachers were assigned to six different white schools, and ten white teachers were assigned to eight different black schools. It should be noted that American Indians and Chinese were considered to be "white" for purposes of pupil assignment.

An analysis of the school enrollment by race reveals several interesting facts. The maximum enrollment of 22,052 for whites was in the year 1932-1933. Clearly, the decline in white enrollment that took place in the 1930s and 1940s was not attributable to desegregation. In the school year 1958-1959 black enrollment exceeded white enrollment in the Richmond public schools for the first time. By 1960-1961, blacks were a majority of the students enrolled in the public school system of Richmond.

During the years of massive resistance the Richmond public schools were not directly involved in the court decisions. Two black students did apply for admission to a white school in 1958 but were turned down by the state Pupil Placement Board, but the students did not file suit. No official reason seems to have been given for this refusal by the state Pupil Placement Board. A retired white Richmond school administrator said recently that Richmond just was not ready for integration at that time. In 1960, four black students applied to attend the all-white Chandler Junior High School. Two were admitted, and two were turned down. In 1961, the number of blacks in the formerly all-white schools had increased to 37; in 1962 to 127; and in 1963 to 520, or about 2 percent of the total black enrollment. No white students had applied for admission to a black school.

Considering all the school desegregation suits in Virginia and in the rest of the south, one may question why so few black students had been admitted to the white schools. There are probably a number of partial answers to the question. There had been little in the way of aggressive legal action on the part of black parents in Richmond. At that time there was no sense of consensus by blacks regarding school integration. Initial reports from other southern schools that desegregated begrudgingly indicated that these initial black pathfinders were not exactly received with open arms by white students, teachers, or administrators—not to mention the white parents and the rest of the white community. Rather than risk the possibility of close personal and social contacts between black and white students, many schools disbanded all extracurricular activities. Thus, black students who transferred from black high schools, or who had moved from an elementary school or a high school, were faced with the prospects of icy and often hateful stares, insults, and personal segregation, being shunted aside in isolated classes or wings of the school.

White students who attended the predominantly black schools in other areas sometimes encountered insults as well, but there was generally no organized opposition to their presence. In several cases in Richmond, black students complained of what they felt were personal insults directed toward them by white teachers. In some cases white teachers were reassigned to different schools because of their opposition to the presence of black students. There seems to have been no opposition expressed by black teachers.

Although many black parents were concerned with the physical safety and the potential psychological effects of the breaking of the race barrier by their children, they also believed that quality education would not be given their children under the existing dual education system. For example, the physical conditions of the black schools were often inferior to the newer white schools; new textbooks would be given to the white schools and the used books sent to the black schools. Many black parents in Richmond felt that the city was not concerned with the education of black students, and they felt that teacher requirements were not similar for black and white teachers. They therefore felt that quality education was worth whatever had to be suffered to acquire it.

Other black parents, though equally concerned with quality education, may have believed that the potential sociopsychological effects of being in a tension-ridden environment would be extremely dysfunctional for their children.

Another major reason why there were so few black students in the white Richmond schools in the early 1960s was the system of pupil placement and of handling requests for transfers from one school to another. At the heart of the pupil assignment policy was a system of dual attendance zones. The city was divided into a number of attendance zones for the white elementary neighborhood schools, but this system applied only to white children. For the black students the entire city was considered to be an attendance zone and students were assigned to the nearest black elementary school. Because most blacks lived in Church Hill in the east end or in Jackson Ward near the central business district, most black students attended schools near their homes. There were, however, quite a number of pockets of black residential sections in the west end, south of the river, and in the northside near the city limits. These children had to travel long distances. There were no school buses, so all children rode special public buses at reduced rates, but even at reduced rates, these school rides were expensive for the poorer families. One of the black high schools was in the far east end and one was slighly northwest of the central business district, so students from all over the city had to travel to one of these. These attendance zones were established by local school administrators and had been the accepted pattern for roughly eighty-five years. As new schools were built, new attendance zones were created, but the dual system was maintained.

Another feature of the assignment policy was the so-called feeder system. Specific elementary schools fed into specified middle schools, which in turn fed into specific high schools. The initial assignment to a school was based on the attendance zone plan just described. In order to move out of this predetermined sequence of schools, a student had to apply to the school board for a transfer and had to give the reasons for the request. To complicate matters, not all elementary, middle, and high schools had identical grade levels, but were arranged so that it would require considerable dislocation to move from one feeder system to another. As an example, the black elementary schools in the northside had grades one through six. The black middle school, Graves, had grades seven through nine, and the black Maggie Walker High School had grades ten through twelve. The white feeder system in this area, however, had a different arrangement. The elementary schools had grades one through five; Chandler Middle School had grades six through eight; and John Marshall High School had grades nine through twelve. (Urban Team 1969: 21).

In addition, a student wanting to transfer out of his or her feeder system had to meet criteria not expected of those remaining in the system. One of the criteria was that the student must have a higher academic record than did those already in the system in order for the state Pupil Placement Board to approve his reassignment. Another feature was a proximity test. The student wishing to transfer could transfer only to a school closer to his home than the one he would automatically be assigned to under the attendance zone portion of the feeder system. In the case of one of the black students who applied to attend the white Chandler Middle School in 1960, rather than the black Graves school he normally would have attended, the state Pupil Placement Board employed a firm of consulting engineers to hand measure the distance from his home to each of the two schools. The engineering firm reported that he lived 8,150 feet from Graves and 8,530 feet from Chandler. His petition was denied. (In one of the ironies of the Richmond school desegregation process, his mother was appointed to the school board in 1969 and is still a member.) This proximity test was not applied to those remaining in the feeder system. This example was reported in the *Times Dispatch* on 16 August 1960, and prompted a number of letters on the use of tax money to employ the engineers. Finally, the state Pupil Placement Board required that the requested transfer be in the best interest of the student, a reason occasionally used for not approving a transfer

Thus the local school officials could retreat behind the legal fiction that the state Pupil Placement Board had the final authority in matters of pupil assignment. This was true in law, but not in fact. Almost without exception, the state Pupil Placement Board accepted the recommendation of the local school officials. There was no appeal from the ruling of the state Pupil Placement Board except through civil suits in the courts.

1960 proved to be an eventful year in race relations in Richmond. Beginning in mid-February blacks began a boycott of several downtown department stores that neither employed blacks in sales positions nor allowed blacks to eat at the lunch counters or in the store restaurant. As part of this protest movement, students from Virginia Union University, a black university in Richmond, held a sit-in at the lunch counter of one of the larger stores; thirty-nine of these students were arrested. In a widely quoted editorial, the *New Leader* commented:

Many a Virginian must have felt a tinge of wry regret at the state of things as they are, in reading of Saturday's "sitdowns" by Negro students in Richmond stores. Here were the colored students, in coats, white shirts, ties, and one of them reading Goethe and one was taking notes from a biology text. And here, on the sidewalk outside, was a gang of white boys come to heckle, a ragtail rabble, slack-jawed, black-jacketed, grinning fit to kill, and some of them waving the proud and honored flag of the southern states in the last war fought by gentlemen. *Eheu!* It gives one pause. (*New Leader* 1960: 427).

The editorial was unsigned, but was attributed to James L. Kilpatrick.

On 16 August, 1960, the state Pupil Placement Board admitted two black girls to Chandler Middle School. In another unsigned editorial, also generally attributed to Kilpatrick, the *News Leader* commented:

Very well. Let the fact be accepted as disagreeable facts must always be accepted, with a view toward making the best of a regrettable situation. It would be unthinkable for Richmonders to manifest their distaste in any sort of public display; at the some time, nothing in the rule book requires that we burst into joyful song.

The two pupils will be at Chandler when school opens next month, so will nearly 700 white students. The city's social order will not collapse overnight; the educational level will not be affected perceptibly; the sun will rise in the morning. So two of the city's 20,000 Negro pupils have been integrated. We don't like it, but we don't propose to have hysterics either. What else is news? (*News Leader* 1960: August).

On 7 September 1960, the two black girls entered Chandler Middle School. When they first arrived at the school they were frightened by the crowd around the door. The crowd was composed of thirty newspaper reporters and photographers who had come to see history in the making for Richmond. There were no problems in or out of school that day (*New Leader*, 1960: 9/7).

ELEVEN YEARS OF LITIGATION: *BRADLEY* I

In 1962, the first serious challenge to the segregated school system of Richmond was the case of *Bradley* v. *School Board of the City of Richmond* filed in the U.S. District Court in Richmond, Judge John Butzner presiding. The plaintiffs in this suit were the parents of ten black children denied the right to transfer to white schools. The lawyers for the plaintiffs were Oliver W. Hill and Henry Marsh, III, assisted by the NAACP Legal Defense Fund. The defendants were the Richmond School Board, Richmond school Superintendent H. I. Willett, the Pupil Placement Board of the state of Virginia, and its individual members. The complaint attacked the feeder system and the pupil placement system on the grounds that the system was designed to prevent even the smallest amount of racial integration in the schools.

The court found that the practices were discriminatory and granted relief to the ten plaintiffs. The court, however, did not grant class relief. This failure to grant class relief was based on the opinion that the school system was taking reasonable steps toward effecting a nondiscriminatory system. This action by the court meant that in the future each plaintiff challenging the feeder system and the pupil placement system would be granted or denied relief as an individual, but that both systems would remain intact.

There was little public response to this decision. Those who had opposed any degree of integration had expressed their feelings during the massive resistance movement and at the time the federal and state courts had overturned the segregation laws of Virginia. The two Richmond newspapers continued to protest against the infringement of federal courts on the powers of state and local government (see Leedes and O'Fallon 1975, from which the above description was taken, for a scholarly analysis of school desegregation in Richmond from 1962 to 1972).

The Richmond School Board appealed the district court ruling to the U.S. Fourth Circuit Court of Appeals asking for a clarification of the injunction as to whether it required the schools to move to a unitary school system. It did not, however, appeal the district court decision ordering the school board to admit the ten students to the school of their choice. The circuit court took a harder look at the evidence presented to the district court. They noted that while the black schools were overcrowded most of the white schools had unused space. The faculties of the schools continued to be segregated and only four of the fifty-four schools in the system had both black and white students. The court also questioned the good faith of the school officials in Richmond; the officials had made no moves toward the establishment of nondiscriminatory practices, and attempted to place the responsibility for desegregation on the state Pupil Placement Board.

The Richmond School Board and the school officials were caught between the laws of the state on one hand and the swiftly changing court decisions on the other. In addition, local white community pressures and the Richmond newspapers were opposed to any steps by the school board to further the desegregation process. There is also some evidence which suggests that many of the black teachers and administrators counseled against rapid desegregation. According to attorney Oliver W. Hill, one of the lawyers in the desegregation suits, many black teachers who had only a "normal teacher's certificate" and who had not done additional studies felt insecure and believed themselves incompetent. According to Hill, some black teachers took it for granted that all white teachers were competent; they had an exaggerated opinion of the competence and preparation of white teachers.

Studies of the displacement of black teachers and administrators in the southern states during the desegregation process indicate that blacks had a legitimate reason to fear for their jobs, for many were fired, transferred, or demoted when desegregation began. This most often occurred when individual schools in small towns and rural areas were merged and there was no need for duplicating administrators and teachers. Though caught between court decisions and state laws, the opposition of some members of the school board to school integration can also be explained on personal and educational grounds. That is, some members accepted the idea of black personal and educational inferiority as a given.

The circuit court did find that it was unnecessary to put each individual through the time and expense of a lawsuit and concluded that class injunctive relief was desirable, but stopped short of ordering steps toward a unitary school system. This would seem to suggest that some measure of "freedom of choice" would be acceptable. The district court on 6 June 1963 entered an injunction ordering the school board and school administration to end discrimination in pupil placement on the basis of race; to end the dual attendance zones; and to end the difficult administrative procedures connected with transferring from one school to another within the Richmond school system.

The response of the school board came in the form of a resolution on 29 July 1963, providing that the initial assignment of a pupil to a school would be based on proximity to the schools, availability of space in each school, and what was deemed to be in the best interest of the student. Transfers could be made if the parents requested the transfer, gave the reasons for the transfer, and did so before 1 June. No promise was made that the transfers would be approved, but only that it would be recommended to the Pupil Placement Board. No mention was made of desegregating the faculties of the segregated schools.

ELEVEN YEARS OF LITIGATION: FREEDOM OF CHOICE

Bradley II began on 16 March 1964, with objections by the plaintiffs in the original suit and by the NAACP to the continuation of dual attendance zones and of the feeder system; of the use of the media as a means for informing parents of the details of transfer requests; and of the failure of the plan to deal with the issue of desegregation of teachers and staff. The district court found the school board plan satisfactory with no unreasonable restraints upon the freedom of a pupil to enter any school of his or her choice or to transfer at any time. Although the assignment of faculty members might be a proper part of the plan, according to the court, its absence did not require the rejection of the plan.

Again an appeal was made to the U.S. Fourth Circuit Court of Appeals. At issue here was the impact of *Brown* I and *Brown* II on local school boards and on the lower federal courts. The plaintiffs continued to plead for a unitary school system with no racially identifiable schools and for the end to the dual attendance zones. The school board, on the other hand, argued that it was its duty not to discriminate on the basis of race, but that this did not mean a duty to desegregate. The plaintiffs further argued that the segregation of faculties and staff resulted in schools labeled and identifiable as black or white.

A majority of the circuit court held that the Richmond plan was satisfactory and that the idea of freedom of choice was indeed in compliance with the spirit and law of *Brown*. It also held that it had not been demonstrated that segregation of faculty and staff had denied students their constitutional rights. A minority of the court, however, felt that the Richmond plan did not qualify as a plan for desegregation of the schools.

The plaintiffs now petitioned the U.S. Supreme Court to rule on the question of whether the segregation of the faculty should have a place in the desegregation of a school system. The Supreme Court ruled that the plaintiffs were entitled to a hearing before the lower courts on this matter. The hearings were never held before the district court. On 30 March 1966 the district court approved a desegregation plan for the Richmond schools. This plan did include an acknowledgement that it was the school board's responsibility to eliminate racial segregation of faculties and to make the freedom-of-choice plan work.

Richmond operated under this freedom-of-choice plan until 1970 without further court battles. This did not mean, however, that there were no changes—there were many important changes. During this time, pupil enrollment remained steady at 42,000 to 43,000. However, the proportion of black students increased from 57 percent in 1961 to 71 percent in 1970, or a little over 6,000 students.

Between 1961 and 1970, the racial composition of the Richmond public schools had changed from 42.7 percent white to 29.5 percent white. There was a loss of some 5,000 white students, in spite of the addition of a number of public kindergartens during this time. During this same period of time the city had lost about 29,000 white residents and gained about 10,000 black residents. This was clearly the continuation of the trend noted earlier of movement of whites to the suburbs and of black rural and small town residents to the central city.

Freedom of choice had had an unequal affect on individual schools. The two traditional black high schools remained all black, as did three middle schools and twenty-one elementary schools. Of the formerly white high schools one was now 68 percent black, one 19 percent black, and one 8 percent black. Of the formerly white elementary schools, fourteen were still over 90 percent white, whereas the others varied from 85 percent to 22 percent white. Clearly the only desegregation that had taken place had been black students electing to go to the formerly all-white schools. Only a handful of white students were attending the black schools.

A clear effort had been made to desegregate the teachers, but it was done to reflect the racial percentages of students in each school, not in the entire system. This means that, after seven years of freedom of choice, nearly all of the schools remained racially identifiable by teacher and student population. Some of this racial identification of schools was of a semiofficial nature—little was done to change the race of principals, coaches, or other staff in the various schools. The supervisors of the different grade levels and of academic subject areas were assigned by race of schools rather than by geographic locations. Clearly, freedom of choice had not resulted in a unitary school system.

During this period in which some of the schools were desegregated, there was little organized community protest; no riots or school closings, and little violence in the schools. There were, however, minor clashes at the schools among individuals or small groups. How much of this was essentially racial in nature has been difficult to determine. It was a period of national unrest among high school and college students. This was also the era of the most aggressive civil rights demonstrations and riots. It would be most unusual if this had not been reflected in the Richmond schools. It is interesting to note, however, that the Richmond newspapers had never before reported fights on playgrounds or in the schools. Now there were frequent news items of "racial unrest" at the schools, designed, no doubt, to instill fear among white parents and to concomitantly discredit the desegregation process.

It was also a time of some unrest among the teachers, each of whom had a "tipping point." Some of the older teachers, unable to cope with the changes, took early retirement. Some of those with several years of experience joined the white exodus and took positions in the growing county schools surrounding Richmond. A few inexperienced teachers lasted only a few weeks. Mainly white teachers left the system; only a few of the older black teachers left the schools. There was no mass exodus in any given year, but a gradual year-by-year erosion of the white teaching staff occurred (Urban Team 1969: 48–51).

The geographic area of greatest change was the area known as the Northside. The high school and the middle school in this area, formerly all white, were becoming increasingly black and by 1968 were majority black, a change that had occurred in a period of only three years. The lower grades in each of these two schools had a greater percentage black than did the upper grades. The racial residential patterns were also changing rapidly. The Northside was an area of older but desirable homes, and blacks seeking better homes and neighborhoods had been moving into the area for several years.

In 1968, the school board, assisted by a grant from the U.S. Department of Health, Education, and Welfare, decided to undertake a study of the resegregation of the Northside schools. A team of five urban specialists from four universities in three states was formed to undertake this study (Urban Team 1969). The Urban Team was directed among other things to find out why this resegregation was taking place, to make recommendations for reversing the trend in this section of the city, and for preventing the resegregation of other schools. The team spent about eight months on the study.

One group that was actively trying to promote stabilized schools and neighborhoods was the Northside Community Association. The Urban Team met with the association a number of times and with individual members even more. The members of the association complained that the real estate interests in Richmond were engaged in "block busting" in the area. They reported that white residents were being contacted frequently by real estate agents urging them to sell their homes before it was too late. They brought letters and printed flyers as evidence in support of this claim. Interviews with both black and white real estate agents produced mixed reactions. Some agreed that the white realtors did split fees with black realtors when a higher price could be obtained from a black family. One white realtor pointed out that many suburban developments were being built and that the houses had to be sold and the apartments rented, and the only way to do it was to get the whites to move out of the city. Others, however, pointed out that "block busting" was a violation of the (white) Realtors Code of Ethics and that the changes were in response to supply and demand (Urban Team 1969: 17–18).

The Urban Team, chaired by the senior author of this case study, made a number of recommendations about such items as racial policies in the schools and changes in educational programs, but concluded that the resegregation of the schools was primarily due to forces beyond the power of the school board to control. They suggested that the passage of a meaningful open housing law, the construction of low-rent housing in all parts of the city, and better enforcement of the code of ethics of the realtors would all help.

There were other school-centered problems during these years. In retrospect they seem unimportant, but at the time they had an impact upon race relations in the schools. Mostly they involved such matters as social activities, cheerleaders, student publications, and Homecoming Queens. In interviews with students and teachers the Urban Team uncovered some more important internal problems. These interviews were only touched upon in the report and were primarily for the purpose of preparing to conduct a human relations workshop for all new teachers in the fall of 1968. There was agreement that whereas some of the schools had been desegregated, they were not integrated on a day-to-day basis. Students continued to eat in segregated groups and to walk in the halls in segregated groups. There were almost no social activities involving both races, and only on the football field and the basketball court was there any real integration.

Many efforts were made by the Richmond public schools to improve both human relations and education during the late 1960s. In the fall of 1967, teachers in the middle schools attended a series of workshops in intergroup relations. These small discussion groups dealt with black-white relations and with differences in social class attitudes and values. The Urban Team conducted a five-day workshop on human relations for new teachers and some administrators in late summer of 1968. For the next few years every school in the system had in-service sessions devoted to the problems of race and social class. Many of the older teachers and quite a few white male teachers felt them to be a waste of time, but the younger teachers seemed to derive a great deal of benefit from them. Few middle-level administrators took part in these sessions.

A number of specialized educational programs were also begun during this period. In the fall of 1967, a new, modern technical center serving both the high schools and the adult education program was opened. That same fall a math-science center was put into full operation, to which students were brought from all of the schools for specialized instruction. In response to pressure from white parents, the John B. Cary Elementary School was turned into a model school in the fall of 1969 and children from all over the city could apply for admission. All of these have proved to be successful. Later elementary school learning centers were opened to provide at least one or two days a week of experience in integrated education. Finally, an open high school was established for those students wanting something different from the traditional high school. Students enrolled at the open high school could take courses in any high school, in one of the colleges, or do independent study.

ELEVEN YEARS OF LITIGATION: BUSING

It had seemed in 1966 that the *Bradley* plaintiffs and the NAACP lawyers had exhausted all the legal means to bring about a unitary school system in Richmond, but by 1970 a number of things had changed. There had been additional Supreme Court decisions raising serious doubts about freedom of choice being the ultimate means of desegregating schools. Judge John Butzner was no longer on the bench of the Richmond District Court. He had been replaced by Judge Robert R. Merhige, Jr. Henry March, III had been the plaintiffs' lawyer in the *Bradley* cases since 1961, but when he was elected to Richmond's city council, he could not continue the case. Also it was becoming increasingly obvious that freedom of choice was not working to desegregate the schools. As long as student transportation was totally dependent upon the commercial bus system, which required at least one transfer to travel from one geographic area to another, the schools remained racially identifiable.

On 4 March 1970, the *Times Dispatch* speculated that the *Bradley* case might be revived (Doherty 1972: 5). On 10 March, the NAACP filed a motion seeking an order directing the school board to develop plans for a nonsegregated unitary system. The court gave the school board ten days to reply.

There were two alternatives open to the school board. One was to admit that they were not operating a unitary system; the other was to defend the present plan. Given the recent Supreme Court decisions, the latter choice was hopeless. The lawyer for the school board admitted that the schools were not being administered as a unitary system. During this pretrial hearing Judge Merhige noted that twenty-six of Richmond's schools were all black; three were all white; twelve predominantly black; and thirty-one predominantly white (Doherty 1972: 6). The school board was directed to come up with a plan for a unitary school system without any identifiable black or white schools.

On 20 March 1970 the school board announced that it had asked HEW to design a plan that would meet the court's requirements. Over the next three months the school board, school administrators, and representatives of HEW worked on plans for a unitary school system. During late spring and early summer a number of community organizations developed plans and attempted to intervene in the case. On 3 June, the Westover Hills Elementary School PTA passed a resolution calling for a continuation of neighborhood schools combined with freedom of choice. The Bellevue Ginter Association and the Sherwood Park Civic Association, both Northside groups, requested Judge Merhige to return to the freedom of choice plan. The Northside Civic Association proposed a plan calling for the pairing of schools in the same geographic area, plus some elements of the feeder system. They were concerned with trying to promote the stability of the neighborhoods and of the schools. All of these groups had both black and white members and were not opposed to integration, but did not want to see a massive amount of busing.

Other groups, however, were strongly antibusing with some element of holding the amount of integration to a minimum. It is difficult to judge the motives of the all-white Citizens Against Busing. Some of them were against busing the children across town, while others wanted to ensure that some majority white public schools would remain. Another organization, West End Parents Opposed to Busing, had similar aims. One black group, Better Education Now, came out strongly against busing. The goals of this group were better education for black students and for more black high-level administrators. This group did not attract a large number of members.

During the summer months the interracial Ad Hoc Committee for Education was formed. This group wanted to ensure that whatever plan was adopted, the schools would be disrupted as little as possible, and they pledged themselves to help the school authorities in every way possible. Many members of this group were parents who offered their services.

When the district court reconvened in midsummer, the plans from the various community groups, the HEW-School Board Plan, and the plaintiffs' plan were submitted. The court rejected all except the plaintiffs' plan. The HEW-School Board plan called for a neighborhood school plan with broad attendance zones, and some busing on the secondary school level. The elementary schools and some middle schools would be paired, and the attendance zones of the high schools were designed to provide for some integration. The court decided that this plan would still not provide for racial balance and would leave some schools racially identifiable.

The plaintiffs' plan called for some pairing on the elementary school level, but for a considerable amount of transportation by public and school-owned buses for the middle schools and high schools. Although this plan was essentially acceptable to the court, none of the details of transportation, pupil or teacher assignments, or curriculum changes were clearly spelled out. The court felt that it was too near the opening of school to put the plan into operation. Instead a fall-back plan by the school board was approved as an interim plan. The court stated that the plan would not be sufficient ultimately.

This interim plan provided for the pairing of most elementary and middle schools and for a certain amount of transportation in connection with satellite zoning. The school board was given additional time to present the final plan to the court. At the same time the court ordered that there be no more school construction until a final plan was approved.

On 24 July 1970 the school board announced the attendance zones. For most of the middle schools and for all of the high schools the zones were noncontiguous. This meant that there would be some cross-town busing. Under this system about 13,000 students would be bused. The school board asked for a stay of the court order until the fall of 1971, but Chief Justice Burger of the U.S. Supreme Court denied the stay.

In the meantime, on 6 July 1970, Judge Merhige wrote a letter to the school board and to the plaintiffs suggesting that they discuss the possibility of merging the schools of Richmond with those of Chesterfield and Henrico counties to form a metropolitan system. The letter soon became an open secret and there was a loud outcry from several quarters. The county officials objected; the Richmond newspapers objected; and a number of protest groups in the counties were organized. Even the Richmond City Council objected and proceeded to pass a resolution asking for a stay of all school litigation in order to prevent chaos and to soothe the feelings of thousands of parents in the metropolitan area. The school board, however, encouraged its lawyers to begin the process of filing a joinder motion.

As the time for the opening of school came, the combination of the limited busing order and the suggestion of a merger of the school systems created a tense situation. There were demands for a boycott of the Richmond schools, especially from the citizens of the newly annexed area. Many black civic, social, and civil rights groups, such as the NAACP and the Southern Christian Leadership Conference, came out in support of busing. A number of white groups chose to evade the busing issue and concentrate on pleas for the support of the public schools. The Richmond Ministerial Association urged the people to keep calm and to work for the improvement of schools for both races.

The Ad Hoc Committee for Education and the Human Relations Commission opened a rumor reply center to answer questions. This center stayed open for the next few years. The Ad Hoc Committee also had 900 volunteers working on the opening days of school to assist the Richmond city students in catching the proper buses and in finding their classrooms.

On 1 September, the schools opened quietly. Governor Linwood Holton took his children to their new public schools. The *Times Dispatch* reported on 2 September that as many as 6,000 students were missing on the first day and predicted that many parents would not send their children to school either because of the busing or because they feared that there would be violence at the schools. School officials insisted that this was not an unusual number to be missing when schools opened before Labor Day. Eventually most of the missing students returned to school, but a sizable number of those from the annexed area never did return. On 15 September, an article in the *Times Dispatch* called busing a flop and said that it had not achieved the degree of integration expected, that it was causing a further exodus of whites from the system, and that it threatened to ignite racial friction.

During the fall of 1970, a number of significant events occurred. On 4 November 1970, the school board moved that members of the state board of education, the state superintendent of public instruction, and the school boards and boards of supervisors of Henrico and Chesterfield counties be joined as defendants. This move caught the plaintiffs by surprise and the lawyers were not sure that they wanted to cloud the desegregation issue by the new issue of merger of the three school systems. The motion, however, was granted. A new step in legal history had been taken.

Response to the joinder motion was swift. The state of Virginia issued a statement that it would oppose the merger. The Richmond City Council officially asked the school board to withdraw the motion, but the school board refused. One member of the Henrico Board of Supervisors urged that Henrico County withdraw from the Richmond Regional Planning District Commission and that the county void all water and sewer contracts with the city. New public groups were forming in response to busing and to the merger proposal. The West End Concerned Parents and Friends was a group of upper-middle-class citizens opposed to busing and to increasing the degree of integration in the schools of Richmond. At least one group was working to organize itself to support the public schools. Citizens for Excellent Public Schools took no position on busing, but urged that people of all races and classes work together to improve the spirit, the image, and the reality of public education in Richmond. This was a broadly based group in terms of membership and probably did as much as any other group to stem white exodus from the public schools and to improve education in the public schools during this era. It still continues to play an active role in the community.

Meanwhile the district court had been giving consideration to the school board's plans for putting into effect the modified version of the plaintiff's plan for further desegregation. On 5 April 1971, Judge Merhige ordered a plan calling for pairing of a large number of elementary schools, placing in the some high school attendance zones widely scattered neighborhoods, and busing of at least 21,000 students. The plan was devised to ensure that each school would have a faculty and student body in which each race would be represented by a ratio equal to at least half of the projected city-wide ratio for that group (at least 17 percent white and 33 percent black). It was projected that the sytem in the fall of 1971 would be 66 percent black, 34 percent white, and that roughly 40 percent of the students would be bused out of their neighborhoods. The school board was required to acquire buses to transport the students. Most of the money for this transportation was eventually to come from a federal grant. The proportion of black students in the Richmond system increased from 69 percent in 1971 to 82 percent in 1978.

When the schools opened in the fall of 1971, white enrollment had dropped to 30.9 percent. The greatly increased amount of busing did not result in any widespread disruption of the schools. The previously mentioned local groups supporting public education urged the parents to stay calm, not to boycott the schools, and to give the plan a chance to work. They were joined by church groups and the media. The two major Richmond newspapers, the *News Leader* and the *Times Dispatch,* urged cooperation with the law, but predicted trouble in the schools, whereas the *Richmond Afro-American* did not predict any trouble. There were numerous bomb threats, and the community was filled with rumors of rioting in the schools.

There was little or no opposition to busing from the black community, but the white groups opposed to busing continued to be active. During litigation over the merger of the three school systems, the antibusing forces in the metropolitan area began to splinter.

EDUCATION IN RICHMOND: THE MERGER ISSUE

Having settled for the time being the issue of Richmond's desegregation plan, the district court turned its attention to the consolidation of the three school systems. At issue was the question of whether the recent U.S. Supreme Court decisions required that the metropolitan area be considered as one unit in establishing a nonsegregated unitary school system or whether the majority-black Richmond system and the majority-white county systems were to be considered separately.

In 1970, when the population of Richmond was 42.4 percent black, Henrico County was 6.8 percent black and Chesterfield County was 11.5 percent black. Although the three areas combined had had about 26 percent black population for several years, the two counties' black population had been a declining percentage of the total population. The differences in school population were even greater. Richmond's school population was 70.5 percent black. The public schools of Henrico County were only 8.1 percent black; several of the schools were all-white and a few had only a few whites in them. Blacks were not equally spread throughout the system. For example, one high school enrolled about 45 percent of all black high school students, whereas 40 percent of the white students were in schools with 1 percent or less black enrollment. A large part of this unequal distribution was due to the pattern of black residential neighborhoods, since a majority of the black population lived in the eastern end of the county.

In Chesterfield County 9.4 percent of the students were black, and an all-black high school had been closed only a few years prior to 1970. At the elementary school level the county operated nineteen schools. One was majority black, one was about 20 percent black, and one 34 percent black. The other sixteen schools had less than 10 percent black enrollment each. This same pattern was true for the high schools and the middle schools.

Although politically the city and the two counties are independent, they are economically intertwined. In 1970, 51 percent of the jobs in Richmond were filled by commuters. This was the nation's highest percentage of commuters in its labor force (Dabney 1976: 358). In addition to jobs, the city supplies the counties with water, sewage treatment, parks, and many public buildings. In fact, until quite recently the Henrico County Courthouse was inside the city limits.

After some months of delay, the consolidation trial began on 16 August 1971. The position of the several parties involved was rather clear. The two counties maintained that they had been approved by HEW as having unitary school systems and that there was no law or any U.S. Supreme Court decision requiring that independent political units be forced to merge school systems in order to provide a racial balance. They argued that the difference in the racial composition between the city and the county schools was not the result of any action taken by the counties or the state to restrict the movement of blacks into the counties, but was the result of forces external to the official actions of the counties.

The lawyers for the city of Richmond, on the other hand, argued that policies and practices of the state of Virginia and of the two counties had contributed to the substantial differences in the racial composition of the school systems. They cited the counties' refusal to agree to public housing projects for the poor or to allow private contractors to build developments for low-income families, and the rezoning restrictions of the two counties. They also noted the rather strict patterns of racially segregated housing supported by local custom and previously enforced by restrictive covenants.

On 10 January 1972, the district court ordered the merger of the three school systems under a single school board. The decision was supported by a 325-page memorandum. In general there was agreement with the position of the Richmond School Board's lawyers. The judge also pointed out that the area was one economic unit and that the political boundaries were somewhat unrelated to land use. The major point was that each of the three systems was racially identifiable and that merger was the only way to remedy this situation.

The Richmond School Board presented to the court a Metropolitan System

Plan that called for the division of the area into six geographic areas each enrolling a student population of 17,000 to 20,000 students. Each school in the system would enroll a black population of from 17 percent to 40 percent. There would be a considerable amount of busing from the city to the counties and vice versa. At the time about 68,000 students were being bused by the three school systems, and a consulting firm, The Lambda Corporation, had predicted that fewer students would be bused and for shorter distances under the merger (*Times Dispatch* 1972: 6/26). The two counties had made no plans for consolidation. The counties appealed the decision to the 4th Circuit Court of Appeals and asked for a stay of the court order and the court of appeals granted the stay pending the appeal.

The U.S. Citizens for Neighborhood Schools called for a rally in Chesterfield County to make plans for a course of action. At the first meeting it was proposed that the residents of Henrico and Chesterfield counties boycott all facilities owned by the city, including concerts, lectures, adult education classes, sporting events, and the like, even the use of a city-owned bridge across the James River. This proposal was adopted by a loud voice vote. When someone suggested that they also boycott the stores in the city there was less unanimity on this point. Finally, it was proposed that those with jobs in Richmond give up their jobs and strike a real blow to the economy of the city, but this proposal received almost no support. The boycotts never were put into practice.

About the same time the PTA of Henrico County adopted a resolution opposing the merger, but it did not support the boycott idea. A short time later the PTA of Chesterfield County took essentially the same action. The teachers in the two county systems were perhaps more strongly opposed to the merger than any other group. Both the Chesterfield Education Association and the Henrico Education Association voiced opposition, and a number of teachers wrote letters to the newspapers stating that many if not most of the teachers would resign if the merger actually took place.

A number of independent groups, such as the U.S. Citizens for Neighborhood Schools, Save Our Schools of Virginia, Save Our Neighborhood Schools, the Henrico Concerned Parents, and some neighborhood organizations joined together in The Richmond Area Cooperating Committee. This group sponsored a march from the Richmond Coliseum to the Virginia state capitol and held a rally on the capitol grounds. About 3,500 to 4,000 people attended this rally, which was held on 10 February 1972. By 22 April 1972, the Richmond Area Cooperating Committee was beginning to break up over differences in philosophy and tactics. Whereas some of the groups were organized to oppose the merger, others had an antiblack orientation. The differences were too great to enable them to work together.

The most massive demonstration against the consolidation of the school systems took place on 19 February 1972, when 3,500 cars joined in a motorcade to Washington, D.C. The chief sponsor of the motorcade was the Henrico County PTA, but all opposed to the merger were urged to join. The motorcade was orderly with no horn-blowing or shouting, and few banners. Leaders of the motorcade met with Virginia's members of the U.S. House of Representatives and Senate. Some had a meeting at the White House with governmental officials.

Nearly all of the people in these groups were white. A number of groups, usually interracial, voiced their support for the merger. The Richmond Area Clergy Association adopted a position endorsing the concept of a metropolitan school system, as did the Richmond Urban League and the Richmond PTA.

Another group, Spirit for 76, supported busing and consolidation as being the only way to save public education. It also took a strong stand in favor of open housing.

Citizens for Public Schools and the Richmond Community Action Program did not take a position on merger but continued to push for support for public schools. It was difficult to find any group outside of the city supporting the merger. One group did emerge that called for supporting a system of public education regardless of the outcome of the court case. This was United for Public Schools, whose members were primarily white, middle-class professionals from Henrico County. Its appeal to the citizens of the two counties, however, was small.

The black organizations in the city and in the counties remained quite silent on the issue of merger. The national headquarters of the Congress of Racial Equality, however, was opposed to the merger on the grounds that it would weaken the black influence in the administration of the schools.

The two major Richmond newspapers opposed the merger on constitutional grounds, but continued to call for the need to follow due process and for opposition to violence or the boycotting of the schools.

On 6 June 1972 the Fourth Circuit Court of Appeals overturned the district court's order merging the school systems. It relied on the fact that the two counties had been operating unitary school systems and that the boundaries of the city and the counties had been established long before the question of school desegregation had arisen. It also found that there had been no overt action on the part of the counties or of the state of Virginia to prevent blacks from moving into the counties. In other words, the court of appeals ruled that there had been no constitutional violation by the counties or by the state.

The plaintiffs appealed to the U.S. Supreme Court and a hearing was held on 15 January 1973. The court denied the petition for reargument and relied upon the transcripts of court decisions and written briefs. Justice Lewis Powell, former chairman of the Richmond School Board, did not participate in the case. By a vote of four to four the Supreme Court upheld the decision of the Fourth Circuit Court of Appeals. This announcement of 21 May 1973 ended *Bradley* III.

EDUCATION IN RICHMOND: RESEGREGATION?

In the seven years following the massive cross-town busing of 1971 many changes have occurred in the Richmond public schools. The number of white students has dropped by 7,444, or 53 percent. The percentage of white students enrolled has decreased from 31 to 18 percent. There has also been a net loss of 2,175 black students, or 7 percent of the black student body. Combined, this represents a total loss of 9,619 students, which represents a loss of 21 percent. A number of factors have combined to produce these changes: the continued movement of white families to the suburbs, the decline of the birth rate of both races, the rise in the number of Richmond white students enrolled in private schools, and the beginning of a black movement to the surrounding counties.

Virginia has had a long history of private schools, some of which predate desegregation and busing in the 1960s and 1970s. In 1950 there were 3,164 white students living in Richmond attending private schools. This represented

16.2 percent of the total number enrolled in schools. In 1971, 4,805, or 19.6 percent, were enrolled in private schools. By 1974, the number enrolled had increased to 5,300, an increase of only 459 students, but because of the decline of the number of white students in the public schools it represented a total of 31.3 percent of the total Richmond white student enrollment.

There is a small, but growing, middle-class black exodus in the Richmond area. Quite a number of middle-class blacks have moved into black suburban developments, and a few into white suburban neighborhoods. Many of these leaving the city are teachers in the public schools or in one of the colleges in the area. Some are the professional elite. Some members of the black community have expressed the view that this means a real loss in terms of leadership for the Richmond black community.

It is almost impossible to get official data on the racial composition of the employees of the Richmond school system. Officially no data on the race of the teaching faculties or of the administrators is available. In 1972, 55 percent of the full-time classroom teachers were black, with more recent estimates as high as 65 percent. No school official would comment on the racial composition of the school administrators. It might be pointed out, however, that in 1970 all four of the formerly white high schools had white principals, the two formerly black high schools had black principals, and the new high school had a black principal. In the school year 1977–1978 there were six black and one white high school principals in the Richmond system. The white principal resigned at the end of the year and has not been replaced.

Based upon such data as college board scores, percentage of students going to college, number of sections of advanced placement honors classes and of basic classes, the Richmond public schools declined academically during the mid-1970s. It must be remembered, however, that different social class populations were being compared. Most of the students missing from the schools were middle class and this would lead one to expect a decline in academic achievement. There seems, however, to have been an upturn in academic achievement in the past two or three years (*Times Dispatch* 1978: 7/9).

The years after the beginning of cross-town busing were years of other problems in the schools. Reports of increasing violence in the schools circulated in the community and were reported in the press. Teachers of both races were insulted and assaulted. Fights among students increased, and the reports of white students, especially in the middle schools, having their lunch money stolen by violence or by extortion increased. Whereas some of these incidents were racial in nature, some were a matter of social-class conflict. One older black student said that the lower-class black males soon learned that the middle-class whites believed that all blacks carried switchblades and gave up their money without a struggle. He pointed out that the black students had learned to say that they didn't have any money or to fight for their property. School authorities blamed much of the trouble on nonstudents roaming the buildings and stealing or starting trouble. In a number of cases it was apparent that troubles that had begun out of school continued at school. These problems seem to have eased in the past year or so, but on 23 June 1978 a first-year teacher at one of the middle schools wrote a letter to the *News Leader* saying that she was quitting because of threats of rape and murder made to her by students and others.

CONCLUSIONS

The story of the desegregation process in Richmond, Virginia is one of responses to court decisions. Black civic and religious leaders supported the court's decisions to integrate the schools, but because the political, economic, and educational institutions were overwhelmingly dominated by whites, and because traditional opposition to racial equality and desegregation was central to the ethos of the ideology of white supremacy, there was little chance that institutional changes would be forthcoming without legal pressure. On the other hand, no local white leadership emerged to further the cause of integration of the schools, except by court order, though several groups and individuals made a plea for order and obedience to the law. There was little violence surrounding the school situation. Parents who were opposed to the court decisions to integrate or who were disappointed in the school system simply moved to the counties or placed their children in private schools. Some have kept their children in private schools. Some have kept their children out of school for several years.

The two major Richmond newspapers seem to have made a 180-degree turn; they now seem to favor freedom of choice and neighborhood schools, both of which they bitterly opposed a few years ago. Somehow the term freedom of choice has now become enshrined as being the historic "American way." Throughout all of their opposition to desegregation, busing, and merger, however, they have continued to urge that the law be obeyed and that there be no violence. There is a touch of irony in this. They must somehow shoulder the blame for the anxiety, confusion, and often misinformation that may have deepened the fears of whites toward the desegregation process. Though they cautioned against violence and against disobeying the law, they presented arguments why the law itself was evil and therefore should be neither respected nor obeyed.

What now for Richmond? The population of the city will probably be majority black in a few years. Annexation seems unlikely in the next decade or so. The school population is predicted to reach 90 percent black in ten years or less. Blacks in the city are assuming more and more responsibility for the management of the city. Richmond now has a black mayor, with a majority black city council; a black chairman of the school board, and a black superintendent of schools.

With such a large percentage of the student enrollment black, some have begun to question the value of busing black children across town to attend an almost black school. Whether there is more busing or less busing, the central issue should be the quality of the education that is offered in the public schools. Many schools across the country have sought to bring diversity into the educational process by developing experimental and/or specialized schools. These schools have, in some cases, added much creativity and have helped to improve the quality of public school education. They have also been instrumental in bringing more white students back into the public schools. But whether whites return to public education or not, the issue is the improvement of public education. There is no valid reason why a black majority public school system in Richmond cannot be successful.

BIBLIOGRAPHY

Bartley, Numan V. 1969. *The Politics of Massive Resistance.* Baton Rouge, La.: Louisiana State University Press.

Dabney, Virginius. 1976. *Richmond· The Story of a City.* Garden City, N.J.: Doubleday.

Doherty, James L. 1972. *Race and Education in Richmond.* Privately printed.

Ely, James W., Jr. 1976. *The Crisis of Conservative Virginia: The Byrd Organization and the Politics of Massive Resistance.* Knoxville, Tenn.: The University of Tennessee Press.

Haynes, Richard. 1976. "Richmond Hassles with the Metro Image." *The New South Magazine.* May/June.

Key, V. O., Jr. 1949. *Southern Politics.* New York: Random House.

Kilpatrick, James Jackson. 1962. *The Southern Case for School Segregation.* New York: Crowell-Collier.

Leedes, Gary C., and James M. O'Fallon. 1975. "School Desegregation in Richmond: A Case History." *University of Richmond Law Review* 10 (Fall): 1–61.

Muse, Benjamin. 1961. *Virginia's Massive Resistance.* Bloomington: Indiana University Press.

Richmond *Afro-American*

Richmond *News Leader*

Richmond *Times Dispatch*

Urban Team Study on Northside Schools. 1969. Richmond Public Schools and HEW.

Wilhoit, Francis M. 1973. *The Politics of Massive Resistance.* New York: Braziller.

Wilkinson, J. Harvie, III. 1968. *Harry Byrd and the Changing Face of Virginia Politics 1945–1966.* Charlottesville, Va.: The University Press of Virginia.

10

The West and Midwest Milwaukee, Wisconsin: Mobilization for School and Community Cooperation

Michael Barndt, Rick Janka, and Harold Rose

The Milwaukee school desegregation case took ten years to decide in the court system. Despite the long period community leaders had in which they could have prepared the citizenry for the desegregation process, none really believed that Milwaukee would be required to desegregate. Part of the failure to anticipate this requirement reflects Milwaukee's self-perception as a small city that does not experience the problems that other large, urban areas face.

When the court handed down its ruling in January 1976, it made clear that community leaders would become part of the process leading to a desegregation plan. A special court-appointed master played a direct political role in the process. A new school superintendent found a platform within the process for the development of educational and institutional themes that interested him. Community and civic leaders were involved extensively in support of the actions of school officials. State legislation helped to underwrite the costs of desegregation. A creative plan that maximized student choice was developed. A conservative school board was overriden when necessary, but was included in the compromises whenever possible. Two phases of school desegregation were implemented without problems. All of these factors led to the claim by Milwaukee leaders that the city was a model of successful school desegregation.

It may be argued that Milwaukee did not confront the difficulties that often accompany school desegregation because it has experienced so little actual desegregation. Fewer than 2,000 of the nonblack students in the school system have been moved from their neighborhood schools. Even the third and last phase of the school desegregation plan, which is currently in doubt because the U.S. Seventh Circuit Court of Appeals remanded the case to the district court for reconsideration, would have continued a pattern of very substantial movement among black students, often under the guise of unavoidable modifications in school enrollment ceilings or changes in school use. The black community has often felt substantially left out of the process and without a political base from which to speak. The liberal white community has often been torn between a desire to support any plan developed in the interest of cooperation with the school system on the one hand, and a recognition that decisions were often made to satisfy the most conservative school board members on the other.

DEMOGRAPHIC BACKGROUND

Milwaukee, like most other major central cities throughout the nation, has lost population since 1960. Much of the population loss has occurred as a result of whites leaving older residential zones for zones of new construction in the metropolitan ring. In Milwaukee, white losses amounted to 70,000 between 1960 and 1970, and 45,000 between 1970 and 1975. The increase in the rate of white abandonment of the city during the first half of the seventies appears unrelated to the court order, for the case lay dormant for a number of years, and even when it was finally brought to trial there were few who believed that the board of education would be found guilty of causing schools to be racially segregated. Thus Milwaukee's total population has experienced a continuous decline since 1960, primarily as a result of white outmigration. Table 10.1 delineates the changes undergone by the city's population during this period.

Changes in Milwaukee's population are structurally similar to those occurring in other northeastern and north central cities during the post-World War II period. Prior to 1960, Milwaukee's black population was relatively small for a city of its size. The continued growth of the black population and a corresponding decline in the white population through outmigration will affect the future racial composition of the city. Even though both sets of rates are now beginning to decline, their influence upon the black proportion of the population has been pervasive.

The racial composition of the city was continuously altered during the period in which black migration to the city was a major contributor to the growth of this segment of the population. In 1960, blacks constituted less than 10 percent of the city's total population, but by 1970 the percentage had reached almost fifteen percent. A special census undertaken in 1975 showed that blacks then constituted 18 percent of the population. These changes in the racial composition of the city's population have had a disproportionate impact on the school system. Because of the youthful age structure of the city's black

TABLE 10.1. Population Changes in the Central City
of Milwaukee, 1960–1975

Total Population		White Population	Black Population
1960	741,324	675,572	62,458
1970	717,372	605,372	105,088
1975	669,022	540,395	123,689

Source: U.S. CENSUS 1960 and 1970. Milwaukee Special Census 1975.

population and the limited use that this group makes of the nonpublic schools, the percentage of blacks in the public school system has always been higher than the percentage in the general population. The black school population is almost double the proportion of blacks in the general population. This situation is further aggravated by the aging of the white population remaining in the city and the age selection movement of younger whites to the suburbs. Changes in the school-age population over this period are illustrated in table 10.2.

In 1970, almost 30 percent of the white elementary-age pupils were enrolled in nonpublic schools, whereas less than 10 percent of a comparable black population were to be found outside of the public schools. The process of white withdrawal from the public school system has had the most severe impact at the elementary school level (see table 10.2).

Residential segregation in Milwaukee, like that in most other American cities, is extreme. Despite the passage of federal fair housing laws, there is little evidence that major changes in the intensity of residential segregation has taken place during the most recent decades. Only a few other cities in Milwaukee's size class were as intensely segregated as recently as 1970. There is a high correlation between the level of residential segregation and the level prevailing in public elementary schools.

During the period between 1950 and 1963, blacks were basically concentrated in what has been described by the Milwaukee public school system as central area schools, which included twenty-five elementary school districts. In 1950, black dominance at the neighborhood level was confined to four northside neighborhoods situated within two miles of the central business district. But even as late as 1965 only sixteen of the central area schools could be described as racially imbalanced. Prior to 1964, the Milwaukee school system did not employ the practice of identifying the racial makeup of individual schools. Of all black elementary pupils, 85 percent were concentrated in central area schools when the school desegregation suit was filed in 1965. Another 5 percent of the black student enrollment was concentrated in five elementary school districts contiguous to the central area.

There was very little change in the pattern of racial imbalance in Milwaukee's public school system during the ten-year period from 1965 to 1975. During the former school year, 72.4 percent of all black pupils attended schools that were 90 percent or more black, and 86 percent attended majority black schools.

TABLE 10.2. Changing Elementary School Enrollments, 1970–1976

Year	White	Minorities*	Total
1970	51,250	24,672	75,922
1971	48,355	26,274	74,629
1972	45,152	26,710	71,862
1973	40,881	26,744	67,625
1974	37,026	27,471	64,497
1975	35,022	27,593	62,615
1976	29,459	28,004	57,463

Source: *The Milwaukee Journal* 1976:10/13.

*The minorities include blacks, Hispanics, Orientals, and Native Americans.

By 1975, the expansion of Milwaukee's black community had spread far beyond the old central area school zone and now embraced thirty-three elementary school districts, including twenty-three schools that were 90 percent or more black, 9 that were 50 to 89 percent black, and 1 that was just approaching a black majority. Likewise, in 1975, 86 percent of the city's black elementary pupils were to be found in majority black schools. This represents an equivalent situation to that which prevailed ten years earlier. The prevailing population dynamics led to an abandonment of previously white majority school districts by parents of school-age children for newer locations in the city. A growing black population inherited previously all-white residential neighborhoods and the schools located in them (see table 10.3).

Two nationality groups have dominated ethnic life in the city since the latter part of the nineteenth century. Although the number of foreign-born and foreign-stock population has declined over time, the residual German and Polish populations still outnumber all other European ethnics. The most recent arrivals from Europe, the Russian Jews, Austrians, Hungarians, Yugoslavians, and Italians did not constitute sizable numbers in the population prior to the census of 1920. The latter groups arrived in relatively large numbers in the years immediately preceding World War I and continued to immigrate to Milwaukee during the decade following the war. European immigration to Milwaukee was substantially slower after 1930.

By 1970, the foreign-stock population had dwindled to less than 30 percent of the total white population. This group includes first- and second-generation populations of European origin. Thus it is difficult to enumerate the magnitude of the ethnic population from first- and second-generation national origin statistics.

In Milwaukee, German ethnics have tended to concentrate in community areas on the north side of the city, whereas Poles are often found to represent the dominant group on the city's south side. However, Germans and Poles share residential space in most southside community areas. One Polish enclave, in terms of ethnic dominance, is to be found on the city's north side in the community area of Riverside West, while the reverse of this situation is found on the south side, with Germans representing the dominant group in the community of Bay View.

The most recent ethnic group to become a significant element in the Milwaukee population is the Spanish-surname population. The Spanish population appears to be almost equally divided among those who have their origins in

TABLE 10.3. Population and Public School
Enrollment Changes, 1970–1975

	Population			Enrollment			
	Total	White	Black	Total	White	Black	Hispanic
1970	717,000	605,372	105,000	132,349	93,023	34,355	3,898
1975	669,000	540,395	123,000	114,180	68,671	39,250	4,808

Source: U.S. Census, 1970; Milwaukee Special Census, 1975; Milwaukee Public Schools; enrollment by ethnic categories.

Mexico and Puerto Rico. By 1970, the Spanish-surname population had grown to approximately 22,000 in number, more than tripling its size in one decade. The 1970 Spanish population was roughly equivalent to the 1950 black population. The possibility of it growing as rapidly as the black population in the same period of time seems a bit unlikely, given the greater distance from the primary zone of origin and a universal decline in fertility rates among all groups in American society.

The Spanish-surname population, like that of other ethnic groups in American cities, tends to be ecologically segregated. However, this population has formed enclaves in older community areas on both the south and north sides of the city. The north side Spanish population is predominantly Puerto Rican and is located along the southern margin of the black community. These groups often compete for residential space in the Polish enclave in the community of Riverside West.

The city's northwest side is a new area, annexed to the city in the early 1960s. There are still working farms in that area, but land is quickly filling with condominium projects and industry. Many of the residents in the area moved from the central city and changing west side years ago. Although not conservative politically, the northwest side is considered a neighborhood of moderates.

The south and southwest sides of the city have the hold on Milwaukee's most conservative residents. The south side is the home for many of the city's Polish. Homes are owned and maintained by generations of Polish families. The neighborhood had changed little in the last decades. During desegregation, the southwest side, long a quiet, suburbanlike community, became the most vocal opponent. Its opposition, however, took the form not of major protests, but rather of bimonthly meetings, attended by only handfuls of people who chatted about constitutional law.

Milwaukee is an industrial center whose industrial specialization has traditionally rested upon the manufacture of machinery, transportation equipment, beverages, and leather goods. In 1970, only 35 percent of the city's residents were employed in the manufacturing sector of the economy. This represented a 7 percent decline from 1960, when this sector was the place of employment of 41 percent of all employment. This is a trend that is evident nationally, but in this instance it might be partially inflated by higher paid manufacturing workers moving to the suburbs and commuting to central city workplaces. Nonmanufacturing employment and its companion secondary employment sources accounted for 45 percent of all employment in 1970. Service employment had come to clearly dominate the employment picture, with the largest percentage increases occurring in the area of retail, health services, and educational services employment. These three categories alone have employed only slightly fewer persons during the latter years than did manufacturing. In the early seventies the greatest employment gains continued to be concentrated in the services.

Milwaukee has been described as a working-class city, ranking fourth among the twenty-five largest cities in terms of working class percentage. Twelve community areas can be described as lower-middle class, ten as working class and one as lower income. The lower-middle-class areas were areas with median family earnings of $10,200 or more in 1969. Working class areas were those with median earnings in excess of $7,596. There is a general gradation in median earnings from those community areas located near the center of the city toward the periphery. One does not encounter upper-middle-class communities before reaching the suburbs. The gradation between community areas in the city and those in the suburbs is more abrupt on Milwaukee's north side than is true of the south side. The north side suburbs generally tend to be more affluent.

THE ROLE OF NONPUBLIC SCHOOLS IN
THE DESEGREGATION PROCESS

In 1970, slightly fewer than one-third of all white elementary pupils were enrolled in nonpublic schools. Only about one-fifth of white high school students were enrolled in nonpublic schools at that date. Roman Catholic parochial schools enrolled the vast majority of non-public school children, with Lutheran parochial schools constituting a secondary nonpublic system. There is evidence that indicates that Catholic parochial schools, like their public school counterparts, have consistently lost enrollment since the late fifties. Yet these absolute losses have not occurred without some local growth. New nonpublic schools have been constructed in areas representing zones of recent residential development, as a means of satisfying the demands of a clientele that is shifting places of residence within the city, as well as the larger metropolitan area.

The numerically dominant nonpublic school, the Roman Catholic parochial school, serves the largest share of blacks attending nonpublic schools. The Catholic parochial schools were thought to enroll between 1,000 and 1,200 black students in 1965. But the largest share of this enrollment was concentrated in four schools. These four institutions, plus eight additional ones, were located in the zone previously described as housing central area schools. Thus these four schools were essentially situated in the path of black residential development and early became sites of concentrated black enrollment. Most central area parochial schools had attained their maximum enrollment prior to 1960 and were in various stages of enrollment decline by 1965. The parochial school districts that were the first to undergo residential racial transition were also the first to take on the racial characteristics of their neighborhoods, although they almost always lagged several years behind their public school counterparts. In the late sixties, a number of central area parochial schools closed down or were converted to community schools.

By 1976, black parochial enrollment had more than doubled as a result of expanding black enrollment in additional northeastern schools and the growing presence of blacks in selected northwestern section schools. The latter section enrolled slightly more black students in 1976 (441) than the northeastern section had five years earlier (434). But as was previously true, the largest number of black students were to be found in only three schools among the eighteen schools located in the northwest section.

THE EMERGING SCHOOL DESEGREGATION ISSUE

Attempts to integrate black and nonblack children in Milwaukee public schools began with a handful of public discussion meetings in the early 1950s. The minority population of the schools then, although never specifically counted, was estimated at well under 10 percent.

The meetings seldom developed into anything' beyond discussion. With small numbers of youngsters involved and attitudes of white superiority still dominating, the problems of black children went relatively unnoticed in a community and state accustomed to farm problems, only brief encounters with urban woes, and certainly little acknowledgment of the special needs of minorities and their importance to the future of the city.

Also at this time Wisconsin was in the midst of a relatively new experience— Democratic leadership. The Democratic party in the state was lacking for decades until the late 1950s and early 1960s. Parenthetically John Reynolds, who was governor during that time, was later to become the federal judge to hand down the desegregation order for Milwaukee.

Even then, however, the route taken by black leaders in the Wisconsin chapter of the NAACP seldom sidestepped accepted, traditional paths. Arguments were made to the superintendent of schools, Harold Vincent, that inexperienced teachers were being forced into heavily black schools because experienced teachers opted out as soon as they got the chance; and that black pupils were being guided into construction, cook, helper, or similar occupations, and away from colleges.

A simple denial from Vincent squelched the issue each time. It should be noted, however, that when the desegregation trial reopened in 1978, an official of the teachers' union testified for the plaintiff's attorneys that Vincent had admitted to him in 1967 that there had been a deliberate policy to steer black teachers to black schools because officials thought they could better educate the children. The defendant's attorney, however, countered with a document from the late superintendent denying the charge.

Turning to the state Department of Public Instruction to mandate changes in Milwaukee schools, the NAACP leaders found similar responses. Officials listened, newspaper stories were written, but no action was taken, and the problems were shelved.

In 1963, it was revealed that the school board was transporting black students from predominantly black schools to predominantly white schools as a result of overcrowding in the black schools. These students were segregated from the white students at the host school, leading to the charge of busing for segregation. The local chapter of the NAACP and other civil rights groups protested this action and sought to have it terminated. Civil rights leaders also asked the schoolboard to desegregate its de facto segregated system. The next year they demanded that the school board cease all practices that led to segregation of pupils on the basis of race. The majority of the members of the board did not agree that blacks were segregated in the Milwaukee school system. However, the board did agree to provide a program of compensatory education to assist blacks in overcoming previous handicaps.

In the early years only three board members accepted as valid the notion that Milwaukee schools were de facto segregated. These board members were attorney John Pederson, Elizabeth Holmes, and Cornelius L. Golightly, the board's only black member. The board president, Lorraine Radtke, only commented that it was the neighborhood racial makeups that determined the racial makeups of the schools and the board was running a neighborhood school system. It was up to those doing the complaining, mostly the NAACP, to prove any charges of wrongdoing, not the school board. The board did form a special committee on Equality of Educational Opportunity in 1963, which the black leaders viewed with optimism, but after several meetings the committee decided that it could not legally act to change the racial balance of the schools.

The refusal of the board to address itself to the issues that had been raised by civil rights groups led to the threat of a school boycott. Many attempts were made to stave off a boycott, but one was finally conducted in May 1964. These were the first steps in a process that eventually led to the NAACP's filing a suit against the public school system in 1966.

After exhausting the traditional routes, Lloyd Barbee, a black attorney and state representative, filed a federal lawsuit against the superintendent and school board on behalf of thirty-two black and nine white public school children (*Amos v. Board of Directors of City of Milwaukee*).

Under guidance from the city attorney's office, the Milwaukee school board members were told not to discuss the case. They quickly and comfortably adhered. In fact, most of them stretched the attorney's advice beyond merely speaking about the case. They simply refused to take any action on any integration plan, claiming it might hurt the board's case in court. Between the time of the 1965 filing and the court decision by Judge Reynolds in 1976, little action was taken.

There was one effort the board approved, on the recommendation of the NAACP and the board's only black member, Cornelius Golightly. That action created an open-enrollment policy permitting any youngster to go to any city school as long as there was space at the new school and as long as the child paid for transportation. Although touted by integrationists as a possible means to help desegregation, that policy was one of many later pinpointed by Judge Reynolds as having contributed to segregation by allowing white students to transfer out of schools that were changing their racial composition.

As civil rights activity in the city moved from the negotiating stage to the activist stage, the school issue moved from the center stage of interest. The housing issue and marches by a militant group of actors helped highlight issues affecting a larger segment of the population. The school issue might have appeared more crucial to Milwaukee blacks of southern origin, but the housing issue was one with which the entire black population could identify. The heightening of civil rights activity in the city and the beginning of a series of long summers nationally began to alter the mood in both the black and white communities. The Milwaukee riot of the summer of 1967 no doubt did much to completely reorganize the agenda in the city, for black demands now focused on issues that were designed to give the black community a share of political power. The black community became more inward-looking as the school issue became one that was being pursued by only a small number of its members. However, prior to the riots, the issue was apparently still alive in the minds of white voters; they aided in the defeat of Cornelius Golightly, who was seeking a second six-year term as a member of the school board. Peaks and valleys in public interest led to a shift in emphasis on issues of social importance. These shifts have been observed in the case of school desegregation in Milwaukee, especially as it relates to the posture blacks have assumed on this issue. Yet many white supporters favoring the elimination of de facto segregation in the early sixties had gone underground a decade later.

THE COURT CASE

With a "neighborhood schools for neighborhood children" argument, the board argued its case in 1973 in federal court, blaming whatever segregation there was in the school system on segregated housing—something the board claimed it could do nothing about.

The judge disagreed with this analysis, however. On 19 January 1976, he ruled that the board had rearranged school boundary lines, making white schools whiter and black schools blacker; built additions onto overcrowded black schools to "contain" blacks in their neighborhoods; assigned new teachers to black schools permitting veteran teachers to flee to outlying schools; bused overcrowded black children intact with their teachers to white schools, refusing to permit them to mix with white youngsters even during recess; and approved open enrollment. In that last finding, Judge Reynolds stated that whites were able under open enrollment to transfer out of schools as the schools became blacker whereas blacks, usually on the lower end of the economic scale, could not afford to transfer. As schools became black, so did neighborhoods, although at a slower pace. This indicated, as the plaintiff's attorneys would argue, that school board actions did have an impact on neighborhoods and housing.

John Gronouski, former Wisconsin tax commissioner under then Governor Reynolds, former postmaster general under President Kennedy, and former ambassador to Poland under President Johnson, was named by Reynolds as special master of Milwaukee's desegregation. It was Gronouski, who with his Polish name and contacts and a gruff exterior picked up the campaign to convince Milwaukeans that desegregation was now "the law of the land." In a series of public hearings throughout the city, Gronouski sold the Reynolds ruling with the strategy that those everyday citizens and parents who for so long had done little or been able to do little about their schools could now become involved in major school changes.

The school board and its superintendent Lee R. McMurrin, were ordered to submit a desegregation plan. The court at first set no racial quotas or goals. Within weeks McMurrin, who had already unveiled a series of plans for city-wide specialty schools in dozens of school buildings, recommended the creation of a citizens panel—the Committee of 100—to assist the board in its planning.

The board immediately appealed the ruling to the U.S. Seventh Circuit Court of Appeals in Chicago and when the ruling was upheld, appealed to the U.S. Supreme Court. It also appealed Reynolds' remedy order a few months later to the Chicago court and continued throughout the desegregation effort to appeal everything Reynolds mandated.

In June 1977, after one year of desegregation had been accomplished and plans for the next two years had been approved, the Supreme Court sent Judge Reynold's order back to the Chicago court and in September 1977, the Chicago court ordered Judge Reynolds to reopen the case. While the remedy remained in effect, the trial reopened in January 1978, with Reynolds first deciding whether the board and school officials intentionally or unwittingly caused segregation of teachers and pupils.

THE RESPONSE OF THE SCHOOL SYSTEM

The constant appeals of the judge's ruling were characteristics of the school board throughout the desegregation process. With each appeal the school board assured the public that it was standing up for the rights of the citizens to determine how to run the schools, and that it was not attempting to keep blacks and whites apart. Even though the board members did place roadblocks in front of every plan to desegregate, there were never any racial overtones to their fighting against the court.

The board is made up of fifteen members, called directors, who are elected at-large for six-year terms with a monthly salary of $50. Historically, the board has been used as a springboard to higher political offices by many of its members. Others have been on the board up to twenty-two years, putting them in the awkward position of being personally involved for decades in the actions labeled by a judge as unconstitutional.

Only five blacks have served on the board in its history—one for a few years during the turmoil of the 1960s and then again when more liberal board members were elected in the early 1970s. Now there are two black board members. Parenthetically, both are married to whites, which at times has diminished their rapport in the black community, although it has strengthened their political influence in the liberal white community.

The board has maintained a conservative-moderate stance on educational issues for most of its history, mirroring a conservative Milwaukee community. The conservative majority rule has bounced from eight, to nine, to ten strong, but has always held strong. The anti-federal court and proneighborhood school directors now number nine. Six other directors have supported desegregation as outlined by the courts. No single characteristic such as sex, religion, or occupation seems to blend the conservative-moderates or the liberals together. Even the neighborhoods the various board members live in do not necessarily pinpoint a reason for the factions. Even though many of the conservatives do live in the city's conservative south, southwest, and northwest sides, some of the conservatives live almost next door to their more liberal board members on the city's progressive east and near west sides.

From the outset, all board members promised compliance with the desegregation order, although the conservative majority pushed for the least amount of compliance possible, often countering the recommendations of the superintendent selected by their own search committee. Lee McMurrin became the fourth school superintendent in the twenty-four years spanning the desegregation issue in Milwaukee. He was hired in July 1975, only six months before the court order was handed down. However, within that half year, McMurrin outlined a network of specialty schools more far-reaching than any other city had planned, and it was that concept the board latched onto for its desegregation plan.

Previous superintendents had not been as innovative as McMurrin in their approaches to educational programs. Harold S. Vincent, superintendent in Milwaukee from 1960 to 1967, ran the schools during the onset of black protests and disenchantment, and in the middle of a baby boom that forced him to become a brick-and-mortar superintendent. When he left the system, a national school board official called him "the last of the father images of superintendents in the country."

Richard P. Gousha, formerly the superintendent of public instruction in Delaware, was hired in 1967 and came to Milwaukee with a different approach to education—a Madison Avenue flare. His job did not deal with racial desegregation, for the board proclaimed at every turn that it could not talk about integration or take any actions for fear of hurting the case still in federal court. Gousha was a superintendent working under the "management by objectives" techniques.

Gousha believed, and later testified during the desegregation trial before Judge Reynolds, that children of different races need not sit next to each other to get a quality education. His strongest and most frequently voiced argument was that it was condescending and insulting to say that the only way for a black child to receive a good education is to sit next to a white child.

Gousha's tenure, although peppered with some controversies over integration, centered almost totally on rearranging a school system administration that was bulging after the baby boom. The board was left to occasional debates on a handful of integration plans, some submitted by new, liberal board members. However, those plans were aired, sometimes debated, and then inevitably shelved.

When Gousha left in 1974, his deputy superintendent, Dwight Teel, took over as acting superintendent—a man merely caught in between superintendents. For a year, Milwaukee public schools had a status quo existence.

Lee McMurrin was a sharp contrast from his predecessors, particularly his immediate predecessor Richard Gousha. McMurrin attended PTA meetings, chatted with parents in his office, and even listed his telephone number. Gousha was a staid, unsmiling man. McMurrin's smile and optimism have become almost overpowering. Even during some of the most controversial desegregation decisions, one Milwaukee newspaper described him as a man "who could find a rose in a septic tank." One of the benefits of the desegregation court order decision coming only six months after the board had hired him was that McMurrin was still in a honeymoon period with board members—the school board is notorious for internal political, philosophical, and personality conflicts, which in time often involve the superintendent.

Because of McMurrin's emphasis on how the desegregation order could help Milwaukee schools by bringing more federal money to the system, allowing for major changes the schools had needed for years, and bringing increased parental involvement, McMurrin was lauded constantly for his efforts by the media, the court, and the court's special master. So when the school board's majority would counter a McMurrin move with one of its own, the board found itself catapulted into criticism. McMurrin's positive image took the limelight and the headlines away from the board members, and many of them, although not a majority, became increasingly uneasy with McMurrin's growing support.

FEATURES OF THE MILWAUKEE SCHOOL DESEGREGATION PLAN

Milwaukee has had several desegregation plans. The first, Phase I, was designed to integrate one-third of the schools to within 25 to 45 percent black in September 1976. The second, Phase II, was initially to bring two-thirds of the schools within these guidelines by September 1977. Changes in guidelines, ambiguity created by court action to review the case, and the willingness of the plaintiffs to relax expectations led to a reduction in the impact of Phase II. The plan for full compliance, to be identified as Phase III, deserves special attention even though it may never be implemented. Its mechanism for desegregation is unique among desegregation plans.

Throughout the planning process, the nature of desegregation proposals was clouded by a rhetoric generated by the school administration that specialty schools with unique styles or emphasis would attract students into voluntary compliance with school desegregation. Behind these proposals, however, was a set of school system actions that left thousands of black students without a normal school assignment. At all times, mechanisms allowing involuntary desegregation were in place if needed. Rarely were the full impacts of school plans understood. This problem stands in strong contrast to plans in other communities in which the specific moves of children, both black and white, were charted in advance by direct assignment of students for purposes of desegregation.

The incentive part of the plan was especially popular with the administration, parents, and the civic community. It represented an opportunity to revitalize the quality and range of educational experiences offered by the system.

At the senior high level, distinctions among schools as neighborhood schools were to fade away. Each school would develop topical areas of excellence—for example, medicine, computer science, business or social service. Students would select the school that fit their vocational interests. The two inner-city high schools would get perhaps the most attractive options—the medical emphasis and a college preparatory sequence. Most programs and most of the movement of students were not expected to occur until the third year of desegregation.

At the junior high and elementary school levels, a select number of schools would be identified as specialty schools. In these schools, the entire curriculum would be oriented to a specific educational philosophy—open classroom, Montessori, fundamental, or individualized, guided instruction. A few schools would also have emphasis programs such as music, German-as-a-second-language, and bilingual education programs.

Superintendent McMurrin envisioned three rings of schools. The outer ring would attract black children directly because of the new, uncrowded, pleasant atmosphere they provided. The inner ring of older black schools would be gradually reduced. Rebuilt schools would serve as city-wide specialties able to attract children from throughout the city. The middle ring would contain schools with substantial variety attractive to both inner-city and edge-of-city youth. The variations would also encourage children within the ring living in not-so-integrated neighborhoods to move to proximate desegregated schools. Most middle-ring schools would not be city-wide specialties. Neighborhood residents would continue to make up a substantial portion of the attendance. Many of the remaining children would be attracted from a series of "sister" schools within the same "league" or "association."

In addition, cooperative suburban transfer plans allowed additional choices for minority students. The plans made it possible for suburban youth to take advantage of the wide range of choices to be available within the Milwaukee public school system.

One major limitation placed upon the specialty school plan was that these schools were to be no more expensive than other schools. Pressures from parents who most desired educational reform led to some modification in that rule. The costs of renovation remained an issue in implementation.

The plan has been publicized as laissez-faire and flexible. Some specialty schools (or merely better schools in the case of black inner-city schoolchildren) were to be selected entirely voluntarily by marketing the choice to parents. Hypothetically, a child could select any school in the city as long as racial balance was not disturbed; however, this selection process was implemented only partially. One limitation upon this process was the substantial pressure upon transportation specialists to provide rational bus routes. Another limitation occurred during Phase I, when black students at selected black schools were "steered" toward selected white outer-ring schools that were not specialties. During Phase II, only a small number of the specialty schools were designated city-wide. The others were limited first to neighborhood children and second to students from league or association schools. These restrictions allowed the movement of students to be more predictable. Other voluntary action was also expected to be limited to league or association schools.

The heart of all school desegregation to date, however, has been the result of changes in school facilities available to students. The effect has involved nearly all black students. The finding of discrimination against the school system had included concerns for overcrowded schools, old, inadequate facilities, and use of temporary classroom units. The neighborhood school policy had served white neighborhoods more effectively than black neighborhoods. In the spring of 1976, just before desegregation was to begin, 34,863 spaces were available for 34,340 white elementary students in majority white neighborhoods, and 19,000 spaces were available for 25,028 elementary students in majority black neighborhoods (a deficit of 6,000 spaces). The additional black students were already attending classes outside their neighborhoods or were fit into classrooms acknowledged as overcrowded.

The Phase I plan substantially aggravated the problem of limited space. All schools were restricted to recommended capacity limits. This meant that many black students were targeted to leave these schools; in addition fifteen elementary schools were designated as specialty schools. For the many already overcrowded schools in black neighborhoods, 2,175 black students were targeted to leave to make room for white volunteers. Only 353 white students were affected. In practice, no white student was asked to leave a school to make room for a black student. And to ensure racial balance in specialty schools, the school populations were dropped substantially—four schools enrolled less than 65 percent of capacity so that the schools could be declared desegregated with a small number of white students. Enrollments at one black high school were substantially cut back because of the condition of these facilities. Introduction of special programs at other junior and senior high schools would be accompanied by movement of black students to make room for white volunteers; 1,970 black students were affected by these actions.

Phase I results indicate that 1,123 white students volunteered to attend specialty schools. Of black students, 8,525 volunteered, and 1,625 attended specialty schools; 6,900 attended other targeted edge-of-city white schools. Most of these black students came from schools targeted for substantial pupil reduction. All students volunteered, but black parents complained that volunteering in black schools was effected under direct pressure from school officials. These results led to complaints about the imbalance of the plan. But school officials countered by arguing that black students were satisfied with the options open to them and quite willing to leave poor school settings for good ones.

The Phase II plans increased the deficit of school spaces open to black students within their neighborhoods. Four additional schools were scheduled to be closed. The students were assigned to adjacent districts already filled to capacity. An additional two schools were designated as city-wide specialty schools where reduction in black enrollment would be necessary. Temporary classrooms were removed from all remaining sites. No white student was likely to be unable to attend his or her home district school as a result of similar action.

During Phase I, a series of specialty and overcrowded schools were selected as targets which were to generate volunteers for other schools. If these targets had not been met, a lottery would have been used to select those students allowed to stay and those who would be required to choose another school. This mechanism was not necessary during Phase I. During Phase II, ceilings were placed upon the enrollments by students of each race for each school. These ceilings were based upon capacity figures for each school. Therefore, they had much less effect in undercapacity outer-ring schools in white neighborhoods.

All students enrolled for fall 1977 by selecting three choices of schools. The first choices were allocated whenever possible. When too many students selected a school, lottery mechanisms were used to determine which choices would be honored. But when spaces were available because students of the other race did not select the schools, students were allowed to stay beyond the ceiling set for their race. This process did not take place, however, until students who had not submitted choice forms were allocated positions. The administration selected schools not formally announced as targets to ensure that a sufficient number of schools would be integrated. The nonblack students who had not submitted choice forms were assigned in large numbers to previously all-black schools. Strikingly, two previously all-black schools were integrated by assignment of large numbers of white students who had not submitted choice forms. This action was later to prove very difficult to implement during the legal confusion that accompanied the opening of school.

The Phase II plan, as first proposed by the school administration in December 1977, was to desegregate all elementary schools. When the objectives were reduced, the process was much more awkward to implement. It became clear in public statements that the administration did not expect white students to volunteer to attend black nonspecialty schools. There was no organized effort to recruit students for target schools, nor were parent groups mobilized by the administration to sell the program. When the choices were being processed by the school administration, the selection of which schools would be affected by ceilings and which schools would be assigned students who had not submitted a choice appeared to be somewhat arbitrary. As grievance procedures were established, many parents were persuaded that the assignments were in the best interests of their children, but many white parents were able to have their children reassigned—if not to their "home schools" at least to one within a white neighborhood.

The net effect of the Phase II plan was not substantial. Affected were 1,885 white and 12,615 black students. Only about 800 students (almost all black) were not given their third choice assignment. More than 2,000 white students and 4,000 black students did not make a choice. About 50 percent of these white students and 60 percent of these black students were assigned to schools that they would desegregate. The total number of white students affected was essentially the same as the total number of white students involved in Phase I. (All statistics, however, were complicated by the changes allowed after the opening of schools, which probably led to a reduction of all figures.)

The Phase III plan would operate in much the same way as the Phase II choice process, except that ceilings would remain in place at each school. The key advantage of the plan by comparison to assignment plans in other cities was that it preserves the expectation of free choice. Almost all students were to receive a school that they had chosen, even if it was not their first choice. This "free market" approach to the process is most consistent with the educational incentives framework: a student may select freely the most compatible educational format.

Operationally, the plan presents certain deficiencies. Desegregation would not in fact occur unless ceilings at each school are reduced with declining enrollments. Schools with considerable space for students can accommodate all residents within the ceiling. Overcrowded districts will always present less of a choice to resident students. The plan would be stable for the years a child attends a single school, but reenrollment at junior and senior high school levels will never be predicted with certainty by a parent. Most schools are composed of a district population of one race and a bused population of the other race originating from a large number of other districts. School bus routes are unwieldy, sometimes impossible; and in September 1977, the school administration, in an effort to reduce the number of taxis being used (about 100) began persuading some children to return to their home schools. The confusion is reduced to some extent by the priority given students within leagues in selecting assignments. But this priority process also leads to differential effects within leagues and associations.

The MPS plan when fully implemented will affect black and white students differently. These differential effects result from the limited school capacity within inner-city schools and excess capacity within the outer ring of schools. Perhaps five times as many black students would be transported by a fully implemented plan—even though racial balance in the school system is approaching 50 percent. The issue of equity has been raised with increasing frequency by the special master and the plaintiffs. However, neither party seems inclined to press the point in the courts. Nor is there much evidence that the equity of plan implementation would be effectively reviewed as a legal issue.

School desegregation through Phases I and II substantially affected black children without affecting more than a very small number of white children. With the exceptions of two schools to which "no choice" children were assigned, white children have not been expected to attend schools in black neighborhoods unless some special programs were being offered at that school to attract volunteers. Spurred by the negative posture of the school board majority, the administration has been careful not to sell desegregation as a value, only as innovative schools. This has reduced the degree of preparation for white parents for more extensive involvement in a final phase. Milwaukee's response to school desegregation will be tested more adequately in the third phase of school desegregation, which has not yet been implemented. The response of the black community has been based upon the realization that equity is not expected to return to the plan with the implementation of Phase III.

During the second year of desegregation the largest enrollment loss ever occurred in the Milwaukee public schools. If a significant share of this loss was associated with the unwillingness of whites to have their children share classroom space with blacks in their own communities, this no doubt portends more severe action in the future. For the greater burden in the third year might possibly fall on that segment of the white population that would be inclined to stay and fight.

The Milwaukee public school system appears to be sensitive to the social class makeup of the host schools into which black pupils are being bused. Most of the previously white schools that were adjudged to have satisfied the desegregation guidelines were located in higher-status community areas. Those community areas in which the larger concentration of eastern European ethnics reside were less often targets of the busing program, although Jackson Park, a higher-status community area on the city's southside, was among those in which a number of schools were targeted. The one-way busing program has been seemingly concentrated in selected higher-status German and Jewish ethnic-dominant communities on the north side. Of course, a larger number of the city's elementary schools are found on the north side.

THE STATE INCENTIVE LAW

One important component of the success of school desegregation implementation has been effected by the passage of state legislation subsidizing school desegregation efforts. The proposal has been heralded because it encourages cooperative arrangements between city and suburban school districts. Each contracts to make space available for a set number of students. These numbers have been small and are considered very likely to remain so. In the second year of the legislation, 420 minority students are transferring to the seven suburban districts, although very few white students are transferring into Milwaukee.

The financial incentive for participation is substantial. The sending school district receives full compensation for the student, the receiving school district receives double compensation. The state also pays the costs of transportation. One suburb, for example, received $247,000 in state aid for accepting 122 minority students into available classroom space. Faced with this incentive, suburban opposition to token participation has been negligible. But few observers perceive this program as having much effect upon racial balance within the city of Milwaukee.

The state law also affects transfers within the Milwaukee school system for desegregation. The costs of transportation and a somewhat increased state compensation apply. This result has been even more important. The costs of school desegregation have been met by state and federal funds, defusing a potentially volatile issue.

CITIZEN PARTICIPATION IN PLANNING AND IMPLEMENTATION

Citizen involvement in Milwaukee must be evaluated in stages. Prior to court-ordered desegregation, participation in school affairs was minimal. During the preliminary planning phase, Janury to May 1976, citizen groups were broadly involved. Decisions for Phase I were completed in the summer of 1976 almost entirely in the absence of citizen discussion. Planning for Phases II and III included some of the broadest efforts of citizen input in Milwaukee history. But again, after December 1976, the decision process was closed to citizens. Decisions regarding implementation were made almost entirely by the school administration.

The implementation of each phase in August of each year included parent and citizen groups to a small extent, as individual schools were able to arrange for participation. Follow-through concerns as school desegregation continues have been even more limited, although the appointment of a citizen monitoring board may change this to some extent.

Despite the unevenness of citizen involvement, the numbers of people and the vehicles created to support their involvement are impressive. The principle of participation was clearly supported by all parties. Participation in practice was limited by some officials' inexperience and by many officials' unwillingness to extend the principle of involvement to actual decision-making activity.

Participation was supported from the beginning by the actions of the judge, John Reynolds. His appointment of John Gronouski as special master signaled a concern for political process. Gronouski was not expected to derive a plan himself but to ensure that planning was taken seriously by school and community participants. The court was determined to give the school system every opportunity to develop its own plan. It was also committed to open channels of communication with other community elements, particularly citizens.

During the spring of 1976, preliminary planning was to take place. The special master attended numerous meetings with parent and community groups. In part, these meetings were to reduce the uncertainty created by the court action and to defuse resistance to the decision, but Gronouski also used the meetings to encourage community input into the process. Parents shared broad concerns about the possible impacts of school desegregation, and communication was effectively therapeutic.

The special master scheduled a special hearing for 12 to 14 May for a discussion of possible desegregation plans. Prior to the hearing, John Gronouski seemed to make it clear that the community groups' input into plans would be taken seriously. Thirty groups testified at the hearings. Many established community groups presented detailed parameters that they felt a final plan should meet. Only two detailed plans were presented, however, and neither was sponsored by a community group.

There were several reasons for the limited nature of initial community input. First, Superintendent McMurrin made it clear that the administration was serious about the planning process. The goodwill created by the new Milwaukee superintendent was sufficient to reduce many community members to a position of waiting for administrative action. Second, the first orders of the court were so vague regarding what would be required of a plan that few knew where to begin or what objectives ought to be met. Third, even long-term activists in the community were overwhelmed with the complexities of school desegregation planning. Although many leaders had read extensively on the subject, they still hesitated to become involved in suggesting alternative courses of action. Fourth, McMurrin himself established the first basis for school desegregation planning, that the first stage of any plan be voluntary and that special schools open to all students serve as a keystone to the plan. The result was that models of direct desegregation adopted in most other cities were rejected broadly. Those who were serious about complete desegregation usually adapted their efforts toward rules for back-up plans within the voluntary incentive scheme proposed by McMurrin.

Another key feature of the first months of planning was the creation of a school-sponsored parents' group, the Committee of 100. This organization was elected in a two-tier process. First, five parents were chosen at each local school;

second, the schools within each high school feeder pattern elected ten representatives to the city-wide body. The Committee of 100 was to include representatives of each organized sector of the community as well, but the school board rejected that model and restricted the organization to parents. The Committee of 100 was charged with the responsibility for reviewing administration proposals and advising the school board on courses of action. After a difficult start because of the ambiguity and size of the organization, the group established itself as an independent force. It took positions consistently more liberal than either the school administration or board, and was to some extent disowned by both.

The first plan was dealt with swiftly. The administration unveiled it to the board, which quickly reduced most of the operative provisions. The Committee of 100 supported nearly all the provisions of the administration's version. The special master, choosing to seek maximum cooperation from the school board, rejected this recommendation on 11 June 1976. Apologizing for allowing too much ambiguity regarding necessary standards for a remedy to the court findings, Judge Reynolds required that a plan that would effectively desegregate one-third of the schools in the first year be brought back to the court within three weeks.

The next phase of planning was conducted entirely in private. Key conservative school board members worked closely with school administrators to come up with a plan which the conservative school board majority would be willing to accept. The school board minority and a number of community groups felt defeated by the emphasis in the plan upon large-scale movement of black students to achieve desegregation. Few, however, testified against the plan in the brief hearings which followed. The plan was too certain of approval; and the time too short to argue with it. The plan was approved by the court on 9 July 1976. Community groups began assisting with the implementation in the short time left before school was to begin.

The plan did contain a strong section on parent involvement in the next segments of the planning process. Parent input had received strong support even from conservative members of the board. Elementary schools were divided into twelve groups to be known as leagues. Each group of ten schools contained a nearly contiguous pie-shaped slice of the city, and was nearly racially balanced as a set. The leagues were to devise plans that would desegregate students among those schools by presenting a plan based upon the best alternatives for that league. The proposal meant that planning could be broken into reasonable scale for parents. It also meant that even though proposals were expected to provide the maximum amount of voluntary, unscheduled student movement, most moves would be expected to occur within the cluster of ten schools rather than across leagues. In addition to the twelve league groups, single planning groups for junior and senior high schools were established. These groups were substantially larger and more unwieldy than the groups established for elementary schools within the leagues.

The parent groups were to begin in August with Phase I implementation. The administration was unable to organize them, however, until late September. At that point, each group was given six weeks to prepare a proposal for completing the desegregation process for their schools. Groups were asked to focus upon the local circumstances of the set of schools they represented. They were given very little data, no options to review desegregation plans, and very little technical or group-process assistance. Nor were any arrangements made to coordinate the efforts of each of the groups. During the process a community group called the Coalition for Peaceful Schools prepared technical documents for the groups and arranged coordination meetings of the leadership of groups. During the six-week period more than 1,000 parents were involved in at least three planning sessions. The commitment of parents was also indicated by the volume of recommendations that came from each group.

But the process was also frustrating for the participants. Leadership developed slowly, and in many cases the school principal retained the leadership role. Time was lost creating agendas, learning about options, and collecting information. Some of the league groups were not effectively able to desegregate using only students within their league. And planning was consistently complicated by conflicting rhetorics—that plans could be voluntary and based upon incentive schools and that involuntary back-up plans were necessary and should be part of the plans. Most planning groups presented plans that recognized involuntary movement, and called for equitable movement of black and white students. Most plans placed an emphasis, however, upon selection of major or minor special focuses for the schools within the league. The technical details for back-up plans were developed only within a few leagues.

For two weeks in November, plans developed by the Committee of 100 were reviewed by its subcommittees. To a large extent, the reviewers were parents who had not been involved actively in the decentralized process. A series of city-wide recommendations were added to the package of proposals. The administration then spent three weeks reviewing this material.

The school administration published a concrete plan on 8 December 1976. The proposal was quickly supported by the community groups that had contributed to it. The key mechanism for desegregation—the rules for selection of schools and acceptance or rejection by those schools—was not an element in plans submitted by the participation process. But this factor did not seem to violate the spirit of those proposals. Selection of special-program emphases at various schools was frequently responsive to community expressions leading to strong support for the plan.

Other than perfunctory review by the Committee of 100 in December, the community was cut out of the next stages. The school board rejected the decision of the administration to present a serious plan and with the advice of the counsel, engaged in a number of legal maneuvers. The special master did not have a working plan endorsed by the school board, but the administration document continued to enjoy strong community support. There was, however, no opportunity to review or refine it as legal arguments continued through a series of hearings sponsored by the court.

The court declared the administration proposal the basis for future desegregation. To reduce the role of the court to an absolute minimum, a limited number of passages in the proposal were selected as court ordered. Additional adjustments followed expressions of concern by Superintendent McMurrin that the court had taken too seriously the intention in the proposal to desegregate all elementary schools in Phase II.

By March the court's final action completed the process, but the exact nature of the plan was still unclear. The administration had done little to provide detail to the proposal. The reduction in targets for Phase II meant that the plan would have a substantially different effect—some wondered whether white students would be affected at all by involuntary moves. School board elections and a prolonged teachers' strike drew attention away from the plan.

Originally, parents were to select schools in two rounds during the month of April. League groups were expected to communicate with parents to help sell the plan and to encourage volunteering The final result, however, was that parents were asked to select schools in one round in June, just before school ended. The league groups were not convened from early November until mid-August the next year. A minimal amount of information was available on the special options for students. And with an assumption that the system did not intend to desegregate schools in black neighborhoods other than specialty schools, parents were reluctant to volunteer their children. With the reduced pressure on all parents, almost all white parents selected the home school as a first choice. The same was true for most black parents.

The result of the selection process was that schools in the fall of 1977 were to be integrated by (1) a hard core of prointegration families who had volunteered for the first year; (2) a large number of black students whose home school was no longer accessible because of removal, capacity reduction, or conversion into a specialty school; (3) students, both black and white, who did not participate in the choice process; and (4) a small number of Catholic students entering the system for the first time, therefore with lower priority.

Perhaps the most dramatic effect of the implementation was the effort to integrate two black schools almost entirely with students who fell into the last two categories. These sets of students led to a new form of participation—protest groups, lines at complaint centers, and withdrawal from school.

In part to press the point that all students would be satisfied by the plan, grievance centers operated throughout the summer and into the fall. Students would be persuaded to accept assignments they were given but had not selected. When this was done successfully, the student could be rated as having "selected" the school. A substantial number of assignments were modified—many of which reduced the impact of desegregation. Action by the U.S. Supreme Court to remand the finding in the Milwaukee case in July, followed by action by the circuit court to remand the decision to Judge Reynolds, reduced the pressure to fully meet Phase II guidelines. Angry parents were able to test the flexibility of the system in this climate.

During Phase I, the office of the special master maintained a consistently low profile. It requested a minimum of overall data from the school system. As problems in individual schools occurred, the special master or his assistant, John Gilligan, would serve as a troubleshooter. No community members were involved in this process.

In the proposal for Phases II and III the school administration suggested a monitoring proposal consisting of research directed and conducted by the administration and reviewed by the Committee of 100. The lawyer for the school board suggested that the special master be stripped of monitoring responsibility. After several months of debate, the special master requested that the judge appoint a monitoring committee to conduct a full monitoring process and to advise the special master.

In August 1977 the monitoring board was created. Of the thirty-seven citizens selected, half represented the Committee of 100 parent structure, while others were sent as representatives of selected community and civic organizations. The panel was substantially more grass roots than blue ribbon in nature. Despite efforts to balance the membership with stable conservative representation, the panel was very liberal in its orientation. As of this writing, the full extent of the monitoring board's role is uncertain. It does represent, however, a separate force with some political and community standing in the unfolding events.

COMMUNITY RESPONSES

There were few protests against Milwaukee's desegregation plan, which changed the system from one of fifteen clusters, or high school districts each with its own feeder junior and elementary schools, to one with zones and unusually shaped leagues set up to achieve racial balance. The lack of protests or demonstrations could be linked directly to the superintendent and the school board's emphasis on voluntary desegregation and specialty schools during the first year of desegregation. Because only those who wanted to transfer had to be involved during the 1976–1977 school year (unless fifty-three schools were still segregated according to court standards of September 1976), the others who wanted no part of desegregation were silent. During that first year, sixty-seven schools were voluntarily desegregated. However, when the system moved into Phase II in September 1977, one hundred and two city schools had to be desegregated. Again, however, a plan that emphasized choices and volunteerism clouded the process during the summer and kept whatever antigroups that were forming from picking up any steam.

It was not until school nearly started the second year and some mandatory pupil assignments were made that protest groups began to form. The white group was small, perhaps fifty in number. This group demanded that the superintendent be fired because of mandatory school assignments. A conservative school board member convinced this group not to boycott the school system. The black group was larger and claimed by the end of the first month of school in September 1977 that they had succeeded in keeping thousands of black children home in protest of a plan that had only one out of every thirty-eight nonblacks riding the buses while black students carried the burden of the desegregation plan. This group presented a list of demands to the school board, including the demand that majority black schools retain a 55 percent black enrollment. The group also demanded that schools in black neighborhoods not be closed and that specialty schools be placed throughout the city, not just in black areas.

There was no violence, nor were there any massive rallies, however. The boycotts received guarded coverage by all the media, but emphasis remained on the fact that the vast majority of pupils was in the schools and that the schools were operating peacefully.

Milwaukee police were never heavily involved in desegregation planning or control. Police Chief Harold Breir issued no formal pronouncements about desegregation, nor were officers assigned to ride on or be near buses or schools any more than they had been before the court order was handed down.

Only two incidents developed during the first year of desegregation. A busload of black youngsters on Milwaukee's heavily white south side was pelted briefly with stones by a car of white young persons. The incident was reported, school officials condemned it, and no recurrences were reported. And, several white pupils and a teacher were injured in a south side white high school when a group of black transfer pupils at the school roamed the halls and "attacked" whoever got in their way. This incident spread over two days with some arrests and injuries. However, school officials quickly set up a racially mixed team of pupils at the school to help solve the problem and this incident too, calmed. The black pupils involved, however, were transferred to other schools around the city.

CONCLUSIONS

The Milwaukee desegregation case was dominated by two personalities: Special Master John Gronouski, who spoke persistently of the inevitability of a fair and thorough constitutional remedy but maintained a caution for the extent of his role that led him to frequently acquiesce to the initiative of the school system; and Superintendent Lee McMurrin, whose role as a mediator, persistent optimist, and supersalesperson flavored the community's understanding, and in many cases misunderstanding, of the plan and its willingness to be responsive to it.

Careful analysis of the Milwaukee plan challenges us to determine whether broad-based community participation is always what it seems to be, whether a voluntary plan was really voluntary, whether court-ordered remedies are fair to black students, and whether community peace is a sufficient objective for those·who seek school desegregation.

BIBLIOGRAPHY

Barndt, Michael. "An Overview and Critique of the Milwaukee Public School 6/25/76 Plan." Milwaukee, June 28, 1976.

——. "Overview of the MPS Administration Plan for Elementary Schools." Report to the office of the Special Master, January 3, 1976.

Beverstock, Frances and Stuckert, Robert P. *Metropolitan Milwaukee Fact Book: 1970,* Milwaukee Urban Observatory, 1972.

Catholic Archdiocese of Milwaukee. Annual school reports. 1971, 1976.

Faley, Reynolds. "Residential Segregation and Its Implications for School Integration." *Law and Contemporary Problems,* Winter 1975, 181.

Greater Milwaukee Conference on Religion and Urban affairs. *City Suburban Newsletter.* Vol. 1., December 1977.

Gronouski, John. "Special Master's Second Progress Report: Response to the Specific Recommendations by Counsel of Record. Changes in the May 24, 1976 Progress Report." Milwaukee, June 11, 1976.

Kingston, Alan. "Impact of Chapter 220, Laws of 1975." Dept. of Public Instruction, State of Wisconsin, June 28, 1976.

Milwaukee *Journal.* "Blacks Vow to Fight for 2-Way Integration." July 28, 1977.

——. "Cab Rides to Schools May be Cut." September 20, 1977.

——. "Panel Urges More White Transfers." August 18, 1977.

——. "Pupils Get Chance to Change Schools." September 7, 1977.

——. "Reading, Riding and Race. Public Opinion and School Segregation in Milwaukee County." March–July 1975.

Milwaukee Public Schools System. Annual enrollment census by race. 1964.

——. *Community Involvement Structure Adopted by the Board of School Directors.* Milwaukee, March 2, 1976.

——. *Comprehensive Plan for Increasing Educational Opportunity and Improving Racial Balance in the Milwaukee Public Schools—First Draft.* Milwaukee, December 8, 1976.

——. *Preliminary Recommendations for Increasing Educational Opportunities and Improving Racial Balance, Pursuant to the June 11, 1976 Court Order of the United States District Court, Eastern District of Wisconsin.* Milwaukee, June 25, 1976.

——. "Report of School District Changes in Central Areas of Milwaukee 1943–1953-1963." January 1964.

——. "Report to the Special Master." October 20, 1976.

Milwaukee *Sentinel.* October 21, 1975.

——. "Gronouski Begins Task with Lots of Gusto." March 13, 1976.

——. "School Figures Fuel Claim on Black Busing." August 19, 1977.

Rauch, Sr. Mary Delores. "Impact of Population Change in the Central Area of Milwaukee Upon Catholic Parochial, 1940–1970." Master thesis, University of Wisconsin-Milwaukee, June 1967, 72, 74.

Reynolds, John W. "Amos et al. vs. Milwaukee Board of School Directors: Decision and Order." Filed U.S. District Court, Milwaukee, January 19, 1976.

Special Census, City of Milwaukee, April 1975.

State of Wisconsin, Section 121.85, Wisconsin Statutes. May 3, 1976 (popularly known as Chapter 220).

U.S. Bureau of the Census, Census of Population, 1960 and 1970.

Van Valey, Thomas, Roof, Wade C., and Wilcox, Jerome E. "Trends in Residential Segregation: 1960–1970." *American Journal of Sociology,* 1977, Vol. 82, 4.

11

Omaha, Nebraska: Positive Planning for Peaceful Desegregation

Dennis N. Mihelich and Ashton Wesley Welch

Omaha, Nebraska was incorporated as a frontier town on the western bank of the Missouri River in 1854. The first thirty years of existence witnessed modest growth, essentially spurred by the fact that it became the eastern terminus of the transcontinental railroad. During the 1880s, as the plains rapidly filled in with farmers and cattlemen, Omaha turned into a veritable boom town as its population exploded to over 100,000 and its economy took on the dimensions of a food-processing center. The drought and hard times for midwestern agriculture that set in at the end of the decade and the nationwide depression of the nineties combined to stunt the city's growth for the remainder of the century.

The return of prosperity, the demand for agricultural products caused by the swift national pattern of urbanization and two world wars, and a liberal annexation policy all ensured renewed expansion. During the World War I era the city annexed all of its contiguous suburban neighbors, and as the area continued to develop westward the process was repeated on several occasions. The decade of the fifties, for example, saw an increase of 50,000 inhabitants; 40,000 came through annexation while the population within the old boundaries jumped by only 10,000. Despite the acquisitions, twentieth-century Omaha grew at a slower pace than the national urban growth rate (144 to 273 percent), but exceeded by far the general rate of increase for Nebraska (Zipay 1967: 7). Today, Omaha is home to about one-third of the people living in this large but sparsely populated state.

Currently Omaha occupies about 200 square miles of territory that holds a population of approximately 380,000 people. Economically the city continues to rely upon its historical base—it remains the largest meat-packing center in the world in addition to being the second largest food-processing center and fourth largest rail center in the United States—although the relative importance of these industries is shrinking. Decentralization of the meat-packing industry during the 1960s resulted in a loss of 50 percent of the jobs in that area, but general growth and diversification of the city's economy largely compensated for the decline. Specific areas of the city, however, continue to be plagued by the change. South Omaha, where the plants were located, became underdeveloped and has not fully recoverd from the disappearance of its economic life-blood, and the Near Northside, Omaha's black ghetto, suffered disproportionately because the packing houses were the largest employers of minority workers. Community-wide rapid expansion in the trade, service, finance, insurance, and manufacturing industries stabilized the overall conditions. Employment data reveal a balanced economy based upon construction, transportation, communications and utilities, trade, finance and insurance, services, and government (Danton 1967: 1–9; OOEDP 1969: 3). The 1978 general unemployment rate of 4 percent is well below the national average of about 7 percent, and of the nation's fifty largest cities, Omaha ranks twelfth in family income.

BLACKS IN OMAHA

Black Omahans do not share proportionately in this prosperity. Educational statistics reveal that blacks drop out of school at a 50 percent rate and that of the total number of blacks twenty-five years of age or older only 29 percent have completed high school (60 percent for whites) and barely 3 percent have graduated from college (13 percent for whites). An official unemployment rate of 17 percent exists, although the Urban League estimates that the actual percentage is double that figure. The median income for a black family of four stands at $7,500, one-half that of its white counterpart. The value of housing in the predominantly black neighborhood averages $7,000 (as opposed to $28,000 for the white sector) and fully 30 percent of the units are classified as deteriorated. That neighborhood also lacks all major health care facilities, and the combination of the above circumstances produces a sense of despair that reveals itself in a very low rate of political participation. In the May 1977, general election only 11 percent of the eligible black voters cast their ballots (League 1978: 10–21).

Historically, the first significant settlement of Afro-Americans in Omaha followed the Civil War; employment with the Union Pacific Railroad served as the major attraction. The number of black residents remained relatively small, however, reaching only 5,143 according to the 1910 census. This represented less than 5 percent of the population, and under such circumstances blacks were dispersed throughout most of the neighborhoods (Chudacoff 1972: 22). This pattern changed dramatically during World War I, when the black population doubled as a result of the migration to work in the booming meat-packing plants. The influx strained race relations, producing a race riot in 1919, and residential segregation also emerged. Two distinct areas of settlement grew, one in south Omaha close to the stockyards and a second, larger zone on the Near Northside in the proximity of the downtown business district (Chudacoff 1972: 22, 155–156).

During the interwar period the black community grew very little and the stability of the residential situation was reflected in the public school enrollment pattern. The city did not maintain a separate system for minority children, but the two elementary schools located within the Near Northside neighborhood evolved into predominantly black units. Other elementary schools on the periphery of the black neighborhoods attracted between 7 and 35 percent minority students. Similarly, students attended the high school closest to their areas; thus only the three buildings located in western Omaha were without black enrollment. The major complaint of the black community was that no minority teachers had been employed by the system since 1910, despite the fact that many qualified individuals graduated from local colleges and were forced to leave the area in order to pursue their profession (Sullenger and Kerns 1931: 18–21). During the thirties the NAACP, the Urban League, and other black civic, religious, social, and service organizations campaigned to get the Omaha Public Schools (OPS) to hire members of their race. The wall was finally breached in 1937 with the retention of a local pastor as a substitute music teacher, but by 1945, the constant stream of protest secured employment for only eleven minority educators (*Guide* 1937: 12/11: 1, 12/18: 1; 1945: 9/8: 1).

World War II encouraged renewed black migration to Omaha, and the influx continued to the present time. The rate of increase was higher than the corresponding white growth and, therefore, the approximately 35,000 blacks now represent about 10 percent of the population. For the city this meant almost a tripling of black residents in three decades; yet, in comparison to other major cities the proportion of minority population remained small. Residentially, the south Omaha neighborhood shrank perceptibly following the closing of some of the packing plants, but the Near Northside ghetto became more dense and expanded northward and westward (Zipay 1967: 11–18; League 1978: 5).

Following the national patterns and buoyed by the expanding numbers, the local civil rights crusade unveiled a new militancy during the fifties that eventually burgeoned into direct action and confrontation during the turbulent sixties. The movement challenged every aspect of de facto segregation and on two occasions, once in 1966 and again in 1968, race riots erupted. In the realm of education, well into the late sixties, the thrust of the civil rights campaign aimed at improving the position of black teachers and at obtaining minority representation on the school board. Between elections the board had the power to fill vacancies, and on occasion it chose a well-known black professional to represent the minority community. On three occasions during the twentieth century a black was appointed to the board and then was able to win reelection. The black board members served as visible spokespersons but remained powerless in terms of reorienting the racial policy of the system. With at-large electtions, however, no black was able to win a seat without prior appointment, and this situation prevailed until 1976, when a district representative system was established.

An Urban League study of 1957 revealed the continued plight of the minority educator, reporting that OPS employed 1,350 teachers, 37 of whom were blacks confined to teaching in five elementary schools located in the Near Northside. Within this group, 22 individuals held master's degrees; another 6 were working toward that degree and 4 were accumulating hours for the doctorate (Lewis 1957: 1–2). Pressure from the black community slowly increased the numbers, and eventually by the late sixties succeeded in getting a few minority teachers upgraded to the junior and senior high level, although assignments continued to be largely restricted to schools located in predominantly black areas (*Star* 1961: 5/6: 1; 1963: 1/15: 1, 11/29: 1).

Increasingly, the emphasis of protest also began to include demands for the improvement of the quality of education, especially through the inclusion of material about Afro-American history and culture. Then, in December 1967 the Urban League called for total integration of the system and the use of cross-busing to achieve the result (*World Herald* 1967: 12/17: B6). The school board called the petition irresponsible and a few months later dissidents, appalled at the unresponsiveness of the white power structure, formed the Negro School Board. They advocated the immediate, total desegregation of OPS, the "proper channeling" of federal, state, and local funds to problem areas, the establishment of a board of appeals for parents with grievances, and increase in the quality of education and the promotion of courses in black history and culture (*Star* 1968: 2/15: 1). The action was dramatic and it mirrored the mood of the community, but the Negro board did not survive long and it did not force its desired results.

THE GREENLEIGH REPORT

At this juncture, a coalition of social service agencies commissioned an independent, professional study group, Greenleigh Associates, Incorporated, to survey the human needs and services in the metropolitan area. The report documented conditions within the OPS on the eve of the legal battle for desegregation. It revealed that the district suffered from a shortage of funds because of inadequate state aid, which began only in 1968. The equalization formula adopted, however, penalized Omaha because of the size of its budget, and the result was an average per-pupil expenditure by OPS that was more than $100 below the national average for cities of comparable size (Greenleigh 1969: 55, 65). The system also experienced the common urban problem of an exodus of quality teachers to suburban districts in order to avoid the problems associated with big-city schools. Of the 2,330 teachers in the system, 144 or 6 percent were black and the vast majority of them were concentrated in ten schools on the Near Northside. Black students in those inner-city schools dropped out at a rate almost three times as high as their white counterparts, and the achievement level of those who remained in school was significantly lower than system wide and nationwide averages. Standardized tests showed that, overall, OPS students fell within or exceeded national norms at most grade levels, but Near Northside scores were one to two years below norms and those from the low-income areas of south Omaha were equally weak. Western area schools located in middle-class to upper-class neighborhoods, however, showed median achievement levels three months to one year above national norms. The researchers concluded that "within the limits of the OPS austerity budget, the citizens are getting a lot for their money, but they are not receiving quality education by any means. If it were not for ESEA Title I money for the special activities programs, the climate in Title I target schools would be intolerable" (Greenleigh 1969: 56-60).

Poor relations between the OPS administration and parents from the disadvantaged areas also plagued the system. Parent-Teacher Associations and other traditional means of communication were ineffective in those neighborhoods, and the School-Community Advisory Committee, which the board had established to advise the administration concerning the quality of education in inner-city schools, was viewed as a rubber stamp or as a "sedentary body whose opinion was never sought regarding policy." On most occasions communication took the form "of a list of grievances and angry demands presented around crisis issues by ad hoc committees, by standing committees of black neighborhood organizations, or by the Urban League." This situation resulted from the fact that many of the parents distrusted the school establishment because of their own negative educational experience, and because, now, most of their contacts concerned disciplinary measures for their children. Yet, according to the research team, even more of the problem arose from "the failure to reach out to the parents and to involve them in working with the schools and in creating an environment which establishes the school as a vital part of the community" (Greenleigh 1969: 62–63).

Finally, the Greenleigh Report documented the existence of de facto segregation. The movement of blacks to all-white schools took place at a slow pace, and schools on the periphery of the ghetto manifested the problem of resegregation. When the racial balance shifted beyond a certain proportion of blacks— usually one-fourth to one-third—a mass white exodus took place. The OPS, the researchers argued, did "little or nothing to reverse the trend," but it did not deserve sole blame; the state department of education, government agencies, and the community at large were more to blame. Prophetically, the report stated, "however, the problem will not disappear and the bill will eventually have to be paid. . . ." It suggested that down payments could be made by hiring more black teachers and administrators, and by initiating teacher-training programs for dealing with minority and disadvantaged children. Generally, the analysts felt that with only a 17 percent minority enrollment, OPS was in a good position to desegregate by careful site selection for new schools, by redefining area attendance boundaries, by establishing magnet schools, and by busing with the consent of the affected community (Greenleigh 1969: 63–73).

THE U.S. DEPARTMENT OF JUSTICE

Subsequently, in 1970, a black who was appointed to the school board presented it with a comprehensive forty-page plan for desegregation (*Star* 1970: 10/29: 1). The board did not act upon the program despite evidence from the U.S. Department of Health, Education, and Welfare that indicated that OPS was becoming more racially segregated. In a period of three years the proportion of blacks attending schools with an 80 percent minority enrollment rose from 55 to 64.4 percent, and the latter figure was 18.5 percent above the national average (*Star* 1971: 1/20: 1). Thus, after years of negotiations that produced minimal changes, a group of black parents brought together by the Urban League filed formal complaints of racial discrimination against OPS with the U.S. Department of Justice (DOJ) in 1972. In April, DOJ notified the superintendent that the system was under investigation, and the district entered a long legal struggle from which it has yet not emerged (CCFO-Desegregation).

In May 1972, DOJ officials visited Omaha and studied OPS records, microfilmed data, and returned to Washington, D.C. for a year-long analysis of the material. Then on 3 June 1973, the DOJ informed the district that it felt the complaints had merit and that it would seek rectification (CCFO-Civil Rights). Specifically, the justice department objected to the construction of the Martin Luther King School, scheduled to open that year, in a location destined to make it predominantly black, and to the use of portable classrooms at several elementary schools with predominantly minority enrollments, while other, nearly all-white schools were underutilized. Furthermore, it argued that OPS discriminated in faculty assignments, and that it increased segregation in certain instances by not redrawing attendance boundaries in accordance with shifting racial residential patterns and by maintaining three kindergarten to eighth grade schools when its general policy was to have junior high schools. Finally, DOJ cited several abuses in the system's open school and open transfer policies. Technical High School, located on the southern edge of the ghetto, and Central High School, in the downtown area but also close to the largest black neighborhood, were operated as open schools, which meant that students from anywhere in the district could attend them. The DOJ charged that the college preparatory courses at Tech were deemphasized, while vocational classes were added to the other high schools; thus the school's magnet quality was lost and white students were encouraged to go elsewhere. Moreover, white students living in attendance zones of racially mixed schools could avoid integration because certain schools had optional attendance zones and the open-transfer policy, adopted in 1964, which allowed a student to change to another school as long as his or her achievement level equaled that of the receiving class and as long as the receiving class was not larger than the one left (CCFO-*World Herald* 1973: 6/27, 7/3). Minority groups supported the policy at first, hoping that it would give blacks the opportunity to attend integrated schools, but they realized quickly that it would not foster desegregation because of transportation costs, the lower achievement levels of minority students, and the fact that inner-city classes were small. A short time before, in order to establish better student-teacher ratios, the administration had reduced all classes in inner-city schools by five pupils. Thus the open-transfer policy did not facilitate the movement of black students out of ghetto schools (*Star* 1964:3/20; 1; *Final Report* II: 4, 20–22).

The school board and the superintendent of schools vociferously rejected the DOJ allegations, and most of the individual members who spoke out warned of the most dire circumstances and counseled resistance. One lone voice from the board advocated "creative and positive action," which, in conjunction with other local agencies, would promote a "program of better community development" (CCFO-*World Herald* 1973: 7/21). The majority opinion, however, claimed that only busing could meet the justice department's directives, and that busing was a "menace" and should be opposed (CCFO-*World Herald* 1973: 7/3, 7/10, 7/18). On 16 July 1973 the board officially voted to resist and it issued a formal point-by-point repudiation of the charges. It argued that the district's policies were racially neutral and that they were determined by its historical growth through annexation, its compliance with national education laws, and its belief in the neighborhood school ideal. Residential patterns and other forces beyond its control produced the segregation that existed, and the board asserted that the DOJ distorted its case by choosing only examples that had segregatory results instead of presenting a balanced picture of the system (Holm and Laughlin 1973).

Community groups taking sides on the issue mushroomed into existence, and established organizations made their position known. Parent groups at various schools supported the board's decision while the city-wide PTA/PTSA Council (some schools maintained the traditional parent-teacher association and others developed parent-teacher-student associations) split over the dispute. The executive committee recommended "all steps necessary" to comply with the DOJ directives, but the full thirty-six-person council argued defiance (CCFO-*World Herald* 1973: 7/10; 7/16). One white group, led by the president of the League of Women Voters and the director of the Omaha Human Relations Department, resolved to support desegregation but believed that the black community should provide the primary leadership (CCFO-*World Herald* 1973:

8/23). The Urban League, the NAACP, and the United Methodist Community Center (Wesley House) were outspoken proponents for desegregation, and a coalition of fourteen black groups organized to promote school integration, eventually urging the initiation of a court suit for that purpose (CCFO-*World Herald* 1973: 7/17; 8/5; 8/19; 8/24). The Urban League, for example, denounced "the recent defensive attitudes and emotional approaches publicly taken by the Superintendent of Schools and some Board of Education members." League officials felt they "raised false issues to confuse and inflame the people of Omaha. They have created the impression that busing is the solution." This, they argued, was "patently not true" (*Star* 1973: 7/19: 1). A survey of black parents revealed that the issue with them was quality education; if busing was part of the solution, that was acceptable because many of their children already rode a bus (CCFO-*World Herald* 1973: 7/16).

During this initial phase of the controversy the press and the business establishment advised calm and cooperation. The *World Herald,* the city's only daily newspaper, editorialized that "consultation not confrontation, would bring the desired results." It criticized school leaders for establishing a false dichotomy of busing or nothing, and it argued that "it would be far better for the community to work out a plan reflecting local ideas and feelings than to undertake a resistance which could result in the imposition of a pattern written by a judge" (CCFO-*World Herald* 1973: 7/12). Business leaders echoed these sentiments and issued several joint statements urging cooperation and planning that would uphold the basic American ideals of democracy, equality of opportunity, and respect for the law. Even though none of these individuals or organizations advocated busing, all felt that the community could arrive at viable alternatives. Two of Omaha's highest ranking executives went as far as to promise to "pass the hat among our friends" to pay the cost involved in the OPS planning for an integration model (CCFO-*World Herald* 1973: 7/12, 7/13, 7/16).

The DOJ, however, was faced with the categorical rejection by the OPS, and on 10 August 1973, it filed suit and also sought a preliminary injunction in federal district court to force compliance with two of its directives for the coming school year—to block the opening of the Martin Luther King Middle School until it could be opened on an integrated basis, and to curtail the open-transfer policy, thus requiring all children to attend school within their own attendance zones (CCFO-*World Herald* 1973: 8/3). Hearings began two weeks later, and four days before school opened Judge Albert Schatz denied the injunction. Schatz, a veteran of three months on the bench, stated that the government failed to demonstrate "substantial probability" that it would win a discrimination suit and that an injunction at that time would "harm" the district and all the children in it. He concluded, however, that his decision should not be misconstrued to mean that the government could not win its case at a full trial (CCFO-Civil Rights; CCFO-*World Herald* 1973: 8/31).

The DOJ now began to prepare its suit, and on 11 October the Legal Aid Society, representing thirty-two black plaintiffs (seven couples and their children), filed a successful motion to intervene as a third party. The Urban League led a drive to raise $10,000 to finance the effort, and three attorneys from the Center for Law and Education at Harvard University were retained as co-counsel. The intervenors entered the case to plead their distinct interests and to prevent an OPS-DOJ out-of-court settlement. The Legal Aid lawyers, both of whom had practiced law for only a few years, decided that the rigors of the case demanded greater expertise in educational litigation; thus they secured help from the federally funded Center for Law and Education at Harvard, which specialized in school integration cases (CCFO-*World Herald* 1973: 10/12; CCFO-*Star* 1973: 10/25; Broom 1978). This was but one more way in which regional or national groups, ideas, or forces aided, influenced, or in some instances harassed the local desegregation process.

THE OMAHA COMMUNITY COMMITTEE

While the litigants began preparing their cases, a citizen's integration group, the Omaha Community Committee (OCC), held its first meeting. The school board had called for the formation of the committee back on 1 August for the purpose of advising the board on segregation problems and to make suggestions on changes in policy that would "enhance the opportunities for all students in the Omaha public schools." Adding to an already monumental task, the board further charged the OCC to study methods for improving and integrating housing, business opportunities, and employment for all of the citizens of the city (CCFO-*World Herald* 1973: 10/12; McCauley 1977). The committee consisted of over 130 members, drawn from a variety of neighborhoods, classes, races, and religions. Each of the ninety-five schools in the district was allowed one representative, and over fifty social and civic organizations were invited to send delegates. Only eight groups refused to participate, but among them were the Urban League and the NAACP. The president of the Urban League considered the OCC a "stalling tactic designed to delay the process of integration," thus it chose not to affiliate (CCFO-*World Herald* 1973: 8/6, 9/28).

The OCC decided to review the history of OPS, to study the DOJ allegations and methods of desegregation, to make recommendations for furthering integration, and to communicate openly and fully with the public in reaching its decisions. To fulfill its goals, the committee, which met from October 1973 to February 1974, held public meetings in all sections of town, conducted telephone surveys, and visited other cities to observe their efforts at integration. Selection Research Incorporated (SRI), a Lincoln, Nebraska firm that specialized in inquiry into educational and community development problems, was hired to provide the committee with a professional staff (CCFO-*World Herald* 1973: 10/2, 10/18).

Historically, the OCC found that changes in the OPS accelerated during the sixties. The employment of black teachers rose from 76 in 1963, to 234 or 9.5 percent in 1974, and minority administrators comprised 12 percent of the staff. In comparison, however, 19.8 percent of the student body was black, and the vast majority of minority teachers were still segregated in building assignments. Human relations workshops were instituted for teachers, minority culture classes and study centers were developed, and sister-link schools were promoted for integrative exchanges, but the OCC concluded that although much had been done, there was "still far to go" (Final Report II: 108). The committee felt that OPS had not sought "the assistance or advice of civic groups, government bodies, or other school districts in the past with regard to the matter of planning for school desegregation," and, in fact, it had "resisted any such attempts at planning. . . ." The OCC, therefore, recognized "that the citizens of Omaha and the Omaha Public Schools have failed to take the necessary steps to guarantee the rights of its minority students," and it advised that it was "time for the School Board to take aggressive leadership in the implementation of school desegregation" (*Final Report* II: 264; III: 1).

The committee's opinion surveys revealed that the quality of OPS education satisfied both black and white parents. Minority respondents, however, did feel, to a far greater degree than whites, that the quality differed with location and that western Omaha and the suburban districts received better instruction. More respondents favored an 80 percent white–20 percent minority racial balance of students and teachers than any other proportional schema. The idea of all-minority schools received little support from either race, but whites strongly favored minority ratios of zero to 20 percent and blacks preferred a 50–50 split (*Final Report* II: 204–205).

Another questionnaire showed that few OPS students (8 percent) rode the bus to school; over one-half walked, another one-fourth were driven in the family car, and the remainder used a combination of the two methods. Seeking responses to particular methods, an SRI survey found that one-half of the minority respondents supported a voluntary-transfer plan to promote integration, but only approximately one-quarter of the whites polled said that they would participate in such a program. A similar discrepancy surfaced in regard to the paired-school concept; less than one-half of the whites signified approval (42 percent said that they would move or put their child in private school), whereas 64 percent of the minority individuals supported the device (*Final Report* II: 245–257).

The OCC supplemented its locally collected data with trips to Tulsa, Witchita, St. Paul, and Indianapolis in order to compare situations and to formulate more precisely its recommendations. All of the committee's activities received extensive media coverage, and the community realized that it would make far-reaching suggestions. On the eve of the presentation of the final report several school board members made it clear to the public that they were not obligated to accept any OCC recommendations, but had only to consider them carefully. The original charge had obliquely referred to implementing "any and all alternatives to its present practices and procedures which are *reasonable in scope, acceptable to the community-at-large* and calculated to achieve the ultimate purpose of providing equal educational opportunities for each student in the school district" (CCFO-*World Herald* 1974: 3/1; *Final Report* III: 2, emphasis added).

Without assessing blame, the OCC report concluded that segregation existed in the OPS, that it was on the increase, and that teacher assignments were not distributed equitably. In response to these conditions it devised an "Omaha Covenant," based on successful approaches used in other cities and designed to obviate the complaints of the DOJ. The program advised other businesses, social and civic organizations, and educational institutions to pursue desegregation in all areas in conjunction with the OPS. It asked the school district to improve its communication with the parents and the community at large, and to work with established civic and service groups to prepare the community for peaceful integration. The report recommended that the administration draw up a plan to begin in 1974 and that it should include citizen participation in monitoring its implementation. The actual program should include human relations training for all teachers and staff, cultural awareness programs for all students, and an abolition of the open-transfer policy. Finally, some combination of redistricting, clustering (grouping several schools into one attendance zone), and the establishment of magnet schools (ones that provide a setting with specialized educational opportunities to attract a cross-section of students) and learning resource centers (places that provide unique programs to be attended by classes from the various neighborhood schools) should be devised to promote a better racial mix (*Final Report* III: 4–16; II: 198–236).

Because the committee was so large and was composed of so many different groups, it was not surprising that twenty-one separate minority reports were filed. Three important attitudinal generalizations manifested themselves. First, many groups from all-white areas strongly opposed busing and desired only a minimal integrative effort. On the other hand, a significant group of blacks demanded a maximum effort that included busing. Third, many whites wanted the other school districts of Omaha included in the desegregation process (*Final Report* II: 324; III: Appendix I: 23, 31, 42–43). Because of the way Omaha grew through annexation, it eventually found itself with three separate public school districts within the city limits (see figure 11.1). The Omaha School

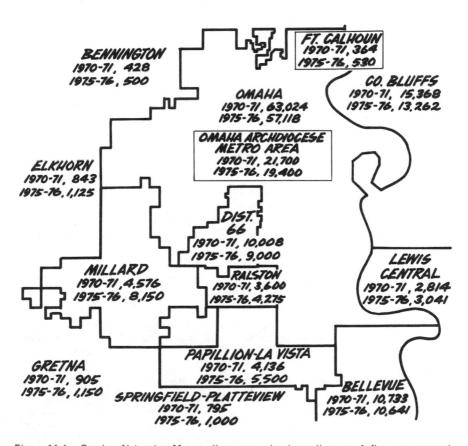

Figure 11.1. Omaha, Nebraska: Metropolitan area school enrollments: A five-year comparison. Most of Millard and all of District 66 are within Omaha city limits but are separate from the Omaha district. Map reprinted by permission of the Omaha *World-Herald*.

District, approximately 145 square miles in area and with over 63,000 students in 1970 is the largest, encompassing the southern, northern, central, and north-western parts of the town. After World War II, the city expanded to the south-west on two separate occasions, annexing large suburban settlements. Because of bonded debt and local politics, in both instances the new additions were allowed to maintain distinct school systems. Thus, in the southwest lie the District 66 School System (12 square miles and 10,008 students in 1970) and the Millard School District (35 square miles and 4,576 students in 1970).[1] The DOJ suit named only the OPS as a defendant; the two nearly all-white, middle-class and upper-class districts were not included in the prosecution. Many whites considered this unfair, that only a part of the community was being singled out for a city-wide problem, and that their exclusion would facilitate the movement of disaffected whites out of the OPS district (CCFO-*World Herald* 1973: 7/10; 1974: 2/). Subsequently, as the long legal battle evolved, a former state senator from Omaha filed suit in Nebraska courts to consolidate the three districts, on the grounds that a 1943 statute mandated that each incorporated metropolitan city in the state shall constitute one school district. In the fall of 1978, the state supreme court rejected the appeal (CCFO-*World Herald* 1976: 2/6; Stahmer 1978). However, in the spring of 1979 the voters in the Omaha School District voted a property-tax cap; because of the conse-quent financial restraints the Omaha district school board is now pursuing the idea of merging the three districts.

The immediate OPS response to the OCC report was another committee, another survey, and more out-of-town visits. Dr. Owen Knutzen, superintendent of schools, appointed a thirteen-person task force of school personnel to evaluate the OCC proposals. It presented pros and cons of the various integrative methods without reaching any definitive conclusion. Redistricting, it found, would preserve the neighborhood ideal while mixing the races, but it would also include the burdens of providing transportation and of redrawing boundaries periodically in order to keep pace with changing residential patterns. The task force liked the voluntary nature of magnet schools and the fact that they would promote innovation while drawing students from every part of the city. On the other hand, it feared that they could lead to a dual system, with the magnets attracting all the accelerated students, and not necessarily promoting integration. The same pluses and minuses applied to the learning resource center, with the added drawback that its part-time nature limited its integrative impact. Clustering was acceptable because it was simple and required little in the way of new facilities or programs. Large expenditures for transportation, however, estimated at $500,000 annually, debilitated this solution. Finally, the task force also called for a reevaluation of the open-transfer policy regarding its relationship to segregation (CCFO-*World Herald* 1974: 4/19, 4/23, 5/30; CCFO-*Sun* 1974: 5/30).

While the administration studied, the *World Herald* surveyed. It discovered that only 27 percent of the 520 people polled felt that the DOJ charges against the OPS were justified. Quite revealing, however, was the fact that whereas only 18 percent of the white respondents answered "yes" to the above question, 70 percent of the blacks replied in the affirmative. In fact, a very definite racial split emerged on every question. Thus, 23 percent of the whites, but 66

1. Statistics provided by the various districts.

percent of the blacks, felt that the OPS promoted segregation; and 39 percent of the whites to 91 percent of the blacks advocated desegregation of the schools (CCFO-*World Herald* 1974: 4/10). Another poll one month later revealed somewhat different attitudes, but its results were more difficult to evaluate because it did not distinguish respondents by race. Two-thirds of the 332 individuals contacted by telephone opined in favor of more integrated classrooms, but three-fourths were against the transfer of students to achieve it. The poll also disclosed that there was less acceptance for integration in each succeeding older age group (CCFO-*World Herald* 1974: 5/4).

THE SCHOOL BOARD

The school board also went about the task of collecting information. First, it sponsored its own one-day visits to Dallas, St. Paul, Tulsa, and Wichita, and then in June it authorized $19,000 to hire the Gallup organization to survey 750 families, 250 black and 500 white. The project was more sophisticated than previous polls and it involved personal, in-the-home interviews using audiovisual aids to explain the various methods of desegregation. Of the four strategies proposed by the OCC, 64 percent of the whites favored magnet schools and 49 percent approved of learning resource centers, but less than one-third supported either clustering or redistricting. Blacks, however, advocated the learning resource center foremost (72 percent), and accepted all the others—magnets (65 percent), redistricting (50 percent), and clustering (49 percent). Of the white households, 43 percent felt that the best advantage of an integrated school was that in it one learned racial toleration. Blacks gave a much more diffuse pattern of responses; whereas 18 percent mentioned the above reply, the more frequent comment (27 percent) was that integrated schools gave a higher quality education. Another dichotomy in basic values surfaced as 37 percent of the whites polled replied that their greatest fear was for their personal safety, whereas the blacks' major apprehension (18 percent) was that they would be treated unfairly (CCFO-*World Herald* 1974: 6/4, 8/28). From all the information gathered it was obvious that white and black Omahans perceived their city and their schools quite differently, that they had different fears and different goals, and that they advocated different methods to bridge the chasm between the two societies.

During the summer vacation period of 1974, while the court suit awaited its hearing, the board did implement policy changes; some were based on OCC recommendations, although it avoided the four major proposals for system-wide integration. The program innovations included the initiation of a rumor control "hot line" to provide accurate information about alleged racial incidents, and the assignment of black teachers to eighteen more schools, bringing the total to seventy-five of the ninety-five schools having at least one minority faculty member (CCFO-*World Herald* 1974: 8/23, 8/26). The board also called for the mandatory enrollment of all OPS staff in human awareness programs, but because the training was planned for after-school hours over an extended period of time with no compensation, the Omaha Education Association challenged the directive. The policy reverted back to a voluntary nature, and then the teacher's organization encouraged its members to participate (CCFO-*World Herald* 1974: 8/13; Thies 1978).

The district also responded to the DOJ allegation and the OCC recommendation by revising the open-transfer policy. The new guidelines forbade transfers that would increase segregation. Using the racial balance proportions of 1973, whites could switch only out of schools that had a 77.5 percent or more nonminority population, and blacks could leave only schools with a 22.5 percent or more minority enrollment. A few other considerations applied, such as medical reasons or to allow students to finish their senior year in the school to which they had been transferring (CCFO-*World Herald* 1974: 5/30). Then, on the other side of the coin, the system moved to promote integration through a limited voluntary transfer plan. The first stage included encouraging 300 black students each to shift from Horace Mann Junior High and Central High to other predominantly white schools, and attracting white students to Tech, including some from the other two districts in the city. The OPS offered to pay the transportation costs of any volunteer who would have to travel more than one and one-half miles (CCFO-*World Herald* 1974: 6/18, 7/2).

Many individuals in the minority community responded negatively to the voluntary transfer plan and, at first, it found little support among black parents. The education coordinator of the Urban League called it a "positive action in the right direction," but added that it could not "be taken as an honest attempt toward desegregation." The spokesperson called for a mandatory plan of black and white transfers. Another critic called it "dishonest" and "racist" because it recruited only blacks out, and the North Omaha Cluster of United Methodist Churches argued that voluntarism would fail and that the policy as devised would work too slowly and would not integrate west Omaha (CCFO-*Star* 1974: 7/18; CCFO-*Sun* 1974: 8/29; *Star* 1974: 8/29: 1). The first contacts with parents produced poor results; of 435 parents approached at Horace Mann Junior High, only 95 indicated they would cooperate. Yet, the final figures in September justified the OPS optimism that voluntarism would prevail, thus avoiding a mandatory reshuffling. In all, 884 students opted for voluntary transfers, although only 7.9 percent were white. Of the total, 238 came at the high school level, 411 at the junior high level, and 235 at the elementary level (*Star* 1974: 7/1: 1; CCFO-*World Herald* 1974: 9/9). The statistics proved parts of the argument of both sides in the controversy; obviously, the program almost exclusively moved blacks, but it did achieve the limited OPS goal of changing the racial mixture at a few select schools.

One month after the fall 1974 term began the district court rendered its decision. Judge Albert Schatz dismissed the charges against the OPS, stating that segregation did exist, but that the district did not create it. He argued that the system followed a "neutral neighborhood policy"; that the building program, the original open-transfer policy, and the hiring practices were not discriminatory; and, therefore, that the segregated schools resulted from other causes, such as housing policy, that were outside the purview of the district (D. Neb. 1974; 8th Cir. 1975). The victory cost the OPS $91,066 in attorney fees, and the board prepared for the expected appeal by quickly budgeting another $80,000 for legal expenses for the coming year (CCFO-*World Herald* 1974: 10/22, 12/3).

The *World Herald*, speaking for at least part of the white community (probably the majority if one takes into account the attitudinal polls discussed earlier), found the verdict "fair," but it also warned against complacency. It prodded the school officials and the citizenry not to "relax their efforts to find acceptable ways to provide quality education for all in a school system which has a better racial balance" (CCFO-*World Herald* 1974: 10/17). The black press and minority leaders, however, viewed the decision quite differently. Most spokespersons felt that the judge ignored crucial evidence, and they called for an immediate appeal. Only the president of a local NAACP chapter cautioned against further litigation, but his skeptical reasoning was based on the fact that the case might eventually go before the U.S. Supreme Court, which with its new Nixon conservative leanings would use the case to reverse earlier prointegration decisions (*Star* 1974: 10/17: 1, 10/24: 5, 12/19: 1). This line of thinking led the local NAACP, heretofore a strong supporter of the desegregation suit, to withdraw from active participation in its furtherance. The NAACP continued to desire the integration of the school system, but it preferred to have other forces bring it about and not have the courts decide the issue.

THE EIGHTH CIRCUIT COURT

The DOJ and the intervenors reflected the majority black opinion by taking the case to the United States Court of Appeals for the Eighth Circuit. The following summer, on 12 June 1975, the appeals court overturned Schatz's ruling, stating that Schatz erred in not recognizing "that a presumption of segregative intent arises once it is established that school authorities have engaged in acts or omissions, the natural, probable and foreseeable consequence of which is to bring about or maintain segregation." Using this reasoning the appeals court countered the district court's opinion in five basic areas: (1) "although the affirmative action program brought more black teachers into the system, the racially discriminatory assignment policies were continued," (2) the open-transfer policy clearly resulted in greater segregation in the system, (3) the optional attendance zones made some predominantly black schools underutilized while it allowed white students to travel farther distances to attend overcrowded predominantly white schools, (4) between 1951 and 1973 the OPS built thirty-nine new schools or additions, and because only one of these schools in the twenty-two years opened integrated, that "was sufficient to establish a presumption of segregative intent," and (5) administration policies made Tech High a school "which was identified as a 'colored school' just as certainly as if the words were printed across its entrance in six-inch letters" (D. Neb. 1974: 101–102).

The U.S. Eighth Circuit Court stated that it realized that integration was "difficult" and that the "pain of transition" was "unfortunate," but nonetheless "racial discrimination in the Omaha Public Schools must be eliminated root and branch." It mandated that the system fully integrate its faculty by the opening of the 1975–1976 academic year. It instructed that "the burdens of integration shall be borne as equally as possible by blacks and whites in all geographic areas of the District." Because of the 1975 tornado, which cut a long, wide swathe of destruction through the western area of the city, damaging several schools in the process, the court allowed the student desegregation to be done in two phases with the completion targeted for 1976. In devising a plan to carry out the order, the jurists directed the district not to shift students in integrated neighborhood schools, to establish a maximum of 35 percent minority enrollment per school, to forbid student transfers that had a segregative effect, and to ensure that future construction will not lead to resegregation. The judges instructed the OPS to report periodically to the district court, which would retain jurisdiction for three years while it monitored the plan to assure its implementation and effectiveness. Finally, the U.S. Eighth Circuit Court empowered Judge Schatz to appoint an interracial citizens committee to aid the OPS in drawing up the plan, and it ordered that the Nebraska State Department of Education and the intervenors be included in the process (D. Neb. 1974: 129–133).

Within a week the school board met and voted 9–2 (the two black members voted nay) to appeal to the full eight-member panel of the circuit court. The school attorneys argued that by using the rule of "presumption of segregative intent," the appeals court shifted the burden of proof from the plaintiffs to the OPS, and that because Omaha was the first northern segregation case before the court, its five other judges should be allowed to consider that point of law (CCFO-*World Herald* 1975: 6/17). On 7 July the U.S. Eighth Circuit Court denied the petition for rehearing en banc, and in a matter of days, the board, by the exact same vote, decided to take its case to the U.S. Supreme Court. Although one board member found the opinion "completely unreasonable" and counseled defiance, the system's lawyers cautioned that such action would bring a contempt citation; therefore, the white majority chose further litigation (CCFO-*World Herald* 1975: 6/17). On 11 October, without stating its reasons, the highest tribunal in the land refused to hear the case. The board's attorneys advised that there was "no further recourse," and another appeal was rejected as "an exercise in futility" (CCFO-*World Herald* 1975: 11/11, 12/4; CCFO-Civil Rights).

Meanwhile, the administration moved forward on devising the first phase of desegregation. For the fall 1975 term, 134 teachers received new assignments to meet the criteria of a fully integrated faculty. In early August the intervenors, the DOJ, and the OPS met with Judge Schatz to agree upon the faculty transfers. Even though the intervenors had other reservations they forced only one change—the reassignment of one more black teachers from five elementary schools (CCFO-*World Herald* 1975: 7/15, 8/2). Judge Schatz told OPS to draw up Phase I of the student plan alone, but that the comprehensive plan for 1976 would necessitate the input of the other groups as designated by the Eighth Circuit Court. Several ad hoc citizen organizations emerged to lobby for their participating. The previous year 480 students visited learning resource centers, 900 volunteered for racial-balance transfers, and 130 attended Tech High on a part-time basis for magnet classes. For 1975–1976, OPS predicted that 4,000 already in existence but increased their frequency and the numbers of students participating. The previous year 480 students visted learning resource centers, 900 volunteered for racial-balance transfers, and 130 attended Tech High on a part-time basis for magnet class. For 1975–1976, OPS predicted that 4,000 students would use learning resource centers, 1,400 would volunteer for racial balance transfers, and 240 would attend Tech on a part-time basis. Also, twenty-three elementary schools were grouped into sister school programs for field trips, class visits, and other forms of integrative experiences. The one new feature at this stage of the process was a series of added requirements necessary for students to become eligible for special-needs transfers. The tightened regulations resulted in the denial of almost 1,000 requests (CCFO-*World Herald* 1975: 7/9, 7/12, 7/24; CCFO-*Star*, 7/10; CCFO-Desegregation).

THE COMPREHENSIVE PLAN

While the administration now began the difficult process of formulating the comprehensive plan, several developments manifested themselves that promoted a positive atmosphere. Twenty-one youths from Burke and Tech High Schools, for example, formed an improvisational group, the Clerestory Window, to spread the message that integration could work. The group opened at a local dinner theater and planned to perform at schools and civic functions. Another encouraging sign was a dramatic shift in enrollment at Tech. In 1975, this school became 16.6 percent white, the highest percentage in a decade, and its total enrollment went up for the first time since 1963. Moreover, about 200 students (80 percent of them white) attended part-time for one to four magnet classes per day (CCFO-*World Herald* 1975: 10/4, 11/2).

In the planning process, Dr. Owen Knutzen, the superintendent of schools, took a low profile; he was involved, but other administrators acted as the public spokesman (CCFO-*Sun* 1975: 7/17).[2] Dr. Norbert Schuerman, director of general administration, chaired the ten-person task force, composed of administrators, principals, and assistant principals from all three levels of education, and OPS resource personnel, which actually formulated the district's version of the plan. Of the members of the task force three were black and one was of Hispanic origin, and four of the ten were women. The group visited eight cities to learn from their successes and their mistakes, to see how they paid for their programs, and to find out how they relieved public fears. The task force discovered ways to generate outside funds, such as through the federal Elementary and Secondary Education Act. The other urban centers also stressed the importance of communication; therefore, OPS decided to "widen its public pipeline on desegregation." As a part of its communication program the district decided to use newspaper stories extensively, and it also held a series of four town-hall meetings during the month of October to explain various plans to implement the Eighth Circuit Court decision. Between 300 and 500 persons attended each of the town hall gatherings at which OPS administrators answered questions and presented information on the status of planning to that date. In return OPS received one message loudly and clearly from the white population in attendance— it strongly disfavored busing. Other aspects of the network included a prime-time television broadcast and meetings with special interest groups (CCFO-*World Herald* 1975: 9/11, 10/4, 10/8).

During the planning process the executive director of the Omaha Education Association felt that his organization played an important supportive role. The administration viewed the teachers' association warily and its role was limited, but it did have significant input in certain areas. First, during the monthly meetings with OPS a "good deal" of informal exchange took place in regard to the desegregation process, especially concerning staff integration. The association supported the policy of no appeal, that is, anyone reassigned had to accept the transfer. The organization also had representation on the committee that established the busing timetables because of the impact it had on teachers' schedules. Originally, for example, the administration planned to assign junior high teachers

---

2. The *Sun* surmised that the reason was because in "other cities where integration was ordered, many superintendents who took an active public role found themselves assailed from all sides. They often wound up jobless."

to ride the buses indefinitely, but this was changed to a program in which the teachers acted as monitors for the first few weeks until the students got accustomed to the ride. Overall, the association pledged to support whatever plan was adopted, and it encouraged its members to make the transition as smooth as possible (CCFO-*World Herald* 1975: 10/20; Thies 1978; Pester 1975).

The state department of education, which the appeals court directed to participate in the planning, actually played a very limited role. The department did not consider itself either ready or equipped to join in the decision-making process—it felt that the issue was a local one that should be handled locally (Campbell 1978). It did, however, establish a task force that attended OPS and community meetings, and that provided technical aid, information, and support. Its supportiveness vexed some members of the black community, who called it a "rubber stamp" for OPS and who complained that it did not know and therefore overlooked the concerns of minority Nebraskans (CCFO-*Evening Journal* 1976: 5/7). The department's one unique contribution was in the area of trying to generate suburban cooperation. The commissioner, Dr. Ann Campbell, urged the surrounding districts to invite OPS classes out to their schools. General policy, however, dictated that nonresidents could attend classes only if they sought educational services not available in their home districts. This precluded almost all transfers out of OPS, although District 66 and Millard did allow a handful of their students to attend magnet classes at Tech High School. On another level of cooperation, the suburban systems issued public declarations that they would scrutinize all requests for transfers and would accept no one trying to avoid busing (CCFO-*World Herald* 1975: 8/10, 12/3; 1976: 2/1).

The intervenors were not happy with their role in the planning or the end product. One of the parents involved declared that OPS "totally ignored" the group, and she predicted that they would return to court. Robert Broom, one of the Legal Aid Society attorneys, felt that his clients were allowed to "make input," but that the board did not consult them prior to accepting a final plan. A spokesman for the OPS task force admitted that in terms of procedure, "we didn't sit down at the same table and work with anyone. But we did arrange to have input from all the groups" (CCFO-*World Herald* 1975: 12/16; Broom 1978).

Similarly, the interracial committee had trouble defining its role in terms of the OPS planning method. The appeals court did not give Judge Schatz guidelines on picking the committee, but Schatz decided it should be small and blue ribbon. Therefore, he chose a group of elite educators and business people, six white and four black. They ranged in age from thirty-two to fifty-five years, all had some college education, all lived within the OPS district, and eight of them had children in the schools. Five held full-time employment in education—three from Creighton University, one from the University of Nebraska at Omaha, and one from Boys Town—while three others were intimately involved through the PTA or on boards of regents. Furthermore, three had served on the Omaha Community Committee (CCFO-*World Herald* 1975: 7/22, 7/28).

After a month of closed meetings the press reported that many members and the public were confused about the actual role of the interracial committee. Part of the problem stemmed from secrecy; the committee did not know when to go public and with what information. Most members felt that they understood their advisory function to the judge, but they did not clearly perceive their relationship to OPS. At one point the chairman announced that the committee would devise its own plan and present it to Schatz, but later it abandoned that goal in favor of giving OPS twelve suggestions, some of which merely restated the Eighth Circuit Court mandate. Its recommendations urged OPS to seek student input, to build better communications links among all the parties involved in the desegregation process, to develop a public relations program that would present desegregation in a positive light, to organize a visible effort by community groups of all sorts to make the plan work, and to establish a student-parent-educator task force to monitor the implementation of the plan continuously (CCFO-*Sun* 1975: 9/18; CCFO-*World Herald* 1975: 8/9, 10/17).

Eventually, the committee's role evolved as a sounding board, not as the commanding decision-making authority in the planning process. The committee visited other cities to gain insight into various plans and it met frequently with OPS, the intervenors, and the DOJ as they developed proposals. The OPS task force worked alone; then, usually weekly, it met with the interracial committee to explain its decisions and to entertain questions concerning any parts of the plan it was developing. Thus, the normal sequence was for OPS to initiate, then the intervenors and the justice department would react, and finally the interracial committee would respond to the above deliberations, possibly influencing a direction but not deciding a policy (Brown 1978).

At the end of November the OPS task force submitted three plans for each of the three levels of education to a special committee of the school board. All the models followed guidelines that sought to hold the number of students reassigned to a minimum, that excluded the transfer of any kindergarteners or first graders, and that tried to strengthen educational programs in the process. Each design presented a variant that combined voluntary transfers, pairing, clustering, rezoning, and magnets; then, depending upon the configuration chosen, it would be determined how many students would be bused.

Then in mid-December the full board approved a final program that called for integrating the high schools exclusively through voluntary transfers. At the junior high level two schools would become ninth grade centers with whites bused to them, and four others would house only the seventh and eighth grades with blacks bused to them. Guidelines for the elementary division envisioned the transfer of second graders from western white schools to schools on the Near Northside, and the busing of third through sixth graders from inner-city black schools to white schools to be integrated with students there (CCFO-*World Herald* 1975: 10/8, 11/26, 12/15). The district submitted its comprehensive plan to the district court on time, on the last day of the year.

The first few months of 1976 were occupied with reactions to the OPS plan and with deliberations between Judge Schatz and the various parties to the suit. Chicanos and Indians now became vocal for the first time, and they reacted against the fact that they were simply lumped with whites in determining racial balance quotas. Two recently formed groups, the Chicano Awareness Center and the Indian Center Industries Association, demanded that children of these heritages be recognized as distinct minorities and that they receive special attention. The tardiness of this protest, the lack of sustained effort, and the diminutive size of the groups—each represented about 300 families, and combined Chicano and Indian children accounted for less than 4 percent of the

OPS enrollment—limited the effect of the demands. The OPS displayed some sensitivity to the concerns by applying for federal funds to initiate cultural and bilingual programs, but the desegregation process continued as a black-and-white issue and the quota system remained intact (CCFO-*Star* 1973: 9/13; CCFO-*World Herald* 1976: 1/23, 3/5, 5/30).

The intervenors felt that the OPS plan discriminated against blacks by placing an unequal burden on them and that it failed to eliminate segregation "root and branch." They objected to the exclusion of first graders, and they claimed many schools remained "racially identifiable." They also complained that black students were reassigned seven or more years out of the thirteen years of school, whereas whites were bused only two or three years. An equal number of white and black students were scheduled for busing, but for blacks the number represented 50 percent of their total enrollment in grades one through six, whereas for whites it represented only 15 percent. The Urban League and other leaders in the black community also strongly supported these objections (CCFO-*World Herald* 1976: 1/23, 2/3, 3/5, 5/30; *Star* 1973: 9/13; 1976: 2/12: 1, 6/24: 2).

The DOJ criticized the plan along similar lines, especially the exclusion of the first grade. It suggested revisions that included busing white third graders (an overall increase of 1,000 white students) and making other technical changes to the elementary and senior high plans. OPS responded by making many of the minor adjustments, and by allowing for voluntary transfers of first graders and expanding the number of integrative experiences at that level—for example, using recess, lunch periods, tutoring, and library work to mix those students with the integrated upper grades. With these changes and with the addition of busing some white third graders, the DOJ dropped its objection to the exclusion of the first grade, and the interracial committee followed suit. They felt that the changes made the burden of desegregation more equitable, and they accepted the OPS notation that statistics from other cities with similar plans showed that when parents had one child transferred to a school they often sent a younger brother or sister to the same school for convenience. Thus, this phenomenon would also produce some first grade integration (CCFO-*World Herald* 1976: 2/4; Brown 1978, CCFO 1976a).

On 27 April 1976, Judge Schatz promulgated the final form of the comprehensive plan. The district court accepted two deviations from the guidelines of the Eighth Circuit Court because it found "no evidence that said deviations will aggravate white flight or make it more difficult to achieve the fully integrated school system": (1) it allowed schools with more than a 50 percent black enrollment to reduce it to 50 percent, not 35 percent; and (2) it allowed schools with a 35 to 50 percent black enrollment to maintain that ratio rather than reduce it to 35 percent. Schatz accepted the modified OPS version despite the continued objections of the intervenors, especially to the exclusion of the first grade. The judge agreed with the district's argument that "long periods of daily transportation would adversely affect the physical and mental processes of first grade children and would inhibit their educational development due to susceptibility to mental and physical fatigue." Furthermore, first graders had to cope with the transition from home to a formal full day of school, they were subject to "frequent illness," they tended to be "emotionally immature and easily frustrated," and learning to read was difficult enough by itself (CCFO 1976b).

For the elementary schools the plan created seven clusters and three pairs for the exchange of students, while kindergarteners and first graders always remained in their neighborhood schools. The clusters combined several predominantly white schools with one predominantly black school. The inner-city school became a kindergarten to third grade center with entire classes of white second and third graders bused in to join blacks who would attend that school because it was in their attendance zone. All fourth to sixth graders from the inner-city school, in turn, would be bused out as classes to the predominantly white schools; thus the other schools in the cluster would accommodate grades kindergarten and first, second or third, and fourth to 'sixth. In the case of pairs, both schools would house kindergarten and first grade while one, for example, would also contain grades two through four and the other, five and six. Overall, the program necessitated reassigning 5,700 students, approximately 2,400 blacks and 3,300 whites.

At the junior high level the plan also used clustering and grade level centers. It created two ninth grade centers and four seventh and eighth grade centers, and seven schools remained as three-year junior high schools. The ninth grade centers were organized with "schools within a school"; that is, in order to provide for equal opportunity in sports, counseling, activities, and other services, each ninth grade center was divided into three distinct units. Each unit was integrated according to race, sex, and school attendance area, and it was hoped that this arrangement would also preserve the personal identification a student would have in a more traditional junior high. These innovations required the reassignment of about 3,600 students, 65 percent of whom were white.

At the senior high level the plan modified the feeder system and the open-enrollment policy as it pertained to specific schools, and it intensified the magnet programs at particular schools. Desegregation of high schools was to be achieved through voluntary racial balance transfers, although a back-up plan of mandatory reassignment was developed (CCFO 1976c).

The city and its largest school district now faced the task of implementing the plan. The period presented a variegated pattern of attitudes and activities that alternately boded ill or boded well for the successful, peaceful desegregation of the school system. Teachers, students, and religious leaders provided positive inspiration; a huge citizens' coalition formed to promote peace; the media strove to allay fears; and the OPS administration intensified its communication network and professionally planned the technical aspects of implementation. On the other hand, the national Republican party initiated an antibusing campaign that influenced local politics and that prompted the school board to undertake a new round of appeals. Moreover, the process spawned several local antibusing groups, which also affected the board's activities and raised the level of apprehension in the community. The most ominous phenomenon was the revival of the Ku Klux Klan in Omaha, although hindsight revealed that it was a weak, temporary organization.

At the first board meeting following the promulgation of the plan, one member demanded a new appeal because, in his interpretation, the plaintiffs drew up the plan that bused too many students and the board gave in without a fight. Several other members challenged his remarks, but only the part about the board "giving in," and they surmised that the statements were politically motivated because the individual was a candidate for county office. The board president expressed its resigned attitude, stating, "it is the law and the Board of Education must uphold the law. We are a nation of laws, a society of laws, and the board is one of laws" (CCFO-*World Herald* 1976: 4/29; CCFO-*Sun* 1976: 4/29).

In March, the *World Herald* interviewed 322 Omahans and only 5 percent of those who responded said that "mandatory classroom integration" would lead to a better quality of education. Another 40 percent felt that the quality would remain constant, but 49 percent replied that it would deteriorate. Later in the summer, even though the paper predicted peaceful implementation, it remained "skeptical of its supposed benefits." Studies from other cities, it argued, claimed busing worked when it did not disrupt, and the editorial staff seemed disheartened by the fact that statements by key OPS officials promised only no reduction in quality. Instead of "no worse education," it hoped, because of the costs involved, that it would "produce better education for all and better race relations" (CCFO-*World Herald* 1976: 3/12, 7/18). Thus, the board, the administration, and a majority of the populace remained unconvinced of positive benefits that were to accrue from the effort demanded of them.

POLITICS

In national politics, President Gerald Ford sought support through the mobilization of the antibusing sentiment. As early as September 1975, the *World Herald* pointed out that the chief executive on the campaign trail became more forceful in his opposition to busing, while at the same time urged compliance with the law. Ford argued that the courts ignored the 1974 legislation that stated that busing was to be used as a last resort, and Congress revealed its attitude again on a Department of Health, Education, and Welfare appropriation bill by stipulating that none of the money could be used to require the transporting of a child to any school other than the one closest to his or her home (CCFO-*World Herald* 1975: 9/16, 9/20). Then in mid-May 1976, Attorney General Edward Levi called for a reevaluation of the busing issue and announced that he was searching for a test case. The president followed up with a White House conference on busing, and in June with the submission of a bill designed to limit the scope of evidence that courts could admit in desegregation cases and the number of years the courts could monitor a plan. Immediately, Majority Leader Mike Mansfield announced that the Ford proposal would not fit on the calendar and on the same day the Senate shelved, by a vote of 55–39, a bill that attempted to prevent the DOJ from seeking court-ordered busing. The courts themselves, however, seemed more attuned to the president's ideas. In late June, the Supreme Court, by a vote of 6–2, ruled that courts did not have the power to deal with resegregation, and in Pasadena an appeals court stated that the city's school board did not have to readjust attendance zones annually to maintain racial balance. In both instances the decisions followed the Ford desire to curb the power of the courts to watchdog plans after their initial construction. All this activity at the national political level buoyed the hopes of local opponents. The school board president hailed one of these decisions, stating, "It sounds like the beginning of positive things coming from the Supreme Court." The board's appetite to resist was whetted by the national administration, and a new round of appeals resulted (CCFO-*World Herald* 1976: 6/2, 6/24, 6/25, 6/29).

State politics played a negligible role in the desegregation of the Omaha School District, except for the effect of the continued low rate of state funding for local schools. No state or local laws pertaining to racially separate schools existed prior to the *Brown* v. *Topeka* decision. At the outset of the controversy in 1973, Governor James J. Exon declared that the matter involved only OPS and the DOJ. The chairman of the Unicameral's (state legislature's) education committee indicated interest in state action, but the Nebraska State School Boards Association lobbied against legislative guidelines for integration measures for local boards. In January 1974, the state legislature passed a resolution calling on the U.S. Congress to initiate an antibusing amendment to the federal Constitution, but it did not pass any state laws regulating desegregation methods (CCFO-*World Herald* 1973: 7/21, 11/9; 1976: 1/15).

Once it was realized that OPS would have to transport students, fourteen greater Omaha state senators pushed a bill to grant special state aid to cover integration costs. Out-state opposition developed swiftly to what some antagonists called "raw greed"; this was another manifestation of a basic division in state politics that frequently pitted small town, rural, agricultural western Nebraska against Omaha, located on the eastern boundary. That bill and several others introduced during the spring and summer of 1976 went down to defeat. The OPS administrators criticized the state's refusal to pick up any of the costs of integration, but the frugal nature of the legislature continued. In 1976, Nebraska ranked forty-seventh among the fifty states, contributing only 18 percent of the local funds (CCFO-*World Herald* 1976: 1/20, 1/25, 2/6, 2/10, 3/10, 6/7, 11/14).

Locally, Mayor Ed Zorinsky spoke out against busing early in the controversy and he maintained that stance throughout, although he always indicated that he would uphold the law. By the time the district entered the implementation period, the mayor became involved in the race for the United States Senate. During the Democratic primary his opponent did not use busing as an issue, but in the Republican camp it became a major question. Second District Congressman John Y. McCollister, looking to change houses on the hill, campaigned on the fact that he had voted against busing thirty times and that he cosponsored the aforementioned Ford bill in the house. The other Republican candidate also attacked busing and said that if black children had "at least equal" teachers and facilities, he did not "see why in the world they would want to be mingled with the whites" (CCFO-*World Herald* 1975: 7/10, 8/10; 1976: 2/2).

Zorinsky and McCollister emerged the victors and kept the issue alive during the entire summer as they campaigned for the fall general election. McCollister publicly associated himself with a group called Omahans Against Forced Busing, and he sent a communiqué to President Ford asking him to intervene in the Omaha case. Not to be outdone, Zorinsky signed the petition of a group opposing busing on the grounds that it forced unconstitutional taxation on local areas, and he personally wrote to the attorney general urging him to use Omaha as a test case. He argued that this action offered "intelligent hope" that busing would not take place in Omaha (CCFO-*World Herald* 1976: 1/31, 5/21, 5/26).

Numerous spokespersons in the community criticized Zorinsky's actions and a group of blacks formed to write a letter to Levi asking him to ignore Zorinsky's request. Even though minority leaders remained disgruntled, the *World Herald* defended the dialogue as a responsible debate (CCFO-*World*

Herald 1976: 1/1, 1/14, 5/31; CCFO-Lincoln *Star* 1976: 5/27; *Star* 1976: 6/3: 1). Despite the argument, the mayor displayed great confidence in a peaceful implementation of the plan. "I give the citizens of our community," he stated, "credit for having more maturity than those in some other cities." His message to the city on the eve of school opening revealed this same sense of confidence and mission. He explained that despite the differences in opinion, "the one common thread that unites us is our belief that Omaha is a community which respects the law and which upholds lawful processes in resolving issues of controversy. . . . I'm sure the pride of Omahans will inspire us to set an example for the entire nation during this transition period" (CCFO-*World Herald* 1976: 4/28; *World Herald* 1976: 8/26: Suppl. 1).

The busing issue also played an important role in other political races. For example, the Douglas County (Omaha) Young Republicans passed a resolution supporting a constitutional amendment that would ban busing for the purpose of school integration. Their adult counterparts adopted a plank in their platform calling for the enactment of "a constitutional amendment or any other legislation possible to prohibit forced busing of school children and to reestablish our neighborhood concept of the public schools" (CCFO-*World Herald* 1976: 2/10, 6/4). This attitude surfaced most dramatically in the Republican primary for the second district congressional nomination in which four candidates flailed away at the issue. The state Democratic Convention, however, unanimously passed a resolution urging party members to work for the peaceful implementation of the Omaha plan and it also advocated finding "ways of influencing community leaders to support desegregation efforts to comply positively with the law." The Omaha City Council, not involved in the election process that year, duplicated the sentiment at the solicitation of citizens' groups and it also passed a unanimous resolution asking for the peaceful implementation of the court order (CCFO-*Sun* 1976: 5/13, 8/26; CCFO-*World Herald* 1976: 5/9, 6/29, 8/6, 8/25, 10/7).

ANTIBUSING GROUPS

The activities of the citizens' antibusing groups dovetailed with the political rhetoric on the issue. Generally, all the groups remained small, they preached resistance but nonviolence, they were led by young adults, and, except for the Klan, their organizations peaked in the spring and atrophied during the summer before school opened. Some groups were directly affected by, or were mere offshoots of, other national organizations, whereas others were of purely local origin. The Black Silent Majority Committee, headed by Clay Claiborne in Washington, D.C., for example, direct mailed material aimed at convincing blacks to oppose busing. Its pamphlet, *Black Brigade Against Busing: What Every Black Family Should Know!,* emphasized the threat of violence against black children and the disruption of life and school caused by lengthy travel on the bus (CCFO-Antibusing).

A local resident attended the convention of the National Association of Pro America in Omaha at which she met some Pasadena, California citizens who inspired her to organize the Omahans Against Forced Busing. The group's leader came from the professional middle class who lived in a well-to-do area in the central section of the city. The organization sought change through litigation and legislation, and it predicted that busing would raise the level of violence in the city, would lower property values by approximately 50 percent, and would decrease the achievement level of students 3 percent annually. The organization's leader also attacked OPS as "a socialistic type of school system"; instead she advocated "fundamental schools" which emphasized discipline and the three Rs, and which rejected federal funds. Omahans Against Forced Busing issued several newsletters during the spring of 1976, brought in critics of the Pasadena desegregation plan to speak in February, and in May aranged for the appearance of a "mystery professor." The antibusing author, who did not use his real name, allegedly was a professor of educational psychology at a midwestern university, but his lecture drew only 250 people (CCFO-Antibusing; CCFO-*World Herald* 1975: 12/14; 1976: 2/26, 2/28, 5/9).

Free Americans for Constitutional Taxation (FACT) arose locally as "a non-profit corporation organized to test whether the judiciary branch of the federal government has the power to mandate an increase in the property taxes for the Omaha School District." The group, also led by middle-class professionals, advocated nonviolence and specifically disassociated itself from the above organization, whose remarks it considered "inflammatory." Yet, to accept court-ordered busing, it felt, was to give up freedom therefore, it filed suit in the U.S. District Court to block the purchase or lease of buses. In mid-April Judge Schatz denied the temporary restraining order that FACT sought (CCFO-Antibusing: FACT flyer; CCFO-*World Herald* 1976: 2/23, 3/13, 4/13).

In late April 1976, Rene Hlavac, chairman of the OPS Health, Safety, and Security Task Force, revealed that organizations, including a neo-nazi-type group, planned to disrupt the school opening. An Omaha police spokesman disclaimed knowledge of such activity, but two days later handbills, imprinted with nazi-like swastikas and advocating white power, were distributed at Omaha's largest shopping center. The flyers listed a return address in a nearby small town. Mayor Zorinsky referred to the message as a product of a "sick mind" and counseled Omahans against allowing outsiders the role of "dictating to us the future tranquility of our community" (CCFO-Lincoln *Star* 1976: 4/28; CCFO-*World Herald* 1976: 4/30). The episode proved to be an isolated incident.

Three other ephemeral groups vied for the attention of the disaffected. The Trust the People Committee was headed by a George Wallace campaign worker who lived in an adjoining city. The organization also disavowed violence and planned to "blanket the city" with 50,000 handbills. On one occasion it distributed literature concerning an antibusing bill in Congress to students as they left about one hundred schools in the area. A local John Bircher founded the Citizens Against Tyranny, and the Citizens Against Busing arose as another indigenous group that planned demonstrations and a boycott of the schools (CCFO-*World Herald* 1976: 4/30).

By midsummer only the Omahans Against Forced Busing remained active, but the group could draw only 28 of an estimated 1,400 members to a meeting. But at this juncture the KKK, dormant in Omaha since 1926, revived itself. The local den, with a membership of only about 20, promised nonviolent protest, and twice it arranged for the Imperial Wizard to speak in Omaha. The Wizard's first visit drew only a handful of onlookers, mostly police and sightseers. Because he spoke in a public park, the city tried to block his second speech, but district court Judge John Burke forbade the restraint under consideration of the First Amendment. The second appearance also produced a sparse crowd, and soon after the opening of school the KKK dissolved as a result of a leadership feud (CCFO-*World Herald* 1976: 7/12, 7/27, 7/28, 8/20, 9/22). The Klan was the only group to stage a demonstration. With the aid of hindsight the episode looks trivial, but then, the threat of the Klan has never come from the number of its members alone.

APPEAL BY THE SCHOOL BOARD

Buoyed by national political activities and buffeted by local protestors, the school board resumed its stance of resistance to the Eighth Circuit Court decision. In early May 1976, the board filed two lawsuits. One suit challenged the constitutionality of congressional action that prohibited the spending of federal funds on transportation for court-ordered busing, although it allowed money to be spent on other integration-related expenses. The second suit questioned the right of federal courts to issue orders that necessitated the spending of local tax funds. The second case was prodded by FACT, which had already filed a similar separate petition (CCFO-*World Herald* 1976: 5/4).

Then, on the same day that President Ford asked Attorney General Levi to seek a test case, a board member advocated a direct appeal to the president and invited the attorney general to Omaha to "request his assistance in obtaining relief from this onerous task." Subsequently, by a vote of 8-3 (both black members registered nays), the board decided to write to Levi and it filed a motion in district court for a new trial. The OPS contended, in line with presidential utterances, that the Eighth Circuit Court violated the United States Civil Rights Act, which prohibited the busing of children past the nearest school for the purpose of integration, and it also objected to the fact that it did not assist in drawing up the racial balance guidelines. Within a matter of weeks Judge Schatz rejected the motion, stating that the plan he had accepted was "for the most part" constructed by OPS and that the few changes were "realistic, feasible alternatives which equalized the burdens of desegregation to a greater extent. . . ." (CCFO-*World Herald* 1976: 5/18, 5/19, 6/8, 6/21; D. Neb. 1974: 165-169).

On the very next day the board voted to appeal to the Eighth Circuit Court on the grounds that its earlier decision was based on ingredients that went "beyond any possible effect the school district's actions could have had" in creating a segregated school system. Again only the two black members voted against the appeal, and again the Ford impact manifested itself, for the president had recently asked for legislation that would instruct the courts not to use evidence unless it showed only the actions taken by school boards. The OPS lawyers argued that the order should rectify only the segregation caused directly by the system and that its recent actions, such as the abolition of the open transfer, corrected its violation; therefore, the order should be withdrawn. At the same time the intervenors filed an appeal to forestall the implementation of the order so that the plan could be broadened, especially to include first graders. Ten days before the opening of school the Eighth Circuit Court rejected both appeals, claiming that the Schatz plan "meets constitutional standards and is consistent with the mandate of this court" (CCFO-*World Herald* 1976: 6/17, 6/22, 6/25, 7/21, 8/24; D. Neb. 1974: 172-175).

School commenced under the plan, but the board continued to pursue the appeals process. Again it took the case to the U.S. Supreme Court, which, on

29 June 1977, remanded it back to the appeals court for reconsideration in terms of the *Arlington Heights* decision. That case established the rule that "official action will not be held unconstitutional *solely* because it results in a racially disproportionate impact," and it also reaffirmed the position that a plaintiff need not "prove that the challenged action rested *solely* on racially discriminatory purposes" (court's emphasis). The Eighth Circuit Court found that OPS was still liable, but remanded the case back to the district court in light of the *Dayton* case to reexamine the remedy. The *Dayton* case established the principle that a system-wide remedy could be used only when it was proved that the system's policies had a system-wide impact. The board reappealed this action by the Eighth Circuit Court, but the Supreme Court refused to hear it in February 1978. Later in that year the district court upheld the plan as it stood. Judge Schatz ruled that the plan would remain in effect for the 1978–1979 academic year (D. Neb. 1974: 176–178). As of late 1979, the Omaha Board of Education has decided against further appeals.

During this hectic period the method of electing the school board also changed. This change added to the aura of uncertainty, but in its immediate impact it did not alter the nature of the board. In 1975, through the sponsorship of state Senator Ernest Chambers, the lone black member of the Unicameral, a bill passed that established twelve constituent districts. The board, the *World Herald*, and one-half the Douglas County solons opposed the bill, which the governor had vetoed twice before, but finally Chambers mustered sufficient support to override the third veto. The law retained the nonsalaried four-year terms and called for the election of six nonpartisan members every two years at the general election. In the 1976 runoff the six even-numbered districts entertained campaigns. Three members whose terms expired in 1976 lived in odd-numbered districts and they had to retire at least temporarily. Two other members lived in the same even-numbered district, meaning the certain loss of another incumbent. Anger at the board's inability to prevent busing contributed to the defeat of two former board presidents, both running in western districts. Analysts also surmised that the fear of backlash caused the acting president not to seek reelection (CCFO-*World Herald* 1974: 1/3, 1/4; 1975: 7/3; 1976: 11/3; *Star* 1974: 1/17: 1, 5/22: 1; *Laws* 84:1: 869–870). Following the election the board had several new members, but it retained its ten-to-two, white-black split and it did not manifest any basic change in attitude. The 1978 elections left it much the same as before. The deliberations of the district court in the fall of 1978 had a more important effect on the attitude of the board than did the change in the electoral procedure.

In this milieu of resistance all the voices spoke of law and order, rhetoric advocating violence was almost nonexistent. The activities of the politicians, the board, and the protestors, however, added an element of uncertainty because they fed rather than allayed the fears of the community. In comparison, many of the students and teachers, the religious community, civic organizations, professional groups, the media, and the OPS administration worked diligently to promote the peaceful implementation of the court order.

The plan's stipulations for high school integration necessitated the recruitment of 750 racial-balance transfers, and by the end of the 1975 academic year over 1,400 students volunteered: 756 blacks and 661 whites. Most of the enlistees (843) did not shift high schools, but were ninth graders entering a new school outside their attendance zone for the first time. Only one school fell a few black students short of the court's 5 percent guideline, and the population of the once underutilized Tech doubled. The administration expressed its surprise at the large response and the *World Herald* editorialized that "the example set by the volunteering students and their parents—of both races—should set a more positive tone for the community's consideration and discussion of the integration task." Furthermore, of the 353 teachers reassigned that summer, only one resigned rather than shift (CCFO-*World Herald* 1976: 3/8, 3/10, 6/9). Thus, the individuals who would occupy the schools established a very positive image. In addition, the high school students, whose attitudes and values are usually firmly ingrained by that age, and who had a greater potential for disruption, contributed greatly to defusing that possibility by making mandatory transfers unnecessary.

During the Christmas season of 1975, seventy Roman Catholics had purchased a half-page advertisement in their city newspaper to urge fellow communicants to become involved in the peaceful implementation of desegregation. The following spring the archdiocese of Omaha directed its priests to aid their parishioners in the pacific acceptance of the court order. The positive-action plan the church developed included a series of three Sunday sermons on the topic, special prayer services, the blessing of families directly involved in busing, the establishment of a network of neighborhood contacts for bused students, a solidarity day, and a series of informational and inspirational coffees for parents. The Rabbinical Council of Omaha, the Omaha Presbytery of The United Presbyterian Church, an interracial group of twenty-four Omaha-area Baptist ministers, and many individual clergymen of a myriad of denominations spoke out in a similar vein. Furthermore, the presidents of the area's six colleges and universities issued a joint communiqué offering the aid of their institutions and staffs to OPS (CCFO-*Catholic Voice* 1975: 12; CCFO-*Jewish Press* 1976: 2/27; CCFO-*World Herald* 1975: 12/18; 1976: 1/27, 3/19, 4/25).

CONCERNED CITIZENS FOR OMAHA

The religious community also helped initiate a large civic coalition that worked to mitigate public fears. In early January 1976, eleven religious and social service groups met to discuss a cooperative venture to obtain Emergency School Aid Act (ESAA) funds to promote a smooth implementation of the court order. At the same time, the interracial committee appointed by Judge Schatz moved to organize the citizens' committee it had recommended to OPS. The two groups decided to cooperate, a development team was established, and eventually it created the Concerned Citizens for Omaha (CCFO). The umbrella organization did not view itself as a blue-ribbon panel; instead it divided itself into ten sectors—business, labor, human services agencies, and so forth—and each was responsible for drawing out the "natural leaders" from its area. In this fashion hundreds of grass-roots volunteers coalesced to create a pervasive communications network.

With the skeleton complete, CCFO went public in early March, seeking volunteers and support for its purpose of "a peaceful and productive" implementation of the plan. Its goals included (1) to establish and maintain relations across lines of difference (e.g., area of town, race, economic situation, ethnic background, and so forth), (2) to provide factual information regarding citizens' questions and concerns, (3) to reinforce people and organizations who intended to comply peacefully, (4) to identify and develop additional community leadership in the direction of peace, (5) to develop and maintain a system of input to locate and monitor areas of particular stress, (6) to identify responsible avenues for the expression of feelings, (7) to be open and encourage people who wanted to participate (ideas and involvement), (8) to strengthen credibility and visibility for CCFO as a means to work toward peace (CCFO-Memo 1975: 12/31; CCFO-Minutes 1976: 4/26; CCFO-*World Herald* 1976: 3/13, 9/12).

Area businesses and the chamber of commerce donated money, equipment, and supplies; they also covered other expenses by printing the newsletter and by loaning to the organization executives who could act as a permanent staff to coordinate the voluntary efforts. Educators from the area's colleges provided the backbone of the research committee and they conducted seminars and training sessions to provide volunteers with skills in particular areas such as conducting small group discussions. The local chapter of the Public Relations Society of America donated its services to produce, direct, and disseminate the CCFO public relations campaign. Television and radio announcements alone that would have cost approximately $30,000 were thus obtained for about $2,000. A local lottery donated $7,500, corporations over $30,000, and many individuals made small contributions; therefore, the entire operation was financed without a single tax dollar (CCFO-*World Herald* 1976: 9/2, 9/12; CCFO-*Sun* 1976: 6/10). The CCFO effort signified a mass outpouring of community concern and civic spirit.

From the outset the CCFO strived to build a good working relationship with the OPS administration. Liaison was established during the developmental phase, and as the summer progressed and the administrators became more confident of the competence of the CCFO staff, a substantial degree of cooperation ensued. The CCFO members attended the meetings of OPS task force committees planning the implementation of the court order, a "hot line" was established between the two institutions' information centers, OPS personnel briefed CCFO phone volunteers on the intricacies of the plan, busing schedules, and other pertinent information, and they cooperated in arranging for a school visitation day. A similar liaison was developed with the mayor's office that also yielded benefits such as official proclamations and the inclusion of CCFO brochures in city pay envelopes (Te Kolsta 1976; Brown 1976a; CCFO-Minutes 1976: 7/13; Clark 1978; Brown 1978).

In mid-May 1976, about 500 persons from sixty cities, including CCFO representatives, attended a conference in Washington, D.C. sponsored by the Community Relations Service of the justice department and the National Center for Quality Integrated Education. The day-long meeting allowed community groups to exchange ideas concerning the peaceful promotion of desegregation. The director of the national center commended the Omaha organization for its unique success in combining the efforts of so many distinct and disparate groups. Subsequently the CCFO sponsored several local seminars to help parents, social service agency volunteers, and the general public prepare for school integration (CCFO-Sector; CCFO-*World Herald* 1976: 5/20, 6/19).

Between 26 April and 16 August 1976, CCFO published seven editions of an eight-page newsletter. It had a direct mail list of 4,700, of which 3,300 went to OPS teachers, while others were distributed through businesses, churches, and civic groups. The newsletter concentrated on disseminating accurate information and focused on a broad range of activities that contributed toward the peaceful implementation of the plan. Of the first edition, 5,000 copies were distributed, and each successive release displayed a remarkable growth rate until the final edition reached a circulation of 27,000. The CCFO news-letter committee also produced a twelve-page supplement for the 26 August edition of the *World Herald*. The separate, magazine-style section, which was included in the 103,000 newspapers sold and delivered in the Omaha area, included a feature called "The First Day—An 'Inside' Story" written in grade school language so that children as well as adults could enjoy it. The supplement also contained questions and answers on desegregation, a summary of the plan, a chart on school assignments, and statements of encouragement from key public officials, parents, and children.

As another component of the network, CCFO operated a telephone center to provide easy access to accurate information and to combat rumors. Its phone number was broadcast regularly over radio and television and published daily on the front page of the *World Herald* along with the number of the OPS center. The CCFO also broadcast its message, simply stated in its motto, "Let's Make It Work," on strategically located billboards, with posters, and on 10,000 bumper stickers, most of which were distributed by volunteer students at shopping centers throughout the city. Television and radio public service an-nouncements, which peaked during the three weeks prior to the opening of school, focused on gaining the attention of a mass audience, while noon lun-cheons with CCFO speakers attracted between 80 and 250 people, and several dozen coffees in the intimacy of a person's home allowed for small group discussion.

In an attempt to blanket the community with information and activities, the religious sector of CCFO also promoted the Purposeful Integration Week-end. The mayor issued a proclamation giving the project official sanction, and the weekend 25 to 27 June began with prayer meetings and coffees "to promote community spirit and brotherhood." The organizers mailed a packet of suggested sermons and lecture ideas to all the clergy of Omaha, and the celebration of fraternity ended with a Sunday afternoon picnic in a public park attended by several hundred people. In another major effort CCFO cooperated with the Omaha Education Association, the Omaha Council of Parents and Teachers, and OPS in promoting a school visitation day. On Sunday, 29 August, about 5,500 parents and children rode buses from their old schools to the new schools, met the new teachers and staff, and had some refreshments supplied by the local PTA. Furthermore, while on the bus, CCFO workers answered questions concerning the mechanics of the plan (CCFO-Sector; CCFO-Minutes 1976: 8/10; CCFO-*World Herald* 1976: 6/11, 8/26).

Some of the opposition groups incorrectly referred to CCFO as a probusing organization; actually, it strictly adhered to its narrowly defined goal of promot-ing the peaceful implementation of the court order. Some individuals and groups within the coalition chaffed from this stricture, but, conversely, the limited nature of the goal made it impossible for CCFO to attract the coopera-tion of such a large number of disparate members and it allowed them to func-tion smoothly in a single direction for a short, compact period of time. Because of its myriad of activities, which touched so many people, CCFO received wide-spread recognition for its major contribution to the peaceful desegregation of the Omaha public schools. The CCFO and OPS received aid from the Commu-nity Relations Service (CRS), although at the outset, the service had created a problem. In May 1974, the national CRS office issued a list of twenty-nine cities in which the government disputes over desegregation in the schools could lead to racial disorder. Omaha appeared on the inventory and Mayor Zorinsky accused the service of "implanting the seeds of dispute" in the city (CCFO-*World Herald* 1974: 5/31). The CRS, however, made up for this early faux pas with numerous visits to the city over several years to meet with the mayor, the safety director, the police chief, OPS administrators and CCFO staff. It was not usually visible, but it provided information and expertise in areas that individuals demanded of it. For CCFO, for example, a CRS communications expert trained eighty telephone volunteers and made tapes of the session that could be used for future training (Clark 1978; Brown 1978; Brown 1976b; CCFO-General Correspondence).

Other significant local groups that cooperated with CCFO also worked independently to prepare their membership to handle the transformation. The Omaha Education Association helped promote the school visitation day by arranging for the teachers to be at the schools to greet the parents. The association also endeavored to build morale and encourage cooperation; it mailed supportive letters to the faculty, and it used the building representative assemblies to create discussion that answered questions and calmed fears about the coming disruption (Thies 1978). Similarly, the Omaha Council of PTA/PTSA had an established communications network that it used to promote peaceful implementation. In comparison to 1973, when the council split over the issue of compliance with the DOJ directives, in 1976 it did not take a position on the plan but instead promoted the single issue of peace for the good of the children.

Representatives from the PTA attended OPS task force committe meetings and gave input on the design of the plan, and their reservations about the inclusion of the first grade was influential in the final decision to exclude that level from mandatory reassignment. In command of the latest information, the council quickly funneled it back to the neighborhood chapters. It helped arrange for the early town hall meetings and encouraged individual PTAs to hold forums. The OPS personnel cooperated fully by attending the many gatherings and explaining the evolving process. The council gathered questions about desegregation from individual members, which OPS answered and published in a brochure that was then distributed on a mass scale. The council president served on an OPS-ESAA grant committee that obtained $1,000,000 to establish integration-aiding programs, and, subsequently, the PTA secured an independent ESSA grant for $42,000 to develop programs in communications and problem solving.

THE MEDIA

The media also played a significant role in pursuing the goal of information dissemination. All of the city's newspapers advanced the cause of peace. The *Sun,* which publishes several weekly neighborhood editions, frequently featured in-depth stories that presented the integration process and its outcomes in a positive light, and its editorials continuously encouraged Omahans to act in concert with American ideals. The *Star,* the weekly black tabloid, reflected and supported the minority community's disenchantment with the process. The paper was a long-standing, outspoken critic of OPS and it remained dissatisfied with many features of the ultimate plan. Still, it counseled cooperation, the essence of its message being: Do not be like some other communities, but show that you are law-abiding, peaceful, and willing to work for meaningful change.

The *World Herald,* the state's largest newspaper and Omaha's only daily, displays a marked conservative political inclination. In conjunction with this ideology, it editorially opposed mandatory busing and, because of the syndicated columnists it published regularly, its editorial pages frequently featured criticism of mandatory busing. However, the paper strongly advocated voluntary integration and peace, and its news coverage presented a balanced picture of the controversy, including stories that contained arguments in favor of busing. The journal *Editor and Publisher* (1976: 18) commended the *World Herald* for the special features it developed to aid orderly desegregation. Daily during the entire summer preceding implementation of the desegregation plan, the paper ran two front-page features, "Get the Facts" and "Questions on Integration." The first ran the telephone numbers of the CCFO and OPS information centers and urged readers to seek the correct facts on any concern. The second, trying to anticipate many of the general concerns, answered questions devised by CCFO about the plan, the mechanics of busing, school programs, schedules, and so forth. Also, the newspaper published and distributed the CCFO supplement the week before classes began.

The electronic media also contributed heavily to the atmosphere of calm. The educational television channel at the University of Nebraska at Omaha produced a five-part series entitled "Omaha Desegregation: A Rational Response," that was rebroadcast over the local NBC affiliate. All the stations developed other information programs, and the news-feature genre shows on both radio and TV gave the issue substantial coverage. The regular news broadcasts presented the process in a positive light and gave a wealth of coverage to OPS, CCFO, and the activities promoting peaceful implementation. In terms of the public service announcements, all the media agreed to make school desegregation the number one issue, and the stations devoted copious amounts of time to messages of encouragement produced by CCFO (Combs 1978).

THE POLICE

Even though almost everyone in Omaha advocated law and order, and even though many groups such as the OPS administration, CCFO, and the media worked diligently to ensure peaceful implementation, planning also went on for the opposite contingency. Over a period of months the Omaha Police Department researched the approaches taken in other cities and held meetings with OPS, the bus company, and the national guard to prepare for any eventuality. A special tripartite command post was established at headquarters to coordinate all police activities concerned with school desegregation, and a separate communications network was devised to integrate all involved—officers out on patrol, the command, OPS, and CCFO. Extra police were assigned to school desegregation duty, vacation requests or days off during the first ten school days were denied, regular patrols were instructed to give schools increased attention, and surveillance officers were assigned to patrol the city seeking potential problem areas.

Memoranda refreshed officers on particular laws and methods of professional procedure applicable in particular situations that might arise. One major problem expected was an increase in the number of lost children. The department established a special phone number and a lost-child center, and it instructed patrolmen to drive home children who became stranded at school. The police also put added emphasis on the educational program for school safety patrols and for the public in regard to school bus traffic ordinances (Friend 1978; Supplements 1976: 9/1, 9/4; CCFO-*World Herald* 1976: 8/26: suppl. 10).

In one instance the police union, however, also added to the discord of the situation. The union sought exemption of the children of officers from busing because it claimed a conflict of interest existed because police would have to enforce orders and their own children would be involved. The *World Herald* called the request "audacious and unreasonable," and the black community viewed it with special cynicism because of the long history of strained relations with the department. The overture fell on deaf ears and the patrolmen did not receive the privileged exemption (CCFO-*World Herald* 1976: 5/26, 6/5).

The OPS also devised a safety and ooourity system for the schools. Each building had security teams, members of the staff had specific positions and responsibilities, and procedures were devised to cover different possible emergency situations. The overall performance of the administration in terms of communication stood in marked contrast to the earlier indictment of the Greenleigh Report of 1968. Interestingly, in this light, the OPS security task force instructed principals to establish more formal and more regular communications channels with faculty, staff, parents, and community groups (CCFO-*World Herald* 1976: 8/6, 8/26: Suppl. 3). If the directive is carried out on a long-term basis, it could prove to be a major tangential benefit produced by the desegregation process.

IMPLEMENTATION OF THE COMPREHENSIVE PLAN

On 8 September 1976 the buses rolled in Omaha without incident; the transportation vehicle that stood as a negative symbol for the majority of Americans and Omahans delivered its cargo safely and without disruption. This feat was made possible through the tremendous expenditures of effort by OPS, CCFO, and the other particular religious, social service, civic, and community groups. The support from Omaha businesses added an important body of opinion from a highly respected and powerful segment of the community whose financial backing and contributed services made CCFO possible. The media through their balanced reporting, their positive editorializing, and their public service announcements also contributed greatly to the pacific atmosphere.

Another important, but intangible, factor was the community respect for the law. This does not mean that Omaha was innately virtuous; violent racial clashes have occurred in the past and police-black community relations were explosive. The possibility of disruption existed, but many leaders such as the mayor displayed great confidence in the basic law-abiding nature of the citizenry. In one sense this helped because the trait was held up as a source of pride, something to emulate, and it combined with the desire of not wanting to be seen nationally in a negative light to aid peaceful implementation. "We won't be Boston," or "We won't be Louisville" was a common attitude. On the other hand, many leaders within CCFO feared that the reliance on the law-and-order theme would produce complacency, and that frame of mind was self-defeating. Thus, despite the fact that almost all of the opposition groups professed non-violence, the organization knew that cities that had positive desegregation experiences had CCFO-type associations, and it diligently went about the task of allaying the fears of as many citizens as possible.

The demography and geography of the city also aided the avoidance of confrontation. Despite its almost 400,000 population, Omaha is not a sprawling, heterogeneous metropolis of deeply divided classes and/or ethnic groups separated into geographic enclaves. Obviously a ghetto exists, and other patterns of division are visible, but to a meaningful degree Omaha maintains a small-town sense of cohesion. Within the town, blacks make up a small percent of the population (10 percent) compared with other large cities, thus reducing the sense of threat felt by the white community. Furthermore, the far southwestern areas of the city did not participate in the program, thus making the area for busing more compact. The opposition to busing was strongest in the northwest, where the distances traversed to an inner-city school were the greatest and where the citizens were struggling to hold back the encroaching black neighborhood. With the exclusion of the virtually all-white District 66 and Millard systems, two areas of potentially vigorous opposition were eliminated from the controversy.

Furthermore, Omaha benefited from the experience of other cities. The OPS, CCFO, the police, the Roman Catholic church, and other organizations all studied the situation in other urban areas. They collected information on what to do, how to do it, and what to avoid. It is probable that, given other positive circumstances, a body of knowledge is developing that makes the desegregation process easier to implement. Omaha obviously profited from the fact that so many other similar cities went through the transformation first.

Finally, the parameters of the plan also mitigated the threat of disruption. It did not affect all white families at once; only selected grades were scheduled for mandatory reassignment. Furthermore, it necessitated the transfer of whites only once during elementary school and once or twice during junior high. Therefore, a white student spent the majority of time in his or her neighborhood school. The exchange by grade level meant that the plan did not change annually, and it allowed long-term planning. This was especially important for families with many children. In comparison, for the black family the neighborhood school virtually ceased to exist; planning meant planning to be on the bus. High school students, potentially one of the more disruptive groups, did not have to fear mandatory reassignment, volunteers committed to the integration of the schools fulfilled the court-ordered guidelines. Thus, for white families, the plan made the transformation easier to accept because they could look forward to only a couple of years of interference with their normal routine.

CONCLUSIONS

In June 1979, the OPS completed its third year of operation under the plan; therefore, only a few tentative evaluations can be drawn and most of them point to mixed results. Dr. Owen Knutzen, superintendent of schools, and other OPS administrators publicly have stated frequently that the plan is working well. In essence this means the schools are operating without confrontation and the mechanics of the educational programs are functioning smoothly. Obviously no evaluation can be made at this time concerning changes in attitudes, skills levels, and other crucial academic areas.

Black views persist along the same lines they have taken throughout the controversey. The community demands integration but still criticizes the unequal burden placed upon minority children. It remains disenchanted with the school board and it realizes that the new form of district elections will not change the board's basic outlook. Some spokesmen also feel that the disciplinary procedures do not operate equally, in that blacks get suspended in a substantially greater proportion than whites (Johnson 1978; Pierce 1978; Stanton 1978).

Several mechanical deficiencies have plagued the plan's operation. In the first year, for example, twelve schools did not comply with the court-ordered guidelines on racial balance, necessitating tinkering with the model. The bus company failed to hire enough drivers on time, and late buses disturbed meticulously designed schedules. The quantity and quality of the bus drivers and the overall bus service remains a pressing problem (CCFO-*World Herald* 1976: 9/8, 10/5, 10/13; 1978: 5/13). The transformation also interfered with financing. The reassignment of inner-city students led to a dispersal of concentrations in certain schools, which thus no longer qualified for Title I funds. This meant a lack of money for special reading and math programs, and for the media center. Part of the loss was recouped through ESAA grants, but most of that money was spent in other areas to aid integration. Furthermore, transportation costs have added $4,000,000 to the annual budget that must be borne by the OPS ratepayers. In evaluating the financial impact, one must also consider the fact that before the latest round of appeals the board spent well over $300,000 in court costs (CCFO-*World Herald* 1976: 1/15, 6/14, 6/23, 9/22; Report 1977–1978; Hlavac 1978).

One of the most controversial areas of impact concerned the plan's relationship to white flight, the phenomenon of whites moving from the city in order to avoid busing. The issue surfaced immediately in 1973, when OPS experienced an overall decline of over 2,000 students. According to one assistant superintendent, the administration predicted a drop of only 500, and he attributed the fourfold increase to white flight in fear of the problems with the DOJ. A few weeks later OPS adjusted the figures, revealing that it originally projected a drop in enrollment of over 1,000, and claiming that the integration suit was only a "partial cause" of the decline. The OPS statistician disclosed that the district did not keep figures on outward migration and therefore did not have the data necessary to make comparisons. The following year witnessed another drop of over 2,000 students, but this time the district argued against white flight. It pointed out that flight percentages were usually far higher than the 3.5 percent rate of decline experienced by OPS, and that the pattern of movement usually accelerated after the first year, whereas it remained constant in OPS. The spokesperson now attributed the decline to the natural causes of a declining birth rate and continued suburban growth (CCFO-*World Herald* 1973: 9/8, 9/23; 1974: 9/6).

The second report, of Dr. James S. Coleman of the University of Chicago, which called court-ordered desegregation a failure and claimed that it forced white flight, kept the issue current during 1975. A *World Herald* study revealed that desegregation had a minimal effect on white flight in the Omaha metropolitan area. It showed that the combined total enrollment of the five largest districts in the area between 1970 and 1975 decreased by 9,000, while the combined total enrollment of nine other districts in the vicinity increased by only 5,300. The OPS had the largest drop in absolute numbers, but it was by far the largest district. Actually, suburban District 66 declined by 10 percent, whereas OPS fell only 6 percent. The newspaper singled out the causes of the falling birth rate, the decrease in population of childbearing-age couples, the availability of new homes in suburban areas, the desire of many to escape urban problems, and, last, flight to avoid busing in OPS. When school opened in 1976, figures from OPS and surrounding areas disclosed that little white flight occurred (CCFO-*World Herald* 1975: 8/3; 1976: 9/6, 9/8, 9/14, 9/16).

Obviously some whites fled, but the excellent community preparation dispelled fears well enough to shrink the percentage. The exclusion of the white middle class (who can afford to move) located in District 66 and Millard also may have held down the rate of flight. Finally, the actions of the other school districts contributed to the low percentage of white flight. As stated previously, the surrounding inner-city and suburban districts promised not to accept transfer students except for strict academic reasons. The Lutherns operated four elementary schools that were at near capacity, and they adhered to the same policy. On a much larger scale the Omaha Roman Catholic archdiocese operated over thirty elementary schools and ten high schools within the OPS district. The system is integrated in a pattern where a number of schools have a small percentage of minority students and a few schools in or around the Near Northside have large percentages. Immediately in 1973, Archbishop Daniel E. Sheehan announced that the Catholic schools would "not become a refuge for students seeking transfers for racially motivated reasons." In 1975, he issued a freeze on new student registrations and conducted talks with representatives of the Louisville parochial system. Early in 1976, the system adopted a set of guidelines on admissions designed to keep the Catholic schools as an educational institution for the children of active parishioners (CCFO-*World Herald* 1973: 7/28; 1975: 12/16; 1976: 2/17; CCFO-*Catholic Voice* 1976: 1/16, 1/24).

Catholic enrollments continued to decline during the period, but at a slower rate. In 1976, the elementary schools located within the OPS area lost 348 students, whereas the high schools gained 332. This represented the smallest decline in eleven years. Most likely more Catholic parents sent their beginning students to parochial schools and the retention rate after six and eight years climbed. The superintendent attributed the rise in high schoolers to recruitment, and this probably explains the situation because those grade levels are not bused under the OPS plan. Significantly, the enrollment figures reveal that whereas a few families may have become instant converts to the benefits of Catholic education, the autonomous parish schools followed the spiritual precepts of the archbishop and contributed to the low rate of white flight.[3]

One very impressive statistic is that there has been no noticeable rise in the number of interracial incidents. In fact, the schools that reported the greatest number of clashes in the past have experienced a marked reduction in this sensitive problem area (Hlavac 1978).

It remains to be seen whether or not the mass community effort that promoted the peaceful implementation of the plan can be marshaled to promote meaningful integration of the schools and quality education. The variegated

3. Statistics provided by the Catholic Board of Education.

pattern of results after three years reveals some problems as well as some signs of encouragement. Generally, the level of acceptance of the plan, especially with the feature of busing, is low. The school board implements the law but the continuing swirl of events within the court system from across the nation continues to have an effect on Omaha.

BIBLIOGRAPHY

Broom 1978. Interview with Robert Broom, Legal Aid attorney for the intervenors, 2 May.

Brown 1976a. Mary Brown to Norbert J. Schuerman, 11 May.

Brown 1976b. Mary Brown to Arthur Peltz, August 16. Letter from general correspondence, CCFO mss.

Brown 1978. Interview with Mary Brown, member of the interracial committee and director of the CCFO information center, 11 May

Campbell 1978. Interview with Dr. Ann Campbell, commissioner, Nebraska Department of Education, 8 May.

CCFO. Concerned Citizens for Omaha Manuscripts, Alumni Library, Creighton University, Omaha.

CCFO 1976a. Letter from OPS to U.S. District Court, Omaha, 17 February, 1976 and "Amendments to the Response of the United States to the Desegregation Plan for the School District of Omaha," 16 March. OPS files, CCFO mss.

CCFO 1976b. "Memorandum Opinion, United States District Court for the District of Nebraska," 27 April. District Court files, CCFO mss.

CCFO 1976c. "United States District Court Desegregation Plan for the School District of Omaha," 21 May, District Court files, CCFO mss.

CCFO-Antibusing. Antibusing groups file, CCFO mss.

CCFO-*Catholic Voice.* Clippings in the CCFO files: December 1975; January 1976.

CCFO-Civil Rights. "Chronology of Events Involving Civil Rights Litigation in the School District of Omaha," OPS files, CCFO mss.

CCFO-Desegregation. "Information on Desegregation Attempts," OPS files, CCFO mss.

CCFO-*Jewish Press.* Clipping in the CCFO files: February 1976.

CCFO-*Lincoln Evening Journal.* Clippings in the CCFO files: May 1976.

CCFO-*Lincoln Star.* Clippings in the CCFO files: April, May 1976.

CCFO-Memo. December 31, 1975, CCFO mss.

CCFO-Minutes. Coordinating Council Minutes, CCFO mss.

CCFO-Sector. Sector files, CCFO mss.

CCFO-*Star.* Clippings from the Omaha *Star* in the CCFO files: October 1973; July 1974.

CCFO-*Sun.* Clippings from the Omaha *Sun* in the CCFO files: March, May, August 1974; July, September 1975; April, May, June, August 1976.

CCFO-*World Herald*. Clippings from the Omaha *World Herald* in the CCFO files: for the years 1973-1978.

Chudacoff, Howard P. 1972. *Mobile Americans: Residential and Social Mobility in Omaha, 1880-1920*. New York: Oxford University Press.

Clark 1978. Interview with Ray Clark, executive director, CCFO, 17 May.

Combs 1978. Interview with Barry Combs, chairman of the CCFO public relations committee, 11 May.

Danton, Lawrence A. 1967. *The Economic Structure of the Omaha SMSA*. Omaha: University of Omaha.

D. Neb. 1974. 389 F. Supp. 293.

Editor and Publisher 1976. "Omaha Daily Aids Orderly School Busing," 18 September.

Eighth Cir. 1975. 521 F. 2nd. 530.

Final Report. Omaha Community Committee: Final Report, Parts 2, 3.

Friend 1978. Interview with Deputy Chief Joseph Friend, Omaha Police Department, 9 May.

Greenleigh, 1969. Greenleigh Associates, Inc. *Agenda for Action.*

Guide. Omaha *Guide.* 1937a: 11 December. 1937b. 18 December. 1945. 8 September.

Hlavac 1978. Interview with Rene Hlavac, assistant superintendent of schools, OPS, May 24.

Holm, Kenneth B., and Gerald P. Laughlin, Attorneys. 1973. *A Preliminary Analysis of the Department of Justice Allegations*. Omaha Public Schools, 16 July.

Laws 84: 1. *Laws of Nebraska*, 84 Legislature, First Session.

League 1978. *The State of Black Omaha, 1978*. Omaha: The Urban League of Nebraska.

Lewis, Milton D. 1957. *Employment and Utilization of Negro Teachers in Selected Communities*. Omaha: Omaha Urban League.

Johnson 1978. Interview with Kenneth E. Johnson, Associated Director of the Urban League of Nebraska, May 22.

McCauley, Mark. 1977. "Desegregation Planning in the Omaha Public School System, 1972-1974." Unpublished manuscript, Creighton University.

OOEDP 1969. *Omaha Overall Economic Development Program.* 1 July.

Pester 1975. Letter from Bill Pester, president of the Omaha Education Association, to the membership. 25 June.

Pierce 1978. Interview with Joyce Pierce, educational coordinator, Urban League of Nebraska, 22 May.

Report 1977-1978. "Omaha School District Statistical and Financial Report."

Stahmer 1978. Interview with David Stahmer, initiator of the school district consolidation suit, 11 May.

Stanton 1978. Interview with Edward Stanton, education coordinator, Wesley House. 25 May.

Star. Omaha *Star*. 1961: May; 1963: January, November; 1964: March; 1968: February; 1970: October; 1971: January; 1973: July, September; 1974: January, July, October, December; 1975: May; 1976: February, June, July. See also. CCFO-*Star*.

Sullenger, T. Earl, and J. Harvey Kerns. 1931. *The Negro in Omaha*. Omaha: University of Omaha.

Supplements 1976. "Division Temporary Duty and/or Information Order 105-76." 1 September 1976, Supp. 1–29 and 4 September 1976, Supp. 33–41.

Te Kolsta 1976. Letter from Dale Te Kolsta to Owen Knutson, 15 March.

Thies 1978. Interview with John Thies, 2 May.

Traub 1978. Interview with Bev Traub, president of the Omaha Council of PTA/PTSA, 15 May.

World Herald, Omaha *World Herald*. 1967: December; 26 August 1976, CCFO Supplement. See also CCFO-*World Herald*.

Zipay, John P. 1967. *The Changing Population of the Omaha SMSA, 1860-1967*. Omaha: University of Omaha.

12

Stockton, California: Education and Coalition Politics

Fred Muskal and Donna Treadwell

THE ENVIRONMENT OF CALIFORNIA POLITICS

The school desegregation issue in Stockton must be examined in the broader context of California politics and culture. In many ways, California politics is a mixture of familiar nationwide values with unique political structures, as is described in a variety of sources (see Lee 1966). The attitudes that dominate California's reformist politics were built on the utopian visions that motivated migrants from the Northeast and Midwest to seek better lives on the West Coast. In political terms, this meant a strong negative reaction to the coalition-based machine politics characteristic of large eastern cities.

The distrust of political parties and coalition politics came to fruition around the turn of the century in the Progressive Party. The Progressives instituted several reforms, among them nonpartisan, at-large local elections and cross-filing. The former structure effectively eliminated parties as a form of local political organization; the latter minimized party power at the state level by allowing candidates to run in all primary elections. Until the 1960s, candidates could win nomination in both Republican and Democratic gubernatorial primaries, thus obviating the need for a general election. As a result, California politics appears elusive and unorganized.

Studies indicate that 46 percent of all Californians move an average of two to three times more frequently than residents in other states. This has several political ramifications. First, high residential turnover suggests that racial change in any neighborhood is likely to occur quickly and relatively quietly. There seems to be little sense of the ethnic territoriality that characterizes many eastern cities. Second, constant population change suggests that traditional political organizing, such as walking precincts, would be less effective. One result of this is the extensive use of mass media for political information and campaigning. The use of public relations firms to market candidates and issues has been developed highly in California over the past several decades. Another significant political factor is California's ethnic makeup.

Mexican-Americans make up the largest minority group with about 2,200,000 people. Second in size is the black population, numbering over 1,400,000. Other sizable groups include the Chinese, Filipinos, and Japanese. For the most part California's minorities are urbanized, although some groups, notably the Mexican-Americans, populate rural areas to some extent. In many cities, including Stockton, there is a large minority population but no dominant minority group. Instead, a number of minority groups make up roughly equal parts of the overall minority population. Although these social features do not define California politics decisively, they do suggest some of the differences between it and other states (Ross and Stone 1973: 152, 154).

Although the primary responsibility for education is with the state government, California delegates this responsibility to more than 1,100 school districts, all locally governed by elected boards.

THE COMMUNITY

Stockton is a central Californian community that is approximately thirty-five square miles in area. In 1975, its population was 117,986. Its metropolitan population is over 290,000. Stockton is the seat of San Joaquin County and the commercial center of the San Joaquin Valley. Its industry consists of agricultural produce as well as shipbuilding, the recycling of paper products, and steel fabrication. Stockton has two institutions of higher education, San Joaquin Delta College, a junior college, and the University of the Pacific, a private university.

Stockton's population includes Mexican-Americans, blacks, Chinese, Japanese, Filipinos, Native Americans, and a smattering of other groups. The Mexican-American population fluctuates seasonally with the flow of migrant labor but has remained stable historically at around 20 percent of the total population. The black population was insignificant until the development of a large naval installation during World War II. Since then, the black community has leveled off at about 10 percent of the city's population. The population of Stockton has grown considerably since 1960 (see table 12.1).

TABLE 12.1. 1970 and 1975 Population of Stockton, California, by Race

	1970	
	Population	%
White	62,757	58.3
Spanish-surnamed	22,841	21.2
Black	11,824	11.0
Asian-American	4,559	4.2
American Indian	448	0.4
Other	5,215	4.9
	107,644	100.0
	1975	
White (including Spanish)	97,045	82.3
Black	12,990	11.0
Other	7,951	6.7
	117,986	100.0

Source: U.S. Census, *City of Stockton, Racial Characteristics 1970 Census; Racial Characteristics October 1975 Special Census.* Washington, D.C.: Government Printing Office.

POPULATION TRENDS AND STOCKTON'S
SCHOOL ENROLLMENT PATTERNS

Natural geographic boundaries in Stockton are formed by the Deep Water Channel and Main Street. These boundaries separate white North Stockton and nonwhite South Stockton (see figure 12.1). Nearly half of the people who are members of minority groups lived in South Stockton in 1970.

There are several reasons for Stockton's racial segregation, including zoning, housing, and school attendance-area policies. Various zoning policies adopted by the Stockton City Council over the past two decades protected residential

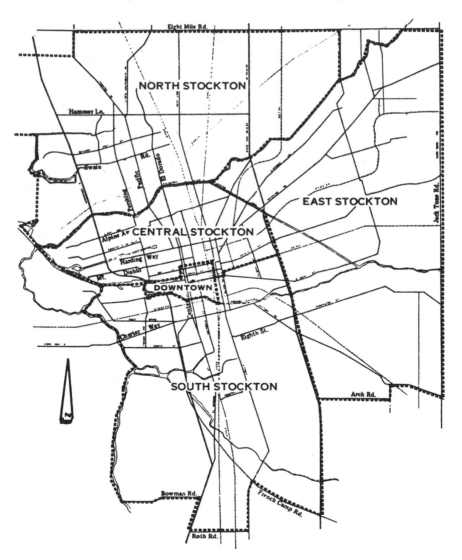

Figure 12.1. Stockton, California: Metropolitan area and subareas. Developed by the Community Development Department, City of Stockton.

areas on the north side while opening south side land to unrestricted use. The overall effect of these policies was to encourage north-side residential development with high land values and to discourage new residential development on the south side. Moreover, unrestricted zoning probably lowered or slowed increases in the value of south-side residential property. Similarly, all low-income housing in Stockton was built on the south side near the navy base during World War II. Attempts to disperse low-income housing on the north side were thwarted during the 1960s.

Historically, attempts of minority persons to move to the north side of town have been fought bitterly. Incidents in the 1920s and 1930s led to the widespread use of restrictive racial covenants enforced informally long after the Supreme Court had outlawed them in the early 1950s. In 1964, the Stockton Board of Realtors supported Proposition 14, which repealed a fair housing law but which was struck down in the state supreme court as being discriminatory. Together with school boundaries drawn in a way that never upset the status quo, these policies resulted in a highly segregated school system.

The current housing boom in North Stockton and the area beyond the city limits is not attributable to any single factor. Although much of this growth has come since school desegregation was implemented fully in 1977, Stockton's housing prices are among the lowest on the West Coast. This has attracted home buyers and speculators from the San Francisco Bay area to the west and the Sacramento area to the north. The northward movment of single-family housing has resulted in increasing dispersion of the minority population in Stockton. As some whites leave to avoid integration, minority families buy homes in formerly all-white areas, thereby increasing residential integration. The net effect of all these variables has been to increase the percentage of whites going to school in Lincoln and Lodi, the two school districts to the north, and to diminish the percentage of whites in Stockton Unified School District (SUSD).

STOCKTON SCHOOLS

Stockton houses three school districts, Lodi Unified School District, Lincoln Unified School District, and SUSD (figure 12.2). There are twenty-six elementary schools, three middle schools, three junior high schools, and six high schools in SUSD. The major portion of the metropolitan Stockton area lies within the SUSD boundaries. The Lodi schools draw pupils from the northern, outlying areas of Stockton, whereas Lincoln draws its pupils for North Stockton, within the ctiy limits. As North Stockton developed, the Lincoln district annexed some areas while the Stockton district took over other areas. Population projections expect 80 percent of Stockton's population growth to occur north of the Calaveras River. All major parcels of land scheduled for development in the near future lie in the Lincoln and Lodi school districts, both of which consist mainly of a white population (Lincoln 90 percent and Lodi 82.7 percent; see table 12.2). Recent Stockton Unified School District enrollment figures indicate a 49.9 percent white population.

The population of the Stockton school district has been decreasing steadily since 1969–1970, whereas the populations of Lincoln and Lodi have increased. The SUSD has lost over 8,000 students in the past decade. Stockton has several

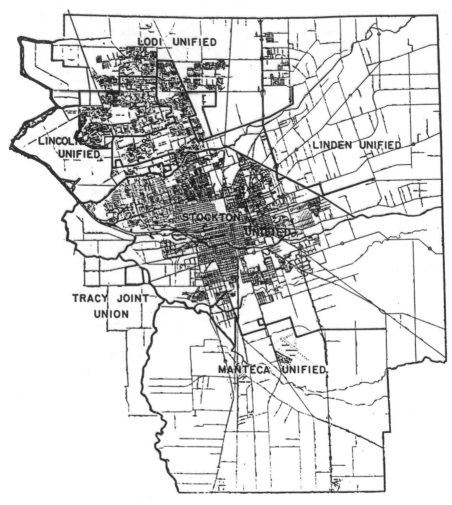

Figure 12.2. Stockton, California: School District boundaries. Developed by the Community Development Department, City of Stockton.

parochial and private schools. The population characteristics of the established parochial school system are similar to those of SUSD, although there are more Spanish-speaking pupils and fewer blacks. Most of the private schools were established around the time that school desegregation was implemented, and seem to have fewer minority pupils, although hard data on this matter are not available. Private and parochial school enrollment has increased since desegregation began, but no firm figures are available.

Overall, Stockton in the middle 1960s was fairly representative of California progressive politics. All elections were at-large, and a city manager administered municipal policies at the pleasure of the city council. Residential change followed typical California mobility patterns in the rapidly developing north side where young families settled, but the south side was far less mobile. Neighborhood stability on the south side diminished school enrollment but provided some base for the significant political campaigns of the early 1970s.

TABLE 12.2. Racial and Ethnic School and Community Populations for Stockton, Lodi, and Lincoln Unified School Districts, 1970

Race/Ethnic Group	School Population (%)	
	Stockton	Lodi
Black	11.0	0.01
Chicano	21.2	7.4
Other	9.5	3.3
Anglo	58.3	89.3

	Population-at-large in Total District (%)		
	Stockton	Lodi	Lincoln
Black	14.5	.05	1.3
Chicano	22.3	12.00	1.3
Other	7.7	3.4	3.4
Anglo	55.6	84.6	90.2

Source: U.S. Census 1970 and enrollment data from the various districts.

THE POLITICS OF SCHOOL DESEGREGATION

The desegregation issue in Stockton illustrates the problems and prospects involved in articulating an issue common to several diverse cultural groups. Blacks generally supported integration as a desirable goal, but the positions of other groups were not so clear. Mexican-Americans remained divided throughout the issue, and no more than a few Asian groups ever committed themselves publicly. Organized political groups tended to favor integration, regardless of which ethnic group dominated their memberships. More traditional social or religious groups showed far less commitment to integration, and south-siders without organizational affiliations tended to ignore or disapprove of the issue.[1] The common ground that eventually united the minority communities was made up of socioeconomic status, some urban regionalism, and an adherence to working within the political system.

Historically, the south side of Stockton was designed to house its poor and ethnic minorities. Various municipal ordinances dating from the 1920s specified that all Chinese, for example, had to locate south of Main Street. Along with the residential and social-class segregation that grew to characterize South Stockton came political exclusion from major municipal offices, principally the city council and school board. At-large elections for these offices tended to favor the resources commanded by the largely white, middle-class north side of town. The north-side majority virtually monopolized city council

---

1. A similar pattern is manifested in the way Californians of Mexican ancestry label themselves. Strongly traditional, conservative individuals call themselves Mexicans. More assimilated but still traditional persons label themselves Mexican-Americans, whereas those urbanized and politicized call themselves Chicanos.

and school board seats until the south side mobilized its political potential in partnership with the white, liberal faction of the north side.

In a series of elections in the late 1960s and early 1970s, the south side demonstrated its growing political strength. Its votes helped pass or defeat a number of school finance referenda. More significantly, both city council and school board elections were changed to district voting systems. In subsequent elections, the south side won representation on both the council and the board, thereby paving the way for a fairly successful court-ordered desegregation program. Taken together, these events span the time between 1966 and the present.

The desegregation issue may be divided into three clear phases over this twelve-year period. In the first phase, 1966–1970, a superintendent who believed in voluntary integration left his position in large part because the antibusing community groups easily outnumbered prointegration groups. The second phase, roughly 1970–1974, marked the political maturation of the south side along with a court order to desegregate the schools.[2] The third phase, from 1974 to the present, deals with the continued legal battle over desegregation and the development of an acceptable plan by the district.

1966–1970: IMPOSED SEGREGATION

In August 1966, James Reusswig was appointed superintendent of schools. He was openly in favor of school integration, a point he repeatedly made clear in interviews with the board. Reusswig rapidly raised the issue of desegregation with the board. His initial success in securing board support was based on two factors: first, civil rights and desegregation were not salient issues yet in Stockton; second, Reusswig enjoyed the traditional sources of power available to school superintendents.

As with most other superintendents at the time and many today, Reusswig controlled the board by managing the information upon which decisions were based. The board had to rely on the superintendent for all information about the schools, including locally gathered data and information about pertinent state and federal legislation. Information management effectively made the board an agency that legitimated the superintendent's policies (Kerr 1964: 34–59). This situation remained firm until controversy led the board to rely on other sources of information—organized community groups. Initially, Reusswig used his advantage to raise the desegregation issue.

Early in his term, Reusswig interpreted recent state and federal civil rights legislation to the board in a manner that suggested that desegregation planning was necessary to obtain federal funding.[3] He proposed a project stressing long-

2. Our discussion relies heavily on Litherland (1978). We have reanalyzed some of the data and recognize the limitations imposed by the first-person account of a participant who came to represent a south side district on the school board. Nevertheless, Litherland's work is invaluable in understanding the Stockton case.

3. The state board of education during this time passed regulations governing the elimination of racial imbalance in public schools, establishing a plus or minus 15 percent variation from proportional representation in a school district as its criterion for a desegregated school. The state board did not enforce its regulations strongly, preferring instead to negotiate or persuade districts to desegregate voluntarily.

term planning and innovation that was funded by the federal government. The Long Range Planning program (LRP) consisted largely of three committees charged with developing plans for the district's future; one committee focused on curriculum development, a second on communications with the community, and the major committee dealt with new school facilities and integration. The committees had broad representation from the community and included both prointegration and antiintegration parents, teachers, and community leaders.

The usual relationship among facilities planning, district boundaries, and desegregation was amplified in California because of the Field Act, which required the structural strengthening or replacement of schools built before 1934 in order to meet earthquake safety standards. The final deadline lay nearly a decade away, but neither financing nor planning had yet begun in Stockton. More importantly, no serious consideration had ever been given to using boundary changes or site placement to alleviate racial imbalance in the schools—a situation used as evidence of systematic segregation in the court's final ruling (*Stockton Record* 1974· 10/13). Reusswig carefully assembled a staff to deal with his twin priorities of innovation and integration.

Buttressed by a board declaration favoring the alleviation of racial imbalance, Reusswig chose only prointegration school personnel for LRP. As one observer noted: "Reusswig wasn't personally talkative, but Long Range Planning spoke for him. It seemed radical at the time. Long Range Planning excluded conservatives; Reusswig kept the committees too liberal and too narrow, and the school board was still conservative at the time" (School principal 1978). Besides restricting administrative representation on LRP, Reusswig had an extremely narrow conception of community participation. His notion was that the community input should be limited to reacting to LRP staff proposals, although a few community people eventually did become involved as LRP staff (see Litherland 1978: ch. 7). Apparently, Reusswig's style was to develop ideal (and idealistic) plans that were to be received by the community as the work of highly trained professionals.[4]

Reusswig made extensive use of outside consulting expertise in training his LRP staff and attempting to orient school personnel toward the goal of integration. In some cases, the effects were negative. Many people were offended by some of the aggressively integrationist consultants and turned against Reusswig and LRP. Other consultants did provide valuable training for integration-oriented staff that was to prove useful later. Overall, however, Reusswig's use of consultants to import needed skills provided an educational training model for his numerically weak integrationist allies. This model was highly useful in implementing desegregation but had limited impact during Reusswig's tenure.[5]

During the period between 1967 and 1969 the LRP integration-building

4. This administrative style dominated school administration into the late 1960s. Essentially it is a medical model wherein the school administrator takes the doctor role in which he diagnoses and prescribes an educational cure for the student, who willingly lends his life to the doctor. For a serious defense of this approach, see Willis (1954: 273–280).

5. Community leaders made similar use of outside consultants. One community group was formed by Cesar Chavez, who in turn had been trained by Saul Alinsky, who also trained at least one prominent local activist during the mid-1960s.

committee developed a total of fourteen plans for desegregation. These included proposals for open enrollment, school pairing, redrawing district boundaries, busing, and a host of variations and combinations. At the hearings on various plans, increasing numbers of antibusing community groups loudly attacked all desegregation plans and demanded Reusswig's resignation. The prointegration position of school administrators on the LRP project spurred increasing anger and political organization on the north side of town. At only one meeting in this period did the prointegration groups outnumber the antibusing groups. Increased pressure from the growing numbers of organized north-siders had demonstrable effects on the board.

The school board tried to walk a middle road between the superintendent and his allies and the angry antibusing groups. Despite repeated symbolic assurances about achieving racial balance, the board discarded all fourteen LRP integration proposals and rejected a plan it had requested from Reusswig. An integration-oriented school replacement plan was allowed to languish without any consideration. Reacting to contradictory demands failed to find neutral ground, so the board was targeted for increasing attack from both sides.

The antibusing organizations developed considerable momentum and ever increasing size as a result of the raucous LRP hearings and apparent board vacillation on desegregation. They gained new strength after an outbreak of student violence at five south-side schools, three junior and two senior high schools. The board quickly canceled its plans to desegregate the summer schools at that point. A combination of retiring board members and intense dissatisfaction with the board led to the development of an antibusing slate for the fall elections, in which three of the five board seats were open. In an attempt to forestall an antibusing takeover of the board, Reusswig resigned. The resignation had no discernible effect as the Citizens for Neighborhood Schools swept to a landslide victory over the coalition slate of north-side liberal supporters of integration. The election marked the high point for the antibusing groups, for they never again were able to gain control of the board. In contrast to this peak, the south-side and liberal groups were only beginning to organize.

From the beginning of Reusswig's superintendency onward it was clear that the prointegration forces clearly were a minority. An early attempt at organizing led to the formation of the Integrated Equal Opportunity Coalition in 1967. The IOEC was an integrated, liberal group that favored voluntary integration whose membership was drawn from both the north and south sides of town. The organization was a loose coalition of about 100 individuals who contributed five dollars per month to build a campaign fund that could be distributed to favored candidates. The IEOC members generally campaigned for their candidates through work in other organizations in which they held membership. For example, IEOC shared mailing lists and membership with the NAACP, Mexican-American Political Association, Council for the Spanish Speaking, and the Black Unity Conference. Candidates favored by these groups came to be known as coalition candidates. Although they were beaten easily in the 1969 board elections, a productive relationship between liberal north-siders and more militant segments of the south side was formed.

The issue upon which the relationship expanded and grew was the denial of south-side representation in municipal offices. At-large elections for the city council and school board strongly favored the resource-rich north side. Even when minority persons were appointed to vacancies on the board, they lived on the north side. One such appointee, a Mexican-American, was a member of the Citizens for Neighborhood Schools slate put together by a combination of north side antiintegration parent groups. The IEOC supplied the necessary political expertise to help the growth of south-side political activism. In effect, the 1969 school board elections were, in the words of one observer, "only a trial run" (SUSD administrator 1969).

The first full test of the coalition's real strength and expertise was the 1970 election to change city council elections from at-large to district voting. The strategy developed by IEOC worked well. Essentially, the coalition worked hard to keep the issue quiet. Organizing and planning were done as discreetly as possible to avoid any publicity in the local paper. The week before the election the coalition mounted a major get-out-the-vote drive in South Stockton. The north side was ignored successfully as the district system was voted in with heavy south-side support. Furthermore, two south-siders were elected at the first opportunity in 1971. (Both are black and still hold their seats. Later, a Mexican-American won another seat, thereby increasing minority representation to three of seven seats.) The quiet strategy maximized the effect of the south-side vote because no opposition ever organized on the north side.

By 1970, the school board was controlled by the conservative Citizens for Neighborhood Schools. While an interim superintendent marked time for a year, the board sought a new superintendent amenable to its views of desegregation. At the same time, IEOC and various south-side groups were expanding their coalition and developing considerable educational and political expertise. The IEOC recognized the difficulties involved in pressing demands on the new board and sought legal help. Although the American Civil Liberties Union local chapter offered its help, IEOC settled on the federally funded California Rural Legal Assistance (CRLA) program. After a period of searching for several months, several minority parents agreed to be plaintiffs in a suit charging the SUSD with discrimination. In *Hernandez* v. *School Board of Stockton Unified School District*, CRLA and the NAACP filed a class action desegregation suit in the state court on behalf of the plaintiffs in April 1970. Meanwhile, the new board had to deal with increasing demands from the emerging voice of the south side.

1970–1974: TWO SIGNIFICANT VICTORIES

The lessons of the election campaign were not lost on the new board. The general exclusion of community input tolerated by the old board had disastrous political consequences, so the new board had to give more attention to community groups. The board was agreeable to the notion of increased input from community groups but at the same time it feared that south-side groups would rekindle the desegregation issue.

The policy framework developed to deal with the south side was the extensive use of federal funding for compensatory education programs. In effect, the board redefined the desegregation issue as one of providing quality education for low-achieving students from poor areas. Because this was a major concern of south-side parents and many groups, the board's position had some legitimacy. The board was so successful in this approach that at one point Stockton received more federal funding than Los Angeles. The board and staff had more problems implementing this policy than enunciating it, however.

Parents at one south-side school examined the compensatory education program at their neighborhood school and found that it was not in compliance with the community involvement regulations. Further examination of records disclosed other irregularities, all of which were dismissed by local school personnel. When the matter was brought to his attention, the acting superintendent recommended an investigation. The board quashed the move and tried unsuccessfully to deal with the parents at private and public meetings. Ultimately, after picketing the school and staging an unsuccessful boycott, parents brought in the district attorney to investigate the situation. The principal was indicted for embezzlement and left the school, but many of the remaining teachers and administrators still resisted community involvement.

Similar problems occurred when the board was forced to deal with IEOC demands and actions. The IEOC pressed the board to integrate at least a single school along racial, social, and economic criteria. The board had little interest in any desegregation program, even a voluntary one. The IEOC focused its efforts on the east side of town, where integration could be achieved with minimal costs through redistricting and slight modifications to the traditional busing program. Altogether the board rejected six such plans before winning state funding to build a new, integrated school. Yet it stalled the integration of the new school until a court order mandated partial compliance with the state contract.[6] A voluntary busing program resulted in the alleviation of some racial imbalance (Litherland 1978: 447). As with the last board, integration was affirmed as an abstract goal and denied in practice. This theme characterized other board actions as well.

In the months before the Field Act bond issue election in 1971, the board had tried to negotiate an out-of-court settlement with CRLA. At the now obligatory public discussion, the entire integration issue was rerun. After a tumultuous meeting with a host of speakers and highly charged emotional statements, the board decided to withdraw from the negotiations and to fight integration in the court system. A school bond issue was defeated by a margin of nearly two to one shortly thereafter. The bond issue proposal contained no plan to achieve racial balance though it did offer a vague promise of multiethnic representation in all schools. Opposition on the south side was strongly organized, and the north-side voting patterns reflected dissatisfaction with the schools.

The board's search for a superintendent amenable to its integration-compensatory education policies ended with the appointment of J. Roland Ingraham, who "wanted the job and conformed to board expectations" (District administrator 1971). Ingraham's main thrust was internal; he preferred working with the staff to dealing with the community and later hired William C. Carey who "supplemented Ingraham's tendencies" (School principal 1971) by providing administrative attention to community concerns while Ingraham dealt with the staff. Within the compensatory education policy framework, he apparently felt some need and some pressure to address the question of race relations among the staff. A minority administrative internship program was started at the University of the Pacific and trained a number of current district adminis-

---

6. The board refused to comply with its state contract because it knew that the state could not take back the newly constructed Martin Luther King School (see *Hernandez* v. *SUSD:* 9).

trators. Ingraham also started one of the first bilingual education programs in the country. Furthermore, he gave official recognition to various minority professional groups within the district, including Mexican-American, black, and Filipino groups. He reinstituted a national recruitment drive for minority teachers to begin the racial balancing of school faculties.[7] Overall, Ingraham's actions were entirely consistent with the compensatory education thrust of the board. He took no action that resulted in integration but tried to meet minority concerns within the board's policy limits.

By the beginning of Ingraham's superintendency, the south side was maturing politically, thanks to an extensive community development drive started by local clergy.[8] Beginning with a small grant, these clergy worked to build community coalitions across racial and linguistic boundaries. In order to accommodate widely diverse interests and views, they used a unique organizational structure and an educational model of community development somewhat akin to Reusswig's approach.

Two separate organizations were set up to structure the project. One, the Educational Concerns Committee, was responsible for administrative support services. The other was an independent policy-making group which used the acronym PEOPLE (Positive Educational Opportunity Provides Lasting Equality) to identify itself, was designed to be free from restraints so that it could work out ideological and political positions without having to answer the complaints of conservative clergy or community people. For example, PEOPLE had to reconcile its internal conflict over integration versus community control of schools. This led to a series of conflicting demands made to the school board until a consolidated position could be worked out internally. In most matters regarding the schools, however, PEOPLE was determined to build the involvement and skills necessary to bring about change.

PEOPLE followed an educational model to bring consciousness and skills to the south side. Besides using college students as researchers and community organizers, PEOPLE employed the services of faculty members from various University of California campuses, who ran many conferences and workshops for growing numbers of community people. Many of these were for highly specific purposes, such as designing an alternative plan for replacing Field Act schools. Others dealt with a broad range of political and educational matters, including integration, tutoring, federal compensatory education regulations, bilingual education, and developing better official responsiveness to community demands. They also hired a community aide and began building communications and coalitions across the south side.

The communications emphasis stressed awareness, the development of individual positions, and ultimately, the development of common positions as political goals for the coalition. As part of its educational approach to community organizing, PEOPLE made extensive use of various media. For example, a movie of the public session dealing with the board's out-of-court settlement

7. In a similar national recruitment drive, SUSD had recruited its first minority teachers in 1947, hiring one black teacher and one Filipino teacher. In addition the district participated in the federally funded Teacher Corps, and the state-funded New Careers programs to train integrated groups of students to teach in low-income areas.

8. Litherland was a prime mover in this effort, which is the focus of his doctoral dissertation.

attempt was used as a consciousness-raising and recruiting device at community meetings. The entire process resulted in specific political positions, which were then implemented using the IEOC model.

The 1971 school board election exemplified the PEOPLE-IEOC political partnership, as did subsequent elections in 1972 and 1973. In 1972, over board opposition, the coalition placed on the ballot a proposal to revise the electoral system for school board members from at-large to district voting. Ignoring north-side attempts to create some sort of political confrontation that would ignite neighborhood school advocates, the coalition held strictly to its quiet strategy. South side organizing for the election went unreported, and no issues were raised. The strategy worked again as a massive turnout on the south side won the election by 4,000 votes.

The 1973 election, at which the old Field Act bond issue was resubmitted and passed, was crucial because all seven of the new district seats were open. Two members of the old board retired and only one of the remaining three won reelection. Five of the new board members were endorsed by IEOC or PEOPLE. (The working relationship between them did not impair the independence of either group.) Three lived on the south side and two of those were PEOPLE members. Only two winners were known to favor busing, but all obviously were more open to community input than were previous boards. Moreover, the seven-member board distinguished itself sharply from its predecessors in other significant ways.

From the start, it was apparent that the board would establish a radically different relationship with its superintendent. The board was reputed not to care much for Ingraham and did not look to him for leadership. Instead, it "took the true role of a board and made policy" (School principal 1973). Ingraham found other employment and the board promoted his deputy, William C. Carey, whose administrative style stressed a participatory, consensus-building approach to community involvement that fit well with the board's character. Carey also felt strongly that the board should be the policy-making body and maintained this position steadfastly throughout his tenure.

After the intensely debated issues of recent years, the board was uniformly in favor of building consensus through community input, and it made every attempt to assert this position. At times it was clear that the board felt that decision-making speed was worth sacrificing in order to reach consensus. Though often criticized for avoiding decisions, the board adhered to its community strategy. Consistent with its assertion of policy-setting, authority and openness to the community were emergent issues relating to federal aid and staff development. Increasingly over recent years the board has questioned its staff more sharply about various funding proposals and demanded supporting evidence from the staff. Furthermore, its interests in basic skills and equal educational opportunity have combined into a strong interest in staff training and development, an understandable need if desegregation is to develop into integration.

The desegregation suit came to trial in early 1974 after four years of pretrial maneuvering between CRLA and the attorney for the district. The four-month trial ended shortly before the judge, John F. Keane, issued an injunction stopping work on the $20 million Field Act bond issue. Judge Keane's reasoning was that segregation might be perpetuated by the planned school replacement program. Not unexpectedly, the judge ruled that the district had deliberately segregated pupils by race and ordered it to "implement a plan of desegregation which will eliminate all vestiges of racially segregated school system, such plan to be submitted to this court for approval" (*Stockton Record* 1974: 10/13).

The response of the board and administration came quickly. Superintendent Carey sent a letter to all employees emphasizing individual responsibility to proceed with "dignity and good will," and added that a rumor center had been established (Carey 1974). Similar feelings were expressed in a letter from the board president to all parents. The research office immediately began studying other desegregation plans. Over the next few months the board debated an appeal, which was thrown out on a technicality. The board raised no further resistance to the desegregation order and set about developing an acceptable plan.

Overall, PEOPLE and IEOC won major victories during this period. PEOPLE succeeded in restructuring the school board electoral system and, as a result, the way the board conducted itself. Even though PEOPLE could develop agreement on the board issue, it never was able to develop a common stand on desegregation. Many south siders opposed it for reasons ranging from worries over children being far from home to community control of the schools. The IEOC always had pursued the goal of integration and fought often for the opportunity to develop integrated educational opportunities. Judge Keane's decision vindicated the long years of work put in by IEOC members and placed a heavy burden on the board and the district.

1975-1979: DESEGREGATION

In contrast to the tumult and political activism of the early and middle years, the recent years of the desegregation issue have been marked by decreased activity. Judge Keane's ruling placed considerable pressure on the board, but its strategy of involving all groups and points of view in the development of desegregation plans apparently defused the issue of exclusion that fueled much of the earlier organizing efforts of community groups. As a result, the community groups weakened, and many simply died off.

The role of various community groups diminished in importance during the third phase for several reasons. Many south-side groups offered to help the schools desegregate while expressing less than total happiness with the board's approach to desegregation. Others committed themselves to working for peaceful school integration. The most political and ideological of all the south-side groups, PEOPLE, has ceased to exist. Its members, however, have continued their interest and, in several instances, their work in the schools.

The antibusing groups have likewise ebbed though not necessarily for the same reasons. After Judge Keane's decision, some north-side parents organized an antibusing group called Stocktonians for Action (SFA), which lasted only a short time and refused to make any membership claims. It gave way to Stocktonians United for Neighborhood Schools (SUNS), who also remained secretive about its size but stayed highly active throughout this period. It sought to develop alternatives to busing and sent two members as friends of the court to make various appeals to Judge Keane. However, SUNS never was able to muster as many as 50 people at any school board meeting, compared to meetings topping 1,000 during Reusswig's tenure. In addition, SUNS launched two abortive recall attempts on school board members, and a third was thrown out for illegal signatures. None of the attempts achieved enough support to make the ballot. Apparently SUNS has dissolved as antibusing parents have moved from the district or found other alternatives to public education.

By and large the small Roman Catholic parochial school system has not tried to capitalize on the desegregation program. It has allowed schools to reach near capacity, but it has not developed any expansion plans. Established private schools have apparently followed similar policies, and new private schools have had mixed success in retaining students.

Perhaps part of the calm since desegregation began is attributable to the role of other community agencies and institutions. The local press has provided balanced, even-handed coverage and editorial policy on the entire issue. The *Stockton Record,* the only daily paper in the community, has reported fairly the positions and feelings on all sides of the issue. Its editorial policy has stressed cooperation with authorities and using desegregation as an opportunity to improve the quality of education in the school district. When the county board of supervisors took a position on busing, the *Record* editorially told it to stop meddling in school affairs. The city council stayed clear of the issue completely except for one meeting during Reusswig's time. Other municipal agencies took much the same position as the press.

The city police and county sheriff have conducted their offices professionally. When school disturbances occur, they provide appropriate support for school officials. No question has ever been raised about police work or involvement in the desegregation issue. This stance has been true also for most political figures and all municipal agencies. No one has tried to become involved in the issue; it has been left as strictly a school matter. All involvement during the planning phase, in fact, was accomplished under the direction of the school board and court.

Between 1975 and 1977, the board developed acceptable desegregation plans with massive community input and relatively little controversy. The board and Superintendent Carey used community involvement as a means of dealing with desegregation as openly and thoroughly as possible. Every view was heard and considered—repeatedly. Board members set up meetings to discuss the court order with their constituents, while Carey did the same for the staff. As the board dealt with the impact of the decision on the community and skirmished over its unsuccessful appeal, desegregation planning began.

One of the first items was the redesign of the Field Act building replacement program, which was revised to take desegregation into account; the judge allowed construction to continue. Gradually, a number of tentative features were set in place. These included using a goal of about 15 percent of the population distribution of the community to determine desegregation, plans to equalize facilities and programs at the three senior high schools, and the continuance or founding of alternative programs in magnet schools.[9] In September 1975, the senior high schools were desegregated quietly.

9. The plus-or-minus 15 percent rule was once a required state criterion but was struck down in *Crawford* v. *Los Angeles* (1976). The decision did not preclude its use, however. SUSD has three elementary magnet schools (multilingual/multicultural education, open classroom, and basic skills) and three alternative secondary programs.

Much preparation had gone into the high school program. The district conducted polls concerning students' attitudes toward desegregation, and a mass meeting for all high school students was held to answer questions and allay fears. A number of students formed a group that has successfully dealt with desegregation problems. The same type of preparation and planning was utilized when the junior high schools were desegregated a year later.

The most sensitive area for the board was the elementary schools, where parental fears were strongest. In dealing with the elementary school planning, the board and Carey maximized community involvement. The board appointed a broadly representative citizens' committee to explore various features of possible plans. All the committee's reports, majority and minority, were presented to the board and debated over the next several months. District personnel conducted more than 135 meetings over a period of months to discuss and survey community opinion on features of the four elementary school desegregation plans it was to consider. By the end of 1976, the board had developed and passed a desegregation plan for elementary schools that proved acceptable to Judge Keane with minor modifications.

The plan called for the retention of neighborhood kindergartens and naturally integrated neighborhood schools. Of the twenty-six Stockton schools, six met desegregation criteria. The remaining schools were to be desegregated through a pairing program. In effect, the board formed a number of two-campus schools in which grades one to three would be taught at one site and four to six at the other. Both schools would retain the kindergarten. As these schools became integrated through residential integration, parents could petition the board to separate them into two autonomous kindergarten through grade six schools. Busing was to be two way; children of all races would be bused to paired schools.

Staffs were also subject to desegregation. The board plan also made a commitment to staff development. One significant feature of the final plan was the provision that the school district monitor the desegregation and report to Judge Keane. The district was given a chance, in other words, to analyze its problems and develop possible solutions. During the 1977–1978 school year, the first year of elementary school desegregation, Judge Keane expressed satisfaction with the way the plan was working. The year had been peaceful and quiet; Superintendent Alton W. Cowan, who succeeded Carey and Interim Superintendent James Shannon, stated: "The survey has confirmed how well the full scale desegregation was accomplished and justified all the praise received when the plan was first implemented last September" (*Stockton Record* 1978: 4/11).

Other interested parties were not so satisfied and sought further judicial action. Judge Keane has considered plans from SUSC, CRLA, two SUNS spokesmen, and eight members of the now defunct board citizens' committee. His willingness to listen to unofficial groups may have been to blunt any reasons for appeal. Even though the judge apparently was ready to allow the current plan to remain as is for the 1978–1979 school year, the citizens' committee group filed a motion to reexamine the plan because four schools vary fully 20 percent from mandated proportions of racial groups. Delays forced the group to withdraw the motion. The board took no action and allowed the appeal to lapse, thereby finally accepting the judgment of the court.

The concern over white emigration to nearby districts is well-founded. The antibusing groups lost in school politics and in the courts, and many white families have left the public schools. Minority-group children form a majority of the district as school population continues a decline begun in 1969. Although the decline has not accelerated, the school districts within Stockton's boundaries continue to grow.

There has been no active or intensive resistance to desegregation. Low housing prices have made the Stockton area boom in population. Because all of the major parcels of land suitable for development lie outside SUSD in adjacent districts, it is difficult to estimate with any accuracy how many families have moved to avoid desegregation. The overflow in the outlying areas has strained capacities of existing schools and created pressure for new school building programs in nearby districts, but the current climate of revolt against increased taxes resulted in many limits on school planning. One nearby district is busing students to equalize enrollments and to maximize use of its present facilities. There have been no objections raised to this busing program, although local politicians refer to it as transportation rather than busing. Some neighboring districts have found that students who do not live within district boundaries have enrolled in its schools; one district expelled more than fifty students on these grounds. Similarly, enrollment increases have strained the capacities of private schools.

BUILDING SCHOOL INTEGRATION

The mixing of staff and student bodies in a way that provides racial variety constitutes school desegregation. From that starting point, the school must build integration, which involves diminishing stereotypes and teaching members of various cultures how to interact with each other. In brief, students are taught to appreciate their own and other cultures in a way that aids intergroup communication. The principles that proved successful in Stockton school politics—maximum involvement, communications, and problem solving—have evidently also been relatively successful in Stockton schools, according to interviews with monitors who have observed the processes during the 1977–1978 school year. Although problems inside the schools still exist, the Stockton experience does indicate that desegregation is feasible. Staff attention to these problems may eventually result in an integrated public school system that is beneficial to all racial groups.

BIBLIOGRAPHY

Carey 1974. Letter from Superintendent William C. Carey to all employees, Stockton Unified School District, 9 October.

Crawford v. Los Angeles 1976. Crawford v. Board of Education of City of Los Angeles. 17 C, 3rd 280, 130 California Reporter, 724, 551 p. 2d. 28.

District Administrator. 1971. Interview.

Hernandez v. SUSD 1970. Hernandez et al., Petitioners v. Board of Education of Stockton Unified School District, Respondents, San Joaquin County Superior Court 101016, April.

Kerr, Norman. 1964. "The School Board as an Agency of Legitimation." *Sociology of Education* 38 (Fall).

Lee, E. C. 1966. *The California Governmental Process.* Boston: Little, Brown.

Litherland, Richard H. 1978. "The Role of the Church in Educational Change: A Case History of a Feasible Strategy." Unpublished D. Ministry dissertation, Department of Advanced Pastoral Studies, San Francisco Theological Seminary.

Ross, Ruth A., and Barbara Stone. 1973. *California's Political Process.* New York: Random House.

School Principal 1971, 1973, 1978. Interviews.

Stockton Record. 1974: 10/13. "Full Text of SUSD Integration Ruling," 1978: 4/11, 5/9.

SUSD Administrator. 1969. Interview.

Willis, Benjamin C. 1954. "The Need for Professionalism in Education Today." *Chicago Schools Journal* March.

U.S. Census 1970, 1975. City of Stockton, Racial Characteristics: 1970 Census; 1975 October Special Census. Washington, D.C.: Government Printing Office.

PART III: COMPARATIVE ANALYSIS

13

School Desegregation
and the Management
of Social Change

Susan L. Greenblatt and Charles V. Willie

To most Americans, the term *school desegregation* has come to mean disruption and strife between whites and members of racial minority groups. As these ten case studies of school desegregation illustrate, such an interpretation is in most cases a distortion of fact. Only in a few instances has school desegregation resulted in violent incidents or severe disruption of a community's social life.

Of the ten communities under study in this project, Boston and Mobile experienced the most severe disruptions. Both of these cities witnessed events that resulted in injury to individuals and to property. Violence in Mobile was clearly attributable to staunch segregationist groups such as the Ku Klux Klan, and many of the incidents in Boston were stimulated by the activities of a group that called itself ROAR (Restore Our Alienated Rights) and several other recently organized protest associations. Protest marches and demonstrations specifically aimed against busing took place for an extended period of time in Boston. Interracial fights within schools occurred in both Boston and Mobile. In these two cities, however, violence was limited to only a few of the public schools.

The other eight cities each experienced at least some type of organized protest movement, but in most cities the protest was minimal. Richmond participated in a massive resistance campaign against desegregation following the *Brown* decision. Unlike the period of massive resistance in Mobile, however, in Richmond there was little if any violence.

With the exceptions of Boston and Mobile, no city experienced an interruption in schooling because of court-ordered desegregation. Antibusing groups were organized in these communities, but they were unable to mount a major campaign to challenge the court's order to desegregate. Most antibusing protest groups became increasingly invisible and ineffective once the desegregation plan was implemented.

In all ten cities, school board members denied that they had intentionally operated dual school systems. With the exception of Erie all of the school boards appealed at least once the findings of the court that segregation had been intentional. Indeed, in most of the cities, the school boards repeatedly appealed the court's findings; in some instances the cases reached the U.S. Supreme Court several times on various legal grounds. Of the ten cities, only the Erie and Stockton cases failed to reach the Supreme Court.

Appeals to the U.S. Supreme Court resulted in a variety of effects upon the desegregation plan. In Boston, for example, the Supreme Court refused to hear the case several times. In both Omaha and Milwaukee, the Supreme Court remanded the case to the district court for a rehearing on the finding of intentional segregation. The final verdicts had not been passed down when the case studies were completed. In Dallas, the desegregation case reached the Supreme Court in 1978 at the behest of the plaintiffs, who contended that racial desegregation of schools had not been achieved, that the majority of black students were still segregated in the East Oak Cliff district. The Supreme Court agreed and ruled that a new desegregation plan be designed for Dallas.

In Mobile, the Supreme Court ruled that the entire county must be desegregated in order to eliminate all vestiges of segregation. The court mandated that school officials investigate all possible techniques of desegregation, including the provision of additional transportation.

Both the Richmond and Wilmington/New Castle County school desegregation cases also reached the U.S. Supreme Court. In the Richmond case, the appeals court's decision that the school system of three counties could not be merged was upheld by the Supreme Court, since no constitutional violation by the suburban counties or the state had been found. However, the merger of eleven school systems in New Castle County was upheld by the Supreme Court, which agreed that official state action had indeed led to racial segregation in these districts.

The New Castle County School District is the first example of a merger of school systems based on a desegregation suit and as such merits special attention. The white suburban school districts fought the merger with the predominantly black Wilmington school district. The negotiations and political manipulations that took place during the long legal process leading to the merger are important indicators of what may occur in future cases aimed at mergers of urban and suburban school systems. The white suburbs controlled the planning mechanisms established during the process. In Wilmington, the black school board was overpowered by the white political structures in the suburban districts. As a result, the desegregation plan placed a greater burden on black students than on whites. Such power struggles can serve as an incentive for blacks in other central cities to maintain their predominantly black school systems in order to retain control over the operation of public schools, although in Richmond blacks urged the school board to seek a merger with suburban school systems; the attempt was unsuccessful. Richmond blacks wanted to merge city and suburban school systems but not city and suburban governments, for city government was coming under the control of blacks.

Geographical location fails to provide an explanation for the differing degrees of disruptions that did occur in the ten cities. Although one southern city in this study experienced disruptions, two others—Corpus Christi and Dallas—did not. In each of these cases, de jure segregation of schools had had a long history; also in these communities, the initial desegregation plans left many minority children in racially isolated schools.

Demographic variables (see table 2.1) provide some insight into the achievement of peaceful desegregation: the group of smaller cities studied (population less than 250,000) were among the most peaceful. Corpus Christi, Erie, and Stockton each experienced relatively calm desegregation processes. Apparently, the size of the city rather than the proportion of the minority population was the more significant variable. These smaller cities with populations less than a quarter of a million had minorities that ranged from 6.8 to 46.9 percent of their total populations. In the medium-sized cities (population 250,000–499,999), Mobile, with nearly a third of its population consisting of minority-group members, experienced substantial disruptions. On the other hand, even though 42 percent of its population was black, Richmond did not experience disruptions similar to those in Mobile. Omaha and New Castle County experienced very little in the way of disruptions; they, unlike Richmond had small proportions of minorities.

Among the three large cities (population 500,000 or greater) Boston and Milwaukee are quite similar in their proportion minority-group members, although their responses to the court orders to desegregate public schools were quite different. Dallas, with a quarter or more of its population black, and a significant though smaller number of Hispanics, experienced virtually no disruptions. In sum, the percent of minority population seems to have only a minimal effect that can be mediated by other factors.

Whereas disruptions were experienced in some but not all of the medium-sized or larger cities of 250,000 or more people, none was observed in the smaller cities of populations of less than a quarter of a million. In cities of all sizes, peaceful school desegregation was observed in some that had relatively large minority populations as well as in others that had relatively small minority populations.

Perhaps more important than percent minority population is the extent of desegregation actually achieved in determining whether the adaptation is peaceful or otherwise. In only six of the ten communities studied were entire cities or metropolitan areas desegregated. In Boston, Erie, Milwaukee, Mobile, Richmond, and Wilmington/New Castle County, the school systems that were ordered to desegregate coincided with city or county boundaries. (In New Castle County the rural district of Appoquinimink was omitted.) In Corpus Christi, Dallas, Omaha, and Stockton, school districts did not include the entire city and in fact did not include several areas within the city limits where upper-middle-class white families resided.

The Corpus Christi case provides a good example of this phenomenon. There was little or no violence in Corpus Christi, its desegregation plan involved only one-fourth of the school-age children. The neighborhoods least affected by the school desegregation plans in most of the cities in the South were those that were middle to upper-middle class. The institutional systems found ways to exempt these neighborhoods because of their isolated geographic locations or distant separation from racial minority neighborhoods. Using community institutional systems to defend them so that the ethnic purity of their schools was maintained, there was no need—especially for middle-class whites—to violently resist school desegregation. Community institutions had done this for them in an official and legal way. A less than comprehensive plan provided numerous opportunities for exemption. In most instances, the neighborhoods exempted from massive desegregation were those that were middle class.

Collective resistance to racial desegregation in Corpus Christi tended to be greater among those institutions dominated by affluent and middle-class people than among those controlled by the working class. Indeed, a working-class-dominated institution—a labor union—actively promoted school desegregation in Corpus Christi. Obstructionists to school desegregation were school trustees and the administrators, individuals in Corpus Christi who definitely were middle class. They had insisted that all charges against the school system be tested in court, and they used ways of evading the full requirement of desegregation. One could say that Corpus Christi was calm because the institutional authorities in education resisted desegregation for members of the majority who opposed it. Because only one-fourth of the school-age population has been involved in desegregation, one can conclude that the institutional resistance was quite effective. Under these conditions, interpersonal violence was unnecessary as a means of control.

The Mobile case indicated that middle-class whites, when not protected from desegregation by institutional means, were as likely as working-class or lower-class whites to engage in violence. Probably violence has been seen more frequently among working-class and lower-class whites because they have been more exposed—that is, their interests have not been protected by institutional actions.

When desegregation no longer could be avoided in Mobile, interracial fights were one unanticipated outcome that appeared with increased interaction between black and white students. One school that substantially desegregated was Murphy High School, known as an elite school that served white students from one of the highest socioeconomic areas in the city. A considerable amount of violence and interracial strife was experienced at Murphy High in Mobile. For Murphy students, desegregation represented invasion of a sacred territory by an alien group; and Murphy white students did everything in their power to repel the blacks whom they considered to be invaders, even to the point of becoming quite violent. Clearly, people of high socioeconomic status were not immune from violent behavior as a means of resisting school desegregation.

The development of institutional means to limit desegregation was a feature of southern resistance frequently utilized by the middle class. Such institutional approaches resulted in limited rather than comprehensive school desegregation. Had larger proportions of whites from higher socioeconomic strata been included in the desegregation plans in these cities, it is possible that the response of their populations and particularly their leaders would have been different, for residents of these areas most likely have available to them professional expertise, financial resources, and political control.

In the Wilmington/New Castle County case, representatives of middle-class white suburban districts were able to use their status and political resources to weaken the decision-making power that the leadership of Wilmington had been allocated by the court-established, interim board of education. The legislature increased the size of the interim board from five to thirteen with Wilmington assigned only two seats on the enlarged board. With each suburb allocated at least one seat (Newark had two seats), the suburbs were able to gain a powerful upper hand in any decision that came before the board. Although they were legally compelled to desegregate their schools and merge their school systems against their will, the suburban districts maintained control over the design and implementation of the plan.

The finding that whites from the upper strata are in many instances exempted from school desegregation suggests that there is an interaction between the variables of social class and race that merits further sociological study. The relationship between these two variables undoubtedly has great effect on practical attempts within the community to desegregate schools and housing and to merge urban and suburban school districts. Because upper-socioeconomic individuals tend to control governmental decision-making processes, it is they who determine whether there will be increased segregation or desegregation in local communities. Even though the Kerner Commission stated that our society is becoming increasingly racially segregated (Kerner Commission 1969; *New York Times* 1978), insufficient attention has been given to linkages between the racial caste system and the social class system. That segregation by socio-economic status is used by upper- and middle-class individuals in cities as well as suburbs to cover up racist practices is a possibility suggested by the data in these case studies.

Legal and other institutional means have been used by the dominant class to maintain segregation. Physical violence is unnecessary when the institutional systems in the community·can be pressed into action to resist desegregation, as the case studies in Richmond and Corpus Christi revealed. However, when institutional control is lost, those who were forced to sacrifice their control are as susceptible to violence as those who never had control. The example of Murphy High School in Mobile is an illustration of this phenomenon. Social scientists who have limited their studies of interracial violence to working-class neighborhoods have left us without any understanding of the activities of high-status individuals and their contributions to a segregated or integrated society.

It is also important to note that in at least one case, the failure to integrate blacks resulted in intraracial class conflicts within the black community. In Dallas, the majority of black students remained in the segregated East Oak Cliff area of the city. Many of the lower-socioeconomic blacks residing there felt betrayed by the upper-status black leaders who had participated in the design of the desegregation plan. In the case of Mobile, many blacks felt that some of their own leaders had given up on that city and had turned their attention to a black-controlled suburban city adjacent to Mobile. The basis for this feeling was the fact that attorneys for the plaintiff negotiated a consent decree that limited what some thought could have been a more comprehensive remedy. Experiences in these cities serve as a reminder that blacks as well as other racial and ethnic minority groups do not hold monolithic set of values, that social class and other factors divide their membership even as whites differ in terms of these characteristics.

POLITICAL LEADERSHIP AND CITIZEN PARTICIPATION

The processes leading to social change inevitably disturb those who benefit from the status quo. Planned social change that is brought about through legislative processes enables proponents and opponents to negotiate compromises somewhat acceptable to both sides. Citizens who are dissatisfied with legislation may attempt to recall or defeat legislative representatives who in their opinion have not appropriately protected their interest. In the case of social change that is brought about via the judicial process, government officials lack the ability to negotiate compromises in the usual manner. Similarly, citizens who disagree with the judicial mandate are unable to obtain different results by replacing court authorities, who are not subjected to popular elections. The only recourse for those dissatisfied with a judicial decision based on a question of constitutional rights is to continue the judicial process by utilizing the appeal system.

School desegregation is an issue that has been brought into the judicial arena by minority-group members and civil rights groups. In regard to the issue of school desegregation, those whites who previously contributed to the intentional segregation of public schools must now play the game according to the rules of law and court procedures. Instead of relying solely on their political dominance and control of social institutions to manipulate the issue, the majority must enter into an arrangement in a court case that is scrutinized for fairness and equity.

For many years, the research literature on race relations has echoed the theme that strong governmental action in support of court orders that require racial desegregation can prevent violence. Weisberg (1969) stated in 1951 that racial violence can be prevented by "decisive and informed government action." Williams and Ryan (1954) echoed this view in a study of twenty-four communities undergoing school desegregation that they conducted prior to the *Brown* decision. More recently, Pettigrew (1971: 130) has maintained that racial violence is rational in the sense that it occurs when leaders hint that violence will be tolerated.

The case studies presented here provide additional data that support the contention that actions by public officials in support of law and order may prevent racial violence. The officials themselves need not be in favor of the court order to prevent violent resistance. Their public pronouncements may be neutral if they take a strong position asserting that the law will be enforced, court orders must be obeyed whether or not one likes them, and violence will not be tolerated. When public officials speak out against court orders to desegregate the public schools, they stimulate resistance by the public at large which may get out of hand and become violent. Judicial appeals of court orders to desegregate by public officials sometimes are taken as a sign that resistance by any means will be tolerated.

Mobile is a classic example of violence that was stimulated by the resistance of public officials, including the governor of the state and the local school board. At the urging of the governor, the state legislature in 1956 enacted massive resistance laws to school desegregation. Ultimately, these laws gave parents freedom of choice to send their children to schools attended only by members of their race. With the highest state lawmakers resisting school desegregation, the Ku Klux Klan embarked on a campaign of terror and intimidation of anyone, black or white, who attempted to desegregate the Mobile schools.

All during the 1960s, the school board of Mobile sought delay after delay. Meanwhile, the White Citizens Council took its cue from the resistance of the highest educational authority in the local community and precipitated some violent incidents that were particularly aimed at preventing desegregation of the prestigious Murphy High School.

By 1971, little desegregation had been accomplished in Mobile. The school board found itself in the court again. This time, the decree required the U.S. Department of Health, Education, and Welfare to develop a school desegregation plan for Mobile, if the school board continued to refuse to develop a plan. Meanwhile, white parents took their cue from the school board and resisted abiding by the desegregation plan that had been formulated by HEW for Mobile. They staged a tumultuous session at a school board meeting.

By 1971, when school desegregation appeared to be inevitable and after a new school superintendent had come on the scene, the Mobile County School Board came forth with their first voluntary plan. The principle of massive resistance had been abandoned, and immediately, there was in-depth negotiating between the defendants and the plaintiffs. This led to a consent decree. The school board had decided to act in a lawful way. The board and the superintendent issued positive statements to assure the public that everything possible would be done to promote racial harmony.

The opening of school following the negotiation of a lawful decree was unlike previous years. There was no outbreak of violence, there was no overt resistance to desegregation. The community appeared to follow the law-and-order leadership of the school board.

Richmond never experienced the violence that was exhibited in Mobile largely because the school board assumed more leadership in responding to the school desegregation court order in a lawful way. Virginia also passed massive resistance laws. When these laws were declared unconstitutional, the local school board sought ways of partially conforming to the court order rather than resisting it outright. For example, the Richmond School Board appealed the court order in the *Bradley* case because it required the development of a unitary school system; however, the board did not appeal that part of the court order to admit ten black students to the school of their choice. The Richmond School Board resisted the court mandate that resources be distributed among all schools in an equitable way but accepted the requirement to desegregate, and their response was more peaceful than that of Mobile.

Omaha's leaders presented a variety of responses to the court order to desegregate. The mayor publicly sided with the antibusing group, signed their petition, and wrote a letter to the attorney general asking him to use Omaha as a test case on the desegregation issue. Nonetheless, the mayor was quite clear in verbalizing his expectation that Omahans would obey the law. Similarly, school board members took a stance against the desegregation plan but in favor of upholding the law. They denied the charges that their actions had resulted in segregation, and appealed the case to the U.S. Supreme Court. However, they upheld the legitimacy of the court order and the school desegregation plan after the appeals process had been exhausted. The board president said, "It is the law and the Board of Education must uphold the law. We are a nation of laws, a society of laws, and the board is one of the laws."

Both the Omaha City Council and the state Democratic Party advocated by formal resolution peaceful acceptance of the desegregation plan and its implementation. Omaha experienced a minimal amount of resistance to desegregation. The few antibusing groups that evolved were short-lived; there were no school boycotts, and there was no violence.

Boston, on the other hand, experienced a great deal of resistance and violence. Antibusing groups staged numerous protests and boycotts; physical violence took place both inside schools and in the community, and students in some schools walked out daily to protest desegregation. The actions of official Boston leaders tended to legitimize these disruptions. An elected official, a city councillor, organized the local antibusing movement. Other city councillors, elected school committee members, and state legislators made public statements supporting the resistance movement. One state legislator managed to have the busing issue put on the ballot as a referendum question. This action led the public to believe that the court order could be changed by voting when in fact the only recourse was appealing the decision through the court system.

Throughout the process, public officials, including the school committee members, were resisters. They refused to cooperate with the court unless under direct order to do so, appealed the decision to the U.S. Supreme Court, and failed to offer any support to any school administrator who attempted to abide by the court order. The superintendent who was responsible for implementing the first phase of the desegregation court order was not rehired at the end of his contract period. Three years later, his successor superintendent, who eventually was named the court-appointed receiver of South Boston High School that had resisted the second phase of court-ordered desegregation, also failed to receive reappointment when her contract expired.

The mayor's role was one of vacillation until the summer of 1976. Prior to the implementation of the order, the mayor made a speech on television that indicated his intent to please parties on both sides of the issue. He contended that he was for integration but against busing. Furthermore, he stated that individuals who were planning to boycott the schools had a right to do so. The mayor also emphasized that his role constituted protecting the children's safety and the public order.

Disruptions in the city continued. During the spring of 1976, several violent interracial incidents occurred. As a result, the mayor formed a committee to study violence in the city of Boston. That summer, he made a speech indicating that the court would not change its finding, that desegregation and busing would continue in Boston, and those who stated otherwise were misleading the public. Since that time there have been minor interracial disruptions inside the schools, but no protests of great magnitude. Some public officials who sanctioned the desegregation resistance movement lost elections. As a viable antibusing organization ROAR fractionated and eventually collapsed. Race relations in Boston became less turbulent within four years of the first desegregation order.

Milwaukee presented yet another pattern of official action. The mayor and city council played virtually no role in the issue. The school board was dominated by a conservative majority that continually appealed the court rulings to the U.S. Supreme Court. The superintendent of Milwaukee schools took the initiative and submitted his own plan for desegregation, which the court accepted. The plan stressed that school assignments would be voluntary, and the superintendent established various structures for obtaining citizen input into the design of the plan. The superintendent also linked the desegregation plan to a series of educational innovations in the school system, including the establishment of magnet schools and a career education program.

Milwaukee experienced very little in the way of community resistance or disruptions to the school desegregation order. There was no violence and the few protest gatherings that occurred were sparsely attended. The major resistance came from the group that was called Blacks Against One-Way Busing that organized a boycott of the schools. This group was established after the desegregation process was well underway, and it did not have a substantial impact.

In Stockton, city officials such as the mayor and city council members played virtually no role and took no stands on the desegregation issue. School board members resisted desegregation when it was first proposed by the school superintendent but complied once a court order for desegregation was handed down. In Erie, the mayor publicly supported the antibusing group while other city officials took no stance. In Dallas, the mayor supported the final desegregation order when it was handed down and rallied the city council to offer its support; the superintendent of the Dallas Independent School District also supported the school desegregation plan ordered by the court.

The analysis of events in these ten cities indicates that public officials may play a crucial role in the prevention of disruption and violence. In cities such as Mobile and Boston, public officials brought a long history of turbulence to an end by finally taking a strong stand in favor of upholding the law. In other cities officials prevented turbulence by indicating at the outset that the law would be enforced.

According to Edelman (1964), political leaders are able to influence citizens' behavior with their own leadership style, which may be as important as their policy decisions. Examples are the contrasting styles of the mayors of Boston and Omaha. Both disagreed with the desegregation order, yet the mayor of Omaha and other Omaha leaders were quick to make clear that they would not tolerate any violation of the law. The mayor of Boston at the outset indicated that violations of the law in the form of school boycotts were up to the individual's conscience, and he did not indicate that he would use his powers to enforce this law. The contrasting responses that these two communities made to court-ordered school desegregation may indeed be a function of the administrative styles of their public officials and the behavior they evoked.

Edelman (1964) also notes that certain words or phrases arouse a severe emotional response that far exceeds their superficial meaning. Clearly the words "forced busing" fit this category. None of the political leaders ever stated that they were against racial desegregation, yet the term "forced busing" connotes legally enforced integration. And many political leaders said that they were against forced busing. One Boston politician who frequently said she was against forced busing usually followed the denouncement with the statement, "and you know what I mean." The crowd always roared its approval of her sentiments against race mixing in the public schools, although she never said that was what she was against. By not verbally opposing racial desegregation itself but claiming to be against "forced busing," political leaders attempted to satisfy those on both sides of the issue.

Some who described school desegregation as "forced busing" did not use the phrase as a symbol to evoke a particular response; they strongly disagreed with the desegregation ruling and felt that the law was forcing them to do what they did not choose to do. Most lawmakers who were opposed to race mixing in the public schools did not wish to oppose the legal system of this nation; thus, they sought to change state or federal law. Virginia is well known for its massive resistance state laws that hampered school desegregation in local communities until they were declared unconstitutional. The state legislature in Nebraska passed a resolution calling for Congress to initiate an antibusing amendment to the U.S. Constitution. Although ineffective, these were real attempts to overcome the U.S. Supreme Court ruling to desegregate public schools. Most of the cities exhibited some resistance to court-ordered school desegregation by citizens or their representatives. The most common example was resistance by a school board, especially in its attempts to appeal the court order.

It is also important to note that leaders have manipulated the language to evoke a positive response to school desegregation. One leader, the school superintendent in Milwaukee, continuously referred to "voluntary" school assignments. In reality, not all students obtained their preferred assignments. Nonetheless, the terminology and the publicity surrounding the "voluntary" plan undoubtedly contributed to the lack of protests in Milwaukee; many citizens believed that they retained free choice in school selection.

In general, public officials attempted to satisfy both opponents and proponents of school desegregation. This was the most prevalent approach in the ten cities we studied and was the strategy most frequently attempted by mayors. Mayors successful in using this approach were those who took a strong stance in favor of law enforcement at the time the court order was issued; this stance was more important in maintaining public order than a mayor's personal opinion in favor of or against school desegregation.

Our study revealed that public officials can deflect some of the pressure of a school desegregation court order when members of their communities are both for and against it by asking for the assistance of citizens, citizens' groups, and professionals. Structures for the receipt of such assistance may include the establishment of groups of community leaders and parents to help formulate or monitor the desegregation plan, the retention of a panel of experts to advise on implementation strategies of the plan, and sponsoring a series of tours to other cities to learn about their school desegregation experiences. The superintendent in Milwaukee established citizens' groups in all schools to assist with the planning process; he developed out of this process of citizen participation his own desegregation plan that was submitted to the court. The Dallas Alliance, a business-dominated citizens' group, was urged by the judge to submit a desegregation plan which was accepted by the court. In both of these instances, community leaders who were not legally required to play a role stepped in to assist their communities meet legal obligations and yet maintain public order. In Omaha, a citizens' group called Concerned Citizens for Omaha took an aggressive role by studying desegregation in other cities, publishing information about the desegregation plan, and setting up a communications network. Officially sanctioned citizens' groups were definitely an asset in achieving peaceful school desegregation in those communities in which they were invited to participate by public officials.

SCHOOL SUPERINTENDENTS AND SCHOOL BOARDS

Williams has stated, "The more direct the lines of responsibility from the highest positions in a hierarchy to the lowest, the more effective is implementation of the policy" (1977: 288). Unfortunately, most cities that have undergone court-ordered school desegregation have been unable to clarify the lines of responsibility for implementation. Although the court has placed the burden of responsibility for the actual design of the desegregation plan on the school board which is often the defendant, school board members usually have been reluctant to comply and in some instances have refused to design desegregation plans. When the school superintendent is named as a defendant in the school desegregation cases, too, problems in administration and accountability increase. Under this condition, the superintendent must choose whether to obey the court or to follow the model of behavior set by the school board. The problems created for the chief school administrator by this dual obligation were revealed in the Dallas school desegregation case. Maybe this fact accounts for the short tenure of superintendents in most cities during the years of the school desegregation controversy. In only one city, Corpus Christi, was the superintendent in office for a decade, that city had not experienced much desegregation at the time of our study.

Previous research on school boards has indicated that most of these groups tend to be homogeneous and they try to avoid public controversy by debating issues in secret executive sessions so that a unanimous front can be presented to the public. Court-ordered school desegregation has blown their cover. The public has become aware of the court orders through the mass media. The possibility of board members maintaining a unanimous front on this issue is likely only when a board is homogeneous ideologically. Even under this condition, it is unlikely that all board members will agree that race mixing in the public schools is educationally beneficial or harmful to minority and majority children.

When a controversial issue must be dealt with publicly, it is likely that divisions will surface among school board members. This may cause much anguish among local decision makers who accepted the role of school board members in the spirit of public service and who were unprepared for the estrangement that the school desegregation issue can cause. School desegregation more than any other issue has made school business public business and has demonstrated the need for a diversified decision-making structure to handle controversial issues. In the future, more school boards probably will be more diversified. The homogeneous boards were found wanting in dealing effectively with school desegregation. Their lines of communication with minority communities were insufficient. When challenged, they responded as if their function was to protect the status quo and the dominant people of power.

As more board members are elected in single-member districts rather than at large, there will be better representation of the various sectors of the population. It is probable that heterogeneous boards will be more open and less secretive in their deliberations, which will result in greater public input. Thus, future controversial issues may be resolved by deliberation rather than litigation, for the school board will include all interests and not just those of the majority or the dominant group.

Previous research has indicated that many school boards function merely as legitimation agencies for the decisions made by superintendents; the professionals and chief administrative officers in education (Kerr 1969; Zeigler and Jennings 1974). Data from our case studies provide some indication that court-ordered school desegregation has changed this traditional relationship to one where political concerns outweigh professional concerns. The Boston case study provided an example of political leaders, including elected school board members, symbolically manipulating the community's response to school desegregation and thereby increasing their control over policy making as well as policy implementation. For the first two years of court-ordered school desegregation, some city officials, including school committee members, were in the forefront of the antibusing movement. School committee members refused to submit a desegregation plan that had been developed by a professional staff supervised by the superintendent to the court; three of the five members were found to be in civil contempt of court for refusing to transmit a plan as ordered by the court. Although the chief educational officer tried to protect the board by preparing a plan, as mandated by the court, the school committee would not follow his advice and was so incensed over his repeated attempts to cooperate with the court that it would not renew his contract. For similar reasons, the contract of another superintendent was not renewed. Clearly the Boston school committee was involved in policy-making and administrative decisions.

In Stockton, the superintendent originated the idea of school desegregation in 1964. At that point, he enjoyed the traditional relationship with the school board described by Kerr. His suggestion that the schools be desegregated resulted in increased politicization of the community and the formation of antibusing groups. The school board, which previously had not taken an active role in policy formation, became more active and finally rejected the superintendent's plan. As a result of these actions, the superintendent resigned. The board then sought out a superintendent who would agree to support their policy on desegregation.

The Milwaukee community was the only one that we studied in which the superintendent retained administrative initiative during the desegregation crisis. Although the school board members were against desegregation and continued to appeal the court-ordered plan, the superintendent's actions, which linked desegregation to educational innovations and greatly involved parents in the planning process, were so popular that the school board would have risked defeat if it had tried to exert more control over him. In essence, the superintendent in Milwaukee utilized desegregation to strengthen his own position in relation to the school board. The relationship between the board and the superintendent was unique in Milwaukee compared with other cities under court order to desegregate.

In general, school board members who are elected at large will attempt to satisfy the constituency that controls the largest number of votes. In most American cities, white voters still outnumber black voters. Thus school board members tend to respond to whites, whom they perceive as opponents of busing and school desegregation. In so doing, they exert greater control over the superintendent's administrative actions as well as set policy.

A superintendent may aggressively support school desegregation and obtain community support for his or her actions under certain conditions. First, a superintendent must be aware of politics and the symbolic use of language and utililize these factors to bring about support for school desegregation. The Milwaukee example reveals that a superintendent can overcome a board that has a negative orientation to school desegregation. However, it must be recognized that Milwaukee has a weak mayoral government and therefore the superintendent did not have to contend with a powerful leader working contrary to his goals. Nonetheless, the Milwaukee example suggests that superintendents who take a strong stance may in fact be able to play the key role in maintaining peace during the desegregation process. This finding stands in contrast to Rossell's (1977) suggestion that the mayor is the only figure with enough authority to control the desegregation process. Rossell's portrayal of school superintendents as apolitical, business-type managers is contrary to what we observed in Milwaukee; the superintendent there was a real professional who knew how to handle community pressure groups.

RESISTANCE GROUPS

In most of the communities we studied, local groups were organized that had the explicit goal of defeating school desegregation. One could call these single-purpose groups. Usually they were ad hoc, not part of an existing institutional system. Even when organized community groups existed that could accommodate local antiintegration interests, school desegregation resistance effort became so specialized that those in charge splintered from the larger group. A characteristic of most of the resistance groups is their relatively short existence. "Forced busing" is the only phrase around which they can rally. The short life span of resistance groups—roughly three years—is prolonged when they receive official sanction or sponsorship. When desegregation resistance groups last for five or more years, they tend to continue because they receive support from recognized community institutions. The disintegration of resistance groups can be due to disinterest, to ideological differences, or to violence directed against members of the ingroup as well as members of the outgroup.

In Richmond, three groups against desegregation appeared in 1970 and attained a reasonable amount of visibility. Two of these groups were white—Citizens Against Busing and the West End Parents Opposed to Busing. A third group was black and was called Better Education Now.

By 1971, opposition to busing from Richmond's black community had dissipated, although active opposition continued in the white community. According to the Richmond case study, "A strange sense of ambiguity was beginning to be experienced by some of the individuals opposed to busing in Richmond. The issue of merging with the surrounding counties created a dilemma for many. . . . During litigation over the merger of the three school systems (Chesterfield County, Henrico County, and Richmond), the antibusing forces in the metropolitan area began to splinter." Apparently, opposition groups can remain intact as long as their energies are focused in one direction. They seem to disintegrate when confronted with alternative choices of creatively dealing with that which is troublesome.

The Ku Klux Klan and the White Citizens Council had little impact in Virginia, but in Mobile these groups were quite active in resisting school desegregation. In due time, they too, disintegrated. In 1964, the White Citizens Council encouraged "almost 300 white students" to participate in a noisy demonstration against desegregating the formerly all-white Murphy High School in Mobile. Around this time, the John Birch Society also came on the scene. It identified the movement for racial desegregation as communistic, and stirred up a great amount of community opposition. Within a year or two, both the John Birch group and the White Citizens Council had been infiltrated by former Klansmen and split over that and other issues.

The Assembly of Christian Soldiers Church, an offshoot of the Klan, was organized in 1971 in Mobile. This group declared war on school desegregation, and established a school "to spare the white children the indignity of attending schools with blacks in the public system." At one time, 300 to 400 people were attracted to the meetings of the Assembly. However, as its identity as an off-shoot of the Klan was revealed fewer and fewer people participated, and the school "came to an early demise."

The ideology of violence also contributed to the disintegration of the group. For example, the Imperial Wizard of the Ku Klux Klan allegedly "shot two of his fellow Klansmen who had raised questions about his managing of the funds of the organization" in a Birmingham, Alabama meeting. The violence that first is directed against minorities or members of the outgroup eventually is directed toward its own members. Violence appears to be uncontrollable.

There was organized resistance to school desegregation in Dallas, but it was not widespread. Most of the members of the elected school board in 1973 were endorsed by a conservative group known as the Committee for Good Schools. By 1977, the endorsement of this group was not significant; a majority of the school board members then neither sought nor received the committee's support. There was token opposition also in the black community to the proposed plan of the Dallas Alliance, which the court eventually adopted. But the black leaders who were few in number agreed not to take action until the plan was further explored.

In Erie, a grass-roots group organized in October 1970 to oppose the possibility of busing children for the purpose of racial desegregation. The group called itself Concerned Parents and Taxpayers and claimed to have a paid-up membership of 2,700 individuals. Between twenty-five and thirty members served on the executive board of the organization and directed its activities, which took the form of protests at school board meetings. In addition, the group presented a petition against busing containing 16,000 signatures.

Despite its early numerical strength, Concerned Parents and Taxpayers failed to obstruct the plan to bus or transfer children from their neighborhood schools. Erie's desegregation plan did utilize transfers that in many instances enabled children to walk to their newly assigned schools. Perhaps the utilization of walking instead of busing was attributable to the pressure of Concerned Parents and Taxpayers; nonetheless, the group failed to completely obliterate busing.

In the spring of 1978, when the Erie case study was written, Concerned Parents and Taxpayers was still in existence, if only nominally. Its membership had dwindled considerably, although exact figures were not available. Its existence was attributable to its two founders and leaders, who had gained reputations in the community as skillful leaders. Although the goals of the organization were ostensibly the same as when the organization was founded, in actuality the group did not continue to deal with desegregation. Instead it focused on bringing about educational change within the school system and at individual schools. Parents' groups that were dissatisfied with curriculum or structure at their own children's school often contacted one of the organization's two leaders to assist them with their appeals to the school board. Thus by 1978, the character of a group originally established to oppose busing had changed both in size and issues to be dealt with. However, the Erie experience is unusual. Few protest groups have been able to change goals and remain viable.

In Wilmington/New Castle County the group that offered the most resistance to the desegregation plan was the Positive Action Committee (PAC) founded by James Venema in February 1975; Venema claimed that his organization mustered 10,000 members throughout New Castle County. The tactics used by the PAC included widespread distribution of literature throughout the county and letter-writing campaigns to newspapers and legislators. Venema's stance was clearly that of an astute politician cognizant of the power of symbols. He used the term "forced busing," but he warned the organization's members that violence on their part would hurt their cause. Venema further contended that an organization as strong as PAC could easily defeat political candidates who failed to oppose busing for desegregation. Inevitably, PAC's tactics did have an impact on the state legislature, which engaged in numerous symbolic gestures to indicate opposition to busing.

By the spring of 1978, when the Wilmington case was still in court, PAC's influence had diminished greatly. By that time it was apparent that busing would be a part of the desegregation plan when it was implemented in September 1978, and the founder (and leader) of the group resigned from PAC in order to run for U.S. Senator from Delaware.

The largest antibusing group in Boston—ROAR—was unveiled by City Councillor Louise Day Hicks in the fall of 1974. It is difficult to collect data on the activities of the group, because its strategy included remaining quite secretive. This group reached its peak during its first year of official existence, which coincided with the first year of court-ordered desegregation in Boston and with a number of disruptive incidents in the schools. During that year, Hicks attempted to make ROAR a national organization, and participated in a march on Washington, D.C., which failed to garner the national support she had hoped.

As the Boston police and official leaders began to take a stronger stance against violence, violent incidents began to subside and ROAR's strength began to diminish. Its diminishing influence was partially attributable to an ideological split between its two top leaders. Louise Hicks and Pixie Palladino, who had been elected to the Boston School Committee as a result of her antibusing leadership, had differences of opinion concerning the strategy ROAR should take. As a result, Palladino and her followers started their own organization known as ROAR United. The fragmentation of the antibusing group led not only to a decrease in antibusing activities but also to the eventual political defeat of both leaders. In November 1977, Hicks was defeated in the election for city council and Palladino in the election for school committee. Four years after its inception as an antibusing group, for all practical purposes ROAR ceased to exist.

In Omaha, Stockton, Corpus Christi, and Milwaukee, no group of desegregation resisters ever gathered substantial strength or stability. Omaha had one group whose strength existed for several months. One antibusing organization in Stockton gathered enough strength to elect its candidates to the school board in the early part of the conflict; it was never able to repeat this success. Stockton had a series of small, inconsequential groups that were established in succession; following the demise of one antibusing group, another would be organized. Corpus Christi had several antibusing groups, but none ever had a substantial impact on the desegregation process. Milwaukee's greatest resistance came from the black community, which organized a group called Blacks Against One-Way Busing. This group protested the fact that blacks were bused in disproportionate numbers to whites. However, the group was established late in the desegregation process and failed to have much impact.

The short duration of groups formed to resist desegregation is due largely to the fact that they have many of the characteristics of crowds or mobs. Joseph Gitler describes the growth and demise of a crowd:

> [It] forms when an unusual event . . . occurs which violates community mores. . . . Anger, excitement, and frequently hysterical assertions mount, and the members interact with one another on an exceedingly emotional plane. Leaders emerge who tend to channelize the crowd's activities in the direction in which they are already moving. The focus of the participants becomes strongly centered on their purposes, and when the high level of emotional tension is reached, the crowd fulfills its intentions. It dissolves after a period of action, when emotions begin to level off and individuals return to a semblance of individual awareness (1952: 85).

Racial desegregation in the public schools is an event that changes practices which have existed in some communities for more than a century. The abrupt change by legal decree generates anger and excitement. When political leaders reinforce that anger by accomodating the crowd they contribute to the crowd mentality of desegregation-resistance groups. Political leaders who propose alternative solutions contribute to the disintegration of the crowd by raising multiple purposes. A crowd becomes a group when it must choose. Even if the crowd is not dissolved by the introduction of choice that precipitates rational consideration, its intensity diminishes after a confrontation—a form of fulfillment after.which emotions begin to level off and there is a concomitant return to individual awareness and rationality.

The resistance groups may have a disrupting effect upon the total community, but they may serve a useful purpose for their members. They keep alive the belief that a miracle will prevent the desegregation court decree from being implemented. Toch (1965: 43–44) states that "miracles provide prospects of change in situations that are objectively hopeless, and offer comfort and a basis for enduring situations that are objectively intolerable." They are a way of "delaying the recognition of defeat. . . . The miracle functions to retain psychologically essential prospects; it not only brightens the future, but validates the present and sanctifies the past." Toch calls belief in miracles "means of self-preservation." Although belief in miracles does not improve conditions, Toch states that "it ameliorates the travails of adjustment. With luck, it permits survival until higher probability solutions become available."

The higher probability solution in a republic that is a constitutional democracy is that the court decree will be enforced unless it is overturned at a higher level of the judicial system. Such an occurrence requires that these emotional groups work within a system that is painfully slow and requires a great amount of financial and professional resources. Although several resistance groups have utilized this approach, none has been successful in the ten communities under study.

The miracles called for by the desegregation resistance groups enable them to slow down the experiencing of the new reality. Those who participate in these groups believe that such action is necessary for self-preservation. Objectively, there may be a better way of adapting to a changing situation. But the members of desegregation resistance groups may not know about them, or if they do, they probably believe that they would not work in their particular situation.

COMMUNITY PARTICIPATION

The ten cities studied represent a variety of patterns concerning community participation in the planning process for desegregation. Most of the cities had no court-established structure designed to encourage citizen participation.

Boston was an exception to this pattern. Court-appointed parent councils were established following implementation of the first desegregation plan in Boston. The goals of the councils were to deal with interracial and interethnic problems as well as to improve communication among parents and educators. Thus part of their mandate was based on the negative presupposition that problems would occur. In the fall of 1974, elections were held at each school in the city to fill the slots allocated for whites, blacks, Hispanics, and Orientals. Participation in the elections was low, as was attendance at council meetings. In addition to the councils at the individual schools, a city-wide parents' group was elected; it consisted of members drawn from the school councils.

The structure of the councils changed the following year, as did the councils' name. In addition, district-wide councils were added as an intermediate level. These councils were not utilized to assist with the planning process for the revised desegregation plan. Court-appointed masters who held hearings and experts assisted the judge with this process. Furthermore, the court also established the City-wide Coordinating Council (CCC), a group of leading citizens, to monitor the desegregation process. Many of these citizens did not reside in the city proper, and few had children in the Boston public schools. The CCC gained the reputation as the group that had the greatest influence with the judge. This fact resulted in resentment among members of parents' councils and, in effect, represented a social class struggle, for members of the CCC were upper and middle class whereas members of the parents' councils were less affluent.

In Milwaukee, citizen participation was part of the desegregation planning process from the outset. The court-appointed master conducted public hearings as his first act. The superintendent of schools established parents' committees at each school and in each district as well as a city-wide committee. These committees, along with school principals, drew up plans for specific aspects of the desegregation plan as it would affect their own schools and neighborhoods. Although there is some question as to how much these plans actually were utilized, citizens did have the opportunity to express their ideas and present them to the school system.

In addition, voluntary organizations in Milwaukee formed the Coalition for Peaceful Schools in an attempt to assist in the peaceful implementation of the desegregation plan. This group obtained federal funding that enabled it to serve as a communications network and a training center for those involved in the desegregation process.

Omaha also utilized citizen participation in the planning process. Even before the court ruling was handed down, the school board appointed the Omaha Community Committee (OCC) to investigate the charge that the public schools were segregated. This group held public hearings, conducted surveys, and visited other cities to observe their desegregation efforts. The OCC concluded that the Omaha Public School System must provide aggressive leadership to desegregate the schools.

Additional citizen participation in Omaha took place through a structure called Concerned Citizens for Omaha (CCFO), established by an interracial committee that was appointed by the judge. In contrast to the blue-ribbon, interracial committee, CCFO drew upon hundreds of grass-roots volunteers to form a communications network. In an effort to implement the desegregation plan peacefully, CCFO worked with school officials to provide the entire community with necessary information about desegregation. In contrast to the pattern of influence acquired by the blue-ribbon and grass-roots groups in Boston, in Omaha the more active group was the CCFO. The blue-ribbon, interracial committee usually functioned as a reaction to CCFO suggestions.

The case studies indicate that the involvement of citizens may help to achieve school desegregation without conflict if proper planning takes place. Community involvement models utilizing citizen participation appear to be most effective in avoiding conflict when participation is allowed at the outset of the planning process. In both Omaha and Milwaukee, school officials were able to garner citizen support for desegregation by involving the community in the early stages of planning. In Milwaukee, citizens were able to participate in the specific details of the plan that affected their own children. In addition, formal grievance mechanisms provided channels to express dissatisfaction. Both Omaha and Milwaukee experienced very little in the way of formal protests and resistance groups. It is likely that the school officials' work with citizens' groups served to pacify or co-opt potential resisters.

In contrast, Boston did not create mechanisms for citizen participation until after school desegregation had already begun and resistance groups had been established. Officials in Boston failed to co-opt potential resisters prior to the establishment of antibusing groups. When citizens' groups were established, they suffered from poor participation particularly in neighborhoods where resistance groups already had a stronghold. Thus it appears that if citizen participation is to be utilized successfully, it must be implemented in the early stages of the planning process.

Williams has noted that participation in conflict processes changes individuals' norms, goals, and organizational structures (1977: 315). Specific examples of such changes were evident as a result of participation in Boston's parents' councils. Although these councils failed to achieve many of the goals for which they were established, they did succeed in teaching parents that collectively they could have an impact on the school system. Citizens in several elementary schools used these councils to protest what they considered to be inadequacies in their schools. When Roxbury High School in the heart of Boston's black community was scheduled to be closed, parents went to the council established by the court order to fight successfully against this closing. Evidently parents had learned that their collective voice could successfully challenge the school system. Furthermore, the existence of the parents' councils provided the parents with an ongoing mechanism that they could utilize. Had it been necessary for these parents to begin organizing without the presence of the council, it is likely that the school would have been closed before the parents were able to mobilize support for their position.

A similar learning experience took place for parents in Erie who originally had organized in an attempt to defeat the desegregation order. Leaders of Concerned Parents and Taxpayers (CPT) failed to eliminate desegregation but realized that they could have an impact on school issues. They became so effective that they continued in their role to monitor the quality of education. When parents became dissatisfied with some aspect of education at their children's school, it became commonplace to contact the leaders of CPT to gain their assistance in protesting these conditions to the school board. Thus the desegregation process taught them to be less passive and how to organize effectively to bring about the educational change.

STATE GOVERNMENT

Edelstein (1977) has noted that the role of state governments has been minimal in the desegregation process. Our case studies provide support for this contention. In several states, legislative representatives and other state officials were in the forefront of the movement to resist desegregation. In Virginia, the governor and legislature proposed changing the state constitution and funding private schools as a means of avoiding desegregation. In Alabama, the Pupil Placement Law was passed as a means of avoiding desegregation. More recently, the state legislature in Delaware acted symbolically to indicate its opposition to busing and a merger of the eleven separate school systems. The state board of education only reluctantly submitted desegregation plans as required by the court, even though the state was one of the defendants in the suit.

The state governments of Texas and Nebraska played virtually no role in the desegregation process with the exception of the Nebraska state legislature's resolution calling on the U.S. Congress to initiate an antibusing amendment to the U.S. Constitution. California at one time had state guidelines requiring that public school enrollments be within 15 percent of the racial breakdown of the population in the community, but this law was struck down in the Los Angeles school desegregation suit. Wisconsin has a statute encouraging the voluntary transfer of students from Milwaukee schools to the suburbs and vice versa to achieve desegregation. The state government did not take an active role in the Milwaukee desegregation case beyond passing this statute.

Massachusetts and Pennsylvania played the most active roles of the states studied in this project. In 1965, Massachusetts passed the Racial Imbalance Act, which the state department of education utilized in its legal case against Boston. The Massachusetts Department of Education threatened to cut off state funding for Boston if it did not submit a desegregation plan. Although the state court held that the state must reinstate the funding, it also required Boston to desegregate. The state department of education drew up its own desegregation plan for Boston, which was later used by the federal judge for this first phase of school desegregation.

The Pennsylvania Human Relations Commission (PHRC) initiated the desegregation case against the city of Erie as well as sixteen other Pennsylvania cities. The Erie School Board and the PHRC negotiated for seven years before a desegregation plan was finally accepted by the commission. Even then, the plan failed to meet the desegregation guidelines set by the state. However, the PHRC and the state department of education took no further actions.

Seven of the nine state governments represented here played either a negative role in the implementation of desegregation or a negligible role. Only in Massachusetts and Pennsylvania did the states initiate legal action to bring about desegregation. In general, state governments did not take an active role in desegregating public schools, although the state government is the ultimate educational authority.

SUMMARY AND CONCLUSIONS

If these ten communities are representative, it is fair to conclude that many communities will have unusual or even unique circumstances surrounding efforts to desegregate the public schools. For example, Corpus Christi's desegregation suit was sponsored by a steel workers' union and resulted in the legal definition of Mexican-Americans as a minority group. The Wilmington desegregation case resulted in the merger of a metropolitan school system despite the efforts of the suburban school systems to prevent it. The Erie desegregation suit was initiated by a state agency, whereas the Omaha suit was started by the U.S. Department of Justice.

Despite the presence of community-specific characteristics and circumstances, similar patterns of behavior by leaders and citizens alike have been discovered in these ten communities.

In virtually every instance, school board members have appealed the court order to desegregate schools. School board members in each of the ten cities were elected to their offices, and their reactions to court-ordered desegregation reflected their perceptions of the white constituency's attitudes. In some instances the board's appeal resulted in a delay of the implementation of desegregation. In none of the ten cities did the board's behavior result in a reversal of the desegregation order. Eventually, even those boards that strongly resisted desegregation at the outset have come to accept it as inevitable and have finally taken action to avoid community strife and disruption of the school system.

It is possible to avoid severe disruptions and conflict as a concomitant of school desegregation. Crain et al (1968) found that school boards were capable of garnering support of their policies toward voluntary school desegregation whether they were segregationist or integrationist. Our study provides data to suggest that this finding is applicable to court-ordered desegregation also. Had school board members supported desegregation from the outset, it is likely that the minimal number of disruptions, protests, and school boycotts that did occur would have been even fewer.

Furthermore, it is possible for officials with a city-wide constituency, leaders with city-wide networks, and community organizations to mobilize the community for the goal of peaceful school desegregation. The ten community studies presented here represent a variety of approaches to this type of mobilization effort. In Dallas, the business community proposed a desegregation plan that relied upon magnet schools, improved education, and provided widespread publicity for this plan. In Omaha, a network of lay citizens, representatives of community organizations, and members of the school department conducted system-wide communications efforts to bring about peaceful desegregation. In Milwaukee, the superintendent and the court-appointed master used citizen input in the planning process, and the superintendent linked the concept of educational innovations to the desegregation plan. In addition, the Coalition of Peaceful Schools served as a resource center for all those involved in the desegregation effort.

The specific mechanisms utilized by communities to peacefully enforce school desegregation will vary with the characteristics of the community and its power structure. The main point is that community organization for peaceful desegregation is possible if community leaders desire it. Cooperation with a court order will be facilitated if the order specifically delegates responsibility for the design of a desegregation plan to leaders who agree to work toward the goal. Emphasis upon law and order and improvement in the quality of education will appeal to the value systems of most citizens and will serve to gain their support.

Those communities that experienced disruptive school desegregation had leaders whose behavior served to incite the disruptions. In both Mobile and Boston, city officials publicly suggested initially that the school desegregation order or "forced busing" was legally and morally wrong. These cues from officials roused the emotions of citizens who had a predisposition against the court order. In some instances, leadership reinforced the public's misconception of governmental processes. In Virginia, the leaders' policy of interposition led the public to believe that the state constitution could negate the federal constitution. In Boston, a referendum on busing led voters to believe that their votes could change a court order. In contrast, those cities that had leaders who indicated that violence would not be tolerated and that the law must be obeyed experienced little or no disruption. These leaders also used symbolically key words such as "law and order," and instilled a sense of community pride in the residents. Evidently the appeal for law and order strikes a set of values more deeply ingrained in the public than those values that reject racial desegregation.

The issue of desegregation has contributed to the increased politicization of educational processes. It is only recently that educators have admitted that public school systems are subject to the same political pressures as other public institutions. With urban areas containing many diverse groups within their population, it has become inevitable that these groups will vie for control of the public school system. Superintendents, who ordinarily are appointed by school boards, are placed in the position of playing political roles for which, in many instances, their professional training has not prepared them. Graduate schools of education must recognize that the additional demands upon superintendents require a new type of training. Superintendents must receive training in the sociology of urban organization, the politics of public administration, and the theory and practice of community organizations that involve negotiating, compromising, and gaining public support for educational policies. Without such training and expertise, superintendents are placed in jeopardy, and they are likely to be replaced by the school board at the first signs of discontent in the community.

Virtually every city has utilized busing to implement its desegregation plan. Each of the cities had a desegregation plan fitting to its own demographic and social characteristics. Although the cities varied in the degree to which they relied upon busing as a technique to achieve desegregation, each of the ten cities used transportation to some degree. Cities have supplemented busing with pairings of schools, magnet schools, and redistricting.

Peaceful desegregation is not necessarily an indication that actual desegregation has taken place or that whites and minority-group members are being treated equally. Some of the most peaceful cities had the least amount of actual desegregation. Dallas, a city that experienced no disruptions, had left the majority of its black students segregated in their own subdistrict. Milwaukee's plan enabled most white children to select the school they wished to attend, whereas black children were forced to "volunteer" to be bused because their neighborhood schools were often closed. In Wilmington/New Castle County, black children were to be bused for nine out of twelve school years, whereas whites were to be bused for only three years.

In several cities, affluent whites were not included in the desegregation because their school systems were separate even though they were inside the city limits. This type of situation often leads to the speculation that working-class whites and working-class blacks are two classes of have-nots who compete for scarce resources and cannot get along. In truth, affluent whites have controlled institutions and policy-making agencies so that they themselves may avoid racial desegregation and violent confrontation.

Desegregation has made subdominant groups more aware of the effect they may have on educational change. Citizens' groups established to support and to oppose desegregation have exposed their members to the operation of the judicial process, the school system, and effective community organizing. These groups have enabled parents who once conceived of themselves as powerless to use their collective influence to rectify situations that are unsatisfactory to them. The realization that grass-roots citizens can have an impact on political processes has already resulted in changes in the electoral processes from city-wide to district elections for the school board and city council in Stockton and for the school board in Omaha. Single-member, district elections have been proposed for several other cities that we studied. In addition, citizens in Boston and Erie who were active in the desegregation process have continued to utilize their collective power to bring about educational change.

Those resistance or antibusing groups that were the most successful were those that had leaders who understood the importance of symbolic politics. Leaders of antibusing groups that continued in their efforts for the longest period of time utilized terms such as "forced busing" to charge their followers with emotion. These tactics failed in most cities from the outset when other officials or community groups provided citizens with the alternative of peaceful desegregation. In those communities where no positive alternative was provided, antibusing groups survived until it became apparent that desegregation would continue despite their efforts. In this situation, the key to the demise of these groups was usually the first day of actual school desegregation, which shattered the members' hopes that they could alter the situation.

In order to make effective use of citizen participation, citizens must be allowed to participate in the planning from the outset. Although much citizen participation in planning is more symbolic than real, it may have a positive effect in avoiding conflict if participation takes place *before* specific decisions about how to desegregate are made. If citizens feel that they have a mechanism that channels their opinions to school administrators, they are more likely to accept the final plan that emerges. Participation through voluntary organizations that help implement the plan and the establishment of information centers may also result in increased citizen commitment to desegregation. It is especially important that citizen participation be obtained in areas where there is likely to be strong resistance. In this way, officials can co-opt the residents to a value system favoring desegregation prior to the resistance group's efforts in these areas.

BIBLIOGRAPHY

Crain, Robert L. 1968. *The Politics of School Desegregation.* Chicago: Aldine.

Edelman, Murray. 1964. *The Symbolic Uses of Politics.* Urbana: University of Illinois Press.

Edelstein, Frederick S. 1977. "Federal and State Roles in School Desegregation." *Education and Urban Society* 9:3 (May): 303–326.

Gitler, Joseph, 1952. *Social Dynamics.* New York: McGraw-Hill.

Kerr, Norman. 1969. "The School Board as an Agency of Legitimation." In Alan Rosenthal (ed.), *Governing Education.* New York: Doubleday, pp. 137–172.

Pettigrew, Thomas. 1971. *Racially Separate or Together?* New York: McGraw-Hill.

Rossell, Christine. 1977. "The Mayor's Role in School Desegregation Implementation." *Urban Education* 12:3 (October): 247–270.

Sears, David O., and John B. McConahay 1973 *The Politics of Violence.* Boston: Houghton Mifflin.

Toch, Hans. 1965. *The Social Psychology of Social Movements.* Indianapolis: Bobbs-Merrill.

Wegner, Eldon L., and Jane R. Mercer. 1975. "Dynamics of the Desegregation Process: Politics, Policies and Community Characteristics as Factors in Change." In Frederick R. Wert (ed.), *The Polity of the School.* Lexington, Mass.: Heath, pp. 123–143.

Weisberg, Bernard. 1969. "Racial Violence and Civil Rights Law Enforcement." In Allen D. Grinshaw (ed.), *Racial Violence in the United States.* Chicago: Aldine.

Williams, Robin M. 1977. *Mutual Accommodation: Ethnic Conflict and Cooperation.* In collaboration with Madelyn B. Rhenisch. Minneapolis: University of Minnesota Press.

Williams, Robin, and Margaret Ryan. 1954. *Schools in Transition.* Chapel Hill: University of North Carolina Press.

Zeigler, L. Harmon, and M. Kent Jennings. 1974. *Governing American Schools.* With the assistance of G. Wayne Park. North Scituate, Mass.: Duxbury Press.

Index